W9-CUJ-247

THE HUMAN TRADITION IN LATIN AMERICA

"Pagu: São Paulo's Flapper and More."
Desenho de Di Cavalcanti, *Revista Para Todos*, Rio de Janeiro, July 27, 1929.

THE HUMAN TRADITION IN LATIN AMERICA

THE TWENTIETH CENTURY

EDITED BY
WILLIAM H. BEEZLEY
AND
JUDITH EWELL

SR Scholarly Resources Inc.
Wilmington, Delaware

The paper used in this publication meets the minimum requirements of the American National Standard for permanence of paper for printed library materials, Z39.48, 1984.

First published 1987
Printed and bound in the United States of America

Scholarly Resources Inc.
104 Greenhill Avenue
Wilmington, DE 19805-1897

Library of Congress Cataloging-in-Publication Data

The Human tradition in Latin America.

Bibliography: p.
Includes index.
1. Latin America—Biography. 2. Latin America—History—20th century—Biography. 3. Latin America—Social conditions—1945- . I. Beezley, William H. II. Ewell, Judith, 1943-
CT503.H86 1987 920′.08 87-12906
ISBN 0-8420-2283-X
ISBN 0-8420-2284-8 (pbk.)

To our parents, Lorene A. and Howard "Red" Beezley, Claude and Betsy Ewell, and Ruth Ewell, vital parts of the Human Tradition

I believe in aristocracy, though—if that is the right word, and if a democrat may use it. Not an aristocracy of power, based upon rank and influence, but an aristocracy of the sensitive, the considerate and the plucky. Its members are to be found in all nations and classes, and all through the ages, and there is a secret understanding between them when they meet. They represent the true human tradition, the one permanent victory of our queer race over cruelty and chaos. Thousands of them perish in obscurity, a few are great names. They are sensitive for others as well as for themselves, they are considerate without being fussy, their pluck is not swankiness but the power to endure, and they can take a joke.

—E. M. Forster, *Two Cheers for Democracy*

Contents

Introduction

Westerners have assumed until recently that the traditional societies that encountered modern values and technology were "people without history," passive vessels into which the liquid of Western culture flowed.[1] The persons in this book, on the contrary, have met head-on the changes that uprooted the traditional certainties of their lives. The disruptions they experienced, often labeled as progress, sometimes shattered lives and, sometimes, inspired creative adjustments to new circumstances. These adaptations in turn have contributed, in small ways, to a changing social environment. These personal and individual responses are valuable for what they reveal about the durability of the human spirit. They also suggest the many levels on which the dissemination and acceptance of modernization occurs in the twentieth century.

Within Western culture there has long been a prevailing belief that change—any change—not only is good but also is an improvement that will fit tongue in groove with other improvements—and within other cultures. Western-style change, so the notion runs, will slowly construct as near perfect a world as humanity can achieve. Western values, especially those liberal tenets that emerged in the eighteenth century, are touted as both universal and modern; Western social science (economics, law, politics, sociology) can guide the reshaping of traditional societies; Western science will provide a value-free framework for modernization.

Latin American voices have been raised since the late colonial period in challenges to some of the premises of westernization. In the eighteenth century, Spanish economic and administrative reforms often spurred prosperity for the port cities along South America's east coast, while for the hinterlands they began the process of isolation and abandonment. These reforms from within the Spanish and Portuguese empires, had they continued, might have gradually found ways to reconcile the European-style urban, liberal sectors of the colonies with the rural traditional elites and their peasant allies. But in 1808 French troops occupied the Iberian Peninsula, ending these reform efforts. Latin American colonials suddenly faced new opportunities and new

[1] Eric Wolf, *Europe and the People without History* (Berkeley, 1982).

challenges. Urban elites, who had had a head start in adjusting to the enlightened trends, seized the opportunities that political independence offered. Even for these elites, however, independence from Spain and Portugal did not mean autonomy from foreigners, economically or culturally. Further, for many, perhaps most, of the Latin Americans in rural areas, the nineteenth century meant the overwhelming or distortion of traditional culture and relationships, as they endured what E. Bradford Burns has called the "poverty of progress."[2]

After 1900 the pressures on individuals and communities became more pervasive. Technology and capital provided roads, bridges, cars, telegraph lines, and radio and television signals, reaching into even the most remote regions of Latin America. In most cases, political rule—still in the hands of the urban elite—assumed a more modern form, using technology and the military to strengthen the dominance of principal cities over rural areas. In most nations, the major city—Mexico City in Mexico, São Paulo in Brazil, Buenos Aires in Argentina, Caracas in Venezuela, Lima in Peru, Santiago in Chile—in effect became the nation and either reshaped or ignored the hinterlands. The modern emphasis on individualism, secularism, and capitalism discounted or destroyed the organized protection offered ordinary people by village, religion, and family. Some rural individuals chose to remain in the countryside, where urban, liberal values had penetrated to a lesser extent. Even there, however, they were often driven by necessity to experience a measure of "modern life," to cross the divide from penurious self-sufficiency to earning pay for work in another man's field. For others, the perils of progress appeared when they left their village and moved to the city, when they gave up their ancestral land to work in a factory or go into domestic service.

Political movements, sometimes inspired by foreign pressures or ideologies, have also contributed to changing the social landscape of Latin America. For individuals, joining or refusing to join with guerrillas or government soldiers, aiding combatants or resisting their demands for the produce from their small corn patches, altered the humdrum pace of everyday life. For much of the twentieth century, the majority of Latin Americans, whether they live in the cities or the country, have inhabited a kind of borderland between the old and new. They have been neither Luddites intent on resisting all change

[2]E. Bradford Burns, *The Poverty of Progress: Latin America in the Nineteenth Century* (Berkeley, 1980).

nor passive sponges ready to soak up all change. They have made decisions based on their best judgment as to their own interests, limits, and possibilities.

These biographies form a balance wheel, a necessary corrective to the great themes used to organize the past—liberation, urbanization, industrialization, modernization, unionization, male chauvinism, political mobilization, capitalism, and Marxism. These grand-sounding words are poor collective nouns for the lives they purport to represent. Recently, social historians, using census and other statistical data, have attempted to identify the everyday people underneath these terms. Their efforts have met with some success, but they too often result in what the intellectual historian Dominick LaCapra calls "a bizarre and vicious paradox whereby a vicarious relation to the oppressed of the past serves as a pretext for contemporary pretensions to dominance."[3] Flesh-and-blood people have seldom squirmed out of the maze of charts and graphs.

Revitalizing our understanding of the lives of ordinary people must begin with breaking up the constant, dreary high seriousness about their history. Humor leaks out of the past despite historians' best efforts to ignore it. Through the centuries, life, for all of its travails, has had its moments of laughter, of pleasure, and of satisfaction. To watch one's children at play, to pick a pocket with a feather-light touch, to joke with one's friends, to dance until dawn, to win a fight, to delight at the abundance of one's fields, to exult at one's skill in weaving a blanket or in patting out perfectly round tortillas—these moments cannot be neglected in any account of everyday life. In fact, those individuals who wrestled with progress did so in order to preserve these good things that they knew, to protect them from change and from those who would diminish them. Anguish, hunger, misery, and death form a labyrinth without escape. Humor, pride in accomplishment, and human warmth afford consolation in the midst of despair.

This book is entitled *The Human Tradition in Latin America* because the heritage so evident is the story of courage, not only to get up and face another day but also to start out with hope, determination, and, sometimes, a smile. These are stories of women and men who lived their lives with pluck and determination. They were not blank tablets on which progress wrote with impunity.

---

[3]Dominick LaCapra, "*The Cheese and the Worms*: The Cosmos of a Twentieth-Century Historian," in *History and Criticism* (Ithaca, 1985), 69.

II

Disillusionment characterizes our time. It has eroded faith in progress, even within our Western culture. Thus an art, literature, and scholarship of despondency has appeared. Some scholarly disappointment with, or sullenness about, the dashed hopes of the century's early years has become the "existential predicament" of the 1980s. This malaise, according to Barbara Tuchman, is a reflection of unfulfilled expectations.

> We suffered the loss of two fundamental beliefs—in God and in Progress; two major disillusionments—in socialism and nationalism; one painful revelation—the Freudian uncovering of the subconscious; and one unhappy discovery—that the fairy godmother Science turns out to have brought as much harm as good.[4]

Tuchman and her colleagues in Europe and the United States have seldom tried to escape their malaise by looking abroad. In contrast, scholars and philosophers of the 1920s and 1930s, distressed at what they thought to be the decadence of Western culture, looked to non-Western societies for inspiration. Latin American writers aided their quest by asserting the vibrancy of their own traditions, a selective mixture of Western tradition and indigenous culture. José Vasconcelos of Mexico lauded the "cosmic race" and Gilberto Freyre praised the contributions of African culture to Brazilian civilization. José Carlos Mariátegui and Víctor Raúl Haya de la Torre turned to pre-Columbian Inca patterns for models for new political movements in Peru. But Latin America also had its prophets of doom, and writers like Ezequiel Martínez Estrada, in *X-ray of the Pampa*, pointed out the darker side of a culture in which frontier roughness and sterile mimicry vied for dominance.[5] Ironically, the general pessimism regarding Western culture often found in Latin America an opposing spirit of creativity and optimism and a vitality that Westerners could both admire and envy. The Western disillusionment that Tuchman describes, like that of the twenties and thirties, is not entirely shared by Latin Americans perhaps because for them Western attitudes and institutions often have been filtered through very different individual and social values.

---

[4]Barbara W. Tuchman, *Practicing History: Selected Essays* (New York, 1981), 269.

[5]See José Vasconcelos, *La raza cósmica* (Paris, n.d.); Gilberto Freyre, *The Masters and the Slaves*, trans. Samuel Putnam (New York, 1956); José Carlos Mariátegui, *Siete ensayos de interpretación de la realidad Peruana* (Lima, 1938); Ezequiel Martínez Estrada, *X-ray of the Pampa*, trans. A. Swietlicki (Austin, 1971).

There is in Latin American history a natural divide that falls roughly at the end of the nineteenth century. After some eighty years had been dedicated to a struggle for progress, events began to undermine confidence in that idea. Tuchman's first example—loss of faith in religion and in progress—had a different history in Latin America. Progress and religion identify two ideals in conflict for most of the nineteenth century. Because Roman Catholicism formed the backbone of the Iberian heritage in Latin America, those who wanted to preserve this legacy took up arms to support the church; opponents who wanted progress through secularization proposed to knock down the major obstacle to their attaining this goal—the church and its clerical bureaucracy. In most Latin nations, the liberal, anticlerical forces like those led by Benito Juárez in Mexico could claim victory by the beginning of the twentieth century, and the Catholic church surrendered for a while much of its wealth as well as its political power. Yet, even as people accepted this weakening of the church's temporal power, they saw flaws in the Western ideologies of progress, principally in liberal positivism, with its emphasis on capitalism and political order. Perhaps, then, could the positive values of the traditional order be incorporated into a more humanistic kind of progress?

The elites had seen, or claimed to see, an irreconcilable split between the church and positivism. Largely unnoted by the elites, however, many people continued to blend their belief in Catholicism with their folk and popular beliefs, much as the indigenous population had been doing from the moment of Iberian spiritual conquest. Indigenous traditions mixed with Catholic ones, *macumba* and *voudoun* existed alongside the formal church, Jews and Mennonites added a different leaven in some regions, and popular nature cults, such as the María Lionza group, took on new life as country people brought them to the urban centers. The wisest spokesmen for the Catholic church recognized the vitality of popular religion (even as some of the first missionaries had in the sixteenth century) and joined that spiritual energy to the formal church in Christian base communities and liberation theology. The wisest political leaders tried to work with folk religion instead of against it. The heirs to the idea of progress, whether politicians who feared church activism or theologians who scorned any deviations from orthodoxy, fought against the popular church. The most Western of all Latin Americans, they would be most likely to share Tuchman's conclusion that people had experienced the malaise that accompanies a loss of faith in God.

Do Latin Americans share the loss of confidence in socialism that Tuchman refers to? Or, although not mentioned by Tuchman, in capitalism? In the 1920s and 1930s some of the experiments with socialism in Latin America—in Argentina, Chile, and Bolivia—failed, but the ideals of socialism continue to live. They live in base communities, in at least the rhetoric of Mexico's ruling Party of the Institutionalized Revolution (PRI) or Venezuela's Acción Democrática (AD), in the growing influence in the 1970s and 1980s of the Socialist International in Latin America, in the "military socialism" of Juan Velasco Alvarado in Peru, in Sandinista Nicaragua, and even in the rigidity of the Latin Communist parties. Others find the expression of communal values more compatible with the Iberian tradition than liberal capitalism. Few Latin Americans espouse a pure or ideal socialism. Most echo the words of Argentina's Juan Perón and other political leaders in asserting that their particular models are "neither capitalist nor communist." The invention of "state capitalism," where government becomes the principal investment entrepreneur, further attests to creativity in adapting ideologies to Latin American conditions. Popular ideas—individual and community choices—have contributed to the eclectic political programs of Latin America. The ideas can be as disparate as Emiliano Zapata's demand to have the community land of Anenequilco, Mexico, returned to the village, and the UNAG's (National Union of Small Farmers) pressure on Sandinista Nicaragua to retain individual ownership of small properties.

What of disillusionment with nationalism? With television, radio, and movies and with more strongly centralized governments, national consciousness has grown. Popular pride in local *béisbol* or *fútbol* teams has become legendary, and Latin Americans avidly follow Olympic sports, hoping for victory for one of their own. National rock music stars are also a source of pride. In the 1980s it is likely that "I am an Argentine," "a Paraguayan," "a Guatemalan" comes somewhere on the list of features by which individuals identify themselves. Negative aspects of nationalism have also become popular. It is the foreigner—the other—who beats up the prostitute, who refuses to marry his pregnant girlfriend, who owns the company that will not negotiate with the union, who buys the guns that terrorize the countryside, who treats a national shrine like a somewhat tawdry version of Disneyland. Latin Americans see nationalism not as a source of disillusionment but as a source of identity and of pride and as a necessary defense against neighbors and the great powers.

On both an individual and a collective level, there is often concern expressed about exactly what national identity is. Their countries overrun by the foreign media, McDonald's hamburgers, and foreign backpackers and multinational technocrats, Latin Americans have forged a popular culture that is neither a foreign import nor an indigenous creation. One both insists on *picante* sauce to flavor the McDonald's burger and borrows from the U.S. fast-food tradition to establish Doña Arepa (the cornmeal sandwich popular in Venezuela) chains. A compatriot singing rock and roll in English may seem as "national" as a U.S. salsa artist. National identities may be eclectic, threatened by the ubiquity of the international mass media, or they may have a deeply negative side, as Octavio Paz points out in *The Labyrinth of Solitude*.[6] Finding the authentic national character becomes increasingly difficult. Efforts to block or just limit the amount of outside culture that comes into a Latin American nation can seem silly, as when the Chilean minister of culture under Salvador Allende declared that Donald Duck was a class enemy—but it is not.[7] Cultural imperialism represents the most insidious colonization and the most difficult to defend against, but defense is necessary if individuals are to determine their own national identities. The consciousness of national symbols, values, and differences can be a source of strength and pride. Latin Americans are at work, like squatters, to shape their own unique corner of the "global village."

Nor has Freud's "discovery" of the subconscious driven Latin Americans to despair. Their folk traditions have honored much of what is in Freud long before he formulated and published his ideas. Amazon beliefs surrounding the freshwater dolphin, or *boto*, for example, suggest that the villagers acknowledged both the power of sexual drives and the presence of an irrational, unconscious desire that could be tapped by the *boto*. Wise villagers looked for "signs" that some of their neighbors or lovers had succumbed to unconscious lusts and tried to bring them back to their "normal" conditions.[8] Also, for some, modern psychology provides a release from crippling social strictures, many of which came out of the Ibero-Moorish traditions of the European invaders of Latin America.

Many contemporary Latin American writers have tried to use the theories of Freud and his follower Karl Jung to unlock the collective unconscious of their compatriots. The unique mingling of national folklore and modern psychology in the novels of Miguel Angel Asturias

---

[6]Octavio Paz, *The Labyrinth of Solitude: Life and Thought in Mexico* (New York, 1961).

[7]Ariel Dorfman and Armand Mattelart, *How to Read Donald Duck: Imperialist Ideology in the Disney Comic*, trans. David Kunzle, 2d enl. ed. (New York, 1984), offers the most perceptive discussion of this topic.

[8]Charles Wagley, *Amazon Town: A Study of Man in the Tropics*, 2d ed. (New York, 1976), 238–41.

and José María Arguedas or the archetypes depicted in the paintings of Diego Rivera exemplify self-conscious efforts at cultural healing and fusion.

Perhaps Latin Americans have never had the same faith in the infallibility of science that many Anglo-Americans have. Since the sixteenth century, modern science and technology have nearly always come from outside the Iberian tradition. As relative outsiders for so many years, Latin Americans could see more easily that science is the source of both good and evil. Science can eliminate malaria with chloroquine or DDT and entire populations with napalm or nuclear bombs. Railroads allow easier access to foreign markets, but access to these markets becomes a reason to seize peasant lands and to produce strawberries for export rather than beans for local subsistence. New tractors are efficient, but they destroy the topsoil. Modern machinery improves production but eliminates jobs. Helicopters transport the sick to hospitals and transport soldiers to intimidate rural communities. Many Latin Americans find their imaginations as captured by the U.S. astronauts' walk on the moon as they were in the 1920s by Charles Lindbergh's flight across the Atlantic. But they are hardly so naive that they believe they can receive the benefits of modern science without paying a price.

No, the malaise and disillusion that afflict the largely middle-class, literate societies of Europe and the United States have not touched twentieth-century Latin America in the same way. On both an individual and a collective level there has been much testing and trying of the material and intellectual culture coming from abroad. The changes produced by this onslaught of foreign values and technology have often caused individual distress and discontentment. They have often altered, sometimes destroyed, communal and family patterns. They have inspired wars and provoked famines. Adaptations and mixing of the old and the new have not always been timely or positive. Indeed, frequently the changes have destroyed the traditional while leaving nothing in its place. Yet the examination of individual responses says much for the resiliency of individuals and of societies. Perhaps the intellectuals and philosophers of the so-called developed world might do well to emulate their predecessors in the twenties and thirties who looked to non-Western societies for inspiration.

For in Latin America, throughout the years of travail that have followed independence, there survives representatives of what E. M. Forster called the "true human tradition." These ordinary people won what he declared to be humanity's only victory over cruelty and chaos because "they are sensitive for others as well as for themselves, they are considerate without being fussy, their pluck is not swankiness but the power to endure, and they can take a joke."[9]

III

The biographies of such people fill this volume. One or two, Forster's few great names, such as Marmaduke Grove and George Westerman, might have left records enough for an individual biography, but the others lived in such obscurity that they cannot be considered alone. Nevertheless, together they make a collective statement about the dogged determination to take the measure of circumstances and make a life despite all obstacles.

Each of these persons actually lived; several are still alive today. Some have chosen pseudonyms, and those instances are noted in the introduction to the essay. Whether these persons bear real or assumed names in this volume, their stories illustrate many of the constraints that face twentieth-century Latin Americans as well as the ways that individuals can nonetheless give meaning to and achieve satisfaction in their lives. What emerges as limiting circumstances will surprise few: nationality, gender, ethnic or racial heritage, economic class, and family status represent real obstacles. What also emerges as the common disregard of these deterministic mechanisms will encourage many. Several individuals in this anthology ignored the boundaries imposed on them by the circumstances of their birth and chose to make a different destiny for themselves. With little alternative but to straighten the backbone and stiffen the upper lip, these persons dived into the life they had, made the best of it, and even on occasion enjoyed it. Of course, their decisions rarely had the hoped-for results, but these actions did change their lives.[10] Few individuals here would oppose changes that they initiate themselves, but progress to most people means change imposed from the outside, a great force that overwhelms any opposition.

Revolution has sometimes been described as progress in that the ordinary person has a say in the changes that occur once the revolution succeeds. Yet, while they are being fought, revolutions mean many things to many people. During the Mexican and Cuban revolutions,

---

[9]E. M. Forster, *Two Cheers for Democracy* (New York, 1951), 73.

[10]Novelist Ken Follett discusses the issue of the role of individual actions versus great forces in controlling people's lives in his thriller, *The Modigliani Scandal* (New York, 1985). See especially the introduction.

for example, some fought for agrarian reform, some for industrialization, some for women's rights, some for personal power, some to be free of foreign control, some for new constitutions and new laws, some for implementation of old laws and old constitutions, some for individual freedom, and some for collective cooperation. Not all of those who were on the winning side won their revolution. For many, especially for women, old people, young people, and, usually, country people, revolution often appeared to be simply more changes imposed from without in the name of revolutionary progress. Latin Americans, already enamored of the quality of machismo, often have to deal with the idealized modern male, the Noble Revolutionary.[11]

Pedro Crespo serves as an example of the Noble Revolutionary. Crespo brought to Yucatán, Mexico, changes in the name of progress that others saw only as a disruption of traditional village life. Ofelia Domínguez Navarro and Leoncio Veguilla endured life under the direction of the Noble Revolutionary in Cuba, Fidel Castro, who once remarked that it is easier to make a revolution than it is to make a revolution work. The truth of this comment can be clearly seen in these two biographies, which illustrate the different priorities that people develop in the name of progress, especially progress in the name of revolution.

Other persons in this book also were caught in revolutionary or reformist circumstances. The experience of Tomasa Muñoz de León illustrates this situation. Tomasa is an Ecuadorian woman who managed to gain access to a small plot of land under the 1964 agrarian reform decree. But she found that her efforts to improve life for herself and her family met obstacle after obstacle because enterprise remained largely the prerogative of men in her society.

To survive in the crucible of change forces the individual to develop a thick hide, a tough attitude, and innovative behavior. Strategies of survival in Latin America demonstrate the diversity of individual responses to modernization and offer important suggestions for students of other Third World nations.

Those involved in twentieth-century survival activities can draw on a rich history of individual and collective responses to change in Latin America. In the Western Hemisphere the process of European expansion and colonization extended over a long period of time. Thus one can see how the indigenous and later the mestizo (mixed-ethnic) groups responded to Western culture during the colonial era. Some

[11]Carlos Rangel examines this development in *Del buen salvaje al buen revolucionario: Mitos y realidades de América Latina* (Caracas, 1976).

managed to adjust and they survived.[12] Then, one sees that beginning in the mid-eighteenth century these same groups faced attempts to modernize them, to draw them into the economic and intellectual world of non-Iberian Europe. Latin America has endured two conquests, first colonization by Iberian Europe and second modernization by Europe and North America. In much of Asia and Africa, these conquests were simultaneous and hence are more difficult to sort out for analysis.

In the last two decades, ethnohistorians have probed the manner in which pre-Columbian cultures responded to their conquerors. Several excellent volumes examine the ways in which indigenous peoples survived Spanish and Portuguese efforts to impose European culture upon them, especially in its economic and religious forms. Charles Gibson, in *The Aztecs under Spanish Rule* (1964), introduced this ethnographic approach, and more recently, Nancy M. Farriss, in her Bolton Prize-winning volume, *Maya Society under Colonial Rule*, explores the strategies—flight, outward acculturation, and accommodation to the conquerors—that enabled the Mayas in Yucatán to survive during the colonial period. Farriss points out that these Mayan strategies also had the effect of modifying the Iberian culture that was developing in Yucatán.[13] For the Peruvian colonial period, two other prize-winning works have analyzed the arduous and complex process of cultural interaction: Karen Spalding's *Huarochirí: An Andean Society under Inca and Spanish Rule* and Steve J. Stern's *Peru's Indian Peoples and the Challenge of the Spanish Conquest: Huamanga to 1640.*[14]

It has been easier to plot the interactions between indigenous and conquering cultures in collective rather than individual terms. An exception is *Struggle and Survival in Colonial America*, in which the editors,

---

[12]For example, William B. Taylor, in *Drinking, Homicide, and Rebellion in Colonial Mexico* (Stanford, 1979), argues that the principal characteristic of Spanish colonial rule was its relative lightness. Indigenous peoples who survived the shattering military conquest of the first fifty years often found that they were left relatively alone as long as they accepted Spanish rule and supplied whatever tribute was required of them. The Spanish had no interest in, nor indeed the resources for, cultural annihilation.

[13]Charles Gibson, *The Aztecs under Spanish Rule* (Stanford, 1964); Nancy M. Farriss, *Maya Society under Colonial Rule: The Collective Enterprise of Survival* (Princeton, 1984). The Conference on Latin American History awards the Bolton Prize for the best book published each year in Latin American history.

[14]Karen Spalding, *Huarochirí: An Andean Society under Inca and Spanish Rule* (Stanford, 1984); and Steve J. Stern, *Peru's Indian Peoples and the Challenge of the Spanish Conquest: Huamanga to 1640* (Madison, WI, 1983).

David Sweet and Gary Nash, have compiled the biographies of twenty-one individuals in the emergent Anglo and Iberian colonies. These life histories reveal successful and unsuccessful efforts to meet the challenges posed by cultural ambiguity. Individuals chose strategies of accommodation or of confrontation as ways to survive and sometimes to prosper. Most of them, as we all do, influenced their families, friends, and neighbors. Some of them found that their individual accommodation or defiance also affected the wider community in which they lived.[15]

The large size of the nineteenth- and twentieth-century societies under study has prompted anthropologists and ethnohistorians to drop down to the village, community, or regional level to study adaptation to change. Anthropologists have perhaps done the pioneer work, often in studies of the effects of change at a given time. The names of Robert Redfield in Mexico, Charles Wagley in Brazil, Lisa Redfield Peattie in Venezuela, and Oscar Lewis in Puerto Rico and Mexico come to mind. Reaching an understanding of the slow process of cultural change can be facilitated if the records consulted cover a long period. Luis González, in *San José de Gracia: Mexican Village in Transition*, lovingly traces nearly two hundred years of the village's history, as roads, trade, and an expansive Mexican government intrude more and more into the community.[16] Several other recent works have followed the pace of change in regions regarded as the hinterlands; the works of Robert Wasserstrom for Chiapas in Mexico and Florencia Mallon for the central Peruvian highlands are two of the best.[17] These studies highlight community strategies to accommodate the "second conquest" of modernization, much as the Gibson, Farriss, and Spalding books chronicle the reactions to the "first conquest" in the sixteenth century.

The Human Tradition in Latin America: The Twentieth Century describes the lives of individuals confronting modernization. The same strategies have been used again, that is, some persons have fled to more remote areas of the countryside or to the city in order to escape the kind of modern life they reject; others have fled to a neighboring

[15]David G. Sweet and Gary B. Nash, eds., *Struggle and Survival in Colonial America* (Berkeley, 1981).

[16]Luis González, *San José de Gracia: Mexican Village in Transition* (Austin, TX, 1972).

[17]Robert Wasserstrom, *Class and Society in Central Chiapas* (Berkeley, 1983); and Florencia Mallon, *The Defense of Community in Peru's Central Highlands: Peasant Struggle and Capitalist Transition, 1860–1940* (Princeton, 1983).

nation in which circumstances seem to offer a more desirable existence. A few have fled through drugs, alcohol, or insanity. Others have modified their lives in outward ways to satisfy the authorities who represent the state, the labor boss, or some agent of the culture (soldiers carrying out civic action, Peace Corps personnel, and priests). Still others have survived because in the process of modernization the traditional population has engulfed the modern society and imposed enough trappings of the old way of life that it looks like home.

These techniques for creating a little room for independent maneuvers within the mechanisms of modern life reveal the toughness of the human spirit in Latin America. They offer points of comparison with responses to change in the other parts of the world that have faced modernization and westernization, and they show the resourcefulness of ordinary people. Perhaps the core of the human tradition is that the techniques are just that—ways of surviving—and they need not tarnish or destroy the individual's integrity or will to live. In colonial times, the Spanish viceroys had the privilege of responding to royal orders with the litany of "Obedezco pero no cumplo" ("I obey, but I do not enforce"). Everyday people, the aristocracy of the plucky, as Forster would describe them, have often demonstrated the same attitude toward the changes that modernization has brought them.

IV

What ways do most persons have of expressing their joie de vivre? Humor, the soul at play, can be a statement of joy and helps set apart humanity from other living things. Humor appears as the final voluntary act of the living—in gallows humor, for example, in which a person quips about his or her impending death. Humor has been used as a strategy, both for expressing the delightful side of life and for coping with the oppression of modernization. Apache Indians enjoy telling jokes in each other's company; some of these stories parody the white man, who has done so much to damage their native culture. In the Republic of Niger, Songhay possession dances before independence incorporated sarcastic portrayals of French colonial officials. Carnival in Brazil and popular festivals elsewhere always include biting humor, usually involving social reversals. Cowboys (gauchos or *llaneros*) in Argentina and Venezuela conduct duels through song. The quickest with a rhyming verse, and often one that is humorous and insulting, wins. In face-to-face, nonliterate societies, oral skills enable some humorists to earn acclaim as virtuosos.[18]

Mirthful exuberance and other sentiments as well find expression in dance. Rhys Isaac argues that the quadrille and jig allowed colonial Virginians to release their feelings in a community in which perhaps only 10 percent could read and write.[19] Essays can be written on Latin American dance—indigenous dances, cumbias, the samba. In this volume, we have included a piece on one of the best-known styles of music and dance, the tango, and on the tango's greatest artistic interpreter, Carlos Gardel. The tango expressed an approach to life that had meaning for an entire generation in Argentina. Today, Latin American rock-and-roll bands, the salsa, and the Nueva Canción movement also represent vibrant mixtures of the old and the new.

Play offers yet another outlet for relaxation and the pursuit of pleasure. Nearly a half century ago, Johan Huizinga, in his classic *Homo Ludens*, argued that it is humanity's capacity to play that separates it from other living things.[20] Miguel Rostaing found respite from his job as a construction worker in Lima on the soccer-playing fields. Pedro Crespo, the mestizo revolutionary, saw baseball as a worthwhile activity for the rebels in the Yucatán Peninsula. Ligia Parra Jahn broke tradition when she played baseball with boys in her neighborhood and continued to participate in physical sports, including basketball and bullfighting, throughout her adolescence. Such interest in organized sport also reflects the social changes that we have come to call "modernization." Allen Guttman persuasively argues that

---

[18]For a discussion of humor in desperate circumstances, see Antonin J. Obrdlik, "'Gallows Humor'—A Sociological Phenomenon," *American Journal of Sociology* 47 (1941–42): 709–16; Keith Basso, *Portraits of the White Man* (London: Cambridge University Press, 1979); and Paul Stoller, "Horrific Comedy: Cultural Resistance and the Hauka Movement in Niger," *Ethos* 12, no. 2 (Summer 1984): 165–89. For an examination of Mexican humor, see William H. Beezley, "Recent Mexican Political Humor," *Journal of Latin American Lore* 11, no. 2 (1985): 195–223; and on gaucho song duels, see Richard W. Slatta, *Gauchos and the Vanishing Frontier* (Lincoln, NE, 1983), 25, 81–83.

[19]Anya Peterson Royce has made the most systematic study of dance and society. See *The Anthropology of Dance* (Bloomington, IN, 1977). For an analysis of an indigenous dance, see, for example, Stanley H. Brandes, "Dance as Metaphor: A Case from Tzintzuntzan, Mexico," *Journal of Latin American Lore* 5, no. 1 (1979): 25–43. Also see Rhys Isaac, *The Transformation of Virginia, 1740–1790* (Chapel Hill, 1982), 80–87, especially p. 81.

[20]Johan Huizinga, *Homo Ludens: A Study of the Play Element in Culture* (1938; reprint ed., London, 1970).

organized sport requires secularization, equality of laws, record keeping, specialization, bureaucratization, quantification, and rationalization of activity. Maya *béisbol* players may have found pleasure in the game, but they played it under circumstances that stood in opposition to the traditional values of their community. Striding onto the soccer pitch was but another step toward modern life for men such as Rostaing.[21]

Still, for others the best part of life, the greatest satisfaction, comes from their personal ability to make something. Whether they are called artisans or craftsmen, the label cannot capture the sense of pride that comes from the activity. The Bolivian weavers Doña Sara and Doña Juana, who must steal time to weave from their daily struggle to survive, make that survival worthwhile by weaving their tapestries. For others, satisfaction comes from the ability to cook an artistic meal, a meal noticed perhaps by no one else but in that even more satisfying in its transitory integrity. Some find that satisfaction in life comes from doing a job well. No doubt sugar cane workers and construction laborers are pleased when they contemplate their skills and strength.

Some people are born organizers and derive pleasure both from leading others and sometimes, if they are fortunate, from the results of their efforts. Chilean Marmaduke Grove had exceptional success in politics as did the Panamanian George Westerman. More typical of the leadership roles played by everyday people are those of strike leader, feminist, priest or minister, and lay leader in a base community. Each role permits the individual at some time to experience the satisfaction that accompanies collective resistance.

Nor should we forget the heady sense of risk that comes with open defiance of authority. To challenge a parent, to take vengeance on a faithless lover, to escape from jail, to defy taboos, to defend an unpopular friend or associate, to seize land or a house, and to pray to God in an unpopular church all are conscious acts of rebellion.

Recognizing the human tradition in Latin America, the resilience of people faced with overwhelming odds, does not mean one ignores inhuman living conditions or romanticizes them as picturesque. Poverty, unemployment, illiteracy, poor health, neglect of women and indigenous peoples, and stunted opportunities for the young all require remedies. Amelioration does not demand modernization in its common guises or a solution copied from the capitalist or Marxist experience; it calls for a commitment to a better life for all.

---

[21]Allen Guttmann, *From Ritual to Record: The Nature of Modern Sports* (New York, 1978), 15–56.

The path toward authentic national development lies perhaps in an accommodation at the national level as creative as those on the personal level won by many of the persons in this book. These individuals survived and sometimes triumphed by using all of the weapons in their arsenals: flight, defiance, cooperation, violence, humor, organization, intelligence, suspicion, adaptability, and love. The most successful recognized that some situations called for watching, waiting, avoiding, and reacting; other situations required asserting, screaming, and demanding. Those who chose the right combination of weapons at the right time joined the ranks of the aristocracy of the sensitive, the considerate, and the plucky. No nation can achieve full modernization without a genuine consideration of its own vibrant and creative human tradition.

Mimicry is not modernization, no matter what material improvements are made. Progress will come with the betterment of life in small ways for persons such as the ones in this volume who represent the human tradition in Latin America and whose lives "make hope practical and despair unconvincing."[22]

William H. Beezley

[22]Raymond Williams as cited in Stanley Aronowitz and Henry A. Giroux, *Education under Siege* (South Hadley, MA, 1985), 142.

1

Juan Francisco Lucas: Patriarch of the Sierra Norte de Puebla

David LaFrance and G. P. C. Thomson

David LaFrance, now at Oregon State University, taught for four years at the Universidad Autónoma de Puebla. He has spent most of his professional career investigating the Mexican Revolution in this region. His numerous essays consider Puebla, the revolution, and Mexican popular culture, especially baseball and political cartoons.

A lecturer at the University of Warwick, Guy Thomson has written articles and a book, *Puebla de Los Angeles: Industry and Society in a Mexican City, 1700–1850* (1986), on the Puebla region of Mexico. His research methodology, called microhistory by Luis González, represents the latest trend in Mexican studies and examines in detail the country's numerous, isolated localities.

LaFrance and Thomson together have resolved many of the complexities of Puebla's history and politics. Here they provide the first assessment of Juan Francisco Lucas, a typical political strongman, called a cacique, in the unique setting of Puebla's Sierra Norte.

Juan Francisco Lucas, a Nahuatl-speaking Indian, exercised a pivotal influence over a large expanse of Mexico's Sierra Madre Oriental, from the Liberal Revolution of Ayutla in 1854 until Lucas's death in 1917. His must count as one of the most enduring regional *cacicazgos* (informal fiefdoms under a personalist leader) to be found anywhere in nineteenth- or twentieth-century Latin America. Each state and national leader was obliged to take Lucas's power into account, and all Mexican presidents, from Ignacio Comonfort to Venustiano Carranza, arranged accords with him. The Lucas *cacicazgo* was all the more remarkable for remaining broadly popular over a period when the local political boss became one of the principal targets of the 1910 revolution. Lucas's power survived three governments after the fall of Porfirio Díaz's dictatorship (1876–1911), and, on his deathbed, Lucas left command of the "Brigada Serrana"—the core of his *cacicazgo*—to a well-groomed, although far less popular, successor, an Indian peasant, Gabriel Barrios, who remained a dominant force in the Sierra Norte de Puebla until the 1940s.

Juan Francisco Lucas, by 1900 commonly referred to as "Tata Juan Francisco" or "Patriarch of the Sierra," was born on June 16, 1834, in the Nahuatl-speaking barrio of Comaltepec in the municipality of Zacapoastla on the southern flank of the Sierra Norte de Puebla. Manuel Lucas, his father, worked on the land of a neighboring hacienda and carded wool to supplement the family's income. The Lucas family's possession of a surname suggests a measure of acculturation, since, until well into the twentieth century, Indians of this region generally had only Christian names. Juan Francisco's completion of primary education in Zacapoastla in 1848 also set him apart from the mass of the Indian population, among whom bilingualism was exceptional. Mastery of Castilian and Nahuatl, combined with literacy, would qualify a man for a village secretaryship or for the position of *preceptor de primeras letras* (primary-school teacher).

Even such modest opportunities, however, were not available to the Lucas family. Comaltepec was a mere barrio of a town inhabited almost entirely by *gente de razón* (the Spanish colonial term still used in the Sierra to refer to non-Indians), descended from a cluster of Spanish families who had settled in Zacapoastla during the eighteenth century. These were families proud of their *limpieza de sangre* and accustomed to racial endogamy. They controlled the town and district governments, monopolized the trade of much of the central Sierra, and owned the only three haciendas in this region of small holdings. The Lucas family's decision, in 1848, to migrate to Altotonga, in neighboring Veracruz, was probably a result of the limited opportunities for them in the Zacapoastla district. The tumultuous political events of the subsequent thirty years would change all this. Indians would experience great suffering, but they also would be presented with unprecedented opportunities as the traditional restrictions on them were modified and they became involved directly in political events.

Shortly before the Revolution of Ayutla in 1854, the Lucas family returned to Comaltepec in search of land. There, Manuel Lucas, with other squatters, became involved in a conflict over land with the owner of the hacienda Xochiapulco. Events at Xochiapulco would soon occupy a central place in the rise to political preeminence of Manuel's son, Juan Francisco. When the revolution broke out, several squatters languished in the Zacapoastla jail. Manuel Lucas took advantage of the temporary collapse of authority to organize a daring attack on the prison, releasing twenty-eight prisoners and taking twenty rifles. For the first time, Indians had organized a violent action in the hitherto peaceful Sierra; in the process, a significant armory came into the possession of people who were not *gente de razón.*

Juan Francisco, who had helped his father in the attack on the jail, was arrested shortly thereafter and sent to the state capital, Puebla de los Angeles, for trial. The recently established Liberal authorities soon released Lucas, who, rather than return to certain persecution in Zacapoastla, where the Conservative movement in the state had its headquarters, enlisted in the forces of Juan Alvarez, the mestizo leader of the Ayutla movement. Lucas participated in his first battle on March 8, 1856, at San Isidro Ocotlán. This event marked the beginning of a long and successful military career during which Lucas established himself as an indispensable force in the politics not only of the Sierra but also of the state of Puebla and, at critical moments, of the entire republic.

Lucas's political importance makes sense only when his career is placed within the context of the conflicts that occurred between Liberals and Conservatives and between Mexicans and foreigners over the twenty years following the Revolution of Ayutla. This period is called La Reforma (reformation) in Mexico. It brought changes no less radical and far-reaching than those brought about by the great revolution that broke out fifty years later. The 1910 revolution, in one sense, may be seen as the culmination of the Liberal reform movement. From the outbreak of the independence movement in 1810, Mexican politics can be understood, crudely, in terms of a prolonged reaction by corporate groups—the landowners, the clergy, and the army—intent upon defending the privileges that they had inherited from the colony. The power of these "conservative" groups was concentrated in Mexico City and in the provincial capitals of central Mexico. The "liberal" forces opposing them claimed to represent those Mexicans who did not enjoy the same corporate privileges. The Liberals were strongest in the northern states, the mountainous zones of the southeast, and the coastal peripheries. The Revolution of Ayutla, led by Alvarez, a veteran of the popular insurgency of the 1810s from the Costa Chica of Guerrero, was the moment at which Liberals finally gained the upper hand. Nevertheless, a long armed struggle proved necessary before a stable Liberal republic was established by Porfirio Díaz in the late 1870s. During this struggle of the 1850s and 1860s, Liberals and Conservatives, as well as the French and Austrians upon whom the Conservatives had called to rescue their declining fortunes, mobilized whatever forces they could persuade to fight. Mexico, for the first time, experienced a generalized, protracted, and bloody civil war. The sierras of Mexico, and the landowning Indians residing within them, offered a heretofore untapped strategic reserve as factional and ideological conflicts deepened. Indian leaders such as Manuel and Juan Francisco Lucas in the Sierra Norte de Puebla, Manuel Lozada in the Sierra de Jalisco, and Tomás Mejía in the Sierra Gorda of Querétaro held the keys to this reserve, and they would, on occasion, lend their influence to outside forces in exchange for recognition of their regional authority.

The strategic value of the Sierra Norte de Puebla was appreciated by all of the forces competing for national power between 1854 and 1876. Pacification of the Sierra was a matter always high on the agenda during the thirty-five-year dictatorship of Díaz. The strategic importance of the Sierra was recognized once more during the uprising led by Francisco Madero in 1910 and throughout the revolution. The Sierra was close to the principal communications axis between Mexico City and the nation's main port of Veracruz. No government could feel secure with this region in enemy hands. In addition, the Sierra possessed seemingly inexhaustible resources for provisioning the armies recruited from Indian villages subject to still influential towns. This source avoided the political embarrassment of recruiting field hands as well as the strategic vulnerability of having to raise matériel from the hacienda districts of the altiplano. Moreover, the Sierra offered men who were prepared to fight if they were exempted from taxes; recruitment proved far more difficult in hacienda zones because the landlords would only reluctantly release their peons and because the peasants, who had no land to defend, stood only to lose from fighting. The Sierra Norte de Puebla, while a military provisioner's cornucopia, did not yield its strategic reserves of men and maize easily. The region had to be organized, and it was in this respect that Juan Francisco Lucas proved his indispensability.

Lucas's usefulness was first appreciated during the bloody Three Years' War (1858–61). The Liberal commander of the National Guard, General Juan Nepomuceno Méndez, from Tetela de Ocampo, promoted Lucas from foot soldier to captain in July 1858. He instructed Lucas to organize the Indian barrios on and around the Xochiapulco hacienda into the National Guard Battalion of Zacapoastla. Since 1855, Puebla's Conservatives had been trying to establish a power base in the Sierra, counting on the presumed conservatism of the region's Indians and their distaste for Liberal reforms. In a few areas they had succeeded. In Tlatlauqui, parts of Tezuitlán, Zacapoastla, and Chignahuapan, large landholding families, aided by Catholic priests in the Indian barrios, were able to provide local support for Conservative and, later, for Franco-Austrian incursions into the Sierra. But the more densely populated districts of Tetela, Zacatlán, and Huauchinango had few, if any, haciendas, a priesthood unaligned with the landholding class, and liberal antecedents, which, in the case of Zacatlán, could be traced back to Francisco Osorno's rebellion during the wars of independence.

In these districts a militant liberalism took root around the leadership of National Guard commanders of humble mestizo and Indian origin. These men had just commanded the local defense forces established to combat the Americans. Then they mobilized to fight the Conservatives and the European intervention. Finally, they supported Porfirio Díaz's bid for the presidency in the revolts of La Noria (1872) and Tuxtepec (1876). They also attempted to secure the leadership in state politics for the Sierra politicians and soldiers who formed the Montaña party—men such as Juan Nepomuceno Méndez, Juan Crisostomo Bonilla, Lauro Luna, and Ramón Márquez Galindo. Lucas's skill in raising National Guard units, provisioning military campaigns, and mediating conflicts between Indians and *gente de razón* was central to the political success of the Liberal and patriotic cause in the Sierra, thereby accounting for his rapid rise within the army.

In 1859, Méndez, now the recognized Liberal caudillo of the Sierra, gave Lucas command of the Sixth Battalion of Puebla's National Guard. In May 1863, Lucas was promoted to lieutenant colonel of the "Batallón de Cazadores de la Montaña," in July 1863 to full colonel, and in February 1865 to general. He took supreme command of the "Línea Militar de La Sierra Norte del Estado de Puebla" in October 1866. Lucas was a brilliant, indeed an invincible, guerrilla commander and inspired extraordinary loyalty from his soldiers. For nearly forty years, certain barrios along the southern flank of the Sierra would provide, at the slightest warning, a majority of their adult males to fight under Lucas. When, on occasion, Lucas would sue for a truce, he generally succeeded in obtaining favorable terms, including amnesty for his commanders and soldiers, from the state and national governments. He would never allow his soldiers to be disarmed. Indeed, many of them kept their rifles until the revolution of 1910, long after the Sierra National Guard was formally demobilized in 1884 and reduced to an auxiliary force within the federal army. As late as the 1890s, Lucas could be found interceding on behalf of his soldiers in their claims for the tax exemptions granted them some thirty years before in recognition of their services to the Liberal and patriotic cause.

Lucas's military strength was in defense rather than offense. He rarely moved his troops beyond the Sierra, although the Sixth Battalion did contribute to the defense of the state capital against the French on May 5, 1862, to the retaking of Puebla from the Austrians on April 2, 1867, and on November 16, 1876, to the battle of Tecoac, which brought Díaz to power. Thus, Lucas served the designs of the Sierra politicians who aspired to power on the state level. He was expected to use his influence among the National Guard at election times to ensure victories for the Montaña party, which controlled the state government between 1876 and 1884. Nevertheless, Lucas was more than simply a servant of the Liberal cause in the Sierra. His continuing popularity and influence among the Indian population rested, above all, upon his ability to shield Indians from forced recruitment, from military service beyond the Sierra, from arbitrary taxation, and from outside political interference during a period of widespread social and political upheaval. Lucas's control of the Sierra National Guard served to guarantee the integrity of the Sierra's Indian communities even as they faced the profound legal and administrative changes and the internal restructuring that accompanied implementation of Liberal reform legislation.

Three further points can be made to explain more fully the pervasiveness of Lucas's influence and the survival of his *cacicazgo*. The first factor was the manner in which Lucas's military authority acquired civilian and institutional form through the founding of a new municipality on the hacienda of Xochiapulco. The estate had been expropriated by the Liberal state government of Fernando María Ortega in December 1864 and renamed "Villa de 5 de Mayo" in recognition of the contribution of guardsmen from the area to the victory over the French in 1862. The hacienda's holdings were subdivided among landless soldiers according to rank; for instance, one *almud de maíz* (measure of corn—about four liters) for soldiers, two for corporals, and three for sergeants. It took a decade, until 1874, for the status of Xochiapulco to be affirmed, and Lucas was instrumental in this endeavor. To this end, he organized a formidable rebellion against the state government between 1868 and 1870, in an attempt to hold the bureaucrats to their word regarding Xochiapulco, provided funds from his own pocket to compensate the owners of the sequestrated hacienda, and supervised and funded the distribution of plots.

Consequently, Xochiapulco became a near-military colony, settled by Indian agrarians armed and willing to serve at Lucas's call. Lucas, with a branch of his family from his first wife resident in Xochiapulco and himself owning the rancho de Tascantla, which overlooked the town, became the new municipality's patron and guiding force. He supervised the construction of municipal buildings, schools, bridges, and roads; donated a massive clock for the town hall; built a sanctuary for the saints of the surrounding barrios; and introduced a Methodist minister for the administration of the cult. Over the course of the last three decades of the nineteenth century, Xochiapulco became one of the most densely populated municipalities of the Sierra Norte. It served as a haven for Indians fleeing repressive ladino village administrations throughout the central Sierra and neighboring highlands. Many of these refugees were national guardsmen whom ladino authorities were attempting to disarm and tax during the 1880s.

The second factor that deepened Lucas's influence in the Sierra was his acquisition of extensive landholdings, the sine qua non of all effective caciques. His second marriage was to Ascención Pérez Contreras of Zautla. Her father, Francisco Pérez, owned the Tascantla ranch, as well as several others in the municipality of Puebla, which were adjudicated in Pérez's favor during the 1860s. By the 1870s Lucas had become one of the principal landowners of the Sierra. His holdings took the form not of latifundia, which were physically impossible in the Sierra, but of small and medium-size ranches scattered over a wide area. Lucas also lent small amounts of money to peasants who then purchased land from these municipalities that were divesting themselves of corporate property. This land often became his after loan foreclosures. Lucas was an energetic and successful farmer in an area where opportunities for commercial agriculture were greater than in most other parts of the Sierra. This situation existed in large part because of the location of a flourishing mining community at Tetela, Lucas's preferred town of residence, and the proximity of his estates to the principal route of communication between the cattle-producing coastal plains and the markets of the plateau. At Tascantla, Lucas fattened cattle, bred pigs, and provided beans and rations for workers in the nearby mines. Lucas's success in acquiring and farming land freed him from dependence on a state salary and pension and greatly enhanced his ability to dispense patronage and to arm and equip the National Guard of the region. He would often settle refugee Indians on his estates as sharecroppers, and, later in his life, he donated several plots to village and barrio authorities for the construction of schools or to meet the needs of war orphans, widows, and infirm veterans.

A third factor accounting for the popularity of Lucas and the endurance of his influence among Indians and non-Indians alike was his importance as a symbol of racial harmony in a region that, as a result of civil war and Liberal reforms, was undergoing substantial modification in the traditional relations between ethnic groups. From the 1850s through the 1870s, the phrase "guerra de castas" (caste, or racial, war) often came to the lips of the *gente de razón* as they anxiously observed the arming of Indian militia and witnessed Indians, hitherto passive, taking direct and often violent action in defense of their land and rights. Frequently, Lucas was appointed to mediate in disputes between or within Sierra communities; he was particularly instrumental in pacifying the major Indian rebellion in the Sierra, in the municipality of Cuetzalan, which was led by Francisco Agustín between 1868 and 1872. The rebels accepted only Lucas's assurances that their community lands would not pass into the possession of *gente de razón* and believed only Lucas's guarantee that the terms of an amnesty would be respected. Clearly, the Indians of the Sierra trusted him. For its part, the non-Indian population, as it acquired extensive landholdings from municipal corporations, introduced cash crops such as coffee, and entrenched itself ever more deeply in control of municipal and district government, must have felt reassured to have Lucas at its beck and call whenever the social order was threatened.

But Lucas was no puppet of the ladino class. His correspondence over the 1870s, 1880s, and 1890s shows him to have been sensitive to the sufferings and anxious to preserve the dignity of the Indian population. He frequently requested intervention from state and national authorities to redress local injustices, even threatening to use, and sometimes using, a mobilized Sierra National Guard to underline his position. In his private life, Lucas remained socially distant from the small-town bourgeoisie of Tetela de Ocampo, where he was described in censuses as an "agricultor," a farmer rather than a landowner. Like all effective caciques, Lucas studiously cultivated a modesty and simplicity of manner and an air of political accessibility and innocence. His granddaughter, Aurora Lucas (d. 1985), described how for photographic portraits General Lucas always had to be pressed to don his military tunic and medals, which hung uncomfortably over his peasant drill and sandals. She recounted how, on one occasion, two federal army officers, instructed by Díaz to visit the general in order to assess his influence, dismounted from their horses in front of Lucas's house on the corner of Tetela's main square. They handed their reins to a waiting Indian, and, shortly thereafter, were received indoors to their astonishment by the very same man, General Juan Francisco Lucas.

With the Tuxtepec rebellion behind him and President Porfirio Díaz firmly in power by the late 1880s, Lucas must have felt that his active military and political career was over and that he could now rest on his substantial laurels. Indeed, for the next two decades this seems to have been the case. Although Lucas maintained his commission in the army and, on occasion, became directly involved in local and Sierra politics, for the most part he remained in semi-retirement, spending long periods on his ranch at Tascantla raising livestock, tending to his crops, and hunting deer in the surrounding mountains. Increasingly, when some matter of state called for his attention, it was Lucas's sons Abraham and Miguel who acted in the name of their now famous but aging father. In fact, between 1891 and 1897 the political situation in Tetela was so quiet that the authorities saw no need to repair the broken telegraph connection between the district capital and the outside world.

In this atmosphere it is hardly likely that Lucas could have foreseen that by the beginning of the second decade of the new century the greatest upheaval in Mexican history would be just getting under way. As a consequence, the Patriarch of the Sierra would again be faced with a formidable challenge to both himself and his people—a test no less great than the one he faced fifty years earlier. From the onset of the revolution in 1910 to his death in 1917, Lucas demonstrated that his stewardship of the northern sierra of Puebla was no aberration. He deftly and successfully managed to make the transition from his role as one of Díaz's principal backers to that of a supporter of the governments of Francisco Madero (1911–13), Victoriano Huerta (1913–14), and, finally, Venustiano Carranza (1915–20). Unlike so many of his contemporaries who failed at this deadly game, Lucas proved to be not just a survivor but also a master politician, always knowing when and how to make the next move. Greatly aiding him in his endeavors was the nearly unwavering support of great numbers of people of the Sierra, people with whom Lucas and his sons kept in constant contact and whom they were always ready to help. Federal and state authorities fully understood this close relationship and therefore saw Lucas, albeit sometimes reluctantly, as the key to controlling the region.

It must have been especially difficult for Lucas to dump his long-time ally Porfirio Díaz. By early 1911, Díaz found himself in an increasingly precarious position as his dictatorship was challenged by the nationwide revolutionary movement of Madero. In February, with uprisings occurring daily in scattered areas of the state of Puebla, Lucas made a deal with the Maderistas in which he assured them of his neutrality in the coming showdown. Díaz, aware of his subordinate's wavering support, urgently requested that Lucas come to Mexico City for consultation. Lucas, claiming that the aches and pains of old age and a fear of the railroad prevented him from traveling such a distance, declined the invitation. Consequently, Díaz had little choice but to write off the strategic Sierra, which had served him so loyally since 1862.

The fall of Díaz only three months later, in May 1911, ushered in the Madero period; the new president formally took up the office in November of that same year. Despite the optimism generated by the overthrow of the Díaz dictatorship, Madero's government proved to be unstable. Elements both from the old regime and from among those who wanted faster implementation of revolutionary change challenged Madero. The new president himself made a series of political and tactical blunders, including keeping intact the Porfirian army while dismantling the revolutionary forces that had brought him to power.

Although Lucas tried, there was little he could do in the long run to save Madero. In the spring of 1912, facing a serious rebellion, Madero persuaded Lucas to come out of retirement and create and lead a special force in the Sierra of some seven hundred men, a force that the federal government promised to equip and pay. Once successful in pacifying the region, Lucas demonstrated his always independent nature as well as his keen sense of politics by exerting direct political control over the towns he garrisoned. He replaced personnel, freed prisoners, and eliminated taxes in an effort to benefit his predominantly Indian followers. These steps directly challenged the state government whose chief executive threatened war with Lucas if Madero did not bring the cacique under control. In the end, Lucas reluctantly heeded Madero's order to disband his force. In the process, he made it clear, however, that he was little beholden to either the state or federal governments and that he remained the central force to be reckoned with in the Sierra.

Recognition of Lucas's importance in the region came once again in early February 1913 when, following a hotly disputed gubernatorial election in the state, two candidates claimed the position. Upon the inauguration of the Madero-backed aspirant, Juan Carrasco, the challenger, Agustín del Pozo, supported by more conservative elements, including the army, formed his own state government in Lucas's bailiwick, Tetela. Madero insisted that Lucas not back del Pozo, and the wily cacique did maintain a neutral stance, waiting, no doubt, to see which way the political winds would blow. Lucas was saved from committing himself when, only a few days later, Madero was overthrown in a coup d'état in Mexico City led by the federal commander Victoriano Huerta.

How to treat the illegitimate Huerta regime so as not to be branded a reactionary yet to protect his political home base became Lucas's next dilemma. His position soon became doubly difficult as, by late spring of 1913, anti-Huerta rebels, operating under the auspices of Carranza's movement based in northern Mexico, began to battle the federal army in the Sierra. Lucas tried to stall for concessions as Huerta put pressure on him to make a deal in order to enable the president to secure the Sierra against Carrancista incursions. Lucas finally got the deal he wanted. In October 1913, Huerta acceded not only to Lucas but also to demands for better security against the Carrancistas from the Canadian-owned Necaxa hydroelectric works near Huauchinango and the American-owned Tezuitlán copper company. In a truly unusual yet beneficial arrangement for the Serranos, Lucas, Estebán Márquez (head of the Carrancista forces in the Sierra), and the Huertista general Mariano Ruíz signed an agreement in Tetela. It called for the withdrawal of the federal army from the Sierra and the creation of a two-thousand-man army under the command of Lucas and Márquez. These troops would replace the federal forces and maintain a neutral peace in the region. In addition, the federal army was to end all recruiting in the Sierra, and elections were to take place to select new local officials.

On paper, the pact gave the people of the Sierra the autonomy they desired, but, in practice, it got off to a wobbly start. By year's end, the agreement had begun to unravel. From its beginning, some elements, including officers such as Gilberto Camacho, who earlier had fought under Márquez, rejected the truce. Then, in December, it received a further blow when Márquez's brother, Gaspar, also denounced it. Despite Lucas's efforts to hold the accord together, it ended in January 1914 when Estebán Márquez disassociated himself from it and called upon the people of the Sierra to take up arms against Huerta. Lucas and his sons, under increasingly bitter criticism from many quarters for their tacit support of Madero's murderer, soon followed Márquez's lead.

By April 1914 the Lucas and Márquez clans headed several hundred troops and controlled large areas of the Sierra. Despite the invasion of Veracruz by the United States that same month, they rejected Huerta's calls for the creation of a joint army to oust the Yankee invaders. Nevertheless, Lucas did agree to a short cease-fire with the federal army in order not to appear to be undermining the nation at such a critical time. The cease-fire did not, however, significantly help Huerta, and he was forced to flee to Europe in July 1914.

With Huerta gone, Lucas continued to back Carranza, but he did so only under the condition that the Sierra remain his bailiwick and his soldiers stay in the area. Throughout the summer and fall of 1914, Lucas secured the region for the "First Chief" and urged local officials to cooperate with the Carranza regime by, for example, allowing the collection of taxes for the Constitutionalist government coffers.

Peace did not reign long. In December 1914, Estebán Márquez accepted the position of state governor for the Conventionalist government led by Emiliano Zapata and Francisco Villa. Márquez established his capital in Huauchinango, thereby directly challenging Lucas. Despite the seeming superiority of the Conventionalist forces, Lucas astutely remained with Carranza and was named head of a brigade under the overall command of General Antonio Medina. Carranza's efforts to secure a negotiated peace with Márquez, using Lucas as a go-between, finally succeeded in May 1915, when the disintegration of the Conventionalist government left Márquez in an untenable position. For the remaining year and one-half of his life, Lucas continued to serve Carranza. He helped put down another rebellion by Márquez and even allowed the First Chief to transfer his brigade from the Third Division of the Army of the East to the military command of the state governor. Nevertheless, the Patriarch fought for and succeeded in getting Carranza to agree that his troops would remain armed and would not be used outside the Sierra districts of Tetela, Chignahuapan, and Zacatlán, except in the case of an emergency. Lucas also began to implement the Constitutionalist land reform program in the Sierra even as Carranza himself increasingly backed away from his commitments to such change in other areas of the country.

In failing health during the whole revolutionary period, Lucas more and more referred to his aches and pains in letters to friends and depended on medicine brought to him from Mexico City. In his later years he traveled little; when he did, it was often in a sedan chair carried by his aides. In November 1916, Lucas caught a cold, and, in the following weeks, he rapidly declined. He died of an intestinal inflammation on February 1, 1917, at the age of eighty-three in Xochiapulco. His oldest son and principal confidant, Abraham, remained at his side until the end. Lucas was buried in the municipal cemetery in Tetela in an impressive ceremony attended by thousands of his loyal followers. Even today, he is fondly remembered in the Sierra.

SOURCES

Archives Consulted

Francisco Madero Archive. Archivo General de la Nación. Mexico City.

Lucas Family Archive. Puebla, Mexico.
Municipal Archives. Tetela de Ocampo and Zacapoastla, Mexico.
Notarial Archives. Tetela and Zacapoastla districts, Mexico.
Porfirio Díaz Archive. Universidad Iberoamericana. Mexico City.
Secretaría de la Defensa Nacional Archive. Mexico City.
U.S. Department of State Records. National Archives. Washington, DC.
Venustiano Carranza Archive. Condumex. Mexico City.

Published Works

Cosio Villegas, Daniel. *Historia moderna de Mexico: La república restaurada, vida política.* Mexico, 1959.
———*El porfiriato, vida política interior.* 2 vols. Mexico, 1970–72.
Galindo y Galindo, Miguel. *La gran década nacional: Relación histórica de la guerra de reforma, intervención extranjera y gobierno del archiduque maximiliano, 1857–1867.* 3 vols. Mexico, 1904–06.
Paré, Luisa. "Inter-Ethnic and Class Relations (Sierra Norte Region, State of Puebla)." In *Race and Class in Post-Colonial Society*, edited by the United Nations Educational, Scientific, and Cultural Organization, 377–420. Paris, 1977.
Perry, Laurens Ballard. *Juárez and Díaz Machine Politics in Mexico.* DeKalb, IL, 1978.

2

Miguel Rostaing: Dodging Blows on and off the Soccer Field

Steve Stein

Miguel Rostaing, much like his compatriot Juan Esquivel (whose biography is also in this volume), sought new opportunities in the Peru of the early twentieth century. While Esquivel went into commercial agriculture, Rostaing turned to the building trades in Lima, the capital city. Despite his working long hours each day, Rostaing found the time to play soccer for the newly developing teams. He enjoyed the game, and it gave him the opportunity, when his opponents were white teams, "to settle the score" with at least some members of the elites who dominated his life off the playing field. This biography demonstrates how Rostaing developed skills that served him in both his sport and his life.

Rostaing's biography comes out of extensive oral interviews conducted by Steve Stein during his research on working-class culture in Peru from 1900 to 1930. Stein's interest in this topic developed during graduate study at Stanford University and, in 1980, resulted in his book, *Populism in Peru: The Emergence of the Masses and the Politics of Social Control.* This work was followed in 1985 by a three-volume study *Lima obrera, 1900–1930*, in which Stein examines popular culture, working-class politics, and urban social structure.

Currently, Stein is a professor of history at the University of Miami and director of the university's North-South Academic Exchange Program and Programs in Great Britain.

INTRODUCTION

Miguel Rostaing (1900–83) was one of Peru's premier soccer players in the early decades of this century. Playing before the sport was professionalized, Rostaing worked full-time (sometimes twelve to fifteen hours a day) as a bricklayer at the same time as he was a member, for nearly fifteen years, of the first string of Alianza Lima, the most successful and popular of all urban soccer clubs. His life on and off the field was representative of the daily hardships and the occasional joys experienced by Lima's lower classes. Through Rostaing's account, we can begin to understand some of the subjective as well as objective components of the daily experience of the Lima poor. On one level, we are witness to certain common occurrences in the popular-sector family in the period from 1900 to 1930, to the formation of the city's earliest soccer teams, and to the virtual racial warfare between "black" teams such as Alianza Lima and their more white, higher-class adversaries. On another level, we learn how a man like Rostaing felt about his life—about being abandoned at an early age by his father, about the cheers of the crowd that greeted him after an especially good play, and about being black in a society that relegated people of African origin to the lowest rung on the social ladder. And it is in this realm of feeling, in this innermost precinct of human existence, that life histories like that of Miguel Rostaing are most revealing.

I was born in Lima in 1900. All my life I took good care of myself because of soccer. That's why I played for many years, from the year 1914 to 1936.

We really fooled around when we were kids. We had to be home at a certain hour. If we were late, we got it. My mother waited for us with a whip and a belt in her hand, those pointed whips that the milkmen used. That's what she hit us with, and we would run underneath the bed. She stuck us with a broom handle to get us out, and at times we wouldn't let her since we were strong. "Let go! Because I'll get you, get you out if I have to kick you!"

Once we went to the circus. We didn't go to school. And a man who knew us told my mother: "I tell you I've seen Miguel and Juan in the circus." We really got it there. My mother beat us on the naked rear end, and we really got it. If she got distracted, we escaped, because we had a door and windows that faced the street. So we escaped, and we didn't come back until after she went to work.

My mother never liked it when we answered her back, or even looked at her. *Uf!* She gave it to us with whatever she had around, even with big metal and wooden spoons. My mother wouldn't let us look at her when she was bawling us out. At midnight and at two or three in the morning, she hit us on the naked rear end because they had told her about something we had done. She got us then because we couldn't escape, because if she fell asleep we escaped and we didn't come back until after she left for work. Since we knew she had to go, when she came back she had already forgotten, then she didn't hit us.

I say that my mother was really tough, she punished us. If not, we would have come out, well, bad. Because in our neighborhood of La Victoria,[1] a lot of boys came out bad. They became thieves. There were a lot of chicken coops in the *corralones*, all that, because chickens weren't raised in Lima because it wasn't allowed, and when La Victoria grew up, almost everybody in the *corralones* and *callejones*[2] raised their chickens. There is where some got robbed. And there were some guys who didn't just steal chickens. They also robbed clothes from inside of houses. They were robbers but not big ones. And they were our friends out in the streets, and that's what my mother didn't want.

We weren't into stealing chickens. We weren't into anything bad, because my mother wouldn't let us. We tried to obey her because it was good. Because if we hadn't paid attention to her, we would have gone bad. Sometimes we stole a few pieces of fruit or some vegetables, just fooling around. That was different.

My mother had been abandoned. My father left us. He left me when I was two years old and my brother was in my mother's womb. I finally met him when I was twelve years old. He came to see us. He wanted to make up with my mother. She wouldn't go along, and us kids, me, for example, we didn't have any respect for him any more. We didn't act badly towards him, but there was no affection, especially because we never got an education. My father was one of the top typesetters of *El Comercio*.[3] He was really sought after. So he could have given us a good education. He left us without an education. When I got to know him, I told him what I thought. Talking, talking, I told him: "For me, you are not my father anymore."

I only went to school for one year because of my mother's situation. Mother had to be helped. My mother was left, you could say, almost a widow, when we were very young. I had to leave school to go to work. I liked mathematics because it helped you with your jobs. I just didn't have enough school. I couldn't continue because we were in need of a lot of things. Especially clothing was a problem. My mother had to buy it, and she didn't have enough.

My mother worked in the most tiring of jobs. She was a cook and a washerwoman. She worked in various places as a cook, and at home she washed for certain people who knew her. We never went hungry, but we had a hard life because we didn't have a father. She worked

---

[1]A lower-class neighborhood on the edge of central Lima established in the early twentieth century.

[2]Two of the most common forms of lower-class urban housing.

[3]Lima's most important daily newspaper at the time.

for a priest who was a really good man. He gave us all his leftovers. I have never met any priest like him. He had us come in: "Take the meat, let's not have any food left over here." And that's why my buddies used to hang around my house, because there was lots of food.

My mother would do the washing early in the morning. She got up at five and washed from five to nine. Then she went to work and came back at nine or ten at night. That's when we would go to the priest's for the leftovers. She had a terrible life. She just worked and worked and never had a rest. She worked all the time. On Sundays she worked until one in the afternoon.

When my mother was working she left us alone. My older brother heated up our food. Once my face was burned. I was two years old, and when my brother was heating up dinner he burned my face. I was sitting at the table, and my brother poured too much fuel in the stove, and he lit a match to see if it would start, and the cooking fuel fell on me. And since in those times they used to dress you up with girls' clothing, I got all burned. I don't know how my mother revived me because I really got burned, even my hands. Since then I've always had this burn on my face, and that's where I got the nickname "*El Quemado*" [the burned one]. And that was my nickname for soccer.

My mother's situation probably forced me to start working. I started to work at the age of nine in construction, as a peon for a man who was a specialist in floor tile. The man's name was Espinosa. I started making five reales in 1909. The situation was bad, and I wanted to help my mom. Because a pair of shoes cost three-and-a-half soles. I realized that we had food, but we needed money to buy clothing. Sometimes there wasn't enough and besides we played a lot of soccer and we ruined a lot of shoes. Sometimes we had to wear broken shoes, and there you could see that we didn't have enough. My mother considered what I made a help. I gave everything I made to my mother, and she gave me fifty centavos on Sundays as allowance.

To get a job, you went to where there was construction, and you asked if they needed a peon. But my mother knew a Sr. Espinosa. a specialist in floors. So helping him mix the cement and lay the tiles he paid me five reales. In construction there were kids working but not many, because at that age you aren't so strong. That's why I got an easy job with the tiles where you didn't have to carry that much, and a little mixing too. To carry bricks you have to be bigger, stronger. Sr. Espinosa treated me like family. He gave me five reales like a tip.

You started off as a peon, and then you moved up to bricklayer, master bricklayer. When you're a master bricklayer then you know just about everything. I must have worked six years as a peon, yes, six or seven years. After Sr. Espinosa I carried bricks to the bricklayer. It was hard work because the bricklayers laid the brick fast; I had to keep him supplied. At the beginning, I didn't carry much. You went on helping the bricklayer with two, three bricks. Guys who were strong carried three. And the bricklayers hurried you up. Most of the walls were made of adobes, not of bricks, and you had to carry the mud mixture or the adobe bricks in a tray on your head and dump it out for the bricklayer. The adobes are heavy. You had to hurry up to supply enough to the bricklayer, but the tray couldn't be very big. Us kids had small trays, but you had to hurry up in order to keep the bricklayer happy. He would call you: "Come on, you, bring me the mud!" You had to hurry up. Afterwards, when brickmakers used bricks, it was something else. And it wasn't so dirty either, because the mud was what made it so dirty. Not a day passed when you didn't get your shoes dirty with the mud. The first years were the hardest. I became a bricklayer when I was around sixteen years old. You learned pretty fast. And I said to myself: "How am I going to continue making so little? I have to go about finding out how to learn more."

When I worked as a bricklayer, most of the time I did piecework. The fastest workers made the most. You had to hurry up to lay the most meters. You always had to hurry up to lay more, because there were a lot of engineers who made you work for a daily wage, and then they paid you less. But there were engineers who paid more when they were in a hurry; they paid by the meter when they were in a hurry. The day laborer worked for a daily wage, that's all. When you're young, you don't feel so tired working fast. It's at the end that you feel tired.

I was a bricklayer for forty some years, and that's why I suffer from bronchitis. You were always very cold as a bricklayer. In bricklaying you felt a lot of dampness, because in the old days to work as a bricklayer you had to dig wells in the streets because you didn't have so much water available as you do now. You needed the water to mix the plaster, the mud. You had to dig wells five or six meters down to store the water. So all this water affected the bricklayer, because almost all bricklayers die from their lungs, from asthma, from things you got from having colds. It was a dangerous, a tough job.

All this time I was playing soccer. Hour after hour we played. Some left, and others continued playing until it got dark. When I was nine, I played with a rag ball. When one of my mother's stockings got torn, we would rob it from her to make a ball. We filled it up with rags. The rag ball was common everywhere, because leather balls were pretty expensive. So we made rag balls, we made them good, they even bounced. Now everybody has rubber shoes. Before, the only thing we had were rope-soled shoes, much cheaper, they cost three soles. We used to play in open fields, that's all. We made goals with little sticks dug into the mud or sometimes just with stones. My mother used to watch me sometimes when she was going around where we played. She used to say that they were going to kick me. She said: "Be careful when you're going to play soccer. When I go by where you are playing, it seems to me that they're going to kill you, they're going to give you some bad blows."

My first team was called Huáscar. We formed it in the neighborhood in 1914 among friends. We were players and founders of Huáscar. Most of us used to train after work. Between five and seven at night we would run and do calisthenics. Some who couldn't go in the afternoon trained in the morning. Those who could went in the afternoon, and others trained at night. On Huáscar every team member paid monthly dues, I think fifty centavos, to maintain the club. We rented a room for the team to get together. If we hadn't charged dues, how were we going to pay for our room? Sometimes we had to buy shoes too. There were times that some players didn't have enough for the shoes, and we had to help them out. Guys that had enough bought their own shoes. We had a president whose name was Don Andrés Broche. He had an Italian name. He was the one who paid the most. Don't you see, he made chocolates. If there was a player who couldn't pay, he took care of everything. He was a great guy. We even helped him wrap the little chocolates, the candies. They used to wrap them in papers, almost the same as they do now, but now they make them nicer. But before they wrapped them in papers and twisted them at each end. Sometimes we also helped him deliver the chocolates. He didn't pay us, but sometimes he gave us candies. He made a lot of them to sell. It was like a little factory.

When I played, I played every position. I was like a one-man orchestra, to be exact. I played right forward, left forward, left wing, right wing, right half, left half, and once I even played center half. And I also played defense. They always changed me around to different positions. I played them all the same. After all, the ball is round everywhere on the field.

I started playing on Alianza in 1918.[4] A lot of us came in that year, and we formed a new Alianza, made up of young guys, because the

[4]Alianza Lima, Peru's first, and most famous, popular-sector soccer team. It was founded in 1901 in Lima.

guys that had originally founded the team were going downhill by that time. Alianza had some sponsors, and they talked to you, if you wanted to join the team or not. But since Alianza was a celebrated team, it had its fans. Any player for them became popular.

When I joined, we had old people on the team, and we had to renew ourselves. We looked first for José María Lavalle. I knew José María for a time from the neighborhood. And we saw him play, we went about pulling him on to the team, and the modern Alianza began to be formed. He was a guy who played in the street; he made adobe bricks. So we saw him play and saw that he was good. So we got him for Alianza. We pulled a couple of players from other teams—Montellanos from Gálvez, Filomeno García from Peruano, "*el loco*" Quintana from Progreso. Alejandro Villanueva played with a team called Teniente Ruíz, and Dr. Soria too. But they preferred Alianza because it was a famous team, and it was better than any other team. And we convinced them with friendship, through friendship, that's all. We knew every one of them, the guys who you met on the street. So we went out and convinced them with: "Come over here, you." Until they came, and that's how the modern Alianza was formed.

They called us the *Intimos* [the intimates], and they also called us the *compadres*. Those names came out sometime after the 1921 Centennial of Peru: '21, '22, '23, '24. They called us that because of the friendship all of us had with each other. We always celebrated our birthdays together at home. We felt like we were related. Somebody's birthday came, everybody went. Another *compadre's* birthday came, and there we were. It was something else. We were intimate friends. We were always together. None of the other teams were like that, just Alianza. In Atlético Chalaco,[5] our friendship was only at the club, not in the home. On Alianza, on the other hand, no.

Alianza became conceited because of their fame. José María was right wing, and he had a really terrible urge, a really bad habit. When he found a halfback who wasn't too good, who you could easily dribble around, he would have a banquet with him. He laughed at him, and he danced the marinera around him. He ran, he stopped, he gave him the ball and took it back. He would spin him around the field. When this happened he wouldn't let go of the ball for anything. Those things hurt the team. He didn't center the ball, and the team couldn't make goals. And he just laughed. Valdivieso [the goalie] had to swear at him to make him pass the ball. He would scream at him from the

[5]An early popular-sector soccer team from Lima's port city of Callao for which Rostaing played in 1930.

other end of the field to stop screwing around with the poor halfback: "All right, come on '*negro*,' get rid of the ball!" José María just laughed. You had to talk tough to him, threaten him. We had to make him center it. You couldn't score a single goal because he was having a banquet with the halfback. That *negro* was a real sly one. He looked like a mullet, that *negro* José María. *Uf!*

Alianza always had players who drank a lot. Most of them were drinkers. I drank, but very little. At times they played drunk and they lost. When we made our first trip to Chile in 1933, the players came in drunk on Saturday night and played the next day. That's why we lost almost all of the games. My *compadre* Domingo García played drunk. If you took away his liquor in the middle of the week, he couldn't play. Although it might seem a lie, he needed liquor to play. Once we were going to play, I think it was going to be against Universitario: "Let's shut *compadre* Domingo in. Don't let him out to drink." And he almost collapsed while playing. I tell you, he didn't do anything that day. So what were we going to do with him? Starting Friday, we made him his fish soup, and he stayed shut in from Friday before the game. But since we took away his liquor in the middle of the week, he couldn't do anything in the game. He was the best of the Garcías; he would go forward even though he was a halfback. He's still alive. But he still has his drinks. Even now we get together to drink.

We would drink cognac during the games but in a very small quantity. This was only on Alianza. We made a preparation of tea, lemon, and cognac, and we didn't feel tired. It was mostly lemon, a kind of strong tea. Sometimes we took three bottles of that to the games. One little glass of that and you didn't feel tired. We would drink it after the first period, just before going out for the second. You didn't get drunk with it. You didn't feel dizzy either, nothing like that. You could say that we revived with that drink. Now Segalá [the goalie] was very nervous. So we always gave him a few drops of Valeriana[6] in his tea because we knew all too well about his nervousness. You would see him even change in color when he was starting the game. He came on to the field all yellowish until he made his first save. And then he became sure of himself. In the second period, three more drops of Valeriana in his tea.

Alianza was always a team of the people, to a certain point, of the blacks. That was the idea of Alianza. Alianza's players were working people. The majority worked in construction, and one or another of

[6] A mild tranquilizer.

us had [a] different kind of job. Sometimes they said to us: "There come the bricklayers," and sometimes, "There come the blacks."

Our fans were from different neighborhoods. Of course, the largest quantity from La Victoria, from Abajo el Puente, from Malambo,[7] from all those places. I used to think: "I'm a player; I'm not making any money at this." I guess I played, at least in part, because the people applauded me. Ah, the fans loved you! The fans would start to buzz, and as you were playing you would start faking out your opponent, dribbling around him. They would call you, for example, "*Quemado* Rostaing!" "Villanueva!" "Lavalle!" They would call to us, and we would dribble by the other guy. *Uf*! We would pass to somebody else. Sometimes he would let the ball go to another teammate. The game opened up there. It was, in fact, the fans who made us do that.

It was there that the olés came. For example, there were a lot of olés when you made a good play; in those times there was a lot of that with the goals. That's where the olé of Alianza came from. Because when Alianza scored one, two goals, then they started screaming: "*Titán, titán*, olé, olé!" That came from Alianza. There was a kind of friendship. For example, you were leaving the stadium and you would always go and have a glass of beer with two or three friends. And since most of Alianza were big drinkers, they liked being treated by the fans. They would stay until they were pretty drunk. The fans paid for the beers.

After every game, that's when the celebrations began, the applause, the cries. The wives and *compadres* and *comadres* went too. We had a rooting section of women. And, later on, Alianza came to have a women's club to put on the fiestas of the team. But most of them were dark. But the fiestas were nice, well set up. All of those ladies were maids, and they even knew about the fiestas of the rich. And when Alianza had a fiesta, it was like a rich people's fiesta. It was just the same.

There was a special section of the stadium where our fans sat. Sometimes our fans got into fights. If there was an argument, you fought, the women too, everybody. A lot of women went, and even they fought with other women there. But the toughest fans were from Callao, from Atlético Chalaco. They were fishermen. They were fierce, the people from Callao, a lot of bad people, those fishermen. They came with dynamite, and the Lima fans couldn't stand up to them.

---

[7]A working-class neighborhood with a large black population.

What did you defend yourself with? You had to get out of there on the run.

They almost blew up a back that we had. He was going to throw in the ball, and they threw a stick of dynamite at him, and they almost blew him up, ball and all. We were playing in those times [1922] for a gold medal. They beat us when some fans cut Segalá in the behind [*el potingo*]. They were in back of the net, the fans on that side. Somebody stuck a knife through the net and cut him. Segalá turned around, and the ball went in the net. They had to take Segalá out and give him five stitches. Chalaco was ferocious. Against Chalaco it was terrible. Their fans were scary. *Uf*! You had to run out of there with your pants in your hands because those fishermen threw dynamite.

There was this rivalry, in terms of sports, with the Universitario de Deportes team. Any team could beat us, and it wasn't so bad, but not Universitario. Universitario was made up of students, and you could be sure that there wasn't anyone on that team who wasn't a student. They were all students. Such is the case that all have university degrees now. That was the difference. To be on Universitario you had to be from the university. Only little white boys. And Alianza's players, blacks, poor, bricklayers, all of us. Maybe stronger, better players.

Alianza was popular, the team of the workers. Those who supported Universitario were university students. Alianza represented the poor people, and Universitario the rich people. That's why they called them black and white. You could say that this rivalry came from the whites. There was this rivalry between blacks and whites, and, well, Universitario was the team that most upset us. There was this rivalry, no, according to my mother, since the blacks got their freedom from Castilla,[8] that the blacks and the whites didn't rub shoulders. Yes, instead, they stuck to their own race, above all the whites.

The blacks don't want to be blacks. The black doesn't want to be a black. The black, for a woman he looks for a lighter one. Because they themselves have been brought up in this rivalry of the black and the white. The black wants to improve the race. Naturally, that's why they look for a lighter woman. If not, how do you explain José María? His wife is a light *zambita*.[9] The majority of the blacks look for whites. Those who look for a black woman are rare unless you go to Cañete, which is filled with blacks. There you see black men with black women, very few whites. In Lima, we've always looked to cross our race. Well,

[8]The Peruvian president who freed the slaves in the 1850s.

[9]A racial mixture of black and Indian.

I think that the black doesn't want to be black up to this day. This from the moment that the blacks themselves imply that the black is detestable, from the moment that they want to cross their race. But it's very rare to find somebody who wants to cross with a black. What blacks have looked for, yes, is to improve their race. I have seen blacks here who look for light women. And, of course, if they get a white woman, they take up with her. It depends on the woman, no?

In soccer I always took pride in being a *pícaro* [sly] player. They call a *pícaro* a sharp person. To be sharp as a player means not letting yourself get kicked by anyone. You could say that you were sharp if you were quick and didn't let yourself be kicked much. Jumping here, jumping there, and sometimes give back a little so that the other player is afraid of you, too. You jumped when a player came after you to cut you down. You had to jump, and then you kicked him, too, with your foot. When you are a *pícaro*, when you fall and are on the ground, you give it to the other player with your foot so that he doesn't jump on you. Once, I got kicked in the ankle by a guy, and he left me limping for two months. Don't you see I was with my head up, looking at the ball, and crack! I even swore at him. "I'm going to get you!" But he wouldn't let himself be caught, and I couldn't do much because I was like a limping rooster. It was then that I learned to give this special blow in a moment that nobody saw you.

You're born a *pícaro*, born that way. I didn't learn it from anybody. It's something I have. I was always that way since I was very young, since I was fourteen when I played on Huáscar and then when I was eighteen and started on Alianza. To face life you have to be that way. Because life is like a soccer game. You have to be quick so that they don't knock you around like that in your daily life. It's like in work. You have to protect your job because they're always trying to sabotage you, to take your job away from you, and you have to be careful.

You played because you liked soccer. There was no material gain. The gold medal, the diplomas, those are the most pleasant memories. We played two times for the gold medal; one of them Chalaco beat us when they cut Segalá in the behind. But the other time, yes, we won. But when times got bad, we had to pawn the medals and they were lost. And the diplomas, now it's just too expensive to frame them.

3

The Rough-and-Tumble Career of Pedro Crespo

Gilbert M. Joseph and Allen Wells

Gilbert M. Joseph, a professor at the University of North Carolina at Chapel Hill, and Allen Wells, who teaches at Appalachian State University in Boone, North Carolina, have made Mexico's Yucatán Peninsula their second home. Both men wrote dissertations, since published, on the political and economic development of the peninsula—Joseph's *Revolution from Without: Yucatán, Mexico, and the United States, 1880–1924* (1982) and Wells's *Yucatán's Gilded Age: Haciendas, Henequen, and International Harvester, 1860–1915* (1985). Their collaboration on articles and on *Henequen y la International Harvester* (1986) led to their election to membership in the Academia Yucatanese de Ciencias y Artes.

In the vignette that follows, the authors examine the career of one of Mexico's outstanding, yet little-known, local power brokers—Pedro Crespo of Temax, Yucatán. His career invites comparison with that of Juan Francisco Lucas, another Mexican who prospered through the opportunities created by the Mexican Revolution. In both cases, the high-and-mighty words of revolutionary idealism are translated into action by individuals variously motivated by a craving for adventure, by envy, by revenge, by social conscience, and by the courage and cussedness of ordinary human beings.

Temax is at the end of the road. A few blocks north of the weather-beaten plaza, the paved road from Izamal runs out; further on, *camino blanco* winds for about twenty kilometers through scrub, then mangrove swamp to the Gulf of Mexico. Eighty kilometers west of the town is the state capital, Mérida; en route one travels through the heart of the henequen (sisal) zone, glimpsing remnants of a more affluent past. Poorly tended henequen fields line both sides of the highway, which is crisscrossed here and there by the rusting and twisted rails of imported Decauville narrow-gauge tram tracks. Blackened chimneys and the ruins of once elegant haciendas similarly bear witness to the grandeur of a monoculture now in irreversible decline.

To the east of Temax, henequen's bluish gray spines soon give way to denser scrub and clearings of grazing cattle; beyond the neighboring village of Buctzotz there is little to see for another seventy kilometers, until Tizimin, cattle country's new boomtown. Hot, dusty, and unprepossessing to the casual eye, Temax appears to be just another desperately poor and sleepy municipal seat that time has long since passed by.

Current appearances, however, mask a turbulent and intriguing recent past. Indeed, Temax has figured prominently in Yucatecan history since the apocalyptic Caste War of the mid-nineteenth century. Poised as it is between the dynamic henequen zone and the marginal sparsely populated hinterland, between the settled plantation society and the zone of refuge for the rebellious Maya campesinos who resisted plantation encroachment on their traditional way of life, Temax has been a strategic periphery or frontier. Consequently, its control has posed a significant problem for Yucatán's modern rulers. And, for much of the first half of the twentieth century, Temax's political fortunes were closely linked to the career of an extraordinary rural insurgent and political boss, Pedro Crespo. State authorities came to realize that the price of peace in Temax was a certain degree of autonomy for Don Pedro. Like Carlos Fuentes's archetypal revolutionary cacique (boss), Artemio Cruz, Crespo knew how to survive. And, much like that of Cruz, Crespo's political career came to embody the achievements and contradictions of the larger revolutionary process.

We know relatively little about Crespo's prerevolutionary career, before he burst upon the local political scene in March of 1911. During the presidency of Porfirio Díaz, Temax was overwhelmingly rural—even today, 80 percent of the working population is employed in agriculture—with a small town-based commercial sector catering to nearby hacienda and peasant communities. Born about 1870, of humble village origins, like many campesinos on the fringes of the expanding henequen zone Crespo grew up determined to preserve the family's status as small but free cultivators. Quite likely, he chose to enlist in the state national guard, to avoid the mechanism of debt that tied an ever-increasing number of villagers as peons to the large and powerful henequen estates.

In short order, Crespo demonstrated his prowess as a soldier and was made an officer in the local guard. How did Crespo regard his duties, which included hunting down and returning runaway peons to their masters, quelling worker protests against brutal, slavelike labor conditions, and implementing the hated *leva* (conscription), which dragooned villagers and drifters into the guard? We'll never know.

No doubt Crespo came to know the social world of north-central Yucatán beyond the boundaries of the rural countryside. Temaxeños remember him as a man with a foot in both worlds: "un mestizo de buen hablar"—a Maya campesino who spoke Spanish well and could handle himself in town.[1] Through his work, young Crespo was introduced to the milieu of urban politics, to the ever-shifting layered networks of patronage and clientele, which tied the local *dzules*—powerful rulers of land and men in their own right—to even more powerful patrons in the state capital.

As an officer in the guard, Crespo was compelled to play this exacting, dangerous game of late Porfirian politics. Although he initially flirted with the intrigues of a disenfranchised faction of the planter elite in 1909, by the eve of the 1910 gubernatorial election, Crespo had allied himself with Enrique Muñoz Arístegui, the "official" candidate of the "Divine Caste," an entrenched oligarchy led by the state's most powerful planter, merchant, and politician, Don Olegario Molina.

Don Olegario was a formidable patron. He was a favorite of President Porfirio Díaz, and, following a term as governor of Yucatán, he served as minister of development in Díaz's cabinet (1907–11). Molina's relations and cronies filled the upper echelons of the state's bureaucratic machine. Indeed, the power of the "Divine Caste" radiated outward from the Molina *parentesco* (extended family), which, apart from its national connections, was greatly fortified by its partnership with the principal buyer of raw henequen fiber, the International Harvester Company. Under the terms of a secret arrangement between Molina's import-export house and the North American corporation, large sums of foreign capital were periodically placed at the oligarch's disposal, enabling Molina y Compañía to affect price trends, acquire mortgages, and consolidate its hold on fiber production, communications, the infrastructure, and banking in the region. Despite the fabulous wealth generated by the fin de siècle henequen boom, the first decade of the new century was a veritable summer of discontent for the vast majority of Yucatecan producers, merchants, workers, and campesinos, who found themselves personally indebted or subordinated, in one form or another, to the Molina *parentesco*.

Francisco Madero's national political campaign against the Díaz regime emboldened two disgruntled camarillas (political factions) of

---

[1]In Yucatán the term *mestizo* differs from the standard usage. It indicates a person or attribute—that is, style of dress—which is at root Maya but has been influenced over time by Hispanic culture.

the Yucatecan planter class and their middle-class allies to organize parties for the purpose of challenging Molinista hegemony in the 1910 elections. Formed in 1909, these rather loose political coalitions, the Centro Electoral Independiente and the Partido Antireeleccionista, were known popularly as "Morenistas" and "Pinistas," after their respective standard-bearers, Delio Moreno Cantón and José María Pino Suárez, who were journalists. But they were financed by their planter supporters, and each faction hastily attempted to construct alliances reaching into the urban intelligentsia and small working class, and, perhaps even more tactically, into the large and potentially explosive Maya *campesinado*.

As a rising military leader able to bridge the cultural distance between *dzules* and campesinos, Crespo was a valuable asset in strategic Temax and was wooed by incumbents and dissidents alike. After testing the waters of Morenismo, however, he chose to stay with the Molinistas. Along with Temax's other prominent functionaries, Colonel Antonio Herrera, the *jefe político* (district prefect), and Nazario Aguilar Brito, the municipal tax collector, Crespo joined the local chapter of the Unión Democrática, the political club working for the election of Molina's puppet, Muñoz Arístegui.

It was not long before oligarchical repression foreclosed the electoral road to Maderismo nationwide and to the moderate political reformers in Yucatán who had affiliated with it. When Morenista and Pinista candidates and their supporters were harassed and jailed, these parties entered into a nominal alliance, plotted secretly, and ultimately rebelled against the established order. In June 1910, 1,500 insurgents—mostly peons led by a local property owner, an accountant, and a hacienda foreman—rose prematurely in the eastern city of Valladolid. Fueled chiefly by hatred of the abusive Molinista prefect, who was summarily shot, this rebellion held Valladolid captive for six days but, lacking effective leadership and focus, did not spread to other localities. While campesinos indulged themselves in celebration and *aguardiente* (the cane liquor of the masses), federal and state troops stormed the city. Justice was served in characteristically draconian fashion: public executions of the leaders, stiff jail sentences and penal servitude in the jungles of nearby Quintana Roo for the lesser lights. The oligarchical order stood firm.

Still Pedro Crespo stood with the establishment. What, then, turned this cautious policeman into a revolutionary? Quite likely he was unable to ignore ties of blood and a claim for vengeance. Like Pancho Villa, whose sister was raped, and countless others who joined Madero's national movement in 1910, a sense of deep personal outrage set Crespo at odds with the Porfirian authorities. Sketchy press accounts and judicial proceedings, which here and there are corroborated by local tradition, shed light on the question of Crespo's motivation. Crespo had been left by Temax's corrupt prefect, Colonel Herrera, who also was Crespo's superior officer in the local guard detachment, to languish for thirty days in the notoriously unfriendly confines of Mérida's Juárez Penitentiary. Crespo would later speak vaguely of "differences he had [had] with the Temax authorities," and his lieutenants would cite the tyrannical abuses of Herrera's local rule. Some old-timers recall that Crespo had been openly critical of the *jefe político's* high-handed tactics in meetings with Temaxeño campesinos. But for Crespo, much more than *mal gobierno* or perhaps even personal rivalry was at issue here: Herrera had killed Crespo's father, Don Cosme Damían, under shadowy circumstances. Apparently, while Pedro was in jail, Don Cosme had balked at Herrera's arbitrary order that he do *fagina* (unpaid, forced road work), whereupon the *jefe político* had ordered his goons to gun the old man down in broad daylight.

Soon after his release from prison, Crespo sought revenge. He mustered up a small band of his kin and clients—most of them peasant villagers—and exploded into revolt. Operating in the chaotic political climate that was Maderismo in Yucatán, Crespo elected to burn his bridges behind him, joining his local vendetta to the larger regional movement against Díaz and the Molinistas. On March 4, 1911, he led his column in a lightning predawn raid on the county seat of Temax. The rebels easily overwhelmed the nine-man guard detachment of Temax's central plaza. (Later, the town police commander would charge that the *guardia* had been sleeping on the job.) Crespo immediately rousted Colonel Herrera and the treasury agent Aguilar Brito from their beds and hauled them, clad only in their skivvies (*paños menores*), to the plaza. All the while, as members of his band shouted "Viva Madero!" and "Down with bad government!," Crespo vented his rage on the stunned Herrera: "You bastard, you killed my father! Before you were on top and screwed me, but now it's my turn!"[2]

The tables were indeed turned. Handpicked as district prefect by the great Molinista planters, Colonel Herrera was the dominant figure in Temax's political life, and his physical presence made him even more menacing to local campesinos. Hulking in stature, with his shaved

---

[2]Archivo General del Estado de Yucatán, Ramo de Justicia, "Causa seguida contra Pedro Crespo y socios por homicidio, rebelión y robo," 1911. Interview with Don Melchor Zozaya Raz, December 31, 1986.

head and long gray beard, Herrera often took on the dimensions of a mad monk or an avenging prophet. Only days before, during the Carnival revels of Shrove Tuesday, although too cowed to make a statement about their *jefe político*, Temaxeños had mocked his subordinate, Aguilar Brito, as "Juan Carnaval," shooting an effigy of the treasury agent in front of the Municipal Palace. Now, in the same central plaza in the wee hours of the morning, Pedro Crespo was cutting the despised prefect down to size. In a final act of humiliation, Crespo strapped Herrera and Aguilar to chairs and riddled them with bullets in the same spot in front of the town hall where Aguilar had been "executed" during Carnival. The bodies were piled into a meat wagon and then dumped at the gates of the town cemetery. (It was ghastly ironic that the treasury agent would later be interred in the same coffin that "Juan Carnaval" had occupied the preceding Shrove Tuesday.)

Before he left town the next morning, Crespo emptied the municipal jail, freeing some campesinos who had been imprisoned for refusing to do *fagina* ordered by the deceased *jefe político*. Crespo armed his new recruits and then, in the manner of the Valladolid rebels, requested food, drink, and "contributions" from local merchants, and took the 300 pesos (one peso equaled fifty U.S. cents) in the municipal treasury. Yet Crespo had learned some valuable lessons from the Valladolid debacle: He made sure that Temax's prominent families were not physically harmed, and he strictly limited his men's intake of *aguardiente*. There would be no premature celebrations in Temax; Crespo saddled up his force—now swollen to about eighty—and divided the men into two mobile bands, one to head west toward Cansahcab, the other east, under his direction, toward Buctzotz. All wore red bands on their hats.

In the weeks and months that followed, Pedro Crespo became Yucatán's most successful insurgent. His hit-and-run tactics, based on an intimate knowledge of the local terrain, were celebrated in the pueblos and hacienda communities of north-central Yucatán, and his ranks continued to multiply. One week after his raid on Temax, his troops mushroomed to 200; by mid-April some estimates placed his strength at 400, in May, close to 1,000. Many free villagers and some hacienda peons joined his campaign willingly, eager to strike a blow against the *dzules*, particularly the despised *jefe políticos* and hacienda overseers who symbolized the encroachments and abuses of the oligarchy. In Buctzotz, a group of villagers rose up upon Crespo's arrival, took the National Guard barracks, and cut out the tongue of the municipal president before executing him. In Dzilám González, dozens of campesinos, including the town's band, defected en masse to the rebellion. The musicians brought their instruments and enlivened the guerrilla campaign in the weeks ahead with a series of impromptu Saturday night *jaranas* (folk dances) in remote backcountry hamlets.

Although many hacienda peons were recruited at gunpoint by the rebels, Crespo sought to erode planter paternalism and social control with clientelist measures of his own. At the Cauacá, Chacmay, and San Francisco Manzanilla haciendas—the estates of the largest henequen planters—he decreed "liberation," canceling all of the peons' debts. Moreover, Crespo provided amply for his recruits, derailing trains, raiding *cuarteles* (barracks) for munitions, and levying forced loans on local planters and merchants. At Cauacá, 150 peons joined Crespo, and suddenly Maya surnames were greatly outnumbering Spanish ones in his ranks. Many planters, hoping to avoid the total loss of their work force, immediately ordered the temporary evacuation of their *sirvientes* to nearby county seats, where they would wait out the rebellion.

Crespo's guerrilla campaign forced the Molinista regime to expend great amounts of time, money, and manpower in a futile effort to pin down the rebels. Soon other risings against government installations and officials—like Crespo's, nominally Maderista—spread throughout the countryside. During the spring of 1911 the Mérida government found itself unable to do more than hold the county seats, leaving the hinterland to the insurgents. Moreover, village-based campesinos increasingly resisted government attempts to recruit them to fight against the rebels, or mutinied following recruitment. Finally, Muñoz Arístegui was compelled to resign, and the new military governor issued an amnesty for all disaffected rebels designed to coax rebel leaders like Crespo to lay down their arms, a desperation move that did little to quell rural unrest throughout the state.

All the while, Crespo moved at will throughout the Temax district and penetrated into neighboring Izamal, Espita, and districts farther east. Early on, he reached an understanding with Juan Campos, a popular insurgent who also had risen against local abuses and later conveniently labeled himself a "Maderista." Campos already was carving out a power base (*cacicazgo*) north of Temax, in the area around Dzidzantún and Dzilám González. In the months and years ahead, Crespo and Campos would wage a number of joint operations and together come to control all of north-central Yucatán for over two decades. *Ancianos* still recall the two chiefs as local instruments through which the revolution put an end to "la época de esclavitud" (the age of slavery). Campos was even more audacious than Crespo in his dealings with the planter class. Local lore has it that he would arrive at an estate, hear the grievances of the peons, and then mete out the appropriate number of lashes to the hacendado or his administrators prior to distributing merchandise from the hacienda's store (*tienda de raya*).

By late May 1911, Díaz had fallen, and Pedro Crespo had disbanded his forces. But, far from being finished, his career was just beginning. For the next thirty years, Crespo arbitrated the political fortunes of Temax, brokering power between elites, villagers, and peons during the most volatile juncture of the revolutionary period.

In the political vacuum that resulted in Yucatán from Díaz's defeat, Morenistas and Pinistas vied for leadership, and rural violence reached dangerous new levels. But, under Crespo's sway, Temax remained relatively calm. The cacique had only contempt for noncombatant civilian politicians like Pino Suárez—soon to become Yucatán's Maderista governor and then vice president of Mexico—who during the insurrection had called upon Yucatecos to join Madero but to avoid acts of vengeance such as those committed at Temax. Unfortunately, once in power, Madero and Pino seemed intent upon employing the same nefarious "bola negra" tactics of political imposition that they had deplored during the Porfiriato. Crespo's sympathies lay with the more popular Morenistas, who now intrigued throughout the state with their former Molinista foes against the ruling Pinistas. At no point, however, during the short-lived Madero regime (1911–13) did the Pinistas feel strong enough to move against Crespo in Temax. Following Díaz's ouster, Crespo had sent his lieutenants to Mérida to serve Pino notice that, although they had been disbanded, his followers remained armed and could be activated at his command on short notice.

Like Maderista liberals, the neo-Porfirian Huertista military leaders who would supplant them (1913–14) saw the wisdom of accommodating the Crespo *cacicazgo*. Nor did the pattern change significantly when the Mexican Revolution in Yucatán moved dramatically left under the socially active administrations of Constitutionalist General Salvador Alvarado (1915–18) and the Marxist Felipe Carrillo Puerto (1921–24). These progressive caudillos also found it wiser to court rather than wrangle with the powerful Crespo as they sought to mobilize campesinos behind their agrarian, labor, and educational reforms between 1915 and 1924. For his part, Crespo was a political pragmatist; he could live with—even actively support—regimes of widely varying ideological coloration, provided they favored, or at least did not intrude upon, his *cacicazgo*.

Particularly interesting is the nature of Crespo's collaboration during the twenties and thirties with the Socialist Party of the Southeast (PSS), led by Carrillo Puerto (1915–24) and his successors. Whereas General Alvarado had brought the Constitutionalist revolution to Yucatán in March 1915 with eight thousand troops, the civilian governor, Carrillo Puerto, was not always able to count on the support of a loyal, progressive military and, consequently, had to rely more heavily on the muscle of local power brokers like Crespo. Moreover, in case of hacendado-backed insurrection against the socialist revolution (a very real possibility), the geopolitics of Crespo's *cacicazgo* were critical: Temax was located on the rich eastern fringes of the henequen zone, astride the Mérida-Valladolid Railroad. Its proximity to the *comunero* hinterland made it essential that Temax be secure since, if it fell into hostile hands, Valladolid and the southeastern part of the state—the base of rebel operations during the nineteenth-century Caste War—might once again be cut off from the state capital in Mérida.

To ensure Crespo's loyalty, Carrillo Puerto awarded him the plums of civil government and agrarian office, either to hold himself or to dispose of as he saw fit. Like other powerful caciques, Crespo combined the municipal presidency with leadership of the local resistance league (*liga de resistencia*), the PSS's constituent unit in Temax. Upon Crespo's recommendation, his ally, Juan Campos, was chosen as the district's federal deputy. Several years later, Crespo succeeded Campos in the Chamber of Deputies.

Generally speaking, Governor Carrillo Puerto was careful not to impinge upon the establishment of economic preserves by such local bosses. During the early 1920s the socialist government was inundated with petitions from campesinos protesting against abuses that, in most cases, were explicitly linked to individual caciques. A sampling of the complaints registered includes: irregularities in the implementation of agrarian reform, as bosses obtained personal control of the best *ejido* (communal lands); violation of landlord-tenant agreements; the use of unpaid communal labor; and the embezzlement of resistance league dues. Carrillo Puerto's response invariably was to promise redress, and, in many cases, he made good on his promises. Yet the frequency of such petitions suggests either an inability or, in certain situations, an unwillingness to act.

In Crespo's case, irregularities were alleged in the press and in petitions to the governor; indeed, some of them are still heard in

Temax. Powerful hacendados like Pastor Castellanos Acevedo, a former *jefe político*, accused Crespo of forcibly removing peons from the large estates and exploiting them as his personal servants. On the other hand, there are some old-timers who claim that Crespo actively colluded with planters to impede the agrarian reform process. In June 1918, Temaxeños petitioned for land, originally belonging to the old Temax *ejido*, which was under the control of neighboring estates. Ordinarily, Carrillo Puerto's PSS was particularly well-disposed to requests for *ejidal* grants from the villages of influential chiefs like Crespo. Critics charge, however, that because of Crespo's alliance with the planters, restitution of the traditional lands was delayed until June 1925, after Carrillo Puerto's fall from power. Even then, the size of the grant was thousands of hectares (1 hectare equals 2.47 acres) less than the area to which the Temaxeños were entitled.

Such allegations are difficult to verify; moreover, there is no shortage of partisan advocates on either side of the question. Certainly Crespo's personal land holdings increased during the twenties and thirties, but not excessively, according to most accounts. We know that, in addition to his membership in the Temax *ejido*, he was granted a medium-size plot ("un terrenito") and one dozen head of livestock by Carrillo's government. In his last years, Don Pedro would donate a piece of this land in Temax for a federal primary school that he named after his father. Despite the charges of economic impropriety, no indictments were lodged, nor was redress ordered by Carrillo's government or by any subsequent PSS administration.

To the day he died, Pedro Crespo lived in much the same manner as his campesino followers: He spoke Maya among friends, wore the collarless white *filipina*, and lived in the *kaxna*, the traditional wattle-and-daub cottage with thatched roof. What interested him most was political power, not wealth. The revolution had offered him a chance and he had seized it. No doubt he viewed himself and came to be regarded in Temax as a *líder nato*—a born local leader, a chief. As such, he did what was necessary to preserve, even extend, his *poderío*, or his local power base. This entailed constant political vigilance and negotiation; deals might be made with powerful planters and bargains struck with the emerging revolutionary state, but it never called upon Crespo to sell out his clientele, to accumulate great wealth and leave Temax for Mérida. Indeed, precisely because he was a *líder nato*, he was incapable of transcending his locality and breaking with the political culture that had produced him.

In return for Carrillo Puerto's preferment and patronage, Crespo performed a variety of services for the PSS. Not only did he selectively bring violence to bear against local opponents of the party to ensure it a political monopoly within the state, but Crespo also doubled as an informal ward boss, guaranteeing, through a variety of incentives, the enrollment of local campesinos in Temax's *liga de resistencia.* Like other loyal party officials, Crespo scheduled weekly cultural events and frequent recreational activities.

Although few in the region appreciate it today, under Carrillo Puerto baseball became a strategic component of the PSS's campaign to mobilize its rural-based revolutionary regime. The sport already was rooted in the regional environment. In addition to its incredible popularity among all classes in Mérida and Progreso, the principal port, campesinos in the larger rural towns had demonstrated a particular fascination with it. Now, the party's goal was to mount a statewide campaign to organize baseball teams "hasta los pueblitos"—in even the most remote interior Maya communities. Such a program would enhance the popularity and morale of the PSS, which might then be parlayed into other programs for social change. It would strike at traditional rural isolation, which impeded the socialist tradition, and would immediately contribute to the party's goal of social integration, even in advance of longer term efforts to improve regional communication and transportation. Carrillo Puerto had no way of knowing it at the time, but his campaign also would have the effect of institutionalizing *béisbol* as the regional pastime, an anomaly in a nation where elsewhere *fútbol* became the people's game.

Pedro Crespo and Juan Campos became energetic promoters of the game in north-central Yucatán. In 1922 these *beisbolistas* petitioned the Liga Central de Resistencia in Mérida for money for gloves, bats, balls, and uniforms, and personally organized ballclubs in Temax, Dzilám González, and surrounding pueblos and hacienda communities. Once this rudimentary infrastructure was in place, Crespo and Campos worked with the presidents of other interior *ligas de resistencia* to schedule country tournaments and leagues and, later, to arrange for tours by the more experienced Mérida and Progreso clubs. To this end, they frequently petitioned Governor Carrillo Puerto for free passes for ballplayers on the state-controlled railroads.

It is not surprising, then, that local nines still bear their names, or that Temax has become synonymous with high-quality baseball, periodically producing bona fide stars for the Mexican League. The backcountry ballgames that these caciques promoted in the twenties and thirties likely echoed with the same patois of Maya and Spanglish that one hears on hacienda and pueblo diamonds today: "Conex, conex jugar béisbol. . . . ten pitcher, tech quecher, tech centerfil!"

("Come on, let's play ball. . . . I'll pitch, you catch, and you play centerfield!")

Carrillo Puerto's socialist experiment ended suddenly and tragically in January 1924, when Yucatán's federal garrison pronounced in favor of the national de la Huerta rebellion and toppled the PSS government, which had remained loyal to President Alvaro Obregón. Carrillo Puerto and many of his closest supporters in Mérida were hunted down and executed by the insurgent *federales*, who had the financial backing and encouragement of Yucatán's large planters, whom Carrillo Puerto had threatened with expropriation. When push came to shove during the de la Huerta revolt, the majority of the irregular bands led by Carrillo Puerto's cacique allies proved unreliable; in fact, remarkably few of them mounted even token resistance against the *federales*. The truth is that few of these local bosses were ideologically motivated or were organizationally prepared to become dedicated socialist revolutionaries committed to a defense of the PSS regime.

Pedro Crespo was one cacique who did not desert his *patrón*. In Carrillo Puerto's vain attempt to elude the Delahuertistas in December 1923 and, ultimately, to gain asylum in Cuba, he stopped in Temax, where he was received by Don Pedro and his intimates. One eyewitness graphically recalls the brief, poignant exchange between the two socialist leaders:

> *Carrillo Puerto*: "We're lost."
>
> *Crespo*: "Where will you go? You can't leave. Wait this thing out here with us. I held out for months in the bush (*en la montaña*); I can do it again. We can survive."
>
> *Carrillo Puerto*: "It's over. I can't compromise you and your people."[3]

Crespo could not persuade his *patrón*, who continued his flight eastward across the peninsula, a journey that soon ended in his capture and execution.

By April 1924 the de la Huerta revolt had been quelled and the PSS returned to power in Mérida but now with a social program more in tune with the moderate politics of national leaders Alvavo Obregón and Plutarco Calles in Mexico City. The next decade (1924–34) witnessed a decline in the membership and organization of the resistance leagues, a reconsolidation of the power of the peninsular bourgeoisie, the infiltration of the PSS by that group, and a sharp falloff in the

---

[3]Interview with Don Melchor Zozaya Raz, December 31, 1986.

agrarian reform, especially in the henequen zone. As the Yucatecan revolution reached its Thermidor, Crespo, now in the autumn of his years, adjusted with the times. In 1930 he was still president of the local resistance league, but now, more than ever, "Yucatecan socialism" was a matter of form, not substance. Led by their patriarch, Temaxeño socialists wore red shirts, spouted revolutionary slogans, and invoked their martyred Don Felipe Carrillo on appropriate public occasions. Yet few serious agrarian or labor demands emanated from Temax's *liga de resistencia.*

Apart from the revolution's ideological drift to the right, the economics of the period left Don Pedro and the socialists little room to maneuver. The henequen boom had crashed on the rocks of world depression and foreign competition. Temaxeños, like other Yucatecan campesinos, were experiencing severe privation and were glad for even the reduced workload that the henequen estates provided. Like most of the PSS' rural chiefs, Crespo was forced to seek an accommodation with the most powerful planters during the Great Depression in order to keep fields in production and minimize layoffs. Indeed, it was his ability to balance and play off the hopes and fears of both *dzules* and campesinos amid the roller-coasterlike political economy of the twenties and thirties that preserved his *cacicazgo* until his death in November 1944.

Even the renewed populist groundswell of Cardenismo, which unleashed a fury of riots and political assassinations throughout the state during the late thirties, could not topple Crespo. Newly formed radical mass organizations like the "Juventudes Socialistas" denounced Crespo and the larger evil of "revolutionary caciquismo," but Don Pedro's alliances within the party and provincial society allowed him to hang on. In fact, it was Melchor Zozaya Raz, perhaps the most vocal of the young firebrands in the Juventudes Socialistas during the late 1930s, who would become Don Pedro's protégé in the early 1940s and ultimately inherit the Temax *cacicazgo* upon Crespo's death.

Now properly reverential of Pedro Crespo's "revolutionary legacy," Don Melchor Zozaya ruled the district into the 1970s, until diabetes and blindness weakened his political grip. Although no powerful individual boss has emerged since, *caciquismo* as an informal institution of power and patronage has endured in Temax. Municipal government, *ejidal* office, and access to work on private sector estates are in large part controlled by a camarilla, which corporately functions as a cacique. A favored few are endlessly recycled through the same offices, thereby assuring the Party of the Institutionalized Revolution (PRI) a large majority at all levels of government. And, while the PRI periodically excoriates bossism in the abstract, the national regime seems reluctant to tamper with the political culture of the institutionalized revolution—in Temax or anywhere else. This is because the Mexican state rests upon a multitiered system of patronage and clientele that always finds new aggressive, upwardly mobile elements to sustain it.

In the Temax of the 1980s, Pedro Crespo also has been institutionalized; Yucatán's branch of the PRI has duly incorporated him into the revolutionary pantheon alongside more famous regional icons like Salvador Alvarado and Felipe Carrillo Puerto. Temaxeño popular tradition, however, has reached a more ambiguous verdict regarding Crespo's *actuación revolucionaria.* "Era cacique . . . gran cacique," old timers pronounce, often with raised eyebrows or a wry smile. ("He was a boss . . . a very great boss.") This rather terse depiction reflects admiration for Crespo's courage, resoluteness, and shrewdness but also registers a sardonic appreciation of his surmounting ambition to control and dispense power.

4

Marmaduke Grove

Frederick M. Nunn

Latin American history and the students at Oregon's Portland State University gained significantly when Fred Nunn decided on graduate study with Edwin Lieuwen at the University of New Mexico rather than pursuing a basketball career. And, despite his protestations, basketball is none the poorer. As a historian, Nunn has examined the soldier in politics in *Chilean Politics, 1920–1931: The Honorable Mission of the Armed Forces* (1971), *The Military in Chilean History: Essays on Civil-Military Relations, 1810–1973* (1976), and *Yesterday's Soldiers: European Military Professionalism in South America* (1983), for which he received the 1985 American Historical Association's C. H. Haring Prize. Nunn spent the 1985–86 year as a Guggenheim Fellow. He is now dean of the College of Liberal Arts and Sciences at Portland State.

Marmaduke Grove's unusual name has always added to the fascination of this colorful Chilean military leader. In the following essay, Nunn examines Grove's career in the tangles of Chile's civil-military politics, his role in the "red airplane affair," his exiles to Easter Island (Pascua), and his participation in the short-lived Socialist Republic in 1932. His career serves in many ways as a prism through which to contemplate how soldiers become involved in politics, especially as happened in Chile during the decades between the world wars.

Marmaduke Grove Vallejo was born on July 6, 1878, in the town of Copiapó, Chile. The son of Marmaduke Grove and Ana Vallejo de Grove, he studied at the Liceo de Hombres in Copiapó. In 1892, just one year after his father had returned from exile for antigovernment activities during the Civil War of 1891, Grove entered the Escuela Naval at Valparaíso. Grove was expelled from the Escuela in 1894 and returned to Copiapó for further schooling. In 1896 he entered the Escuela Militar, from which he graduated two years later.

Grove's political career spanned the interwar years and lasted until 1949, five years before his death. He was a contemporary of some of Chile's most important civilian leaders. He was soldier, rebel, dissident; he was exiled and relegated; he was a senator, *golpista* (rebel), party leader, and presidential candidate, a fervent admirer of military glitter, and a peripatetic defender of the downtrodden. His name is familiar to Chileans who never knew him through the aphorism: "¿Quién mandó el buque? ¡Marmaduke!" ("Who's behind all this? Grove!")

Grove became an artillery officer and, early in this century, was an adjutant at the Escuela Militar. By 1906 he was in Germany, one of the Chilean Army's elite. This was the heyday of Prussianization under General Emil Körner, and Grove was one of those Prussianized. He spent time in a German artillery regiment and received a diploma from the Charlottenburg Artillery School. Ever the wit, he tired of being talked down to by *Graffen* and *Freiherren* so had calling cards printed up to read: "Marma Duque de Grove."

In 1910, Captain Grove, now back in Chile, joined the Maturana Regiment as a battery commander. He was a sometime participant in a Young Turk-like movement, the Liga Militar. In the year that the Great War began, Grove, by now a staff officer, joined the Velásquez Regiment in northern Tacna. He married doña Rebecca Valenzuela, daughter of the Escuela Naval commandant who had expelled him years before.

When the world returned to the chaos of peace in the 1920s, Major Grove was on the Division I staff. Soon he returned to the Escuela Militar as assistant director. He made a name for himself by speaking out against the cynical "Mobilization of 1920," an administration ploy to divert attention from attempts to rig the presidential succession. For his efforts he was posted to a southern garrison in Traiguén.

Arturo Alessandri, the new president, restored Grove to the Escuela staff, and there he stayed, as Colonel Arturo Ahumada Bascuñán's right-hand man, until they both became involved in the tumult of 1924. At the age of forty-six, Grove, the professional soldier, found himself on the brink of a second career—that of political activist. His presence was somehow significant in all important events of the next fifteen years. They were intense years indeed, dominated by controversial figures.

II

Chileans divide their opinions on political leaders in direct proportion to their achievements and proximity to the present. Time was when Bernardo O'Higgins was considered not only the "father of his country" but also an inspirational figure. Diego Portales, Manuel

Montt, and José Manuel Balmaceda, the autocrats of the past century, were revered, but in a selective way. Above all, they were *historical* figures—nineteenth-century figures.

Around the end of World War I, the strength of political opinions began to blend with those expressed by historians and by participants in their own memoirs. Expansion of potential readership and of political participation coincided with a sharpening of sociopolitical issues, bringing traditional historical points of view to bear on both traditional and current issues. In 1920, Chile entered a twenty-year period of constant, heated controversy, as fundamental issues became inextricably tied to social and economic problems. Grove was active in the process, at times in ways he wished he were not. However divided scholarly opinion may be on O'Higgins, Portales, Montt, and Balmaceda, the accomplishments and failures of Alessandri, Ibáñez, Frei, Allende, and Pinochet—and of Grove—more directly affect life today.

Arturo Alessandri (president, 1920–24, 1925, 1932–38), ever the opportunist, linked social reform to the increment of executive power. Throughout the previous century the struggle between parliament and president had dominated Chilean politics, and concerted attention to socioeconomic matters had not been forthcoming. That political baroquism, the Parliamentary Republic (1891–1925), was incapable of providing government action; not all of its leaders were convinced any action was necessary. Meanwhile, workers and miners struck for better pay and decent living conditions, and the unemployed collected their possessions and fled the nitrate fields for cities. The contrasts between urban and rural, and upper and lower strata, became more visible, and an ambitious middle sector wanted access to power.

Many cognizant of the need for action, and most of those opposed to it, were diehard parliamentarians. To them a strong president was nothing less than a dictator. Alessandri, a former parliamentarist par excellence, became the advocate of government responsibility in the fields of labor-capital relations, public health, welfare, education, and economic development—the spokesman for a greater role (equivocally defined) for the entire governmental structure. A Liberal, Alessandri was only a perceived threat to the status quo, only a perceived champion of *las masas*.

By the end of 1924 he was more than a perceived failure. He was an ex-president on his way to Europe after being forced to resign by military leaders. Led by the army, they made demands on congress for action on issues Alessandri had talked about since the campaign of 1920. Congress caved in to army pressure, but the high command prevailed, and the movement of 1924 was twisted into little more than a means to get the offensive arrivé Italo-Chilean out of office and restore "the right sort" to La Moneda, the presidential residence.

Marmaduke Grove was involved deeply in the military movement of 1924 and was a member of the cabal that restored it to its original purpose in 1925. And so his political career began. So, too, did his personal rivalry with Carlos Ibáñez. An Alessandri appointee like Grove, Major Ibáñez was director of the Cavalry School in 1924. He and Grove had been together in the 1912–14 session of the Academia de Guerra.

Ibáñez (president, 1927–31; then again 1952–58, after Grove's political career was over) became Alessandri's nemesis. He had little use for politicians and thought them untrustworthy; he saw the need for reform, enjoyed holding power, and brooked no opposition in his efforts to bring order to political life and prosperity to all Chileans. Hardly a menace to the status quo, Ibáñez did threaten tradition. He toyed with parliament, enjoyed the benefits of revived foreign investment (from the United States), applied the theory if not the letter of those portions of the 1925 Constitution that increased executive power, and provided for palliative socioeconomic reform. Ibáñez's military career—coincident with Alessandri's rise through parliament and Grove's early meanderings—was distinguished but hardly spectacular. He was doughty, sometimes diffident, as opportunistic as Alessandri, and he did not like competition of any kind. He was a shrewd observer of all that transpired in Santiago during Alessandri's ill-fated presidency. To his first administration goes much of the credit for policies and action generally attributed to the Radical era (1938–52).

Grove found himself at various times an ally, an enemy, and a general thorn in the side of both of Chile's dominant political figures. His role at every stage has been disputed. He and his followers claimed that his was a pivotal, selfless role, one of leadership. Alessandristas, Ibañistas, and those on the far left portray Grove as at best a well-meaning malcontent, at worst a scheming, unbalanced dupe or demagogue.

Whatever his role, Grove did figure boldly, first of all in the crisis of the mid-1920s. He was a spokesman for those younger officers who recognized the need to clear the *escalafón* (list of officers) of superannuated seniors whose training was not up to current standards as a concomitant of political and social change. For example, on September 5, 1924, at a meeting of the Junta Militar, he stated: "In order to perform the work of regeneration, it is necessary to begin by purging [this] institution of those who have played at politics during the last few years, and of all those without aptitude who clutter up the ranks because of defective laws and present day disorganization of the army." He neglected to include himself among those to be purged, ignoring his various public utterances in the weeks previous to the pronouncement of September 5. From what we know about what went on in late 1924, it seems reasonable to assume that whereas many were willing to act and follow, Grove was ready to speak out and desired to lead. He was more adept at the former and was not allowed much opportunity to do the latter. The dashing, articulate hothead was not trusted by many of his colleagues in uniform.

He served as liaison with the navy in September and October and was briefly associated with an anti-Alessandri clique of army and navy officers, but he broke with this group rather than serve reactionary interests. In November his newspaper article, "There Are None So Deaf As Those Who Will Not Hear," made it clear that the perpetrators of the September movement had no idea of turning things over to Alessandri's reactionary foes. He repeated this argument on several occasions but never quite succeeded in dispelling rumors that he and his confreres had been manipulated by the high command and their parliamentary allies.

When Conservative party luminary Ladislao Errázuriz became the military government's candidate for the presidency in January 1925, the manipulation rumors grew stronger. By midmonth Grove and others were hard at work to prove their sympathies were with Alessandri and his reform policies. Grove assumed titular leadership of a cabal bent on returning the president.

Grove was indeed the key figure, for Ibáñez was under surveillance, and a broken leg suffered by "don Marma" just before Christmas convinced the government that he could not be very active. Grove was a quick healer, apparently, for he was meeting regularly with pro-Alessandri army officers in Santiago and planned the Ibáñez-led *golpe de estado* of January 23, 1925.

For his efforts Grove became director-general of the air force (still little more than an army corps). Ibáñez became war minister, and Alessandri was invited to return to La Moneda. Grove, in effect, had been shunted aside, and he never forgot it. Soon after the president returned, he alienated Grove by passing up his younger brother for a post in the army medical corps. Grove's stock was at a low point, and he ceased, for the time, to be a frontline political figure. He published the odd essay in a leftist tabloid, *La Acción*, was associated with each and every rumored and real conspiracy, and spoke to any and all about what was going on in the army and navy, including, on occasion, the U.S. ambassador.

Barely one year after his *golpista* labors of 1925, Colonel Grove found himself in England as chief of an air force procurements mission. Alessandri had ended his term and had left Chile's destiny to an elected nonentity—a voice from the past. Ibáñez was still war minister—a voice of the present. Grove was, in effect, in exile.

Soon Alessandri would join him, and together they would begin the next stage of Grove's political career—man on the outside willing to use any means to get back in. The cause of all this was the rise of Carlos Ibáñez to the presidency in 1927, one of Latin America's earliest examples of inverted civil-military relationships. Numerous politicians from right, center, and left found themselves confronted with a choice: join Ibáñez and his clique or oppose them from outside the political system. Alessandri, himself now a voice from the past, had to leave the country along with many others.

In March 1928 incriminating documents were found on the person of Major Carlos Millán, an Alessandrista arrested in Santiago. The documents were used by the government to link Alessandri, Grove, and Communist party leaders in a plot to unseat Ibáñez. One month before, Grove, still an attaché in London, supposedly met with Alessandri and others in a pub near the Dover-Calais ferry terminal on the Kentish coast. Grove affirmed his presence in his autobiography but claimed that Alessandri himself was not there—to assume most of the credit himself, one suspects, or in truth, owing to Alessandri's propensity for using cat's-paws. Grove did affirm a meeting with Alessandri in January at which they each signed a pledge to work for the overthrow of Ibáñez.

Grove and General Enrique Bravo Ortiz, fellow exile and archenemy of Ibáñez, continued to correspond during 1928 and 1929, and the two established contacts with dissidents inside Chile. By 1930, when the earliest effects of the Great Depression began to devastate Chile's economy, internal disaffection had grown.

In the meantime, Grove's career had foundered. News of the nebulous "Complot de Dover" (the Dover conspiracy) gave Ibáñez the excuse to sack his old comrade. Grove was relieved of duties in July 1928 and cashiered in November, officially for embezzling nearly £10,000 of Chilean funds. His name also appeared among those involved in another scheme, this one to kidnap Ibáñez at his annual January reception for the high command. He was also associated with plots hatched by Chilean exiles in Buenos Aires.

In Argentina, the reelection of Hipólito Yrigoyen in 1928 encouraged the transandean Chilean colony, for they saw him as sympathetic to Alessandri and others. General Bravo arrived from France in March, at about the time the Dover papers were discovered in Santiago, and began to coordinate activities in Buenos Aires and to act as liaison with moneyed Chileans in France and England. Grove arrived in Buenos Aires after being cashiered, bringing with him a good portion of the money he claimed was owed him for salary and expenses. The scheming was thick and heavy for the next twenty months, with the Yrigoyen administration cautioning Grove and his activists more than once.

The aging, failing Argentine leader was deposed in September 1930. His successor, General José Uriburu, was no friend of Ibáñez's foes, so Grove and Bravo decided to move, convinced, as they were, that Ibáñez was ready to be toppled.

The plan they devised was unrealistic; it had Grove written all over it. They decided to fly across the Andes and lead southern Chilean garrisons into revolt. To accomplish this they purchased a used Fokker trimotor, a red one; and thus began the affair of the "Avión Rojo." In one of the most bizarre episodes of his colorful career, Grove flew over the cordillera along with Bravo and other Alessandristas. Piloted by one Edward Orville of Oklahoma, they made the passage in September, landing at a field near Concepción after a routine flight that would have bored Saint-Exupéry. Expecting to be met by home-front conspirators, they were stunned to find that the few Concepción garrison officers who had pledged support either had backed out or disclaimed involvement when the time to act arrived. The passengers and crew of the Avión Rojo were jailed and tried. Grove and Bravo were sent to Easter Island, 2,600 miles out in the Pacific.

Within six months Grove was off Pascua, "rescued" with the aid of European exiles. He ceased to be a significant part of the anti-Ibáñez movement, which itself had little to do with the general's ultimate fall in July 1931. But he was by no means through with plotting.

In March 1932, Grove was back in Chile, professing no more interest in politics. If that was indeed so, he must have been the only disinterested Chilean. The administration of Ibáñez's elected successor, Juan Esteban Montero Rodríguez, was beleaguered. Rumors of *golpes* circulated daily. Montero listened to the wrong people and made Grove air commodore (equivalent to brigadier general) and commander of the El Bosque Aviation School, giving him control of the fledgling air force and restoring to him retirement years lost since 1928. Montero hoped don Marma, back in uniform and in good graces, would be a counterpoise to Ibañista forces. The "disinterested" Grove very quickly established contact with Nueva Acción Pública, Chile's embryonic Socialist party, led by Eugenio Matte Hurtado. Grove, the former dissident officer, the erstwhile putschist, exile, and brief sojourner on Easter Island, was now to become a socialist. As he did, Chilean socialism became a more popular alternative for desperate citizens who could not bring themselves to align with the communists.

By the end of May, the contours of Chile's first experiment with Marxism was discernible. The country was already under a state of siege, and the military, now administered by a civilian defense minister, was split. Changes of command were frequent and brusquely accomplished. There were frequent clandestine meetings (shades of 1924), now, however, with two foci: the Ibañistas and the Grovistas. It was only a matter of time, we can see in retrospect, until Montero fell.

On June 2, Grovistas and Ibañistas temporarily joined forces. The next day Grove was replaced at El Bosque. He took this rather hard, putting his would-be replacement under guard and pronouncing against the government. Santiago units refused to move against him, and, on the evening of June 4, following a buzzing of La Moneda by Grove's pilots, Montero resigned. Carlos Dávila, the Ibañista spokesman of the moment; Matte, the protosocialist; and General Arturo Puga Osorio proclaimed "La República Socialista de Chile." Finally, it appeared, Grove had won out, or had he?

If the Avión Rojo was the most bizarre of Grove's adventures, the Socialist Republic is the most intriguing. Alessandristas and Ibañistas were involved from the beginning. Ostensibly acting at Montero's behest, Alessandri had gone to El Bosque to mediate. Grove later asserted that the former president tried to insinuate himself into the movement. When Grove refused to renew the once comfortable relationship, Alessandri allegedly had replied: "No afloje, coronel." ("Don't let up, colonel.") Sources differ as to Alessandri's intent, but surely it meant that he favored Montero's ouster, if not the success of the Grovista *golpe*. Ibáñez even telephoned from Mendoza, where he was enjoying exile, to offer his services to Dávila, Matte, and Puga. His offer was refused flatly.

Within one week Puga and Dávila were out of office, disgusted with the continual scheming, and more than concerned with Matte's militancy. Grove became defense minister, which raised some eyebrows and caused a number of high-level resignations. Then, on June 16, Grove found himself unceremoniously deposed, roughed up, and hustled off to Valparaíso, bound again for Easter Island. Matte went with him this time. Nueva Acción Pública's program and Grove's presence were simply too much for most men in uniform, for they were likened to communism, not socialism. The idea of an oft-discussed "Soviet state" in Chile appealed to few.

Carlos Dávila emerged as provisional president of the Socialist Republic and named Ibáñez as ambassador in Buenos Aires—a sharp contrast in exile life-style to Grove's. Soon after Dávila's own fall from power in September, Chileans reelected Alessandri to the presidency. It is in Alessandri's second term that Grove's career took still another new turn.

Under Alessandri, Chile painfully recovered from the economic devastation of 1930–33. The functionally democratic political system was restored, and a purged military was sent back to barracks, hangars, and bases. Grove had been a presidential candidate in 1932. Soon he would be a senatorial candidate. His entry into electoral politics marks the end of his conspiratorial career and his entry into the category of "grand old man," "conspirator emeritus."

Grove was fifty-three years old during his brief tenure as defense minister in 1932, and the years had been eventful ones. Most of the next twenty-two years of his life would be less eventful (although he would still be associated with "para-politics" and conspiracies until the late 1930s), as he became a member of the political establishment, more a party creature than a true leader. Youth gave way to middle years, then old age, and as it did Marmaduke Grove ceased to be so colorful and controversial a figure.

When Alessandri took office in 1932, he did so again as a coalition candidate. Chilean politics by this time, however, was even more fundamentally influenced by socioeconomic issues than it had been twelve years earlier. Alessandri certainly received more support from the right than he had in 1920; there was a rival Liberal candidate. A communist ran, and the Socialist party nominated Grove. He ran second, losing by 120,000 votes—and did it after being allowed back from Pascua only a few days before the election. This was his finest hour, and it formally marked the transition from adventurism to systemic participation.

The early days of return to political stability were still marked with scheming. Grove's name was occasionally mentioned in association with various plots, and he was detained for his public uttering in 1934. Later that year, in a special election to fill the Santiago senate seat of the late Eugenio Matte, Grove replaced his old friend. *De la cárcel al Senado* (from prison to the Senate) was his slogan, and there are those who are still convinced that that election was the only way he could have left jail. *El que mandó el buque* (Grove) was now an elected legislator.

As a senator, Grove was by most accounts less than impressive, owing to oratorical skills of touching modesty and to lack of other political skills generally associated with the give and take of legislative activity. Despite this, he won reelection eight years later and was a founder of the schismatic Authentic Socialist party in 1943.

During his first term Grove did have one final hurrah as a national political figure. Prior to consummation of the Popular Front alliance for the 1938 presidential election, Grove was the socialist standard-bearer. The strength of the administration's hand-picked candidate, Gustavo Ross, and the tragic events following the Ibañista-Nazi putsch attempt of September 4–5, 1938, however, convinced opposition leaders—Marxists, Nazis, radicals, and others—to be strange bedfellows. Frontist Pedro Aguirre Cerda succeeded Alessandri in 1938. That event relegated Grove to political obscurity more surely than any of his trips into exile.

III

"Establishment" opinions of Grove will never change. Nor will those of his followers or his opponents on the left. For reasons noted above, he will remain "don Marma"; be ever associated with *el buque*, Pascua, the "Avión Rojo," the "Complot de Dover," *la cárcel y el Senado*. And that is as it should be. For that is what he was, and what made him a historical figure and put his name in Chilean biographical dictionaries, not his mediocre senatorial career.

"Establishment" opinions, however, do not reveal Grove's symbolic significance to the Chilean left. Relegated troublemaker or quixotic historical character that he was, he was also an early mover and shaper of Chile's Socialist party. It should be remembered that one of his socialist colleagues, the then-obscure Salvador Allende Gossens, began his own political struggle just as Grove's career began to fade; that Chile's tough-minded communists asserted themselves legally during his early years as legislator; and that Christian Democrats had their origins at the same time. Grove's symbolic impact and his own thought and self-perception are important areas to consider in studying his times.

Grove's transition from jail to parliament became something of a metaphor for champions of the downtrodden, later a semiotic device to arouse support from the masses. It was Alessandri who relegated Grove to Melinka, that inhospitable island in the Chonos archipelago, south of Chiloé. There he suffered (briefly) privations later experienced by leftists after the military rising of 1973.

Following Alessandri's 1932 reelection, military-civilian relations were still tense, and Grove (all the while drawing his army pension!) and his associates admittedly sought a confrontation by "adopting measures that were expedient." Grove lashed out at Alessandri in May, June, and August 1933, in exhortations to workers and socialists. In August he was accused of sedition. From this point forward he saw the need to iterate in writing and orally that he had no personal political interests whatsoever, and never had. In these iterations we see Grove as he saw himself, and as he wanted to be seen by others. His early years of political activity, he asserted in a letter from the south, were imposed on him by conniving "reactionaries . . . the same who hammered at the doors of the barracks with their lies and promises [and who] drove me to the movement of September [1924]." Willingly he had allowed Ibáñez to become war minister in 1925, and seven years later again stepped aside for others, even though "I could have, and possibly should have, assumed power." He saw himself as selfless, the victim of his own sincerity. Upon his return from Pascua in 1932, he had stated publicly that he would oppose any government that was not "socialist" in orientation, and that he would not sell out to any administration. In his own mind then, his actions were justified.

Moreover, Grove also would write more than once that Chilean socialism itself was misunderstood. He foresaw no campaign against private property, and socialists were not opposed to the civilian militia of the early 1930s, as alleged by some. The militia had been formed to intimidate the military, and the government that allowed it was in the wrong. His old loyalties to the army led him to assert that Chile did not need two armed groups; one or the other should be abolished, preferably the militia. It was, after all, a political creature, deliberative in essence. It had been created, he thought, to lead Chile toward a "capitalist dictatorship backed by the bankers, the clergy, and the reactionaries." He was persecuted, in fine, for opposing injustice—persecuted unjustly. He had no political ambitions, never had. He was a victim of reactionaries and bourgeois institutions.

On April 8, 1934, Grove, now a senator, addressed his new colleagues. Socialism had grown since 1932, he said, owing to the political, social, and economic crises evident since the early 1920s—here, a cause-and-effect justification of political evolution from parliamentary democracy to socialism, now held at bay and denied its rightful place in the evolutionary sequence by an outmoded system and its supporters.

Chilean socialism in 1934 was more legitimate than that of traditional "parties," for it was a fusion of five separate organizations (in 1933). These were not cliques, he asserted, but parts of a more important whole. History, of course, has shown us just how fusion led to fission in socialist ranks. In this speech Grove repeated his oft-made claims about 1924, 1925, et seq.: he had no ambitions, had stepped aside for others, had made the sacrifice.

Ibañismo, he explained, had grown in popularity only by default, for what the people really wanted was stability, and this Ibáñez gave them. Ibáñez's enemies had sought him (Grove) out for their own purposes, and he had joined them out of sympathy for all Chileans under the yoke. He denied misappropriation of funds; the allegedly embezzled monies were used for "patriotic and revolutionary ends, and to guard my family from hunger and misery." False friends in exile had used him and the money to put together the 1930 Avión Rojo affair. He was being unjustly accused of taking part in the 1931 naval mutiny to boot.

After the fall of Ibáñez, he went on, he had returned to head the air force only when he was assured he was needed to avert an Ibañista-military plot against the Montero administration, an administration living in the past. He denied any involvement in the 1932 scheming and pronounced only because he was unjustly relieved of command.

Guileless and guiltless, he went ahead with the June 1932 rising after Alessandri had uttered the words "no afloje, coronel"; not because he was serving Alessandri's interests, as had other officers in 1919, 1924, and 1925; not because of sympathies from the 1928–30 years, but because Chile needed something different. "The times, Honorable Senate, were distinct, and in the new context there came together men and ideas devoted to a profound change of the social order in the life of our country." His conscience was clear, and "his" socialist movement had failed only because of insurmountable difficulties brought about by the economy and by the machinations of the enemies of the people. A tiny minority had foiled the majority. Those who doubted his sincerity and resolution, and the strength of socialism, he warned by saying: "They have eyes but do not see; they have ears but do not hear."

One of the country's greatest needs in this area, he insisted, was agrarian reform. Only it would provide land to those who worked it and would prevent latifundistas from abusing those who worked for them. Hacendados would no longer live as parasites, *al margen de la justicia, del la moral, y del orden.* Basic necessities—food, shelter, clothing—should be plentiful, easily obtainable, and cheap; socialists would see to that too. Chileans would control their economic destiny, not foreigners. This was probably Grove's finest speech.

The relegation, then the triumphant return to Santiago as senator represented in official socialist sources a redemption, a vindication of Grove and all socialists. The establishment had struck, but the people had spoken. Grove had been victimized by the enemies of the people, then saved by the people, brought back from the frontier to the center. Justice had triumphed. Further triumphs were inevitable. Only injustice could prevent the inevitable, but socialism would remove the causes of injustice. Socialism was a logical consequence, a Chilean phenomenon. To see it any other way, by innuendo, was to ignore history and reality, to betray Chile. However poor the logic, many bought Grove's and the party's message.

Grove's self-perception and that of his party were very much the same in socialism's formative years. An official publication of 1937 referred to him as a "revolutionary," "victim," "loyal Chilean," and "democrat." "Comrade" Grove was a citizen from Copiapó, after all, "a city of revolutionary tradition." If not "erudite," he was a "man of action" and of effort, "eloquent" in a "sober, exact, and biting way." "He expounds on the most complex subjects with clarity and simplicity, in such a form that even the least versed in political problems understands him perfectly." For this reason "Comrade Grove is adored by the masses, for through his words laden with faith and optimism . . . they understand this sincere and valorous man who has no other ambition than to achieve the emancipation of the exploited masses."

On January 26, 1936, the Socialist party proclaimed Grove's candidacy for the presidency. Until the final formation of the Front, he had support from other, leftist groups: the Democratic party, the Stalinists, and other communist factions. These reaffirmed their support for his Frontist candidacy the next year, and the brief campaign was under way.

The socialists invited their Frontist friends to join with them in the creation of a government to organize a state-directed economy, nationalize foreign-owned extractive industry, launch an agrarian reform program, stabilize commodity prices, provide tax reform and other social legislation, nationalize all education, and aggressively resolve Chile's housing, health, and welfare problems. Following the platform's acceptance on March 9, 1937, by socialists meeting in Talca, the "Marseillaise" was sung, then the candidate spoke. Grove's speech that day is further evidence of the developing revolutionary-military-victim-hero image, so important in the launching of socialism as the party of the masses.

"I served 35 years in the army," he said, "and I learned to be disciplined at all times, and to do my duty and see to it that others did theirs. Today, serving in the people's army of socialism, I assume this new responsibility, with the same tranquility and zeal with which I have confronted others . . . commended to me." He promised to serve not as a caudillo, but with the "eagerness and discipline of the socialist soldier that I am and will always be, whatever the result of this great struggle."

He promised that he would not govern "playing the same political game of others: the dividing of the spoils of power while the hunger and misery of the people grow to incredible extremes." He would struggle against all injustice, he assured his listeners. Government in a truly democratic manner would come about through peaceful means, not violence, and it would be a harbinger of a future "Confederation of Socialist Republics of America."

Internationalism [not to be confused with Aprista (Peruvian), or Soviet-style socialism] was the true destiny of Latin America in its struggle against "hunger, fascism, war, financial oligarchies, and all forms of capitalism that are driving the world to the abyss of collective madness." Grove equated his confederation with Simon Bolivar's concept of a Spanish-American confederation, thus diverting any possible associations with Peruvian Víctor Raúl Haya de la Torre: the past triumphant over the present—for political purposes.

The past was justification of present politics as well. Grove and Matte's rude eviction from power in 1932, "by the efforts of the traitors of the people and sell-outs to imperialism," convinced them "to swear to dedicate our lives to the cause of the workers and the oppressed." They were certain that their commitment would evoke a response from the "ample and generous heart of the people." "From that moment the Socialist Party has grown in strength parallel to the awakening of the masses. . . . I accept this new charge of my party because this candidacy is a challenge to the oligarchic classes that have exploited and oppressed my Fatherland for more than 100 years, and because I am profoundly convinced that the presidential palace of Chile must be occupied on behalf of the people."

Material in other political tracts of the time compared Grove to Lázaro Cárdenas in Mexico and Luis Carlos Prestes in Brazil (but not Haya) as leader of workers and peasants, as army officer, anti-imperialist, populist, internationalist—and nationalist. Grove was all things to all people: Chile's savior.

He also was presented often as metaphoric hero-victim. His expulsion from the naval school in 1894 came about because of student protests over meager rations and hard bread: oppression of the lower classes. He sought entry to a special program at the military school in 1897 because of a war scare with Argentina: devoted servant of the Fatherland. He graduated at the top of his class in 1898: a hardworking youth. His service record was excellent, but his criticism of the outrageous "Mobilization of 1920" got him a transfer: oppression of the devoted servant. He was returned to grace at the request of a superior officer following Alessandri's first election: the hardworking youth and the indispensable man. He fell from favor in 1924–25 because his ideas were too advanced for his colleagues: a prophet crying in the wilderness. Ibáñez sent him to Europe (where, he claimed, he began to study Marx), to get him out of the way. He was a victim of Chilean exiles. The Avión Rojo conspiracy was betrayed; so was the Socialist Republic. At all times he had acted only in the name of Chile, never for himself, only as a loyal officer or comrade-in-arms, never as a caudillo. He did not seek power but wanted only to serve. Grove could have written all the party documents by himself, so consistent were their arguments with his own.

A glimpse of Grove's image as seen by "the other left" reveals another dimension of the man. To communists, fearful of the Socialist party's rise to prominence and Grove's popularity, he was not a revolutionary at all. Rather, he was a fraud, a bourgeois dupe of Alessandri, Augustín Edwards, and British bankers who feared the growing influence of Wall Street in Chile, especially during the Ibáñez presidency. Grove had been an ally of Ibáñez, then of Alessandri—even into 1932.

He was "a fascist" for he advocated an active role of the state. His call for a government of all classes, moreover, was a denial of "class struggle." He was associated with the army, and his (negligible) role in the 1931 navy revolt was not clearly enough defined to make him a man of the people. He was, in fact, not a man of the people, but a "principal obstacle to the workers' and peasants' revolution." Used and dropped by the right, reviled by the far left, Grove personified the dilemma of Chilean socialism from its inception. He was a product of his times more than an event maker, and his times could have not expected much more from him.

IV

"I swore to my good mother that if destiny prepared me to be a revolutionary, I would truly be one. And thus it has passed." And so it did. Marmaduke Grove Vallejo was, within the confines of his preparation and destiny, a Chilean revolutionary—at least until the creation of the Popular Front. He was the nearest thing to a revolutionary that Chile had until the heady days of the 1960s and 1970s when socialists finally did achieve national power, finally did create a government close to the ideals of those other heady days—the days when Grove acted and spoke, and Chileans listened and followed.

The Popular Front signaled the true passing of Grove from the limelight, and it is not necessary to provide a treatment of his later legislative career when he was not a force to be reckoned with. As the Socialist party became a legitimate party to governmental affairs, Grove's flamboyant past lost its political appeal. As ideology, programs, policies, and platforms became more important to socialists, Grove was less a factor, more a symbol, never quite an embarrassment. Some socialists no doubt wished to forget him. Communists ceased their attacks.

However moot his actual significance in specific instances, even in the greater scheme of things, Grove remains the colorful adventurer, the self-styled revolutionary who succeeded in establishing Chilean socialists as a force. His historical role is unforgettable. He will remain in the minds of Chileans as do figures like José Miguel Carrera and Francisco Bilbao of the past century and Luis Emilio Recabarren, founder of what became Chile's Communist party: pioneers in the struggle for democracy and social justice in a country that still cries out.

Notwithstanding interest in his role in the development of the Socialist Republic rekindled between 1970 and 1973, Grove's entire life is "Maytaesque." As with Vargas Llosa's eponymous revolutionary, there are still so many conflicting views, unanswered questions, anomalies, so much lore. There will come a day, I suspect, when, owing to the passage of time and lack of documentary sources, a biographical treatment worthy of the man may no longer be feasible. And this is a pity, for it would be enlightening to know just how much, in those critical years for socialists, he really did or did not *mandó el buque*.

SELECTED BIBLIOGRAPHY

With the exception of works by Jack Ray Thomas, I have refrained from citing English-language sources. Any scholarly treatment of Chile during the years in question, or of Chilean politics in general, has material on Grove. The Chilean items cited here were used in the elaboration of this essay.

Aránguiz Latorre, Manuel. *El 4 de junio*. Santiago, 1933.

Bedoya, Manuel. *Grove, su vida, su ejemplo, su obra*. Santiago, n.d.

Charlin O., Carlos. *Del avión rojo a la república socialista*. Santiago, 1972.

Grove V., Jorge. *Descorriendo el velo: Episodio de los doce días de la república socialista*. Valparaíso, 1933.

Grove V., Marmaduke. "Discurso pronunciado por el senador socialista Marmaduke Grove V., 23 de mayo de 1934." *Nucleo* (July 1934): 3–22.

———. *Toda la verdad*. Paris, 1929.

Partido Socialista. *Grove a la presidencia*. Santiago, 1937.

———. *Grove el militar y el ciudadano: Una vida al servicio de la nacionalidad y del pueblo*. Santiago, 1937.

———. *La relegación de Grove*. Documentos parlamentarios. Santiago, n.d.

Rojas, Chelén. *Tres hombres: Carlos Marx, Recabarren, y Grove*. Chañaral, 1939.

Siqueiros, Juan. *El grovismo, principal obstáculo para la revolución obrera y campesina en Chile*. Santiago, n.d.

Thomas, Jack Ray. "The Evolution of a Chilean Socialist: Marmaduke Grove." *Hispanic American Historical Review* (February 1967): 22–37.

———. "Marmaduke Grove: A Political Biography." Ph.D. diss., Ohio State University, 1962.

Vergara Montero, Ramón. *Por rutas extraviadas*. Santiago, 1933.

5

Juan Esquivel: Cotton Plantation Tenant

Vincent C. Peloso

Vincent Peloso, a history professor at Howard University in Washington, DC, helped organize Peru's Archivo del Fuero Agrario in the summers of 1972 and 1973. Today, this center, located in Lima, is Peru's agrarian archive and a resource for scholars. It was the source of the information on the life of Juan Esquivel.

For too long the lives of tenant farmers such as Esquivel existed beyond the historical spectrum. Their history was unseen and unheard, like ultraviolet light or high-pitched whistles, and, therefore, ignored. In this essay, Peloso describes the experiences of an ambitious tenant and, by implication, explains the hopes of many of the Andean villagers who left their homes for the factories and plantations of lowland Peru.

Peloso has written on peasant problems in numerous articles and on contemporary developments in several Latin American nations for encyclopedias. Having made an unusual turn in his research, Peloso now studies Peruvian food and culinary patterns. His article, "Succulence and Sustenance: Region, Class, and Diet in Nineteenth-Century Peru," appears in *Food, Politics, and Society in Latin America* (1985).

A labor contractor from Peru's Pisco Valley went looking in 1898 for farmhands for the expanding cotton plantations of the Aspíllaga family. He made one stop in the Chincha Valley where, as usual, he went to the village tavern to find recruits. He wanted, he said, men who had the skills and daring to improve their future.

Juan Esquivel listened closely. A black villager, son of a former slave, he had a vision of a comfortable future that would put him, his wife, and children in a better social position than the one they endured. He had little formal schooling, but he knew from experience how to till the soil and from instinct when to plant and when to harvest to get maximum results. He had confidence in his skills, and he believed he had found an opportunity to escape his village for a greater chance to use his abilities.

After the labor contractor bought him and his friends a round of drinks, Esquivel did not resist much when offered a contract. Vaguely worded, the agreement required no cash from Esquivel; he would pay his rent with cotton. A good crop, the contractor suggested, would leave a shrewd tenant with cotton to sell on the open market. Nor did it hurt the recruiter's argument when he shook a few silver soles, Peru's currency, onto the table in the *chingana* (tavern) as an advance on Esquivel's earnings as a cotton farmer on the Hacienda Palto.

Esquivel made the decision to abandon the village where he had grown up and the people he had known to try for a more exciting life. Pisco was not so far away, so he could always return to his village if things did not work out. With his wife and sons and their few possessions, most importantly the farming tools and a pair of oxen, he traveled south. Not far down the desert coast road the Pisco River formed an oasis somewhat smaller than the one they had left in the Chincha region. There the port town of Pisco, with its few wharves, lay alongside the river. Where the rushing streambed fanned out into a gurgling alluvial dribble as it met the Pacific tide, the Esquivels turned left. Facing east toward the distant escarpment of the massive Andean range that hid the river's origins, they walked another six kilometers until they reached the imposing gateway of the Hacienda San Francisco de Palto.

As a new tenant, Esquivel joined a group of thirty-four men and women and their families who also had abandoned their villages for the hacienda. Many young Peruvians, lured by the promise of wages and drawn by curiosity, left their Andean villages in the waning years of the last century. Some of them went to the new towns sprouting on the edges of the reinvigorated copper and lead mines, others to the big cities, especially Lima, and still others sought out the expanding, lively, aggressive coastal plantations.

The Esquivels could sense the energy from the noise on the hacienda made by the workers, shouting and talking as they labored by hand. People daily turned over the soil, planted, weeded, built or rebuilt dikes and water channels, mended fences and buildings, herded animals, and harvested and stored crops. The only machinery to be found on cotton plantations were the deseeding and pressing machines that were used to prepare bales for shipment.

Excitement filled the region because of the renewal of commercial agriculture on the coastal plantations at the turn of the century. Critical to maintaining rural society in the nineteenth century had been an ideology of authority based on force. Until midcentury, slaves and indentured Asian laborers harvested grapes, sugar, and cotton on the plantations. When demand for cotton rose sharply both in Peru and on the world market, landowners sought ways to develop commercial cotton, but they conceded that a system of authority based on persuasion had to replace force. They gambled that they could persuade free farmers to assume the risks of producing large amounts of cotton without requiring a major increase in labor or new technology.

Caution governed the efforts to stimulate commercial cotton agriculture. Owners made few technological changes, relying almost exclusively on animal and human power until nearly World War I. They found it much easier to limit the cost of labor than to resist technological change, thus encouraging them to begin to expand production. For a decade after the Chilean War (1879–83), cotton planters experimented with various combinations of tenantry. The experiments yielded valuable lessons, and after 1895 many of the large landowners settled for a contract labor system with two categories.

Farm workers became tenants, meaning that they were hired to live on as well as farm the plantations. Among the tenants, distinctions emerged that proved to be of some economic importance. In the southern coastal valleys, some tenants were called *arrendatarios* (renters, or tenants), a designation that initially meant they enjoyed certain privileges, especially the one of paying a fixed rent in kind. However, most of the resident laborers were *compañeros*, a term peculiar to the southern coast and later dropped for the more widely used term *yanacona* (sharecropper). The sharecroppers usually paid 50 percent of their crop for rent, rather than a fixed amount.

Differences between the two types of resident labor were meant to be sharp. The landowners hoped that by providing a bit of freedom from credit and planting restrictions for some tenants, while placing some restrictions on others, they could reduce their costs, especially in times of low prices for cotton. The ratio of sharecroppers to tenants on a plantation sometimes changed when the market or land use policies intervened. The tenants seemed to enjoy a more favorable social status and have more independence in choosing the mix of cotton and other crops they would plant than did the sharecroppers. At least this was true as long as a fixed-rent labor population was important to the growers. Later, when the *arrendatarios* had outlived their usefulness, the owners did not evict them wholesale from the land, they merely altered the rules that governed tenantry.

The owners of the coastal cotton plantations apparently were confident that they had found the right formula. After 1895 they began to increase the amount of land in production on their plantations. Between 1900 and 1910, cotton exports from all coastal plantations doubled, and, in the next decade, they doubled again. The increased land in use was rented to tenants and sharecroppers, who then were provided with field hands if they needed them. Migrant workers were scarce throughout this era; for this reason, plantation owners sought peasant families to fill the roles of tenant and sharecropper. To help the sharecroppers and tenants, the cotton planters would have liked to hire migrant laborers who could be paid by the week or month when the need arose, such as at harvest time or when a road or dike had to be built. But the number of day laborers was small at the turn of the century, and they commanded high pay. Nevertheless, the owners continued to hope that enough of them would become available at critical times to meet production needs. In any case, whether there was enough labor or not, the landowners seem to have minimized the risk to themselves by passing it on to the resident tenants and sharecroppers.

Hacienda Palto, the plantation that had lured the Esquivels and others, was a medium-size, 460-hectare property. It was the cotton plantation of the Aspíllagas, one of the most powerful families in Peru. They had turned this rather neglected, bedraggled estate into a commercially sound plantation, its warehouses bulging with cotton ready for shipment to consignment houses in Europe. The four Aspíllaga brothers owned Palto and other properties along with other business interests. Their business connections were built along vertical rather than horizontal lines. All of their ventures were related to real estate (the use of the land), whether they were in agriculture, warehousing, banking, shipping, or commerce. A large, productive sugar plantation, Hacienda Cayaltí, in the north coast's Zaña Valley, which the Aspíllaga family first had managed for and then bought from a wealthy shipowner, was their earliest successful undertaking in commercial agriculture. They owned several homes and office buildings in Lima and Pisco that they rented. Their offices were located in the capital, where they held positions on the boards of several banks. By the turn of the century, this wealthy family, whose sons had married well, showed little interest in living on a plantation near a small port town. The Aspíllagas preferred the cosmopolitan life, including membership in a prestigious social club in Lima and dabbling in municipal and national politics.

Their reluctance to live in the countryside of Pisco did not mean that the Aspíllagas had little interest in Palto. On the contrary, the extent of their commitment to the plantation and to cotton was evident. They had received numerous offers over the years for the property, and, although tempted in 1891, they held on to the land. It produced a steady, even growing, income for its owners but needed careful and attentive management to produce these profits, so the family hired an administrator to handle the plantation's affairs. The manager had to enforce the contracts drawn between the owners and each individual tenant at Palto.

The rental contract was a vaguely written agreement for the most part, but it was also the instrument that would explain to the tenant how plantation society functioned. No longer would a tenant be linked by the family to a community, with obligations to neighbors and expectations that they would reciprocate if need be. Those obligations ended at the gates of Palto or of any other plantation and were transformed into an unequal relationship with the owner that was based upon certain responsibilities. The expectations, meanwhile, became vague promises.

Although the most attractive contracts stipulated that a tenant could remain on a specific portion of the plantation for three years, contract terms were flexible. In practice, tenant and sharecropper agreements were revised if the manager demanded it or when the owners needed the tenants to keep the land producing. One element in the contract was its list of rewards and punishments. Tenants were to be rewarded for making some kinds of farming decisions under the manager's supervision, for providing their own animals and tools, and with ample room for seeking credit in the marketplace. Tenants could keep their gardens free of pasturing animals. On rare occasions, they might correspond directly with the landowner. This chance to communicate with the owner no doubt was offered for the same reason as other privileges, to make tenants feel like they were more than hired field hands, that they were autonomous farmers in an informal partnership with the owners.

When Esquivel accepted his contract at Palto, he did not recognize that he would need to develop a close working relationship with the plantation's manager. This was something new to him. Although the manager was the owner's spokesman on all matters large and small on the hacienda, he was not the owner. Details about which debts must be paid first—outstanding loans or rent or an owner's option on crops above rent—would have to be discussed with the manager. But there seemed to be no reason why this relationship should prevent Esquivel from becoming a successful cotton tenant.

The manager enforced the contracts and wielded daily authority on the scene, so owners wanted someone who would remind the tenants of the owners, who could identify with the Aspíllagas. Preferably a family man, the administrator was expected to handle the details of plantation management as if the estate were his personal property. The Aspíllagas did not trust a stranger much. For that reason, one of the brothers periodically made a hasty trip to the Pisco Valley, where he checked the condition of the fields, buildings, and equipment and reviewed the account ledgers. A similar visit took place each time a new manager was appointed. The new man received detailed instructions outlining every plantation operation and how the Aspíllagas expected it to be handled. He was instructed to communicate at least once a week by letter with the owners; they especially wanted his judgment on how well the tenants carried out their contractual duties and how the other workers performed their jobs.

The Aspíllagas hired only a few managers for their estate. Usually, these men were recommended through family connections, and they developed their managerial and commercial skills in large farming through on-the-job experience. Their understanding of labor, perhaps the most important element of their profession, was based on attitudes and behaviors common to the elite. These notions included strong negative stereotypes of villagers and other farm workers as people who were slow to learn and who only poorly understood modern work methods. Provincial elites, including plantation managers and accountants, usually looked down on persons of African or Amerindian descent as people "without culture." The owners, thoroughly disdainful of all country dwellers, occasionally reminded their managers to be tactful but firm in their dealings with tenants and other farm workers.

Esquivel's decision to become a tenant was shaped by two factors. One, tenantry, which was already in limited use at Palto for a decade when Esquivel arrived fresh from the north, seemed to be the most independent yet secure form of farming available in the cotton valleys to the person who knew enough about growing cotton to gamble on the size of the next year's crop and who was bold enough to bet his team of oxen on it. Moreover, Esquivel was the right person for the time. Favored for his reliability and productivity and blessed with a strong wife and three young sons who could work in the fields, he did well when others were losing their contracts. When the Aspíllagas raised his rent, Esquivel answered this challenge by renting still more sections of the plantation.

The start was hopeful. Esquivel went to Palto with considerable assets for a village dweller. He owned tools, a team of oxen, and the equipment that he needed to work the animals. But Esquivel took a look around and decided that he did not immediately want a tenant contract. Instead, he settled for a *compañero* arrangement. This made him a partner of the plantation owners, for whom he worked specified fields as a resident laborer. Part of the time he spent working at jobs under the manager's supervision.

The manager assured Esquivel that if he worked at his assigned tasks for a time he could save money, perhaps even enough money to avoid large loans. Esquivel accepted. He worked as an *arriero* (mule skinner), periodically escorting the plantation's mule train loaded with cotton to the warehouses of Pisco where it awaited consignment. Between cotton shipments he tended the animals and wagons and did the regular field work assigned to all workers at Palto—caring for the all-important irrigation system and tending the fields. After the harvest, the raw bales of cotton were hauled off to be sold to English textile factories in Liverpool. Esquivel, as a mule skinner, was paid wages plus meals and given a horse and the tools of his work (spurs, bridle and saddle, blanket, and horse feed, among other things) by the plantation manager, leaving use of the rest of his meager wage to his discretion.

Esquivel had committed himself to working hard for the owners of Hacienda Palto; all his actions showed this, and the manager responded favorably to him. Despite the manager's skepticism about such agreements, he was impressed with Esquivel's talent and his eagerness to work for the plantation. He recommended to the owners that they allow Esquivel to pay a fixed annual rent in kind. The Chincha farmer thus became one of fourteen tenants at the hacienda who together rented over ninety-seven hectares of cotton land. Over the next few years, he quietly and carefully tripled the land he leased, acquiring command of thirty-three hectares of the plantation and paying five thousand pounds of cotton a season in rent. He was by far the largest and most productive tenant at Palto.

After a few successive seasons of larger and larger cotton crops, Esquivel realized that his family's hard work meant that he had accumulated certain privileges, perhaps even rights. Not the civil rights of a citizen in the political world—of those Esquivel had no real awareness as yet—but the privileges of a tenant who regularly fulfilled the obligations of his contract, paid his rent, and canceled his debt each year on time, and who sent workers when the plantation needed them for jobs not directly related to the production of cotton in his own fields. Patiently, with a regularity that made him and his family predictable, he sent his sons, Demetrio, Manuel, and Ernesto, to the manager each week to perform the labor services that the plantation demanded of its tenants and sharecroppers.

One son, and sometimes Esquivel's brother, Apolonio, who had joined the family at the hacienda, would spend a portion of each week, depending on the season and the plantation's immediate needs, mending fences and sluice gates, cutting and hauling wood, tending the herds of goats, oxen, and horses, and, especially, clearing the irrigation channels of debris. Juan continued to work occasionally as a mule driver. His wife tended the garden that helped to cut food expenses, harvested the cotton fields when the time came, and performed a variety of other tasks necessary for the family's livelihood.

The most abominable of all the labor required on the plantation was deepening and widening the channels that led to the swamp at the hacienda's edge and into which all its waste drained and collected. Smelly, grimy, and unhealthy as it was, this work paid only a little better than any other. Yet it was a vital task, for without periodic attention to the waste system the plantation's entire irrigation network was endangered and the threat of flooding increased. It was rivaled in importance and repugnance only by the highly dangerous job of building dikes along the river to control flooding from sudden river swells. Many of the country men could not swim, and occasional drownings intensified the awe felt by the workers for the river that held their crops and their lives in its grip.

Esquivel thought he was up to the challenges hurled at him by the manager of Palto. He paid his rent on time, in full, and with few complaints despite the increases that threatened to reduce his family's income. But the rising price of cotton in the Pisco town market, reflecting the world demand, kept Esquivel even with his rental payments. After 1905 world demand for Peruvian cotton continued to support the endeavors of the Palto tenant and his family. In spite of worsening relations between him and the plantation manager, the Aspíllaga family did not give Esquivel any special attention. Indeed, in 1908 the owners once again acceded to his request to rent more land, raising his total holdings to over fifty-five hectares. At the same time, they demanded that he hire more wage laborers to help keep up production and, despite the added cost, Esquivel complied, but only when the owners threatened to evict him if he did not.

One year later the manager reported that Esquivel was harvesting 13,775 pounds of cotton annually and paying 8,111 pounds of it in rent. Meanwhile, he had planted vegetables and corn in parts of his fields and taken on sharecroppers as well as day laborers to meet his production schedule. The owners had in Esquivel at this point a tenant in whom they had made a considerable investment and upon whom they depended for a large portion of the success of their cotton operation in the Pisco Valley.

Not that Esquivel was alone in producing larger amounts of cotton at Palto, but he was representative of the tenants and sharecroppers who lived there. In total, the plantation's fields yielded 108,770 pounds of cotton in 1909 and 105,895 pounds in 1910. The increases in cotton production that occurred at Palto between 1900, when the plantation's total cotton crop amounted to only 81,491 pounds, and 1909, with the introduction of cotton into larger numbers of fields, paralleled the rise to prominence of Juan Esquivel. Between 1901 and 1905 the entire plantation harvested an average of 86,375 pounds of raw, unseeded cotton a year. During the following five years, from 1906 through 1910, Palto yielded an average of 102,447 pounds of cotton a year. The two figures indicate that the yields extracted from Palto's labor force increased sharply, by over three-fourths, after 1906.

Palto's manager insisted that these increases could not be attributed to the industriousness of the tenants. He found much to complain about in the work habits of these families, and old wounds that had been buried in the press of getting out the cotton in the past were now reopened as the owners demanded even greater increases in production. Some of the hostility was precipitated by bad floods. In 1907 several of Esquivel's most productive fields lying close to the riverbank were flooded, making it difficult for him to meet his rent bill.

Esquivel and the Palto administrator argued vehemently over the total amount of rent the tenant owed after the 1907 flood. The manager insisted that the flood was not the plantation's fault and that Esquivel was responsible for the full amount of rent stipulated by his contract, flood or no flood. To the tenant, this position was a bad sign of changing attitudes. Under harmonious conditions, managers were prepared to accept nature's fickle ways and to forgive a portion of the rent that was lost in a disaster not of the tenant's making. But in this case, the manager was insisting upon tacking the loss onto the tenant's debt. Why had he become so inflexible?

The issues most likely to spark arguments between the manager and the tenants were not directly related to the production of cotton. Often disagreements arose concerning maintenance of the plantation. The floods were one instance when the plantation owners had advised the manager that they would not pay for the damages. Therefore, the manager attempted to pass the cost on to the tenants, but some of them resisted. Those like Esquivel, who saw themselves as victims of the poor maintenance of dikes that usually stemmed the river's tides, refused to absorb the cost. Esquivel argued that he should not have to pay rent for those fields in which the floods of 1907 had ruined the cotton plants. In 1908 the tenants of Hacienda Palto banded together in order to argue more effectively with the plantation's manager over proper distribution of the cost of cleaning the drainage ditches.

Credit was also a matter of dispute. From the beginning, Esquivel received few loans from the owners of Palto. The Aspíllagas were unwilling to share the risk of cotton farming with their tenants. That is why they had sought tenants in the first place—to have others who would have to absorb the immediate risks of cotton farming. Esquivel was able to manage tenantry only because he found suitable lenders, small merchants in Pisco who demanded a portion of his crop as collateral. Thus, each year, after he paid his rent and debts to the plantation, Esquivel would settle his loan.

In each year of this practice, with what remained of a crop after the rent going to pay the principal and interest on the loan, and with nothing left, a tenant would need another loan to finance the next season. The loan-debt cycle seemed like an endless trap, with the high interest on short-term loans making them difficult to pay off. This cycle left tenants with little room for dealing with calamities. Still, Esquivel could point to a growing number of oxen in his stable, and to his growing sons and his wife, as family assets whose contributions to the harvest meant stability in the family's life.

As the demand for cotton rose on the world market, the owners of Palto sought to tighten their hold on the fiber produced on their land. They no longer allowed their tenants to arrange for loans with speculators in Pisco, and they developed practices meant to give them control of all the cotton produced at Palto. The most important of these was to insist that tenants give the landowner first option on the remainder of the crop above rent. The most dangerous aspect of this arrangement was the required loan guarantee. The crop itself was not enough; the owners of Palto insisted that the tenant put up his field animals as a hedge against a lost crop.

In effect, tenants were forced to sell to the plantation owners at below the market price. Esquivel resisted this latest intrusion into what he regarded as his independent farmer status. For years he had argued with the manager over the correct interpretation of his contract: Did he owe back debts first to the hacienda, or did the obligation to pay his creditor come first? At times, the manager became so incensed that he used racial epithets rather than rational arguments to counter Esquivel's behavior. "Colored ingrate," he thundered more than once; "devilish black" and "games player" to suggest that the tenant was deceitful. And, on one occasion, the manager subjected Esquivel to the worst possible humiliation by commanding that he spend the day in the plantation stocks, a punishment ordinarily reserved for drunks and brawling field hands.

Despite the conflicts and setbacks, Esquivel remained at Palto. His stubbornness in the face of insults and demands by the manager and owners of the plantation at first seems incredible. But Esquivel survived because he knew farming. As cotton demand fell off after 1910 he increased the number of fields that he planted in vegetables and corn. Yet, to satisfy the owners, he continued to produce cotton, partly by taking on new sharecroppers and partly by extending the size of his loans. At one point, he had as many as three creditors, and, more than once, he used one crop to guarantee another.

A bewildering maze of loans and guarantees began to characterize his activities, but as long as the crops continued to do well Esquivel was able to pay into his left hand with what he held in his right. All the while, the amount of his indebtedness increased. Between 1910 and 1913 his debts accumulated ominously when flooding again ravaged the fields of Palto and his cotton crops repeatedly fell short of his promises. He was about to give up when the Aspíllagas decided that it was time for the landowners to invest in flood control. However, they accomplished very little. A few more dikes were built along the riverbank, and loan payments were extended, but the plantation system remained intact.

Not long after the owners' halfhearted effort, Esquivel's situation brightened for one final moment. He was, once again, the plantation's most prized tenant farmer. The holder of over thirty-five hectares of land, more than 90 percent of it planted in cotton, he was the most productive and, no doubt, the most influential person at Hacienda Palto aside from the chief administrator. For the first time, however, the manager decided to tell Esquivel what to plant. Astonished and mortified, Esquivel could not let this challenge go unanswered. He now felt comfortable enough to take the steps necessary to protect his contractual rights and ensure his family's security. When he did, the actions he took were a grave threat to the manager's authority. On one occasion, the manager tried to deny him access to the plantation woodlot. Esquivel insisted that he had a contractual right to cut firewood there, and he complained long and loud until the manager, who received no support from the owners for his position, gave in. Years later, the manager notified him that he was required to allow the landowners' cattle to pasture on his fallow fields. Esquivel refused to permit it. If his own oxen did not get enough healthy grasses, would not his cotton production be severely affected? Shortly thereafter, Esquivel and other tenants fenced in their fields with wire. For the moment, the Aspíllagas did not respond to the manager's complaints, and this action went unchallenged. Again, Esquivel's activities had caused him no difficulty with the Aspíllagas. True, the manager was unhappy, but the owners seemed willing to uphold the difficult parts of their contract with him. Perhaps they cared more to honor their agreement with their tenant than to make life easier for their manager.

Calculating that this was so, Esquivel composed a careful letter to the owners the next time he and the manager collided. The moment came in 1918. Of course, it was not possible to come directly to the point. First, he asked after the health of one of the Aspíllaga brothers who had spoken to him on his last visit to Palto. This was Esquivel's way of reminding the owners that it was not a nobody writing to them. On the contrary, he had been singled out in the past as an especially industrious and successful tenant. Surely they must remember him?

Once he had established his credentials, Esquivel explained the discord that had arisen between himself and the administrator, making it clear that the man had no right to insist that Esquivel grow no vegetables at all and that he plant only cotton. Finally, he asked the question that was gnawing at him and that revealed his contempt for the administrator. Juan Esquivel could not contain himself, he had to know: Had the administrator really received such an order, as he claimed, to tell Esquivel to grow only cotton? Esquivel could not believe that the owners, knowing his record, would allow the manager of Palto to treat him, a loyal tenant for so many years, in such a degrading fashion. And, he ended, "If this is true, then I do not understand your patronage very well."[1]

It was an easy step to the end of the tenant system. That point was reached when the tenants at Palto lost control of their pastures, their last bulwark against being reduced to sharecroppers. In 1919 the Aspíllagas announced that the tenants would no longer be allowed to fence in their gardens and that fixed rents would be abolished. Thereafter, all tenants were in effect reduced to sharecropper status.

Soon the plantation manager was talking about the new machinery the owners had introduced into Palto's fields in 1920, especially the Fordson tractor they had purchased from an American dealer. The plantation had become more independent of its tenants, and Juan Esquivel was a marked man. His name disappears from the records

---

[1]Juan Esquivel to Ramón Aspíllaga y Hermanos, Lima, September 9, 1918, Hacienda Palto, Accounts and Correspondence, 1867–1949, Archivo del Fuero Agrario, Lima.

altogether in 1920. The manager had refused to renew his rental contract and "canceled" his debt to Hacienda Palto.

The value of all of Esquivel's assets were totaled against the value of his outstanding debts to the Aspíllagas. Whatever was left over was his to keep when he departed. In fact, he and his wife exited the plantation gates with nothing but the clothes on their backs. While together with their sons they had grown tons of cotton that added significantly to the plantation's coffers, and to its value as a capital asset, their return for such work was hard to see. Even the animals and tools they had brought to Palto had gone to pay off debts. Though Esquivel was a skilled farmer, the plantation system had betrayed his skills, reducing their importance and rewarding only their value as labor rather than as specialized knowledge of farming.

He was not alone. From 1917 to 1925 most of the tenants who had farmed alongside Esquivel at Palto found their debts canceled and their services rejected. None of those still alive show up on the rolls of the hacienda in 1925, and few of them left the plantation with anything but a small amount of cash and an uncertain future. Left on the plantation were about one hundred tenants and their families, a total population of about three hundred fifty or four hundred men, women, and children according to an informal count by one of the Aspíllagas. This labor force of sharecroppers and day laborers was producing an annual cotton crop of roughly 177,000 pounds.

Juan Esquivel's farming success in the Pisco River valley blinded him to the realities of Peruvian society in the early twentieth century. Esquivel expected his skill in cotton farming to be recognized by the owners at least enough to gain respect for his judgment in farming decisions. He forgot that the owners and the manager paid attention to a different set of criteria. This led him to challenge the system of administrative control of tenants, not by striking out violently against the plantation manager but by personally challenging the manager's authority in a discreet manner, through a letter to the owners.

By questioning the manager's views, however, especially by calling attention to the manager's "mistakes" as early as 1909, Esquivel exposed himself to the charge of disobedience. He appeared thereafter to be an unreliable tenant, and only his ability to produce cotton in the face of difficult conditions saved him from eviction before 1919. The plantation owners wanted a clear line maintained between a tenant's working hard to meet the plantation's needs and his challenging the manager's authority. "Silent" hard work was viewed as constructive, while personal challenges, although they might in special circumstances be tolerated for a short time, were seen as ultimately threatening the system of plantation command. If the tenants learned that the manager could be opposed, it would only be a short step to their challenging the authority of the owners. The Aspíllagas were sensitive to such an eventuality. A farm workers' movement was under way in the Pisco Valley, and the Aspíllagas had heard about a strike and demonstrations in Pisco. The workers on some of the plantations had struck for higher salaries, and the demonstrations reportedly had paralyzed commerce in the town for a short time.

Toward the end of his stay at Palto, Esquivel had begun to recognize that there was no room for compromise on the matter of tenant choice and managerial authority on the plantation. Tenants worked under severe tension generated by the competing demands of the export plantation world. On the one hand, they were expected to work in harmony with the overall management goal of achieving greater productivity on the plantation while, on the other hand, they were encouraged to use the land as if it were their own. The explosive mixture of authoritarian management and individual choice overshadowed the tenants' daily lives. Ordinarily, such conflicts were submerged beneath the routines of farming, weeding, feeding of animals, harvesting, and other chores, thus preserving the illusion that the tenant on a commercial cotton plantation was an autonomous farmer. The moments of crises that floods, insect plagues, poor harvests, and similar disasters induced caused great stress on the plantations, disrupting the Pisco Valley countryside and filling the air with the discordant sound of clashes between independence and authority. At these moments, when they were treated like field hands, the tenants came face-to-face with the horrors of the plantation world.

SOURCES

The social and economic activities of Juan Esquivel and his family on the plantation were reconstructed from the letterbooks and accounts of Hacienda San Francisco de Palto that are located in the Archivo del Fuero Agrario, Lima, Peru. Other aids were necessary. Of critical importance were the following collections and studies: Pablo Macera, *Tierra y población en el Peru (ss. xviii–xix)*, 4 vols. (Lima, 1972); Jean Piel, "The Place of the Peasantry in the National Life of Peru in the Nineteenth Century," *Past and Present* 46 (February 1970): 108–33; Bill Albert, "Yanaconaje and Cotton Production on the Peruvian Coast: Sharecropping in the Cañete Valley during World War I," *Bulletin of Latin American Research* 2, no. 2 (May 1983): 107–15; Eduardo

Arroyo, *La hacienda costeña en el Peru: Mala-Cañete, 1532–1968* (Lima, 1981); Manuel Burga and Alberto Flores Galindo, *Apogeo y crisis de la república aristocrática*, 2d ed. (Lima, 1981); Carlos Samaniego, "Peasant Movements at the Turn of the Century and the Rise of the Independent Farmer," in *Peasant Cooperation and Capitalist Expansion in Central Peru*, edited by N. Long and B. R. Roberts, 45–71 (Austin, TX, 1978); W. S. Bell, "An Essay on the Peruvian Cotton Industry, 1825–1920," University of Liverpool, Centre for Latin American Studies, Working Paper 6 (1985); and Rolando Pachas Castilla, *Economía y sociedad en el valle de Chincha: 1860–1918* (Lima, 1976).

6

*Angel Santana Suárez: Cuban Sugar Worker**

Ana Núñez Machín
Introduction by Louis A. Pérez, Jr.

The interview with Angel Santana Suárez first appeared in *Memoria amarga del azúcar* (1981) by Ana Núñez Machín. Rural schoolteacher, poet, journalist, and member of the Instituto de Historia del Movimiento Comunista y de la Revolución Socialista de Cuba, Núñez Machín compiled and edited this series of interviews with Cuban sugar workers. She notes in her introduction to the book, as Angel Santana does in his interview, that the old sugar workers want younger generations of Cubans to understand the bitter misery and suffering that the sweet crop brought to the workers in the past.

Louis A. Pérez, Jr., is graduate research professor of history at the University of South Florida. He is the author of numerous works, including *Cuba under the Platt Amendment, 1902–1934* (1986) and *Cuba between Empires, 1878–1902* (1983). Pérez's interest in social history is further displayed in "Vagrants, Beggars, and Bandits: Social Origins of Cuban Separatism, 1878–1895," which appeared in the *American Historical Review* (December 1985).

INTRODUCTION

The depression came early to Cuba. It started in the mid-1920s, as the price of sugar began to drop, a decline that would not end until the following decade. The government of Gerardo Machado (1925–33) responded to the crisis with the Verdeja Act, an effort to halt faltering world prices by decreasing Cuban supplies. President Machado secured congressional authority to limit the size of the sugar crop by establishing a quota system for production in each province and mill based on estimated acreage. The length of the harvest season was shortened from 136 days to 87 days. The 1926 crop was fixed at 4.5 million tons, a 10-percent reduction from the 1925 harvest. Subsequent decrees imposed a moratorium on new planting and fixed the start of the harvest for January 1927, a month later than usual.

*Translated by Judith Ewell.

Cuban efforts proved futile. Instead of stabilizing world prices on reduced supplies, the curtailment of Cuban production served to stimulate increased sugar production elsewhere. Prices continued to drop. The 1924 price of 4.19 cents a pound fell to 2.57 cents in 1926 and 2.46 cents in 1928.

Cuban efforts to conform to international production strategies as a means to combat declining prices had calamitous repercussions on the island. The economy slumped and stopped expanding. Hardest hit were sugar workers. The shortened *zafra* (sugar harvest) meant effectively less work for tens of thousands of Cubans already suffering the bane of either unemployment or underemployment.

A chilling consensus emerged. Cuba appeared to be moving ineluctably toward an economic crisis of monumental proportions. Distress and dissatisfaction spread across the island, and especially in the more important agricultural and commercial areas. "Importers find themselves suddenly overstocked and the market going down," U.S. Consul Francis R. Stewart wrote from Santiago de Cuba in mid-1927. He continued:

> Restriction of the sugar crop . . . has failed to alleviate conditions in this territory. Field hands upon whom merchants depend for a large portion of their trade have received the lowest wages in many years, in many cases barely sufficient to support their families, and as a majority of the mills of this district have already ceased operations, the men thrown out of work are facing eight months of idleness.

In Guantánamo, Stewart reported, the "poorer classes already are subsisting on sugar cane and boniatos [sweet potatoes], and the diet must continue until the next crop." Poverty was "apparent everywhere" and business was stagnant with "many firms being particularly bad off." A similar condition prevailed in Antilla. "Due to the presidential decree limiting the current sugar crop by several months," U.S. Consul Horace J. Dickenson reported, "unemployment and destitution is everywhere in the province." Dickenson continued:

> To date centrals Marcane, Alto Cedro, Cupey, Miranda, Maceo and Preston have terminated their crops, so that a large number of unemployed men have been left in those localities to face a period of enforced idleness. . . . Conditions will become worse during the coming months when the savings of the workingmen accumulated during the brief period of the past crop have been exhausted. It is anticipated then that there will be a large influx of labor into the port towns and other centers offering hope of employment in other agricultural lines. Such a tendency has already been noted in Antilla, where vagrancy and mendicancy are more marked than at any previous period of [*the*] town's history.

In Nuevitas, the twenty local *centrales* suspended operations months earlier than usual, producing large-scale unemployment. Local joblessness led to a decline in import and retail trade, which, in turn, resulted in the discharge of countless numbers of employees in those sectors. Similar conditions existed in Matanzas. "There has been very little movement of sugar so far this year from the ports in this district," the U.S. consul in Matanzas reported. "The slow movement of sugar . . . tends to increase the unemployment as the stevedores and sugar warehouse workers are forced into idleness awaiting the shipping period. There is considerable unemployment in this district and it has been stated that the poor and laboring classes are finding difficulty in providing a livelihood."

Conditions deteriorated markedly after 1929. The worldwide depression wrought utter havoc to the already ailing Cuban economy. New reversals were not long in coming. In mid-1930, the United States passed the Smoot-Hawley Tariff Act, which increased duty on Cuban sugar. Domestic producers and island possessions gained a larger share of the U.S. market at the expense of Cuban sugar. The Cuban share declined from 49.4 percent in 1930 to 25.3 percent in 1933. A year later, Cuba joined six other sugar-producing countries in the Chadbourne Plan, a strategy to raise floundering prices by restricting exports for five years.

The cumulative effect of these developments was devastating, and everywhere the auguries of calamity were visible. Sugar production, the fulcrum upon which the entire economy balanced, fell by 60 percent. Cuban exports declined by 80 percent, while the price of the island's principal export, sugar, fell over 60 percent. Cuban planters found themselves with surplus sugar, in search of new markets, at a time of declining prices. Producers struggled to remain solvent by lowering wages and cutting production through labor layoffs. The *zafra* was reduced again, this time to a sixty-two-day harvest—that is, only two months' work for tens of thousands of sugar workers. Distress spread quickly to other sectors. The value of tobacco, the island's second largest export, declined from $43 million in 1929 to $13 million in 1933. Salaries and wages were reduced, workers laid off, and businesses and factories closed. Unemployment soared. Two hundred fifty thousand heads of families, representing approximately 1 million people out of a total population of 3.9 million, found themselves unemployed. Those fortunate enough to escape total unemployment found temporary work difficult to come by and wages depressed. Pay for agricultural workers fell by 75 percent. In the sugar zones, wages dropped as low as twenty cents for a twelve-hour workday. On one large estate, sugar workers received ten cents per day—five in cash and five in credit at the company store. In some agricultural districts, laborers received only food and lodging for their work. "Wages paid . . . in 1932," one wage survey indicated, "are reported to have been the lowest since the days of slavery." Wages for the urban proletariat decreased by 50 percent. Wages for carpenters, mechanics, electricians, and painters declined from sixty cents per hour to thirty. Linotypists who formerly received fifty-two dollars per week earned thirty-five dollars. Cannery workers who in 1930 earned twelve dollars per week, in 1932 earned eighty cents per day. Dock workers who earned four dollars per day received two dollars. And as wages fell in absolute terms, the value of the peso decreased in purchasing power. The peso was worth twenty-eight centavos less in 1928 than 1913. Profits plummeted everywhere.

Commerce came to a standstill. Local industry and manufacturing reduced production in response to reduced purchasing power of the population; this, in turn, sparked a new round of unemployment and new wage cuts. The cycle seemed to have no end. Commercial, banking, and manufacturing failures reached record proportions. Business failures produced another spiral of unemployment and new rounds of shortages and price rises. Between 1930 and 1931 the government inaugurated a policy of drastic salary cuts for all public employees except the armed forces. Pay reductions of as much as 60 percent were not uncommon. A year later, budget cuts resulted in the first of a series of sweeping layoffs of civil servants. Highway construction projects that had employed some fifteen thousand workers in 1928 were suspended, creating immediate hardships in thousands of additional households. In the second half of 1931 alone, the government closed 200 post offices, 9 diplomatic legations, and 7 public hospitals, as well as several nurseries, schools, and agricultural stations. And for most who remained on state payrolls, public employment offered diminishing consolation as salaries fell hopelessly in arrears. By 1932, the salaries of the vast majority of civil servants had fallen six months behind. By 1933, more than 60 percent of the population lived at submarginal levels of under three hundred dollars in annual real income; another 30 percent earned marginal wages between three hundred and six hundred dollars.

As economic conditions continued to deteriorate, impatience with government policies spread. Political opposition increased. So did government repression. Arrests, torture, and assassination became commonplace. Government critics were routinely kidnapped, and most victims were never heard from again. Censorship and harassment of the opposition press silenced public criticism of the government.

Through the late 1920s and early 1930s the conflict deepened and confrontations intensified. Labor continued to organize, union membership expanded, and the frequency of strikes increased. In 1927 cigar workers organized the Federación Nacional de Torcedores, uniting some thirty thousand workers in all six provinces. In 1928 electrical workers organized nationally into the Unión de Obreros y Empleados de Plantas Eléctricas. In 1932 sugar workers established the first national union, the Sindicato Nacional de Obreros de la Industria Azucarera (SNOIA). By 1929 the Cuban Communist party (PCC) had established control over large sectors of organized labor. Mass demonstrations and hunger marches increased. Between 1929 and 1930 labor struck a number of industries, including sugar, cigar manufacturing, metallurgy, construction, and textiles. In March 1930 the Confederación Nacional de Obreros Cubanos (CNOC) organized a stunning general strike. Involving some two hundred thousand workers, the strike paralyzed the island. It ended only after a wave of government violence and repression, but not without lasting effects.

Open warfare broke out in Cuba after 1931. Repression increased, but so did reprisals. Government opponents were murdered, and the murderers were assassinated. Every member of the Machado government was a potential target. Assassinations, bombings, and sabotage became the principal expression of opposition. But the price for success was dear. The government responded with mounting fury and indiscriminate violence. Jails filled with government opponents, and they were the fortunate ones. More often, suspects were executed summarily at the site of capture.

There were regional variations to these conditions, to be sure. Conditions were worse in the countryside than in the cities, worse for rural wage laborers than for farmers. Other forces were at work, less visible, less understood, but no less devastating. Economic distress could not have come to Cuba at a worse possible moment, and Angel Santana could not have been at a worse possible place at that moment. Decades earlier, at the close of the Cuban war for independence in 1898, the island experienced a spectacular rise of fertility rates. The postwar baby boom affected all of Cuba. Between 1899 and 1907 the population under 5 years of age increased from 8 percent of the total to 20 percent—a national increase within the 0–4 group of 156 percent, from 130,878 in 1899 to 342,652 in 1907. The baby boom was especially pronounced in Las Villas province, and indeed, Santana Suárez was himself part of that population surge—one of twelve children. In Las Villas, the increase in the under-5 population was more than 205 percent, from 26,101 to 79,763.

What made the collapse of the Cuban economy during the late 1920s and early 1930s especially devastating was timing; it occurred just at the moment that the postwar baby boom population was reaching economically productive age. Nearly 750,000 Cubans, between the ages of late twenties and early thirties, had recently entered the labor force, many with newly established families of their own, and could not find work. In 1931 the baby boom generation constituted 20 percent of the population, and children nine years and younger made up another 28.8 percent of the total.

These conditions were pronounced in Angel Santana Suárez's home province of Las Villas. Between 1899 and 1931 the population of Las Villas increased more than 128 percent, from 356,536 residents to 815,412. The baby boom generation in Las Villas made up 25 percent of this total. In no other province was the percentage of marriages higher, or the rate of divorce lower. The average family size in Las Villas was 5.7 members, the second highest in the republic. It also had the second highest percentage of families over the size of ten. The depression caused havoc in Las Villas. In 1931, unemployment was more than 68 percent. Even though the province had gained population after 1899, between the late 1920s and early 1930s a significant out-migration was occurring. Between 1919 and 1931, Las Villas registered the second lowest population increment in the island. Almost one-quarter of all municipalities lost population during the intercensus years of 1919 and 1931. The municipality of Zulueta, the birthplace of Santana Suárez, declined by almost 30 percent. By contrast, the population of Camagüey, where Santana migrated, increased by more than 78 percent, in large measure due to the opening of new sugar mills during and after World War I. The municipality of Morón, Santana's new residence, increased by more than 81 percent.

Angel Santana Suárez's life during the late 1920s and early 1930s is representative of countless tens of thousands of agricultural workers during economic hard times. He was part of a large floating population, refugees in their own land, constantly on the move searching for work. Even in good times, this was a precarious existence. After 1926, it was transformed into a problematical one.

I was born in the Las Villas *colonia*[1] in Zulueta region on 16 August 1904. I was the fourth of twelve children, and, since my father was a farm worker, we children had to work in the fields from an early

[1]Sugar plantation.

age. From the time that I was seven or eight years old, I did agricultural labor, sometimes guiding the oxen in the fields and most of the time cleaning and cutting cane during the *zafra* [harvest season]. When we couldn't load the cane because we couldn't reach the bed of the cart, we piled it up for our father to lift it in. When we weeded the fields we walked in front of Papa's furrow so that he could check what we were doing, since the overseers said that we children left too much grass. Other times, the old man had to check the work to see that it was all right. That was what my childhood was like, as it necessarily was for all farm workers who had the misfortune of living in our country's sugar *colonias*, in the so-called postindependence era.

When it came to education, no matter how much a large family tried—even if there was a school two or three kilometers away—most of the children of farm workers could not attend. The family needed the modest labor force that the child produced to be able to help sustain the home—if one could call a home a thatched hut lined with palm bark, usually with a dirt floor and with the most unhygienic conditions that could be imagined. I remember that our household goods could be transported on two or three horses and that happened quite often, since my father was very rebellious. Although he was illiterate—a product of the environment in which he lived—he did not stand for any overseer or *colonia* owner to call him a blockhead. For that reason in 1918 we had to leave the zone where I had been born and moved to the 15.5-kilometer mark of Simón Reyes, the municipal boundary of Ciego de Avila.

As I said before, we moved very often, and that's how we came to live in the zone of the San Pablo *central*,[2] rather close to the *ingenio* [sugar mill]. I was then eleven or twelve years old. There we did everything. Papa and my brothers worked in the fields, and I, who was the weakest, worked guiding the oxen in the *batey*,[3] sometimes skimming the first froth from the cane juice when it was boiled to make sugar and at other times guiding the narrow-gauge cars in the weighing area. In the *tiempo muerto*,[4] we washed the sugar off the sugar sprouts, and we weeded the fields.

But there was an overseer who was nicknamed "Pepe el Isleño" [the Canary Islander], who was famous for being abusive, since he liked to gallop his horse over the workers. That man had problems with my father, and one day he pulled his machete on my father. If

[2] Modern sugar mill. It purchased and ground sugar from the surrounding *colonias*.

[3] Group of buildings around a sugar mill, including living quarters.

[4] "Dead time," or time between harvests, which could last for many months.

other people had not intervened, we don't know what would have happened, since Papa also took out his machete. Later when I was in Camagüey I heard that a worker had killed the Isleño, which put an end to his insults and abuses.

Then, after the move to Simón Reyes, we landed at the Stewart *colonia* [renamed Venezuela after 1959]. My father had a brother who was a mechanic-overseer, and he found work for him and for two of us youngsters; my brother in the *batey* office and me in the carpenter's shop. This was during the *zafra*. In the so-called dead time, we worked in the field at whatever jobs came up when there was any work at all.

In 1919, in the time of the "fat cows," so called because of the sudden prosperity of the sugar industry, for the first time, in spite of my youth and ignorance, I realized that something was not right. The workers, led by some companions named Fabregat and Bello, as I recall, agreed to strike against the sugar mill. That strike was broken up violently by soldiers wielding machete blades.

They took the workers of the *batey* from their houses by force, especially those who lived in the large bunkhouses, and made them work. Many of our companions lost their jobs and others had to disappear, since the persecution unleashed by the army, headed by a Lieutenant Cárdenas, ended the first strike that I ever saw. This was during the 1919 harvest.

In 1920 sugar reached an astounding price. Most men did not want to work in the sugar mills, since they could earn up to twenty dollars a day in the fields, without much effort. That lasted only a short time because the next year, when the North American sugar industry had recovered from World War I, sugar prices fell from ten or twelve centavos a pound to less than one centavo. That caused the banks to fail and what was called the Moratorium followed. General Menocal governed the country then. He was also known as "the man of the *timbales* [drums]," a nickname he earned because, as people said, he liked to tan the hides of the workers.[5]

Those were very hard times for us workers in the sugar industry. Everybody had given up the cultivation of food crops, and then we suffered from hunger because there was nothing to eat. Many people

[5]Mario G. Menocal had a long and varied career before becoming president. He had spent much of his childhood in the United States and Mexico, fought in the War for Independence, been chief of police in Havana, and helped found (with an investor from Texas) the Cuban-American Company, which became the largest sugar operation in the world.

died for lack of food in the sugar fiefdoms! Things went on that way for two years until the situation stabilized.

Now that I was older, and encouraged by my mother, who was more zealous of my education than my father was, I began to attend school. I took night classes with other guys of the same age and kept on until I had passed the fourth or fifth grade of primary school. I was learning what was bad and what was good, as well as about the social inequality that existed in the world.

When the 1924 harvest ended, for the first time I left to work away from home. I went to the Morón *central* [today called Ciro Redondo], and I began to work in the carpentry department.

Around the month of August the workers began to spread rumors that a strike had been called, which I already knew about. I am not sure if it was the seventh, but that night we agreed to refuse to go to work the following day until they reinstated a group of companions who had been fired. The administration had discovered that we were organizing a union and that our companions were the ringleaders. They were José Lugo, Marcelino Cuervo, Venancio Trem, and others that I don't remember. All workers of the Morón *central.*

Our unforgettable Camagüeyano leader Enrique Varona, who was a railroad worker, organized the strike. Varona was the true leader of that movement, since he knew well the conditions of semislavery that sugar workers lived in. We worked twelve hours a day, and we were victims of multiple abuses, not only from the men who gave orders in the sugar mills, but also from the army, who were their lackeys.

There's no need even to dwell on the history of the agricultural sector, since the situation of the rural areas is a microcosm of the history of our country. The landlord, the great *colono,*[6] and the great foreign enterprises had at their service in that period—in addition to their own resources—the service of the Rural Guard to squelch the workers' protests or signs of rebellion. The so-called *Tercios Tácticos* [division of the guard] were in charge of guaranteeing peace during the *zafras* to aid the exploitative owners. I had the privilege of hearing about this from Varona—that was when I realized the inequality in which we were living.

I understood that there was a minority that enjoyed all privileges, who were lords of all the wealth and had enslaved the great majority of people who produced everything, didn't have enough to eat, and were victims of all kinds of abuses. This, I repeat, we heard from

[6]Owner of a *colonia.*

Varona, and it took root in our brains and we feel it in our hearts up to today. That was a great struggle; we won the strike, although unfortunately at the high price of the life of that incorruptible leader. Many others also died during the struggle.

Enrique Varona González had an exceptional organizing power. In that month of August of 1924 he led almost all of the *centrales* of Camagüey province to strike. The railroad workers supported the strike by not allowing anything to be transported to the sugar estates.

The work stoppages in each unit were formidable; the workers understood the role that they were playing. They selected the best workers in each place as leaders. We won a victory for the first time, a result of the workers' determination and of the good and honorable leadership of Varona and of the group that followed him. The victory was short-lived.

On 20 of May of 1925 a tyrant took over the presidency of our country, a servile assassin in the service of North American imperialism. At a banquet given for him by North American bankers, he had the effrontery to declare that "no strike would last more than twenty-four hours in his period of government." That was General Gerardo Machado y Morales, known later as the "jackass with claws," as our unforgettable Rubén Martínez Villena called him.

So it was that Machado took charge and put in as Secretario de Gobernación[7] another just like him, comandante Rogerio Zayas Bazán. Immediately the secret meetings began between the imperialistic companies, the U.S. embassy, the landlords, and others of the same ilk. The *ingenios* called a strike, with the Stewart mill leading the way. The strike was broken up by force. The other *ingenios* followed. They freed Varona, who had been jailed on the charge of dynamiting a train in Cuba's north line, and two days later, they assassinated him in Morón on September 19, 1925.

Persecution intensified, blacklists were drawn up of those workers who were known to be with the strike movement; forty-seven of us were expelled from the Stewart mill. We were branded as communists, and our names were circulated to the other foreign companies. They wanted us to die of hunger in our own country, and the same thing that had happened in the Stewart mill also happened in the other *ingenios*. We were lucky that they only put us on the blacklist, since the repression was barbarous; crime was the order of the day, and, naturally, the country was in an uproar.

---

[7]Minister of the interior, in charge of internal order and security.

Zayas's government—which at least had tolerated the right of assembly—had allowed the progressive currents of the October Revolution to enter our country. Leaders such as Julio Antonio Mella, Alfredo López, Carlos Baliño, and many others absorbed this current and openly defended the sublime ideals of redemption of the working class by the end of Zayas's term. At the same time, the students were waking up from their self-satisfied lethargy, which became evident in the "José Martí" Popular University—created by Mella and a group of university professors, who suffered the wrath of those in power—where workers and students grew ideologically and gained the necessary knowledge to prepare favorable conditions for our victory. Also in that year 1925, in August, the Second National Workers' Congress and the Confederación Nacional Obrera de Cuba (CNOC)[8] met in Ciénfuegos.

Trade unions sprouted up like that of the Industria Fabril y Gráficas [manufacturing and graphics industry] in Havana. The Movimiento Sindical Azucarero [Sugar Workers' Trade Union Movement] was already well organized from the year before. And so it was that imperialism, the plantation owners, and great landlords were scared. They had to do something to squelch the liberating ideas and the aspirations of the working people, led by Mella and so many of his companions. It was then that they turned to Machado, already known for his action as minister of the interior in José Miguel Gómez's government. He was the "strong man," which became clear later, through his chain of crimes such as the assassinations of Varona, Mella, Alfredo López, and others. One could name hundreds. Those were sad days in which we Cubans lived in stupified terror because we never thought that such a thing could happen.

At the end of 1925 I began to work in the Velasco *central*, of course using my mother's surname, since whoever dared to give his own name and surname when he was on the blacklist was kicked off the *batey* by the guards and the army, or more likely became a prisoner, depending on the charges against him. Many cases like this occurred.

What sugar worker of my generation doesn't remember the highs and lows of the economy in those days of Machado: Chadbourne Plan, Restrictions, Tarafa Law, Law of Quotas, and destruction of the Elevado of the Crucero of Quesada. That's why the Jagueyal and Velasco *centrales*, where I was working, stopped grinding, leaving hundreds of families like orphans. They had to go out on life's roads to look for somewhere to earn a crust of bread.

---

[8]National Workers' Confederation of Cuba.

In full crisis of 1930, you should have seen the misery of the sugar workers. How could we forget those years when the starvation kitchen in the sugar *centrales* during the dead time lasted at least eight months a year: the "puff" of boiled wheat and the black or *caritas* beans, with their accompanying scum of weevils and worms, since what the company supplied was the garbage that had no market. This will seem to you like a story to exaggerate the sugar workers' hunger but it isn't. It is easy to prove by asking people of that era, many of whom are still living. We had to work for three days a week in fixing up the *batey*, repairing the roads, etc., and I can tell you that we had to do the work, and we only received one meal a day.

We will never be able to forget those years from 1930 to 1933. What a contrast! After the victory of the revolution, everything is different.

But let's leave this and go on. Machado fell, a result of the struggles carried on by groups of courageous Cubans, many of whom sacrificed their lives, and by a general strike—even though he had said that in his presidency no strike would last more than twenty-four hours. Ironies of destiny!

In the convulsion of that revolution, the sugar workers began to feel a little relief. The Pentarquía paraded,[9] the *golpe* [coup] of the 4 of September took place, and the "hermit of Cunagua," General Mendieta, emerged. He and General Batista attacked the working class with Decree Law No. 3, which prohibited strikes. And we again became victims of the reprisals of the administrators of sugar mills. I was fired and ordered to leave the *batey* of the Violeta *central* [since the revolution called the 1st of January] where I had worked after I left the Velasco *central* when it closed in 1930.

The marriage between the U.S. embassy and the ambitious politicians mutilated the revolution. Batista betrayed the revolution, he assassinated Guiteras in "El Morrillo," he deceived Miguel Mariano with the complicity of a puppet congress, and he used Laredo Bru and the "man of the napkin," or Dr. Barnet. But I should add that at that time I got my job back.

The eight-hour law that Guiteras promulgated, and other laws, such as the law of nationalization, meant that they had to hire more people and that saved me because they needed a cane grinder. I was rehired, but not without first being reprimanded and having the riot act read to me.

---

[9]Five-man junta that took over the government in September 1933 after the revolution had caused Machado to flee. The members were Ramón Grau San Martín, Porfirio Franca, Sergio Carbó, José María Irisarri, and Guillermo Portela.

When that 1935 harvest ended, after the March strike, I had to get away from that place and leave my family, in spite of having had our first child. Then I went to Santiago, Cuba. There I heard of the death of Guiteras on the 8 of May of that same year. In November I returned and was rehired.

During those years, up to 1954, our lives as sugar workers were always dominated by the market price of sugar. The restrictions and the Law of Quotas meant seventy-day harvests and a dead time of up to eight months. Our situation didn't get better; it was all hunger and misery. We couldn't look for any other work because there wasn't any. The Constituent Assembly of 1940 conceded tolerance toward unions and some other guarantees and social benefits, a result of the alliance of the Socialist delegates with some Auténticos.[10] We had been organized since 1939, led by that great man Jesús Menéndez, who was assassinated by imperialism and the creole oligarchy on 22 January of 1948.

To tell the truth, our situation improved quite a bit, although always the dead time was our nightmare. The Federación Azucarera led by companion Menéndez forced the sugar magnates to concede some positive economic and social advantages to us. I was elected leader of our union several times. I had the honor of participating in the struggles of our companion Menéndez from 1939 until his death. I knew quite a bit of the *Grausato*[11] and the *Priato*,[12] and in February of 1952, I left the union leadership because the workers' movement had become incredibly corrupt and had lost prestige. Mujal and his gang, instead of defending the workers, "negotiated" their demands and surrendered the gains won in the times of Menéndez.

Corruption and rotten politics ruled. One of Menéndez's hard-fought battles had won for us the sugar differential since as technology spread and production rose, there were fewer days of grinding. That directly affected the workers' economic situation, which already was desperate.

We were already used to that state of misery, but it became more common to see hundreds of companions walking the roads at the beginning of each harvest season, carrying their possessions in *jolongos*

[10]Members of the Partido Revolucionario Cubano Auténtico, which had been reorganized by Ramón Grau San Martín after the failure of the 1933 revolution. The Auténticos returned to power under the presidencies of Grau (1944–48) and Carlos Prío Socorrás (1948–52).

[11]Presidency of Ramón Grau San Martín, 1944–48.

[12]Presidency of Carlos Prío Socorrás, 1948–52.

[straw bags] and asking the unions to help them find work. How many times they asked us to let them cut a bundle of cane so they could continue on their way or to let them work a half day in order to earn "water and charcoal"! Hundreds, thousands of times! And what hurts the most is that there are sugar workers who have forgotten all these calamities and abuses.

But one day after the 10 of March of 1952 in which Batista returned to power with the approval of the U.S. embassy, there was a 26 of July. And after that 26 of July there was a disembarking on the Coloradas Beach in Niquero and the beginning of a real revolution. Our comandante Fidel went up to the Sierra Maestra, then came down to the plains, aided by the unforgettable Camilo and Che and their brave companions. They defeated the tyrant's army at the end of 1958 and put the dictator and his gang to flight.

Now, after the triumph of the revolution, my situation, like that of all the sugar workers, improved one hundred percent. The hated dead time disappeared, and the enterprises which had exploited us so much passed into the hands of the people.

7

*Cristobal Arancibia: The Life of a Bolivian Peasant during the Chaco War, 1932–35**

René Arze Aguirre

Professor René Arze Aguirre, director of the history degree program at the Universidad Mayor de San Andrés in La Paz, Bolívia, conducted this interview with Cristobal Arancibia as part of the oral history project on the Chaco War that he initiated. Arze has published some of his research as *Guerra y conflictos sociales: El caso rural boliviano en la campaña del Chaco, 1932–1935* (1987). He turned to the techniques of oral history because of the high illiteracy rate among the war's veterans and because official documents are either inaccessible or unreliable. Oral history has allowed him to follow the experiences of the anonymous common men who fought in the war and who will not leave written documents. Arze did his interviews in Sucre and the surrounding provinces with Quechua-speaking campesinos. He has called for others to interview veterans whose first language is Aymará from the altiplano and those whose first language is Guaraní from the Bolivian east before these former soldiers die. He states, eloquently, that each death of a veteran before he is interviewed is equal to the burning of a library.

The Chaco War (1932–35) indelibly marked Bolivian history. Fighting between Bolivia and Paraguay had actually begun earlier in this remote scrubland region. Both countries wanted to compensate for territorial losses suffered in nineteenth-century wars. In addition, Bolivia was seeking an ocean port through the La Plata River system. Their rivalry was intensified when Standard Oil of New Jersey began exploring for oil in the region. The financial and human costs of the Chaco War devastated both nations, with the loss of life reaching fifty thousand for Bolivia and thirty-five thousand for Paraguay. In Bolivia, the wartime exploitation of Indian conscripts from the highlands, who suffered from a lack of equipment, supplies, and training, contributed to national unrest. The new awareness of the nation's indigenous population ultimately resulted in the revolution of 1952.

---

*Translated and edited by William H. Beezley.

Cristobal Arancibia was born in the locality of Segura, Canton of Juana Azurduy de Padilla, Department of Chuquisaca, Bolivia, in 1917. Arancibia worked before and after the Chaco War as a peasant farmer. This interview took place in the Chuquisaca Veterans Federation, Sucre, on November 26, 1986.

Question: Where do you live now, Señor Arancibia?

Cristobal Arancibia: In Segura, the Canton Juana Azurduy de Padilla.

Question: How did you come from there?

C. A.: By animal. . . . I left two days ago for Monteagudo. I came from there yesterday in a car. I arrived this morning. We traveled all last night without sleeping.

Question: Do you have a family? Did you have a wife?

C. A.: Yes, we lived as husband and wife only. We didn't have any babies. The woman had daughters; they are married. The son typically is a prodigal, so in this way my son has gone.

Question: Señor Arancibia, I want you to tell me about your childhood. Did you go to school?

C. A.: No! No, I knew nothing of school. I never went to school a single time. The landowners used to say, "Those who know how to read will go to the war, and they are gonna get killed there." They used to tell our parents that, so that's why they didn't want to send us to school. In this way they scared us. Only those in the town learned to read, and they had us in the countryside to work like dogs, tending the sheep and the cattle. They didn't want us to walk into school. For this reason, we didn't learn to read. The owners didn't let us.

Question: And did you want to learn to read?

C. A.: Oh! How it could have been now, well . . . here it could not have been. Because we didn't know how to read I didn't put my passbook in a safe place [this military passbook is discussed later]. Clearly, those who know how to read, don't suffer. If you don't know how to read you suffer plenty. If we want to get someone to read a letter we have to walk a long way. We have to look for someone if we want to make a letter. It is a very bitter life. We only live like animals. We don't know anything; we can't account for anything. By knowing how to read then you more or less know how to understand.

Question: Weren't you a tenant farmer? What was your life like? What did you do as a tenant?

C. A.: Everything. . . . We planted *ají* [a kind of chili]. I used to get up at dawn. Cornelio Guzmán, the owner, used to make us get up at dawn. He was always the merchant. He would travel to San Pedro de Buena Vista, Guañoma. He would come here to Rosario, each year, without fail. And he would make us plant the corn and hoe the *ají*. He would make us work by the week. They made us work by the week without wages, depending on our age. He had the kids care for the sheep and cows, that is what he had us kids do. It was halfway forced service [the *mita*]. The old people had to bring goods here to Sucre and to Sopachuy. It was obligatory that they do it. Or, they had to bring some letters like a mailman. This is the way they kept us busy.

Question: And did they pay you?

C. A.: Nobody paid us anything.

Question: What did you receive in exchange?

C. A.: Your ration, your food. They didn't know how to pay wages. They would give a meal. They would give you a break three times a day. Sunday, we looked after the sheep and cows. Hard work, you see, year around, doing everything—carrying firewood, making *muko* [corn flour that is chewed to make *chicha*, a native liquor], spinning wool—we did everything.

Question: What did the women do?

C. A.: They would spin, weave, chew *muko*. There was a standing obligation to hand over six *arrobas* [a variable measure of about twenty-five pounds of liquid] of *muko*.

Question: And if you didn't have work on the owner's hacienda, where would you go?

C. A.: They were obliged to throw us off their lands, and it was necessary to look for another patron, another similar landowner. Some bad ones wouldn't even give us meals. Some would give us snacks, some would give lunch, more would give us dinner. Some would give us a meal, not a ration, just in a basket; if we didn't work we got the whip. We had to work. Some owners brought fifteen, twenty, thirty peons. They got them from town, because there were no more around Monteagudo, so they had sixty or eighty peons. They made them work long and hard.

Question: Tell me about the Chaco War.

C. A.: They drafted me when I was fifteen years old, more or less. I had been working for thirteen years, for ten years plus three more. In those thirteen years, I was a shepherd. From there they sent me to the barracks; at fifteen, I was a kid. They never paid any attention if you were a boy or an old man, if you were blind, or crippled. They would draft anyone who was male. . . . They would grab you. I went in the last recruitment . . . we walked to Charagua on the new road to Monteagudo.[1] In Charagua, we recruits presented ourselves to the army.

Question: Did any of you want to hide out from military service?

C. A.: Not at all. We were working on the Monteagudo roads, opening the road to Monteagudo. They suspended it and left only the military engineers. Every last one of the workers went to the army. Then they went to the war. Back then I really wanted to go because several of my brothers already had gone; about eight of my brothers were in the war. I wanted to go, too. They hadn't wanted to take me in Tarabuco, nor here [in Sucre], because I was a youngster. I was broke and I left Sucre. I went to Monteagudo for that whole year; when I returned they finally drafted me. I was content then.

They wanted to send me to the rear guard, to Río Grande. To all the youngsters they said, "These guys are not going to go to the front." I wanted to see the war.

Besides I had seen deserters. Some they killed. . . . Yes, they killed them. Some they sent to the front lines. Punishment shouldn't be this way. For one thing, we were supposed to be defending the country. Should punishment be to go to the front line of combat? Seeing that they sent deserters to the front, I ran away from Charagua for a week. I always wanted to see the war, to know how the war was. In this way I was sent to Toledo Regiment, Nineteenth Infantry. From there, we entered the war.

Question: What was better—working on a hacienda or going to be a soldier?

---

[1]The absence of roads and transport forced the Bolivian soldiers to march to the battle lines in southeastern Bolivia.

C. A.: Becoming a soldier.

Question: Why?

C. A.: For the experience, Señor, for the sake of defending our flag, because everyone else went. Those who didn't go were idlers, cowards, chickenhearted . . . a disgrace.[2] People laughed at them. This is why I decided to go.

Question: Then you went to Charagua?

C. A.: Yes, there we received a uniform, and they gave us training. From there, I joined Toledo Regiment, Nineteenth Infantry, in Santa Fe. There we entered the last battle on November 27. . . . It was the battle of Irindague. I was going to say that I fought more, but it was indeed the last battle. We fought our last battle. On the same afternoon, the Paraguayans captured some other Bolivians from Santa Fe and Charagua who were wounded. We rescued them from Paraguayan hands. Indeed, later on the following day—later we were taken prisoners the day they advanced from Santa Fe to Charagua. And it ended there.

I was the courier of a Lieutenant Zobieta, I forget his first name. He was from Cochabamba. I was the courier for that man; they killed him with seven shots. His guts, his belly hanging down to the ground like it had sprouted from there and like it had a hold of him. Still the "Pilas"[3] came toward us, a lieutenant and six soldiers came. Then they shot him again. . . . They killed him with that one.

Our whole regiment got rid of its entire baggage train; the soldiers threw away absolutely everything they had with them. Some made their escape by being immobile, looking dead, because the "Pilas" were already approaching us. Then the lieutenant said to me, "Go 1,500 meters into the woods!" He said to me, "Guide yourself to the side where the sun enters the sky and the moon stops." "Don't let them catch you," he told me. And so, I wandered for nineteen days, day and night, without anything to eat, without anything to drink. How? . . . because this [pointing to his stomach] had already shrunk. Nineteen days exactly I was in the woods.

Question: Were you lost?

---

[2]During the war, some Bolivian peasants protested with armed uprisings against the army and the government of President Salamanca.

[3]Slang for Paraguayan soldiers. Perhaps the name comes from "dung heaps or piles."

C. A.: Yes, well, I had gone into the woods. I didn't take the roads because the "Pilas" were already all over, everywhere; they were already up ahead. We left everything burning at Fort November 27, according to the orders of division command and so everything was burned. This one gentleman . . . Salamanca came out to see the fighting in the Pecuiba Irindague sector. In the afternoon, at four o'clock, and then he left later at eight in the evening. He had come by our position. Then they told me, "That man is Señor Salamanca." "The President," they said. He took a walk around through there. We saw him go through there. He went to meet the command. We in the ranks were paying attention, really paying attention to the "Pilas." And he escaped as well as he could in his little old car.

Question: And you walked for nineteen days?

C. A.: Nineteen days and nights. I counted nineteen days there, and I was ready to die. At dawn, I collapsed from the biting pains in my stomach; there was scarcely anything left of me. I was ready to die. The "Pilas" caught me there. They took all my equipment and my clothes from me and divided them among themselves. They kicked me and hit me with their rifle butts, then they beat my head with a club; they left me really beaten up. They almost killed me. Then the "Pilas" captain says, "This dead guy must be waiting for the other regiment that is coming from over there." So they asked me, "What is your regiment that attacked here? Where is Captain Zubieta, Captain Marzana?" "I don't know. I don't understand," I told them. This is the way it happened. They were kicking me like I was that bag [pointing to the interviewer's satchel]. . . . They kicked me like kicking a soccer ball.

I was already dead, oh yes, really. Skinny. Nineteen days without drinking water, without eating, already a deserter. . . . Frankly, I didn't even have any pee. I peed in a little glass and I drank that stuff myself; at the end, there was nothing but a little red stuff, not even a thimble full, came out. I couldn't take it anymore. I went through the territory of the "Pilas," and they were up ahead, on one side of Santa Fe. Others came from the back, they passed each other.

And within an hour another regiment came. I was still beaten up and naked, the way they had left me. They had taken everything from me. And then another Paraguayan regiment came, and when they were a short distance away they saw me. "Are you a 'Boli' or are you a Paraguayan?" "Hands up!" What did it matter to me? Even if they killed me, I wasn't going to talk. Then a major, it had to be a major, a German, he was not a Paraguayan, said, "You wait for me over there." Then he came over to question me. I told him that a Paraguayan regiment had beaten me up like this, every one of them hit me. Then the regiment took every little thing I had. I suffered, I told him. They also took my clothes.

"And now what do you think, son, which offensive brought you through here?"

"From the offensive that advanced from the Picuiba Irindague sector, Fort November 27. I am from that one," I told him.

"And where can you find your regiment . . . Captain Santa Cruz, and Captain Marzana?"

"They must be far away now."

Then the Paraguayans came with their rifle butts on the ground, like they were carrying staffs. They were really close to the Bolivians. . . . They came singing with their guitars. They went everywhere around the place. They surrounded the place. And later another regiment encircled the Bolivians again. They attacked the Bolivians, advancing against Fort Santa Fe. From there they went toward Charagua. The "Pilas" took Charagua on the same day. I was taken prisoner at seven in the morning. At four in the afternoon, the wounded "Pilas" had already passed, going back to Asunción. At four thirty, or a little later, the Toledo Regiment of the Nineteenth Infantry, the rest of the regiment, Captain Santa Cruz, even the priest, every last one of them had been taken prisoner. That had been the last column. That's the way it happened, Señor.

Once I was a prisoner, they took us over near Encarnación, close to the border with Argentina, near Brazil. I was at a military garrison, called Colonia San Miguel. This was later on. We were a long ways from Asunción. They took us to divide up as field hands to hoe, as workers in the countryside, as campesinos. I was there for a year and half in the hands of a Paraguayan, don Juan Cardozo. I was there from the moment that I arrived for a year and half.

Question: Where was it better to be—on the hacienda of a Bolivian landlord, in the war, or on the other hacienda of a Paraguayan landlord?

C. A.: In the war. . . . Well, but there we were taken prisoner. They locked us up, while the other Bolivian regiments escaped. Some were killed. They made us prisoners there . . . quite a few of us. What were we going to do? We had to go. Later they took us to the barracks, we had to work. What are we going to do? That's just the way things go.

Question: Then you had to work hard as a prisoner in Paraguay?

C. A.: Oh, yes! Just like here. You had to hoe tea [*yerba maté*], yucca, sugarcane, oranges, cotton, and rice. They had some of us doing that; and some they had in the stable, doing whatever jobs they had; some were shoemakers and rope makers. Some horse breakers tamed colts. We were the ones that were useless for anything special; we had pickaxes and machetes, we had to hoe, to pick cotton, peanuts, tobacco, garden stuff, rice. This is the way we passed the time. . . . We were suffering a long time, strained by overwork, until the Bolivian and Paraguayan leaders reached an agreement. Then we got some freedom, then, then, we just got the chance to go walking on Saturdays and Sundays. Until then, nothing else. Nothing more than they would tiptoe up and with a blow of a machete they would kill someone.

Question: You saw them kill people?

C. A.: I saw it.

Question: Before the negotiations, you weren't allowed to rest on Saturdays and Sundays?

C. A.: No! Like slaves. Everything was work. They controlled everything that we did. Others must have had more feeling. After the government gave us this freedom, nobody touched us; we were respected. Before then, we were in a bad situation.

Some tried to escape from Paraguay by swimming the river. They caught some four or five . . . eight. . . . They and the whip made them go back again to Paraguay. The one person who escaped was alone. There was one guy in that place, named Jorge Lloque, that was a real macho. He escaped by swimming to the shore of Argentina. He left from near Villa Encarnación. He kept going until he reached the Bolivian consulate, and it was said that they sent him back to La Paz on an airplane. What a tough guy!

A group of six soldiers, who couldn't bear it anymore, tried it. They were fleeing toward the riverbank. There the "Pilas" got ahold of them again; they beat them with the whip. They killed two, and they made the other four come back like oxen, wearing a yoke made of Lapacho wood that weighed fifty pounds. They yoked it on the necks of the four, and they tied it with thick rope. In order for one to sit, they all had to sit; they all had to get up to eat and to go to the bathroom, too. Their guard always had a whip. Thus we learned to get along. When the governments of both countries reached an agreement, only then did we get our freedom.

Question: Then you suffered a great deal as prisoners?

C. A.: Yes. We were wearing gunnysacks . . . tied with a bow. We didn't have shirts. We entered Paraguay that way. At the front they had destroyed our clothes; there weren't any more. We had come from all over with little peasant pants, and they destroyed these peasant clothes. They had made those shirts from burlap gunnysacks.

Later they brought us all together in Puerto Casado. On an island they had all the sick, there in the harshness of the sun, rain, cold, or heat, drinking the dust. We saw the sunup and the sundown in that place. Every twenty-four hours they gave us a meal, a little spoonful. Breakfast—for twenty-four hours they gave us three biscuits, a half spoonful of breakfast.

Question: Did you get sick?

C. A.: Yes, with dysentery. Then I was wounded. Here, through here [pointing to his leg]. A musket shot went into me, the bullet ricocheting off the bone. Another through here [pointing to his arm]; a little lead splinter stopped here. . . . For sure I recovered. They didn't heal me of anything.

Question: They didn't take the bullet out of you?

C. A.: It came out by itself. It had only gone through the flesh, under the skin. Well, the bullet was already spent.

Question: And how had the war been then? Inasmuch as you wanted to go to war, what did you think of your experience?

C. A.: [laughing] OK. We had the luck to have bad commanders. They didn't lead us. They sent all the soldiers to the front, and they stayed behind. They didn't give us a single thing to eat nor a single thing to drink. There was no water and no food. The soldiers were slowed by hunger, they were weakened by hunger. For this simple reason they collapsed . . . they died.

Question: You went hungry then?

C. A.: Oh! For weeks we didn't eat, we didn't drink . . . we didn't come to any water. The "Pilas" had two common tins of water for each group and a canteen with water to use to wash their faces. And the Bolivians had nothing for us. They treated us poorly. In that way, they failed in the war effort. Many died.

Later on, for tomorrow, I have a witness that I fought in the front line of the Picuiba-Irindague sector. For tomorrow's deposition, he will bring a friend; we were there together. After that my friends died or went to Santa Cruz. Outside of my friend there is not a single one of my companions that survived. There were Paceños [Aymarás from La Paz], some from here in Sucre, and some Cochabambiños [from Cochabamba].

Question: How were the Aymará soldiers? How did they do in the war? Can you tell me something about this?

C. A.: Well, they were in [a] bad situation! They couldn't say anything. I couldn't understand them at all. Over there in the war, they mopped them up.

Question: Were there lowlanders [called Cambas, from eastern Bolivia] in your regiment?

C. A.: There were some; there were a few drafted, too. Those guys were very tough, very crooked, they really kept to themselves! Like thieves! Some had learned to speak Spanish better than Christians. The officers weren't able to punish them ever. If they deserted, they just deserted. . . . The lieutenant with his whip tried to punish them because one of them had run away from the garrison. They said that the lieutenant would desert, too, just as soon as he found an opportunity. That's how they answered him.

Question: By chance, were there any women out there in the Chaco?

C. A.: Well, there were some Chaco women. Then the commanders had to put up with them.

Question: Were there any rain forest girls?

C. A.: Well, yes.

Question: Did you see any of the rain forest women?

C. A.: They came from here. . . . The commanders might have ordered them. . . . There were Mataquitos . . . the one kind they wanted, and the other they didn't. There they were grabbed, they were taken prisoners. They couldn't speak our language at all. They couldn't understand a single thing. They were naked . . . men and women . . .

There were Cochabamba people, also some from La Paz, enough of them. There were miners, too.

Question: And what were the Paraguayans like?

C. A.: Like . . . some were poor, poorer than Bolivians. Their houses too, sad . . . houses of straw thatched on a lattice of little sticks. They lived the best way they could. They worked a couple of hectares, or a hectare and [a] half [200 to 250 square meters]. They didn't have a single cow. Those who were rich, those with the good houses, were foreigners.

Question: Were there a lot of foreigners?

C. A.: *Uf!* Plenty of foreigners. They had the nice houses, the good accommodations. They had cattle, they had the livestock. The "Pilas" didn't even have a place to sleep, they didn't have beds. They had to sleep on bedsteads made of sticks.

Question: So the Paraguayan soldiers were campesinos?

C. A.: Yes, campesinos that were poorer than the Bolivians.

Question: And you were peons in Paraguay?

C. A.: Peons. Bad, then . . . the ones in charge controlled everything. . . . Later they treated us OK. We had breakfast, we had lunch, dinner, but they never gave us any clothes. Some were as poor as us. The women were the workers. The men drank, and the women worked with the Bolivians.

Question: Why didn't you get married there?

C. A.: What was I going to marry? The place? Not one Bolivian wanted to stay; not a single one wanted to stay. Some had said they were going to become Paraguayan. Then all the Bolivians decided to come back. Some women, some with babies, some without, came back to Villa Formosa with the Bolivians. They went with the Bolivians to Villa Formosa. The Bolivians said, "You can go to Bolivia." They believed it and came. When they got to Villa Formosa, the Bolivians were told they couldn't take anyone with them. "Why are you going to take the enemy's wives with you?," they asked. The women were left crying. They had to go back. A few were taken to Padilla and to La Paz. They brought back a few "Pilas" women.

Question: Do you know any Paraguayan women?

C. A.: In Padilla, the woman of this guy Julio Balderas. . . . He brought his woman. She was plain, not very pretty. His father-in-law has come, has come to Padilla. Now I don't know where he is going to live. It could be here; it could be in Padilla.

Question: Señor Arancibia, when you came back from the war, where did you go to work?

C. A.: My place, well, the same hacienda for several years, some three years. . . . But I couldn't get used to it. I went back to Monteagudo. I was in Monteagudo some five years; from there I went to Tarija a couple of years. Recently I just came back again to live in Segura, Juana Azurduy de Padilla, they call it.

Question: What did you receive from the Agrarian Reform [a result of the 1952 Revolution]?

C. A.: They give me a little bit of land. . . . It was a bad measure. The owners reclaimed the lands. They annulled the reform. That's the way it happened.

Question: And now you have nothing?

C. A.: Nothing, I have nothing.

Question: How do you eat? How do you live?

C. A.: My wife has died. She had some pastureland. We worked there, on her land. I was sick, I was very badly sick. So I sent my brother-in-law when they gave the land. Then they ordered another commission; they made me get up. They pulled up the stakes. . . . The secretaries annulled it. "That belongs to us," they said. That's the way they annulled them, never anything else. We only worked the property of my wife.

Question: Señor Arancibia, do you want to tell me why they don't pay you your pension for national service?[4]

C. A.: It is because I never claimed it before. I lost it [referring to his military service booklet]. My little house burned up where I was keeping it. I was in the field . . . when I saw it burning. All my documents burned there. My clothes and everything burned up. That's [the] way I lost my military service book.

Question: How did you find out that they were paying the veterans' pension here in Sucre?

C. A.: Recently they sent someone to find out why I didn't claim it. That's how I came to learn about it. It wasn't very important to me before. As a boy all we did was work, and we didn't have any interest in such things. We never took any interest, so . . .

Question: Now you are completely worn out and you can't work like you did before, so you are trying to get the pension?

---

[4]All veterans of the Chaco War are supposed to receive a subsistence pension.

C. A.: Yes. Recently now we remembered it, Señor. We'll see if I can get it or not.

Question: Are your records in La Paz?

C. A.: They ought to be. I went to the office. "They're not here, they're not here," they told me. They pretended to try and find them. And they said, "They're not here." "Come back, come back." And when I went back, they said, "They haven't turned up." "You should come back again soon." For three years, I was in total agony with my feet. I couldn't walk. For this reason, I couldn't go back. That was six, seven years ago. I couldn't walk. And now they tell me, "There are no records." They have looked for them, and, "There are no records," they tell me. Surely they were not returned to La Paz. They refused me for changing our last name. In the service booklet, since we didn't know how to read, they marked me down as Vallejos. That's the way it is in the service book, so they said in La Paz. My father was raised by a woman. Like we say, he was her orphan. Because of that he is a "Cascaco" by adoption, but he and I are real Vallejos, Vallejollipulli. And later, my father's last name was Arancibia and my mother's Bocanegra. Two family names. But it can be fixed. Tomorrow I am going to bring my carnet [memorandum book] to convince you. It gives the year I was born, too.

Question: Were you changed when you returned from the war?

C. A.: You bet! Braver. I was already kinda brave when I signed up at the garrison. But war made me more of a man, more respected, well, one who knows how discipline is. Before I was just like an animal. And now, as we are grown old already we have just exhausted the feeling. . . . We were having a good talk, and just this minute I forgot what we were talking about. I don't remember. . . . Later, of course, at the garrison we learned everything.

Question: And when you returned from the war, did the owner continue treating you badly or not?

C. A.: Now he respected me. I was the only soldier from that property. The rest were cowards. They didn't go to the war. With his son, there were only the two of us. Now he has died. They respected me, they didn't oblige me to work, they didn't call me to work. They no longer forced me with the club or the whip to work.

Question: If they had whipped you, would you have done it?

C. A.: I would have had to show up for work.

Question: And did some rebel against the owner?

C. A.: Ah, of course. Some were going to stop working like that, ones who had gone to serve in the army. Those who didn't go were timid.

Question: Then the war changed you?

C. A.: Ah, yes. It made us understand respect, respect for all people, big names and everyday people both.

8

Pagu: Patrícia Galvão–Rebel

Susan K. Besse

The impact of industrial capitalism on the lives and values of Brazilian women in São Paulo has fascinated Susan Besse since she began her dissertation at Yale University. The following essay is one of the earliest results of her research and provides the intriguing biography of Patrícia Galvão. Popularly known as Pagu, Galvão flaunted the rules of Brazil's polite society and established herself in the 1920s, while still a teenager, as a flamboyant crusader for women's rights, workers' causes, and libertine culture. Eventually, jailed by Brazilian authorities and abandoned by the Communist party, she grew disillusioned and frustrated.

Besse, now a professor of history at the City College of New York, has studied in Switzerland, in Chile (as a United Nations intern), and in Brazil. At Yale and at City College she has taught courses in Latin American studies.

In Brazil's most modern city, São Paulo, the "modernists" pronounced Patrícia Galvão the "ultimate product" of the late 1920s. She was a rebel who broke all the rules, who declared war against the status quo. Startlingly free of inhibitions, she used her mind and body to subvert the social, economic, political, and gender order. (In)famous for her scandalous behavior and free thinking, she became the quintessential symbol of all that was new, revolutionary, and dangerous. Patrícia was the child of a period of social and intellectual fragmentation, a period when rapid urbanization and industrialization were eroding the restraints imposed by São Paulo's old agrarian-commercial economy. She seized the opportunity provided by this historical moment of "crisis" to experiment with redefining the categories of acceptable thought and behavior and altering the structures of power. As a woman, she assaulted the boundaries imposed by the patriarchal order, prying open new social arenas and assuming roles that had been previously denied to members of her sex. As an artist, writer, and critic, she struck blows at worn-out conventions, helping to pave the way for daring new forms of creative expression. As a member of the middle class, she sided with the proletariat, advocating social revolution to topple São Paulo's exploitative industrial-capitalist economy. Patrícia (like most rebels who fight battles doomed to lose in the short run) was ultimately shunned by the society she so viciously attacked and is barely mentioned in the historical record. But the story of her intense engagement in the great social, intellectual, and political conflicts of her time is a part of the larger story of the Brazilian and Latin American peoples' prolonged struggle to destroy old hierarchical arrangements and make way for a more just social order.

Born in 1910, Patrícia grew up during a period of tremendous ferment in the city that was the catalyst of Brazil's economic growth. São Paulo's coffee economy produced fabulous wealth, transforming the state's capital from a commercial outpost of 64,934 people in 1890 to a thriving metropolis of 579,033 people in 1920. Within a period of little over a generation, São Paulo was propelled into the modern age. European immigrants who flooded into São Paulo after 1890 swelled the ranks of the urban proletariat working in the mushrooming textile mills, food-processing plants, and small enterprises. Economic boom also fostered the growth of the middle classes, made up of bureaucrats, civil servants, professionals, merchants, small businessmen, and military personnel. Political conflicts exploded between the old rural oligarchy, which was losing its monopoly of power, and the new urban middle and working classes, which were struggling under precarious conditions to achieve social mobility. Politics, which had been the prerogative of a small elite of literate men who negotiated deals behind closed doors, moved into the streets. Successful labor organization by anarchist and anarcho-syndicalist trade unions led to waves of strikes during the 1910s and 1920s, which were met by brutal police repression. The middle classes expressed their restlessness over exclusion from political power in campaigns against political corruption and in the formation of the middle-class Democratic party. Young military officers staged a series of barracks revolts during the 1920s, vaguely calling for honest government and social legislation. To contemporaries, the forces of radical economic change and social upheaval seemed to be tearing the social fabric asunder.

Paulistas reacted to modernization with ambivalence. On the one hand, they were fascinated by "progress," took enormous pride in the newly acquired status and power of their city, and pushed for institutional reforms to meet the new needs of the rising industrial economy and the complex social order it had produced. On the other hand, the rapidity of change undermined old certainties and created profound anxieties about the supposedly "corrupting" influences of "progress."

Among the most conspicuous of changes, and one that was considered extremely dangerous, was the seemingly radical transformation of women. In Patrícia's grandmother's generation, women's roles had been narrowly circumscribed. The majority of women from middle- and upper-class families married as teenagers, raised an average of six children each, and devoted their lives to preparing food, sewing clothing and household linens, and providing health care and education for their families. Not until 1890 did Brazilian law outlaw forced marriages, and even after that it was common for parents to play a decisive role in selecting spouses for their daughters. Alternatives to marriage were few and unattractive. In 1893, only 146 Brazilian women and 64 foreign women found jobs as schoolteachers, which provided a meager living. Apart from schoolteaching, little respectable employment was available for middle- and upper-class women, leaving those who remained unmarried in a position of humiliating economic dependence on parents and siblings who typically maintained constant surveillance over these "spinsters'" personal lives.

In a society where concubinage and "free love" were considered little different from prostitution, families zealously guarded the virginity of their unmarried female members. "Respectable" women had little to no opportunity to escape the narrow physical and mental confines of the household. Rarely did they venture into public spaces, and when they did so they were always accompanied. Peddlers and merchants sold their goods door to door, entertainment was still provided by family members and friends, women's social and charitable organizations were nonexistent, and low literacy rates delayed the rise of the popular press, which only later provided women access to the outside world. Nineteenth-century fashion emphasized the separateness of gender roles. Whereas men cut figures of aggressive public actors with their dark suits, beards, and canes, women projected the image of submissive and sheltered domestic ornaments in their highly elaborate and cumbersome dresses. The public silence of women further testified to overwhelming male dominance.

Patrícia was born into a new age when the old social and sexual proprieties appeared to be no longer binding. São Paulo's booming economy gradually commercialized household production, drawing women into the marketplace as consumers of ready-made clothing and household linens, modern appliances, and processed food products. Shopping became both a daily necessity and a social institution;

alluring advertisements, glittering window displays, chic department stores, money-saving sales, and the availability of credit drew in ever larger numbers of female customers.

Technological innovations in communications further encouraged women's entrance into the sphere of the marketplace. Hollywood films arrived in Brazil the year Patrícia was born and quickly captured the popular imagination. Female moviegoers gained as role models the sexy flappers and independent "working girls" portrayed on the screen. At home, radios provided women with daily exposure to new information and ideas. And the spectacular boom in glossy magazines (spurred by the soaring female literacy rates in São Paulo, from 22 percent to 52 percent between 1890 and 1920) also helped promote new values and aspirations for economic independence and social freedom.

Women of Patrícia's generation enjoyed a formerly undreamed-of range of options. Middle-class families, straining to make ends meet in face of inflation and rising pressures of conspicuous consumption, educated daughters to be economically independent in case they failed to marry. Daughters, absorbing bourgeois society's emphasis on independence and taking advantage of new educational opportunities, sometimes prepared themselves for professional careers. Although marriage remained the most secure and the preferred female "career," women delayed marriage, bore many fewer children, and boldly protested their subjugation in marriage. At the same time, more and more middle-class women filled the new respectable white-collar jobs in social services, commerce, finance, and government administration. Even wives who chose not to take paid employment could find an independent source of social identity in one of São Paulo's new female voluntary associations. As middle-class women moved into the male world of work, they also began to move into the male world of politics. A small group of "feminists" organized in the 1920s to fight for legal and educational reforms and won female suffrage in 1932. The "new woman"—independent, active, and sexually provocative—became the symbol of the new age.

The image of the "new woman" figured prominently on the covers of glossy magazines, but critics were terrified by the prospect of a revolution in women's consciousness that could profoundly disrupt traditional gender relations and family organization—leading, in the worst of scenarios, to a "tremendous cataclysm." The flood of cartoons satirizing women who usurped traditionally male roles and the barrage of normative literature instructing women on how to create stable but modern families revealed deep social anxieties. During this period of social disorder, the Brazilian state, the liberal professions, and the

Church all struggled to reconcile modernity with traditional values. The result was a confusing mix of contradictory messages. Women were called upon to cultivate an outward appearance of modern sophistication while carefully preserving the qualities of female modesty and simplicity. They were to be enlightened, resourceful, and independent on the one hand and satisfied with the restrictions of the role of housewife on the other hand. In short, women were somehow supposed to be both symbols of modernity and bastions of traditional family life.

In the context of the deep anxiety over threats to the gender order, Patrícia's adolescent rebelliousness attracted enormous attention and comment. As was typical for daughters of middle-class families, she attended normal school; there, girls received a high-school education designed to prepare them to be good wives and competent mothers, and, if necessary, to earn a living through schoolteaching. But Patrícia flaunted her disdain for the traditional canons of proper behavior by adopting the most modern and extravagant fashions. She wore the shortest skirts, daringly low necklines, transparent blouses, false eyelashes, heavy black eye makeup, and bright red lipstick. She let her hair frizz out of control and carried a conspicuous, furry, puppy-dog purse. More shocking was her smoking in public, which had traditionally been the prerogative of men only. Even worse, her brazen flirtation with students at the law school and her outspoken, uninhibited responses to their wisecracks were considered to be scandalously aggressive behavior for a woman. Patrícia's wholesale embrace of the fashions and styles of the "jazz age" was an initial outward sign of defiance, which (as those she scandalized probably feared) was to run much deeper later in her life.

In 1927, at seventeen, Patrícia began to cultivate contacts with São Paulo's artistic and intellectual community. Filmmaker Olympio Guilherme became interested in the writings Patrícia submitted for publication in his newspaper column, and they had a short love affair before he left for Hollywood. Her flirtation with the young, flashy Reis, Jr., led to another brief affair. Within the circle of São Paulo's artists, these affairs led not to Patrícia's disrepute and doom but rather provided her an entry into the elite community of the Brazilian avant-garde. In October 1928 poet Raul Bopp, playing around with the syllables of her name, dubbed Patrícia "Pagu" and published a poem in a popular weekly magazine that extolled her seductiveness. The first verse read:

Pagu has soft eyes
Eyes like I don't know what

When you're near them
Your heart begins to ache
    Ah, Pagu Hey!
    It aches because it's good to cause pain.[1]

By this time, Pagu had come under the wing of novelist Oswald de Andrade and his wife, the painter Tarsila do Amaral, gurus of the Brazilian modernist movement that was launched in São Paulo in 1922. Adamantly rejecting stale nineteenth-century European formulas, they sought inspiration in Brazil's primitive, indigenous past. From this retreat to "primitivism," Oswald went on to launch the radical "Antropofagía Movement." His May 1928 manifesto advocated a ritual, symbolic "devouring" of European values in order to wipe out patriarchal and capitalist society with its rigid social and psychological boundaries. In March 1929, Pagu's drawings began to appear in the second phase of the *Revista de antropofagía*, the movement's magazine.

It was Pagu's public debut at a fund-raising event at the São Paulo municipal theater in June, however, that caused the greatest stir. Dressed by Tarsila in an extravagant white dress and red-lined black cape, she recited three poems, including Bopp's poem on her seductiveness and her own poem about her lewd cat who had a long tail and imagined she was a serpent. If the audience was stunned by Pagu's daring, they were also captivated. Thunderous applause was followed by reviews that proclaimed her appearance a "total success." For the next few months, Pagu occupied the spotlight as the person who more than anyone else embodied the antropofagist creed: "[to] constantly and directly consume the taboo," or "[to transform the] taboo into totem." Her admirers, in awe of her shocking and audacious defiance of social conventions, pronounced: "Pagu abolished the grammar of life." "She would be capable of devouring various venomous bishops."[2]

Irreverent and liberated, Pagu went on to scandalize even the avant-garde community that had so eagerly embraced her. On the one hand, she lavished praise on her mentor and friend, Tarsila. In a newspaper interview given on the occasion of Tarsila's August 1929 exhibit in Rio de Janeiro, Pagu identified Tarsila as her greatest hero. "I'm in love with Tarsila. I would give her the last drop of my blood. As an

[1]Raul Bopp, "Coco de Pagu," in *Pagu: Patrícia Galvão: Vida-obra*, ed. Augusto de Campos (São Paulo: 1982), 38.

[2]Campos, *Pagu*, 321–23.

artist, I admire her superiority."[3] She noted that she had entrusted Tarsila with her autobiography, the "Album de Pagu," which consisted of a series of free-spirited drawings and "sixty uncensored poems" dedicated to the Brazilian director of film censorship. But several months earlier, Pagu and Oswald had already begun their "romance of the anarchist epoch." Oswald, captivated by Pagu's irreverence and drawn to her for inspiration in his search for revolutionary paths, betrayed Tarsila. "If Tarsila's home totters," he scribbled on a napkin at a fancy dinner party, "it is because of Pagu's intrigue."[4] In September, Oswald arranged a farcical marriage between Pagu and the painter Waldemar Belisário do Amaral, who had been raised by Tarsila's family. So secret was the real plan that Oswald and Tarsila were the best man and bridesmaid at the wedding. Tarsila gave Pagu a painting as a wedding present, and Pagu's family was delighted by the marriage. But as the couple was driving to the coast for a honeymoon, Oswald met them on the highway and took Waldemar's place. The marriage was officially annulled the following February. By that time, Oswald and Pagu had already consummated their "romance of the anarchist epoch" by "marrying" in front of his family's tomb in the city cemetery—in Oswald's words, "the ultimate defiance." And Pagu was pregnant with a son, Rudá, who was born in September 1930.

Wifehood and motherhood occupied little of Pagu's time and energy. She probably never considered retiring to the "secluded charm of her home" as middle-class wives were supposed to do, or submitting to the routine demands of housewifery. But her refusal to do so was highly deviant at a time when a barrage of articles in women's magazines was trying to convince women that the sole path to true happiness and personal fulfillment lay in accepting the "important and difficult task" of building "happy and fragrant homes." Instead of dedicating her life to overseeing the intellectual and moral development of her child (which her own education, the medical profession, and the normative literature of the period insisted was women's God-given "primordial mission"), Pagu hired a nurse to care for Rudá. She summed up her attitude toward marriage in an article written later in her life:

> Women in all civilized times have only known one goal—marriage. Her place in the sun, sheltered by the virile and protecting shadow of a man who takes

[3]Clovis de Gusmão, "Na exposição de Tarsila," in Campos, *Pagu*, 60.
[4]Campos, *Pagu*, 324.

> upon himself all the initiative. All [women's] longings and needs are cut off at this point, with the consequent suffering implicit in the contract.[5]

Exactly one month after giving birth, Pagu participated in the political demonstrations that erupted around the "revolution" of 1930. The stock market crash in 1929 had devastated the Brazilian economy, thus eroding the power base of São Paulo's coffee-exporting oligarchy and throwing the country into political crisis. In the face of the fierce political battles that ensued and the intense radicalization to the right and the left, members of the artistic avant-garde were forced to choose sides. With Oswald, Pagu joined the Brazilian Communist party (PCB) in 1931, followed its orders to "become a member of the proletariat," and took up the cause of socialist revolution. She immersed herself in the lives of the proletariat, working at the worst of jobs to the point of becoming sick. Having experienced firsthand the arrogance of bosses and the humiliation and rage of women workers, she participated in strikes and fought in the front lines of the PCB to bring about the revolution. In August 1931 she became the first woman political prisoner in Brazil, held for a short time for being an "agitator" in a demonstration that became violent. But it was this period of total commitment to the cause of social revolution that Pagu later remembered as the "happiest time of [her] life, during which [she] had faith."[6]

Pagu's unshakable faith in Marxist ideology and her vision of a future utopia achieved through political struggle changed the focus of her writing. With Oswald, she published an irreverent, satirical, aggressively polemical pamphlet called *O homen do povo* (*The Man of the People*). (It was closed down by the police in April 1931 after only eight numbers, following rioting by law students who were insulted by Oswald's denunciation of the São Paulo law school as a "cancer.") Pagu's column, "A Mulher do Povo" ("The Woman of the People"), commented on the behavior and values of São Paulo's female population. It viciously attacked the hypocritical, sterile bourgeois (and Catholic) morality that prevented women from using their minds and bodies freely, thus fostering triviality and neurotic perversions rather than healthy sensuality. Pagu's condemnation of the bourgeois feminist movement was especially ardent. She mocked the notion that Brazil's feminists, a small group of professional women, were in any

---

[5]Quoted in Antonio Risério, "Pagu: Vida-obra, obravida, vida," in Campos, *Pagu*, 18.

[6]Campos, *Pagu*, 325.

sense a "vanguard" or had anything "revolutionary" to propose. Pagu scornfully dismissed their campaigns for sexual liberation, "conscientious maternity," and female suffrage as elitist and naive. Instead of fighting for female suffrage that was irrelevant to the majority of women (who would be excluded because they were illiterate), Pagu proposed that they should fight to transform radically the social and economic structure of Brazil. According to Pagu's vision, women could only achieve equality and sexual liberation after poverty and class exploitation had been eliminated.

The theme of female oppression and liberation was taken up again in Pagu's "proletarian novel," *Parque industrial*, written in 1931–32, but only published in 1933 at Oswald's expense. It describes the lives of the Paulista female proletariat with a frankness that was shocking at the time. Pagu openly discusses the sexual exploitation of female factory workers by bosses and the tragedy of working-class women who were seduced by bourgeois men with promises of marriage, impregnated, and abandoned to a life of prostitution. The villains of the novel are the morally corrupt and decadent bourgeois "parasites," among whom are feminists whose "freedom" depended on their exploitation of maids, and members of São Paulo's modernist movement who were ideologically coopted by continued economic dependence on the rich aristocracy. The victims are the politically unconscious proletariat. The heroes are two women who join the ranks of the Communist party and struggle to raise working-class women's class consciousness in an attempt to help bring about the revolution. The novel uses the modern literary technique of piecing together short cinemalike scenes, and it pioneers the movement toward social realism of the 1930s. But its concern for artistic innovation is subordinated to heavy doses of doctrinaire political propaganda and a call for revolution as the solution to the human problems created by São Paulo's booming capitalist economy.

If the biting satire and vulgar street language of *Parque industrial* made it offensive to bourgeois society, the sexual explicitness and radical feminist perspective that underlay its Marxist analysis made the novel unpalatable to the puritanical Brazilian Communist party. At the insistence of the party (which did not consider women's exploitation to be an urgent political issue), Pagu published her novel under the pseudonym Mara Lobo. In the memoirs of two activists are other hints of Pagu's conflicts with the party hierarchy over her nonconformity. Octavio Brandão held up his wife Laura as a model; in addition to organizing female workers, Laura worked behind the scenes of the PCB to keep morale high, she performed administrative tasks, and she raised children. Octavio praised his loyal wife for having "protected [his] life, health, and liberty" and for having helped to uphold socially acceptable sexual behavior. Perhaps partly in reference to Pagu's deviant behavior, he wrote: "In the Brazilian Communist Party between 1922 and 1929 mutual respect and 'revolutionary ideology' always prevailed. Laura contributed much to this. There was never any case of an amorous adventure or a sexual scandal."[7] Another activist, Leôncio Basbaum, attacked Pagu directly as a "pernicious" influence, who, he claimed, like other middle-class intellectuals, approached her activism in the ranks of the PCB as "supremely entertaining and exciting."[8]

Gradually, the physical exhaustion of daily political work, combined with the emotional exhaustion of confronting not only police harassment but also condemnation by party members, wore Pagu down. Between December 1933 and November 1935 she traveled through the United States, Japan, China, Germany, and France, working as a foreign correspondent for three Brazilian newspapers. Years later, Pagu revealed the motivation for her trip abroad:

> From the age of twenty to thirty, I obeyed the orders of the Party. I signed the declaration that they gave me to sign without reading. This happened for the first time [during the 1931 demonstration in commemoration of the execution of Sacco and Vanzetti] when I guarded the dying body of the black dock worker Herculano de Souza, when I stood up to the military cavalry in the Government Square in Santos, when I was imprisoned as an agitator—taken to Jail 3, the worst jail in the continent.
>
> Then, when I regained my freedom, the Party condemned me; they made me sign a document that exonerated the Party from all responsibility [for the demonstration]. All of that, the conflict and the bloodshed, was the work of a "provoker," of an "individual agitator, [who was] sensationalist and inexperienced." I signed. I signed with my eyes closed without sensing the collapse that was occurring within me.
>
> Why not?
>
> The Party "was right."
>
> Step by step I descended the stairs of degradation, because the Party needed those who had no scruples, those who had no personality, those who did not argue, those who simply ACCEPTED. They reduced me to a rag that left one day for distant places, because the Party grew tired of using me as a scapegoat. They could no longer use me for anything; I was too stained.[9]

---

[7]Octavio Brandão, *Combates e batalhas: Memórias* (São Paulo, 1978), 303.

[8]Leôncio Basbaum, *Uma vida em seis tempos (memórias)*, 2d ed. (São Paulo, 1978), 119.

[9]Patrícia Galvão, "Verdade e liberdade," in Campos, *Pagu*, 188–89.

On the surface, Pagu's around-the-world trip was glamorous. She was offered a contract in Hollywood, which she turned down, declaring: "My goal is much larger and more difficult to achieve." In China she attended the coronation of the last emperor, gained access to his palace, and accompanied him on bicycle rides through the palace grounds. Through the emperor, she arranged for the first soybeans to be sent to Brazil. In China, she also met Sigmund Freud. And in Paris, she became friendly with the most famous surrealist poets and attended courses of the leading Marxist professors at the Popular University.

Pagu's trip abroad also marked the beginning of her profound disillusionment with political activism. She wrote to Oswald from Moscow: "This here is a cold dinner without imagination." Later, she recounted in greater detail the shock she suffered in Stalinist Russia:

> My ideal collapsed, in Russia, in face of the miserable children of the gutters, the bare feet, and the eyes full of hunger. In Moscow, a large luxurious hotel for high bureaucrats, tourists of communism, and rich foreigners. In the street, children dying of hunger; this was the communist regime.
>
> So when an enormous banner pronounced in the streets of Paris "Stalin is right," I knew this was not true.[10]

Nevertheless, when she arrived in Paris, Pagu obtained a false identification and enlisted in the youth wing of the Communist party. A bad injury suffered at a demonstration landed her in the hospital for three months. Then, after three detentions, Pagu was imprisoned as a foreign communist agitator. But the Brazilian ambassador protected her from being tried in France and saved her from being deported to fascist Italy or Nazi Germany by arranging instead for her repatriation to Brazil.

Pagu returned to Brazil in November 1935, separated definitively from Oswald (who by that time was living with another woman), and moved into her sister Sidéria's apartment. Once again, she quickly became embroiled in politics. Bitter ideological conflict between the right-wing Integralist movement, which in many ways resembled European fascist parties, and the left-wing National Liberation Alliance (ALN), which was run from behind the scenes by the Brazilian Communist party, exploded in street battles. Finally, in November 1935, the ALN launched a poorly planned insurrection, a desperate

[10]Ibid., 189.

last-ditch attempt to capture power. Pagu's participation in this fiasco led to her imprisonment for four and a half years. In jail, Pagu still refused to submit despite periods of solitary confinement and torture. She went on hunger strikes which seriously damaged her health, escaped on one occasion only to be captured and sent back to prison, and delayed her release for several months by refusing to pay homage to the authorities.

Pagu left jail in July 1940 in miserable physical condition, weighing eighty-eight pounds. More serious, perhaps, was her existential crisis. Profoundly disillusioned and embittered, she resigned from the Communist party. Although she never renounced her socialist ideology, she did discard her utopian vision of the inevitable and liberating revolution and abandoned political activism. Her experience had taught her to distrust the dogmatic left wing as much as she despised the reactionary right wing. Later, Pagu explained that her worst experience in jail was the psychological torment she was subjected to by fellow political prisoners. In her words, they "had nails to drive into my head, and on the point of each nail, was the word YES. To which I responded NO. They affirmed that the Party was right, that I had to yield, that I ought to submit to orders: YES. 'Yes, because You are wrong.' And I always responded: NO."[11] She was relieved to be transferred to a jail for common criminals, where she escaped from the "nails" of the party.

For the rest of her life, Patrícia (the name she used after her release from jail) waged a continual struggle against sickness, exhaustion, and massive depression. She survived several suicide attempts, one soon after her release from prison, another in 1949, and another in 1962, a few months before she died of cancer. Initially, she refused to speak to even the people she loved, and always remained withdrawn in public. But ultimately, she found consolation in a stable private life and in art, literature, and theater. She went to live with literary critic Geraldo Ferraz, by whom she had a son in June 1941 and with whom she remained until the end of her life. Despite the stigma attached to her name, she was gradually able to obtain work as a journalist. She redirected her energies into writing polemical columns on the world of art and literature. She introduced European avant-garde authors to Brazilian audiences. And finally, she led a campaign to promote theater in Brazil.

Patrícia's second and final novel, *A famosa revista*, which she co-authored with Ferraz in 1945, was born of her struggle to find a

[11]Ibid., 188.

substitute for political activism. Its message inverts the message of her first novel. Whereas *Parque industrial* had been an apology for the party, *A famosa revista* denounces the evils of the monolithic party: bureaucratization, corruption, opportunism, and debasement of human values. The first sentence of the novel announced: "This is a love story between Rosa and Mosci: a protest and a blow against the vortex that outlaws love." The plot follows Rosa and Mosci's transcendence of the pettiness and corruption of the party to their refuge in art, intellectual life, love, and an insistence on an absolute moral purity that admits no compromise. Patrícia's concern for developing a "poetic" literary style signaled her rejection of the subordination of literature to immediate partisan political goals. Having been betrayed by politics, she returned to literature as a means of liberating mankind through the expansion of mental horizons and the fostering of the imagination.

Patrícia died at home in 1962 at the age of fifty-two, her body riddled with cancer. She had paid a high price for the many heresies she committed: abandonment by friends, political persecution and years of imprisonment by the establishment she threatened, betrayal and condemnation by her comrades in the Brazilian Communist party, physical sickness, and tremendous disillusionment, anguish, and pain. But she never shrank from the inevitable consequences of her idealism, intellectual honesty, and personal integrity. Upon her death, her husband Geraldo Ferraz wrote that "she considered her setbacks and defeats, the blows of destiny, attacks by police, prison, and the scandal that shrouded her name and her actions to be the crosses of a struggle that would bring her face-to-face with death."[12]

Patrícia, being too far ahead of her time, was gradually but systematically marginalized. Her revolutionary vision never fit within the project of the PCB, within the program of Brazil's feminists, or within the narrow confines of the country's intellectual life. Moreover, by the mid-1930s, it was apparent that the social and intellectual space opened up by the disruptive forces of economic revolution was closing. With the imposition of the authoritarian Estado Novo in 1937, a new bourgeois economic and cultural hegemony emerged. Dissident voices were repressed, and the threats to the hierarchical order that had been posed by women and the working class were safely contained. Women's domestic roles were reenshrined (for the good of the patriarchal family and public order) through protective legislation that kept women out of higher paying "male" jobs, through female education

[12]Geraldo Ferraz, "Patrícia Galvão: Militante do ideal," in Campos, *Pagu*, 263.

that continued to prepare women to be competent housewives, and through propaganda issued by the Church and the medical profession insisting on the "naturalness" of women's role as wives and mothers. The working class was incorporated into political life, but not as a source of social renovation. Social legislation, a new labor code, and unionization carefully controlled by the state undermined working-class autonomy and militancy. The period of "creative disorder" that fostered the relative freedom Patrícia experienced as an adolescent and young adult proved to be temporary.

Following her release from prison in 1940, Patrícia's continuing attacks on the new (but still hierarchical) social structure and power dynamic in Brazil passed largely unnoticed. Only in the late 1970s was she rediscovered and resurrected from oblivion by a new generation of Brazilian intellectuals struggling to overcome the legacies of a decade and a half of military dictatorship. The example of Patrícia's lifelong search for intellectual, social, political, and sexual freedom has inspired those resisting authoritarian mentalities and political control today. And her unwillingness to compromise, even in defeat, stands as a proclamation of her conviction that no social order is immutable—that people, thinking and acting, can change their world for the better and have the responsibility to try to do so.

SOURCES

Mystery still shrouds many of the intimate details of Patrícia Galvão's life. But the persistent efforts of Augusto de Campos, who spent years searching for lost pieces of Patrícia's life and assembling her widely scattered writings, resulted in the publication of his invaluable anthology, *Pagu: Patrícia Galvão: Vida-obra* (São Paulo, 1982). It includes several essays on her life and work; facsimiles of two manuscripts, Pagu's 1929 autobiography, "O álbum de Pagu," and Oswald and Pagu's diary, "O romance da época anarquista"; autobiographical passages from Patrícia's 1950 political pamphlet "Verdade e liberdade"; Patrícia's poems, a selection of her articles published in the press, and excerpts from her novels; contemporary reviews of her writings; testimonies by Patrícia's last husband, Geraldo Ferraz, and her sister, Sidéria, as well as by others who knew her; homages to her; photographs; a detailed itinerary of her life (which constitutes an outline of a biography); and the most complete bibliography of works by and about her. Facsimile editions are available of Patrícia Galvão's *Parque industrial, romance proletario* (São Paulo, 1981), as well as of the journals *Revista de antropofagia* (São Paulo, 1975) and *O homen do povo* (São Paulo, 1985). Background information on women in early twentieth century São Paulo is taken from Susan Kent Besse, "Freedom and Bondage: The Impact of Capitalism on Women in São Paulo, Brazil, 1917–1937," Ph.D. diss., Yale University, 1983.

9

Ofelia Domínguez Navarro: The Making of a Cuban Socialist Feminist

K. Lynn Stoner

Lynn Stoner, professor of history at Arizona State University, has become the leading voice in the United States on the status of women in Cuba since its independence from Spain in 1898. Her investigation of this subject began at Indiana University and resulted in her dissertation on the Cuban women's movement. Before going to Arizona State, Stoner was a consultant at the World Bank, worked for the National Endowment for the Humanities, and taught at Kansas State University. During a 1986 research trip to Havana, she had the opportunity to lead seminars at the Federation of Cuban Women.

In writing about Ofelia Domínguez Navarro, Stoner explores the role of women in Cuba against the background of that nation's history before Fidel Castro's revolution. A number of themes emerge in Ofelia's story that invite comparison with those seen in the experiences of other individuals, especially other women, found in this volume. Her political attitudes should be compared with those of her Brazilian contemporary Pagu, the erstwhile communist. Ofelia's imprisonment alongside prostitutes is another vantage point from which to view the exploitation of women that marked Soledad Fuente's life as described by Oscar Martínez. The biographies of the other Cubans in this book (Angel Santana Suárez and Leoncio Veguilla) offer different perspectives on what it means to live in Cuba. Finally, Ofelia's story—that of a middle-class woman—reveals options and opportunities denied women of the lower classes, such as Tomasa Muñoz de León of Ecuador and Doña Sara and Doña Juana of Bolivia.

Radicalization in Cuba during the 1930s was a response to thirty years of frustrated democratic aspirations and political corruption. Following independence in 1898, Cuba's military and economic weakness in the face of U.S. domination deprived Cubans of their sovereignty. A series of presidents depended upon Washington's approval to govern and, consequently, put U.S. interests above national needs.

In 1930 worldwide depression exacerbated Cuban frustrations and led students and workers to rebel. The repressive tactics of President Gerardo Machado incited the opposition of students, workers, middle-class businessmen, politicians, and women who took to the streets to protest his alleged dictatorship.

Ofelia Domínguez Navarro joined this opposition. Instead of choosing the predictable avenues of protest open to middle-class women and feminists, she became a socialist feminist. As a lawyer, she defended radical students, socialists, and communists against government-ordered arrests and imprisonment. She was jailed and endured exile for her beliefs in democracy and broad-reaching social change. Incarceration, rather than discouraging her socialist principles, hardened her commitment to revolution.

Ofelia was in her prime between 1923 and 1946. During this time she suffered the trauma of cutting herself off from her friends who were not radical enough to see imperialism, economic disadvantage, and male dominance as the causes of injustice. Her direct experience with political and social inequity took an otherwise privileged lady and created a revolutionary.

Ofelia's high ideals, courage, and intellect came from both sides of her family. Born on December 9, 1894, in Mataguá, a suburb of Seibabo, Las Villas, she could recall the last years of the Cuban War of Independence, in which her parents were active participants. Ofelia's father, Florentino Domínguez, joined a revolutionary group in 1895 and moved to San Juan de los Yeras, where his parents lived. It was a dangerous time for rebels, whom the Spanish imprisoned, exiled, or executed. Ofelia's mother, Paula Navarro, aided rebel forces by smuggling arms to them and making them hammocks. When she drove her cart into the countryside, the contraband strapped to her body, she told Spanish soldiers that she was showing off her child to relatives. She carried along Ofelia, her firstborn, to convince the soldiers of her mission.

In 1895, Florentino was arrested after a member of his revolutionary group informed the Spanish government of his sympathy with the revolutionary forces. Florentino and his co-conspirators were sentenced to exile in Chafarinas, a penal colony near Algiers. There he worked in a rock quarry, yet he held stubbornly to his revolutionary activities. He and other prisoners printed a newspaper, *The Exile*, in which they demanded Cuban independence. Upon his return to Cuba, Florentino again became involved in the revolution. The Spaniards rearrested him and this time sentenced him to a lengthy exile in Mexico. His family accompanied him.

As a child, Ofelia experienced the harsh realities of the independence struggle. She and her mother lived briefly in one of Cuba's infamous concentration camps, which were rife with disease and hunger. An aunt who had married a Spaniard watched her four children starve to death while her husband flourished in the Spanish army. Another aunt watched helplessly as her son, caught aiding the patriots, was tied behind a horse and dragged. In desperation she tried to yank him free, but instead she had to witness as his body was broken on the rocks, his brains and body parts left on the streets.

These experiences contributed to the development of Ofelia's principles and courage. Exile and imprisonment, rather than being shameful punishments, signified stalwart adherence to the principles of independence. While this alone did not make Ofelia a revolutionary, the example of her parents made radical action in the name of nationalism acceptable to her.

Peace and stability did not automatically follow Cuban independence. Political disruption and violence characterized the early republican period, and misgovernment, corruption, and U.S. manipulation of national affairs soon alienated Cuban nationalists. In the first decade and a half of the republic, white Cuban elites vied for the administrative power abandoned by the departing Spaniards. National parties were merely launching pads for political careers and had no ideological bases. Politicians used assassination to remove opponents from office, and those who ordered assassinations were immune from arrest. Political campaigns were carried out in the streets, not in the polling booths.

Ofelia learned what political immunity meant as a young adult, first in 1911 when she took a teaching job in Jorobada, a small rural community outside Aguas Bonitas in Las Villas, and later in Havana where she practiced law. Her teaching experience brought her into direct contact with people who had little hope of escaping poverty, illness, drudgery, superstition, hunger, and premature death.

There was no school building in Jorobada, and the few children who attended classes met in the house of Lao Pérez, an old friend of the Domínguez family. Nineteen-year-old Ofelia had to jerry-build a schoolroom: each day she carried a bench from the park for seats, used an oilcloth as a blackboard, and turned a piece of wood and a barrel into a desk.

Offering the students a modern curriculum threatened the peasants' religious understanding and principles. Some parents were ambivalent about bringing their children to school. They objected to Ofelia's curriculum, which included reading, writing, arithmetic, singing, and physical education. In the P.E. class, the boys marched and jumped hurdles while the girls jumped rope and marched. Some parents complained that their children were being sent to school to learn to read and write and not to ruin their shoes. "For that," one said, "the children could join the circus."

Other parents eagerly brought their children. One father, dragging in his kicking and screaming son, told Ofelia, "I have brought this kid so you can learn him . . . so that between his ears letters will flow along with the blood."

After school, Ofelia read newspapers to the townspeople, who commented on and interpreted national and international news according to their own experiences. She also read their letters to them and then wrote replies. As her life became intertwined with those of the campesinos, she came to respect their essential integrity and honesty, and she began to understand how difficult was their struggle for dignity and the necessities of life.

The principal arm of the government in Jorobada was the *rurales*, a rural police force that "kept the peace" in the countryside. Young peasant males clamored to join the *rurales* because by serving in the force, by donning its well-known yellow uniform, they could earn a steady salary, hold power, and achieve status. Repression and corruption were unconcealed facts of life in Jorobada, and bribes were the modus operandi in local politics. Anyone could become the victim of police extortion. Victims had no recourse because such actions were not regarded as crimes.

Torture was a common means of extracting information about local discontent, theft, and anything else the police wanted to know. The police station opened onto an alleyway beside Ofelia's makeshift school, and she and her students could hear the screams of tortured prisoners.

One day, a local officer, Sergeant Nardo, came to the window that faced Ofelia's desk. In front of the class he challenged her to approve of his activities. "Can you hear it, teacher? We are beginning the torture again. Any man leaving this jail leaves in tatters."

Heedless of the consequences, Ofelia exploded with indignation. "Students," she said to the class, "corporal punishment is prohibited by our constitution, and the first time a uniformed bandit lifts his whip or machete against you, kill him and do not tolerate the affront."

"Teacher! Teacher!," the sergeant roared while the students applauded, "you don't know what you are doing!"

"Yes," she answered, "I am doing what I should do."[1]

---

[1]Ofelia Domínguez Navarro, *50 años de una vida* (Havana, 1971), 49–50.

Ofelia was not exempt from political exploitation simply because she was a teacher. During her first year of teaching, she earned forty pesos a month, just enough to cover food and clothing, yet she also had to donate money to build a school. When the people of Jorobada learned of the arrangement, they built the schoolroom and paid her rent for one year. She used what extra money she earned to defray the expenses of her younger sisters' and brothers' educations.

Sometime later, the government raised teacher salaries to eighty pesos a month, but the teachers had to donate half of their pay to build a house for the minister of education. Incensed, Ofelia went into action and refused to pay for the home of a man who had wealth and lucrative businesses. Although Ofelia thought she was alone in her protest, teachers at the normal school, most of whom were women, demonstrated publicly.

While Ofelia taught in Jorobada, she also was studying for her *bachillerato* (high-school diploma). After completing the degree, she decided to attend law school. Her father wanted her to study for a doctorate in pharmacology because it was a popular degree among educated, elite women in Havana. Ofelia prevailed. She completed law school, mostly through correspondence courses, and moved from Jorobada to Santa Clara and then to Havana to practice law.

Ofelia learned about the seamier side of life through her experience as a criminal attorney. She defended murderers, prostitutes, and thieves. She also saw how public office could be used to subvert the legal system and how legal power often benefited the privileged class. Ofelia could have become cynical about the legal profession and human misery, but she did not. Although she was repelled by crime, she often felt compassion for the victims and the accused. A delinquent, to her way of thinking, was the product of an exploitative system, and ignorance and desperation were the real motivations for crime. Ofelia was most compassionate toward prostitutes. Without denying the immorality of the occupation, Ofelia felt that prostitutes were made to suffer for the transgressions of the men who were their customers. She argued that jurists, who often saw prostitution as a "necessary evil," never considered the women's destitution, which, in Ofelia's opinion, was the fundamental cause of this activity. It was through her defense of these women that Ofelia became a feminist.

Ofelia was not the first to raise the question of women's rights in newly independent Cuba. Women of her mother's generation had fought for independence alongside their husbands and brothers, and they had won respect and recognition for their efforts. Yet, after the signing of the Cuban constitution in 1902, these same heroines found themselves disenfranchised and sent home with nothing more than monuments and poems as rewards for their sacrifices. The principles of independence apparently did not include equality between men and women. Women's rights did not receive attention until women took up the cause for themselves. In 1917 women of good education and high breeding challenged male politicians to reform the laws so that women would have the same rights as men.

Middle- and upper-class women who became leaders in women's organizations were first to connect women's legal and political disadvantages with the promises of independence. They demanded universal suffrage, representation in court, government welfare programs, and control of their own and their children's lives. They believed that the freedoms they sought for themselves would benefit all women regardless of race or class. These early feminists became self-appointed leaders of a women's civil and legal rights movement. They were part of a ruling class that expected to lead and to define new rights in terms of their own understanding of freedom and justice, but they were reluctant to give power to women of the laboring classes so that they might articulate their own notions of justice.

On the surface, Ofelia Domínguez Navarro appeared to be a typical member of Havana's highly educated, cosmopolitan middle class. She was a lawyer and a founder of the Club Femenino de Santa Clara and the Alianza Nacional Feminista, two feminist organizations. Ofelia's colleagues were progressive women of property and influence, who traveled in Europe and the United States. Yet Ofelia's background also included struggle and hardship, and she was sympathetic to the needs of the poor. She supported the women's movement, but she opposed its philanthropic programs for disadvantaged women. In time, she broke with the middle-class women's organizations over the question of poverty, the rights of illegitimate children, and political activism.

Ofelia first became nationally known as an advocate of women's rights in 1923, when she attended the First National Women's Congress. The Club Femenino de Cuba, one of several women's organizations, had called the congress to assess the state of Cuban feminism and set directions for the women's movement. Delegates from thirty-one organizations and all seven of Cuba's provinces attended. Advocates for change spoke about women's comparative legal disadvantages, and the delegates enthusiastically passed reform resolutions. The harmonious atmosphere was disturbed when Ofelia, Dulce María Borrero de Luján, Hortensia Lamar, and others proposed a resolution to correct the unequal status of legitimate and illegitimate children. At this point, the congress erupted into pandemonium. For many feminists, Ofelia's resolution, that illegitimate children receive the same assurances of care, shelter, and love as legitimate children, was scandalous. According to many conservative delegates, the protection of unwed mothers was not a feminist matter but a moral question that revealed a woman's, not a man's, immoral character. The delegates, many of them also influenced by Catholic Church directives, defeated Ofelia's resolution, although they did put it on the agenda for the next national women's congress, scheduled for 1925.

If Ofelia was disgruntled by the conservatives at the first congress, she must have been appalled at the Second National Congress in April 1925. She again addressed the issue of equal rights for all children, regardless of their parents' marital status. Since the last congress, she had gathered evidence about the living conditions of unwed mothers and the hopelessness of their children. But rather than consider the plight of these women and children, the conservative faction accused Ofelia of being a communist. They argued that she, as a single and childless woman, could not understand mothers and children, and that in her arguments she was merely espousing communist ideology, which sought to destroy the family by supporting divorce, free love, and concubinage. The kindest criticism called her a stupid sentimentalist.

What had been pandemonium over the issue in 1923 turned into a near riot in 1925. Women pounded tables with their shoes as they vied for the floor. The conservatives threatened to walk out, but Ofelia and her supporters upstaged them and left first. After the progressives' departure, the reactionary Catholic elements met in secret sessions so that they could control the voting on all issues. As a result, the congress passed nothing more radical than a suffrage resolution.

After this congress, Ofelia increased her activity in the Club Femenino, one of the more radical groups within the women's movement. The Club differed from philanthropic organizations in its demand that the state take more responsibility for the poor and that women have the same civil and political status as men. The Club joined student militants who were fighting in the streets for the release of Julio Antonio Mella, the founder of the Cuban Communist party, who was being held in jail without bond. Although the women in the Club were not communists, they did sympathize with the students' protest against corruption and gangster politics.

The Mella incident was crucial in Ofelia's political development, for Julio Antonio Mella was a friend with whom Ofelia shared some ideological ties. She had been his guest at the Popular University when she gave a talk about the equality of children.

Mella went on a hunger strike, protesting his arbitrary arrest and harsh treatment in prison. Many Cubans thought his arrest was unjust, and they feared that Mella would be allowed to die. The Club Femenino, led by Ofelia, supported the nationwide demonstration. Together with the students of Santa Clara, she planned a massive protest. Sánchez Arango and Gómez Guimeranez organized factory workers, and Ofelia brought out the students from the institute, the normal school, and the law school. In less than three hours, the students, workers, and others marched peacefully upon the provincial government. They held a meeting in Santa Clara's central park and then dispersed.

But Ofelia was not through. She led a contingent of delegates to the home of President Machado's parents, who lived in Santa Clara. Ofelia told them of the arrest, the hunger strike, and the misuse of the law. Señora Lutgarda Morales was visibly moved by Ofelia's description of Mella's fragile condition. She immediately telegrammed her son, asking him to release Mella. "We beg you as your parents who have loved their children to order the release of the poor young prisoner."[2] In Havana even larger demonstrations had been held to demand Mella's release. At the eleventh hour, Machado released Mella, thus sparing his life.

Ofelia's association with students and workers broadened her understanding of oppression and of how to organize against government retaliation. Her interest in reform was no longer defined solely in terms of the women's movement. Despite her enlarged perception of what constituted social injustice, she remained loyal to women's issues. Between 1915 and 1928 she participated in national and international women's meetings to which she carried her message about the rights of illegitimate children. She met other Latin American feminists, such as Paulina Luissi of Uruguay. She also encountered the North American feminists who proved that they were no friends of Latin American women at the 1926 Interamerican Women's Congress in Panama. The delegates from the United States abstained in the vote for a resolution that Latin American nations grant women their civil and political rights. These delegates said that they were not convinced that Latin American women were ready to exercise their rights. This episode reinforced Ofelia's anti-U.S. sentiments.

Women's suffrage turned out to be a political issue inextricably linked to the overthrow of the Machado government. As such, it initially pulled together the conservative and radical elements of the

---

[2]Ibid., 84.

feminist movement. General Gerardo Machado became Cuba's fifth president in 1924, and some hoped his administration would be different from previous, corrupt regimes. Machado acknowledged the need for improved public works and for the elimination of corruption. Many of his projects, especially the trans-Cuban railroad, were popular. At the urging of his supporters, he appointed a constitutional assembly in 1927 to rewrite the 1902 constitution to extend the presidential term from four to six years, thus allowing him to succeed himself. To deflect allegations that he was a dictator, Machado declared his support for women's suffrage. He wanted to convince Cuban dissidents that he was broadening the electoral base and favoring democratic rule, despite his consecutive terms in office, abolition of certain parties, and repressive tactics.

By 1927 essentially all feminists, regardless of their political leanings, supported universal suffrage, since that had been their cause for ten years. Even Ofelia spoke before the constitutional assembly in favor of Machado's resolution. She argued that votes for women would dignify the electoral process and give women the same rights as men, which they should have had immediately after independence.

The constitutional congress's decision to reject universal suffrage sharply disappointed the feminists, many of whom had stood vigil outside the capital to await the decision. Although the delegates had felt free to tinker with the constitution and provide for an irregular presidency, they claimed they did not have the authority to grant women the vote.

Outraged feminists formed a group called the Committee for the Defense of Women's Suffrage. They interviewed the most prominent men of the constitutional assembly, made declarations to the press, and presented a petition to Dr. Antonio Sánchez de Bustamante, president of the convention, demanding that the assembly write women's suffrage into the constitution. The members of the committee knew they would be unable to convince the assembly, but they wanted to keep the issue alive and before the public. Ofelia, along with Hortensia Lamar, Pilar Jorge de Tella, Rosaria Guillaume, and Rosa Arredondo de Vega, carried the petition to Dr. Sánchez during an assembly meeting. She and her associates also denounced the claims made by some of the delegates and medical doctors that women were physically and mentally inferior to men.

In the wake of the setback, a group of women decided to create a united feminist front with members from all social sectors of the republic to fight for the civil and political rights of women. In 1928, Pilar Jorge de Tella and Ofelia invited feminists to an organizational meeting. Pilar urged them to continue the feminist struggle, stating that women's rights were necessary for the well-being of the nation and world peace. Ofelia spoke about the legal status of women, reminding those present that laws included problems of criminality and the economic subjugation of women. Upper-class women such as Elena Mederos de González initially supported Ofelia.

Within days of the meeting, Ofelia invited women working in tobacco factories to become part of the organization. Working-class women, teachers, factory workers, professional women, and the wealthy formed the Alianza Nacional Feminista on September 6, 1928, in the Salón de Actos of the Reporters' Association of Havana. The women called themselves the "*mambisas* for the new army of justice, ideals, and rights."

On behalf of the Alianza, Ofelia sent a letter to President Machado demanding that women have the vote and full citizenship. She argued her case not only in terms of women's rights but also in terms of the rights of the poor. The president promised only to send a message to congress supporting women's suffrage. Whether he fulfilled his promise is not known, but no resolution came before the assembly.

Popular opposition to the Machado government was in its infancy in 1928, and Ofelia was in its vanguard. She wrote for opposition journals and newspapers, several of which were published by the Communist party. She also did regular radio editorials on Havana stations. Fascism was rising in Europe, and some of its repressive tactics were being adopted by its supporters in Latin America, whom Ofelia strongly criticized. But she differed from many of her *compañeros* in the Communist and Socialist parties because of her feminist views that women must advance both as members of the proletariat and as women.

Ofelia's radical leanings were not lost on the moderate feminists in the Alianza. Although their stated purpose was to include women of all classes in the fight for women's rights, their vision for change would primarily benefit the middle class. The Alianza focused on legal changes to improve the civil status of women and labor laws. Many members of the Alianza, rather than tailor their program to include prostitutes, peasant women, tobacco workers, domestic servants, blacks, and mulattos, believed that discipline, education, and better health standards would improve the poor's standard of living. Until poor women could become respectable women, the moderates thought, feminists could aid them only through philanthropy and educational programs.

Ofelia broke with the Alianza in 1930 after losing the organization's presidential election. The membership had tolerated her radical views as labor vice president, but it would not accept her as its leader. María Collado, the leader of the Suffrage party and a vigorous opponent of Ofelia's views, claimed that Ofelia lost the election because she was egotistical and tyrannical. Ofelia's memoirs offer another explanation:

> Because of the heterogeneous composition of the Alianza, we could not do any more than act for civil and political rights for women. We could not incorporate poor women and address their needs. Since rich women predominated, they could not reconcile their interests with those of tobacco workers, sales clerks, or teachers, etc.
>
> For my part, I confess that in spite of the high intellectual and moral values represented in the Alianza, they were skewed enough to make me feel uncomfortable because I had to limit my activities which favored the social rights of working women. . . .
>
> The Alianza had a number of issues and activities. I eventually left this group for no other reason than ideological convictions. The group did not address the needs of people outside their economic and social class.[3]

On May 30, 1930, Ofelia and Bertha Darder Bebé formed the Unión Laborista de Mujeres, which was intended to attract women of all classes to fight for a broad program of reform. The new group focused on women's issues, but it also was anti-imperialist and nationalistic. It differed from the Alianza by identifying poverty, gender exploitation, and North American capitalist imperialism as the sources of women's oppression. It called for collaboration between women and men to create new economic bases and opportunities for all Cubans, especially for those who worked. Ofelia insisted that the Unión be free of Church interference and the influence of members' husbands. Women of prestige and status filled the administrative positions, but they were women whose loyalty to socialist values was unquestionable. The Unión soon had the support of many progressives in the press, among the veterans of the wars of independence, and from the international feminist community.

At this point in her life, Ofelia was a socialist feminist, not a Marxist-Leninist. She did not advocate the destruction of democracy through revolution, nor did she support a totalitarian state or communism. She also refused to let women's issues be subsumed by the proletarian struggle. She worked within the democratic system, and she argued for reform in democratic terms. Because her organization called for major economic and social changes and because of her alliance with

---

[3]Ibid., 118.

other political groups, Ofelia was swept into the political turmoil that erupted between 1930 and 1934.

Four months after the founding of the Unión, Rafael Trejo, a student at the University of Havana, was assassinated. His murder by police during a demonstration galvanized opposition to Machado's regime. Until then the targets of Machado's repression had been striking workers and outspoken opponents of his administration. When Trejo, a student who had had no previous association with revolutionary groups, died, Machado was serving notice that he would use indiscriminate violence to preserve his presidency.

Trejo's death prompted accusations of police misconduct. Students rushed to newspaper offices to publish their denunciations. Trejo's friends, defying repression, carried his body first to the emergency room of a nearby hospital and then to his parents' home where it lay for public viewing. Ofelia and the women in the Unión stood vigil all night.

President Machado declared a state of siege until after Trejo's funeral. He ordered that only family members could accompany the body to the cemetery, but women from the Unión and other prominent radicals marched at the head of the funeral procession. Unión members were pallbearers and carried the casket on their shoulders from the chapel to the grave site. For once, being female had an advantage, for soldiers stationed along the route were reluctant to shoot women who were doing what women do after outbreaks of violence—mourn the dead. Ofelia delivered the eulogy, intended to unify everyone who objected to Machado's repressive tactics.

The Unión did not stop with its participation in Trejo's burial. Its members demanded the firing of the university's rector, who had called for police intervention, and insisted that the police be brought to justice. For those efforts, the Unión became the target of police investigation. Occasionally, policemen interrupted Unión meetings and disrupted the recruitment of new members. They also searched Unión offices for evidence of seditious activities.

Undaunted, the Unión leadership kept up public protest, but they always conducted themselves like ladies and avoided violence. On one occasion, the executive committee of the Unión, along with Dr. Candida Gómez Cala, the niece of Maximo Gómez, one of the greatest generals to survive the wars of Cuban independence, visited Camp Columbia, the military headquarters in Havana, to protest police brutality. The police, who were used to society ladies visiting police headquarters to see that prisoners were clean and well fed, cordially received Gómez and the delegation. When Colonel Castillo, the commander, realized that their purpose was to criticize police behavior, he stiffened and asked that his staff members leave the room. Gómez humiliated Castillo by impugning his nationalism and accusing him of betraying the objectives of independence by repressing Cubans as the Spanish had done. Castillo, chastised, only mumbled that he had no answer to their accusations. The women left unharmed and returned to their homes.

As his administration came under increasing fire from opposition groups, Machado searched for a way to appease some of his opponents. An obvious ploy was to offer votes to women. As proof of his support for suffrage, he reminded the public of his 1927 constitutional resolution, blaming the congress for rejecting the measure. Although few feminists believed Machado, his maneuver succeeded to some extent in dividing the movement.

Most of the women's groups—the Alianza Nacional Feminista, the Partido Sufragista, the Club Femenino, and even the Lyceum—called for an end to the dictatorship and for women's suffrage, but they did not insist upon major political or economic changes. The Unión, on the other hand, was a more radical feminist organization. Ofelia and the executive council accused the government of trying to dilute the strength of the women's movement by using the vote to draw feminists' attention away from more difficult problems. Ofelia called on feminists to forget about suffrage for the time being and concentrate on economic, racial, and gender issues. She went so far as to say that, by paying exclusive attention to suffrage, the feminists demonstrated that women were a retarding force in revolutionary movements.

Machado's desperate attempts to appease opposition elements were unsuccessful, and 1930 marked the beginning of three years of bloody repression. The president outlawed public gatherings during the November by-elections. Newspapers threatened with censorship closed. Police hunted down and killed students because they were members of the Directorio Estudiantil, and they shot and killed protesters and suspected conspirators with their infamous "shots into the air." Violence only begat violence, and groups such as the ABC, a middle-class organization that advocated the violent overthrow of Machado, joined the fray.

At first, the Unión did not endorse violence as a means of ousting Machado. The women became radical only after helping families search for fathers, sons, and brothers who had disappeared. The experience taught them the lengths to which Machado and his supporters would go to crush rebellion. After they had visited prisons as defense attorneys for jailed students and workers, Ofelia and the women of the Unión openly advocated revolution, although they would not bear arms themselves.

Ofelia was first arrested on January 3, 1931, when she and others were recruiting students from the normal school for the Directorio Estudiantil. The meetings were always secret, but the special police (the "Porra," or experts) learned that the students were meeting at 106 Linea. There were two such addresses, and the Porra went to the wrong one. By chance, Ofelia and Dulce María Escalona de Rodríguez, another celebrated female activist of the time, happened past and recognized two police lieutenants. The women knew it was only a matter of time before the police found the correct address, so they drove quickly to Teté Suárez Solís's house, where the meeting was being held. By the time they convinced the students of the danger, the police arrived. Ofelia and several other women pretended they were celebrating Teté's birthday. The police found them listening to the Victrola, with no students in evidence. When the police demanded that they be allowed to search the house, Ofelia collapsed on the bed as if she were ill, for she did not want the police to enter the bedroom where many of the students were hiding.

Her efforts failed. The Porra arrested everyone in the house and packed them off to jail. At first, Ofelia thought she would be spared because she was not put in the wagons with the students. However, one of the policemen invited her, in the name of Lieutenant Calvo, the most infamous of the Porra, to join him in the police car. She suspected that the policeman was taunting her, so she refused and went to one of the wagons with the students. The route to the jail, located downtown at the base of the Prado, meandered through the business center and colonial quarter. Along the way, the prisoners shouted, "Down with tyranny! Down with assassination! Down with Yankee imperialism!" Ofelia recalled Torriente Brau's strong voice calling out, "Who killed Mella?" The answering chorus rang out from the other wagon, "Machado, Machado!"

All gaiety ended at the prison. It was a cold January afternoon, and the prison had no heat. Ofelia's cell, which was ten to twelve meters long and four meters wide, was dark when her jailers opened the barred door. The cell's only fresh air came in through a duct, too high to serve as a window, that faced a bracken marsh. The duct's bars and metal mesh limited the amount of air that could enter, and the only light came in through two windows in the ceiling. The cell was so dank that it took Ofelia two days to dry her handkerchief.

Cold and damp chilled to the bone. The cell had eighteen narrow beds, a few steel chairs, one wooden table, and some small boxes nailed to the walls for storing personal possessions. The prisoners had to share one toilet. On each side of the entryway were small dungeons reserved for solitary confinement.

Ofelia, Dulce María, and Teté found Carmen Gil, a Venezuelan poet, in one of the solitary confinement chambers. She was burning with fever, and she told the women of her terror over the previous seven days. She had been tied to her bed and subjected to the grossest kinds of sexual abuse, all this when she was essentially postpartum, having had a baby only three months earlier. She was suffering from internal infections.

The women hardly slept that night. From down the stairway, they could hear sounds coming from the men's quarters, so they knew who had been arrested and who was being tortured. Dulce María could hardly contain herself at first because of worry over her two small children and then because she could hear the voices of her husband and brother in the adjoining male prison of the Castillo Príncipe.

Two days later, Ofelia and the women were released. Still enraged by Carmen Gil's plight, Ofelia went directly to the offices of *El País*, the communist newspaper, where she reported what had happened to Carmen and her husband. The following day, Ofelia protested to the secretary of government, Dr. Vivanco, who threatened repressive measures if she did not keep quiet. But threats of reprisal did not intimidate Ofelia; if anything, they ignited her defiance.

Police arrested Ofelia four more times on manufactured charges, for she never violated the law. In her first arrest, the allegation was conspiracy, although the government never prosecuted Ofelia. Future imprisonments followed charges of conspiracy and inciting riots, but she was never convicted, even in the one case that came to trial.

Another common characteristic of Ofelia's arrests was that the police offered her preferential treatment because of her class, status, and occupation. On one occasion when the police arrested her at the Unión office, they realized that she was not well, and they offered to put her under house arrest. She refused. On another occasion, Ofelia had a broken leg and was running a high fever. Again the police wanted to put her under house arrest, and again she refused. Preferential treatment saved Ofelia's life on two occasions. In 1933 and 1937 she fled Cuba after receiving warnings from people who were close to her family that she would be assassinated if she did not flee.

Until March 1931, when Ofelia served her second prison term, she was a socialist feminist with a commitment to democracy and to radical social reform. She sympathized with the communists, but she had not joined the party. She was a defender of the right to political dissent, a principle of the independence movement but not necessarily one of communism. The isolation of her cell, the contact with prostitutes and thieves, the filth and the bad treatment made her despair. Her only support came from communist women who befriended her and offered some reason to endure the suffering. They taught her to hope. The final break with her old allies, the progressive feminists, came as she found stronger bonds of compassion and support behind prison walls. Prison made her a revolutionary.

When Ofelia went to prison in 1931, she became both a prisoner and a reporter. She wrote graphically about her arrests, her treatment, and her relationships with common and political prisoners. She experienced firsthand what people on the outside could never know: the smells, the tastes, the sights, and the feel of prison. She knew of the prisoners' hopelessness, despair, ignorance, illness, and suffering. Stripped of her social and political protection, she stood defenseless before the abusive wardens and officers. She lived alongside prisoners who could be violent and duplicitous. She suffered physical illness and mental anguish. With nothing but her intellect as a tool, Ofelia identified her moral convictions, and she deepened her commitment to revolutionary socialism without forgetting her allegiance to feminism. Only socialism, she resolved, considered the motivating factors for crime, and only feminism helped women assume a new consciousness about their victimization in a patriarchal society.

When Ofelia entered Guanabacoa prison in March 1931, nearly all of its 140 female inmates were serving sentences for prostitution. Most of them were disease ridden, and they knew how to steal, swindle, and cheat. Most probably would die a premature death by murder or from venereal disease. Ofelia had understood before she entered prison that a lack of skills and education limited women's chances of obtaining gainful employment, but prison showed her other cultural factors that contributed to women's entrapment in prostitution. Hopelessness and superstition ruled their lives. Santerías, Afro-Cuban rituals, were the sources for supernatural cures, curses, and hoaxes. The women wore red colors in their clothing, patted out rhythms with their feet, used cleansing ceremonies, concocted special drinks, and fulfilled promises to Santa Bárbara to cure themselves. During these ceremonies they often shrieked and fell into trances. The women used rituals to reduce their sexual passions, and they also took out curses against their enemies in prison or against the clients and pimps who were exploiting them. Ofelia saw the tragedy in the santería, for it was an artificial cure for the profound problems that confronted these women. Their minds were darkened by confusion and supernatural forces, leaving them helpless in the face of their oppression.

With no effective outlet for anger, shame, or desperation, the prisoners frequently fought among themselves. A fight might begin between two persons, but it usually ended in a brawl between gangs. The issue might be insignificant or a facade for deep resentments between a homosexual couple. No one was exempt from the violence. The women's snarling and cursing, often consisting of racial slurs and taunts about what sort of beast another woman was screwing, shocked and horrified Ofelia.

Soon Ofelia felt some of her fellow prisoners' passions. She, too, experienced intense hatred, especially toward the jailers, whose authority was represented by the huge key used to open and close her cell door. The key became an icon of her contempt for her oppressors. She despised the stooges who went to the wardens with stories of prisoner disobedience. She hated the warden, who was stealing prison provisions and selling them for profit. Ofelia used her own alienation to understand the self-destructive behavior of the women with whom she lived.

Nothing shielded Ofelia from the horrors of drug addiction and homosexual and heterosexual rape. Many of the prisoners were alcoholics and marijuana smokers whose pimps brought them drugs on visiting days. Without their chemical means of escape, the prisoners often became mean and abusive. Prisoners and guards both were involved in perverted sexual adventures, such as rape and bestiality, violations that occurred between prisoners and between prisoners and guards. Homosexuality seemed almost normal. Some of the women pointed out their lovers to Ofelia and told her they were engaged.

Ofelia despaired for these women, but was especially distressed by problems of venereal disease. Mothers arrested for prostitution were allowed to bring their youngest children to prison with them, and since the mothers were often syphilitic, their children also carried the disease. None of the prisoners understood hygiene, and, even if they had, cleanliness in the prison was impossible. Only prisoners who could afford private medical treatment received it, and even they depended on the prison officials to notify a doctor. Venereal disease was so prevalent that Ofelia learned to recognize it by its appearance and smell. Yet prison officials took no precautions to prevent its spread. The prisoners used everything in common: cups, soap, sheets, towels, and spoons. They shared three showers and three toilets.

Nothing sickened Ofelia more than the syphilitic children who were mentally and physically defective. Children who entered the prison healthy stood little chance of leaving it that way. Healthy and sick children played together in one corner of the prison and shared food and toys that they put in their mouths. Their mothers would pick up their children and kiss them with mouths full of syphilitic sores. During the night, children screamed from the pain of the disease, and one girl had to be restrained from tearing at herself where lesions had appeared. The adult women often used drinking utensils and common water supply for santerías intended to cure their disease, a practice that exposed everyone to contact with syphilis and gonorrhea.

Desperate to contain the spread of disease, Ofelia encouraged the prisoners to take precautions and sent letters of protest through the Unión Radical de Mujeres (the new name of the Unión Laborista de Mujeres) to the secretary of health. She was unable to convince the prisoners that there were "bugs" in the water, and they saw no reason to separate the sick from the healthy children. Worse yet, the doctor sent by the secretary of health to investigate Ofelia's complaints never entered the prison, though he did write a letter denying her charges.

Perhaps Ofelia's greatest accomplishment while in prison was the effort she made to understand the psychological composition of her jailers, who brutalized and mistreated prisoners. They not only forced the prisoners to follow arbitrary orders but also insisted upon humiliating them. The guards' actions demonstrated to Ofelia that they were no better than the "criminals" who were prisoners. She discovered that most guards were frightened or embittered widows and single women. Life had been hard for them, and so they channeled their fury against the only people whom they could control, the prisoners. Nothing stopped them from taunting or accusing a prisoner, and on occasion, a prisoner committed suicide following cruel encounters with the guards.

In her darkest moments, Ofelia drew strength from the more seasoned revolutionaries around. Prisoners who were members of the Communist party tried to organize the others so they could protect themselves from abuse. They also got news from the outside and kept in touch with the revolutionary movement. They paid the price for their actions, though, for they were constantly under surveillance and subjected to harassment by the guards.

One evening, a nurse who was their contact informed them that some would be taken to the Isle of Pines. Ofelia was marked to go, and the news was nearly more than she could bear. She had endured this imprisonment with a broken leg, and she was ill and depressed. Her communist *compañeras* helped her pack her few things and hide her notes. Her misery increased with the knowledge that most of the other prisoners would not know about her move until after she had gone. When the guards came at midnight to take her away, the political prisoners shouted, "Down with tyranny! Long live the revolution!," and sang the "Marseillaise" and other revolutionary songs. As Ofelia followed the guards out of the prison and into the awaiting police wagon, she heard from the highest prison galleries the boisterous voices of her *compañeras* singing the "Internationale."

At that moment, Ofelia made the spiritual conversion from an intellectual socialist to a revolutionary whose identity originated in socialist values and community. She ceased to identify primarily with middle- and upper-class intellectuals, choosing instead the solidarity of revolutionaries, for they were at her side during her moments of need.

Although Ofelia thought she was going to the Isle of Pines, she in fact went to the Calixto García Hospital where doctors treated her broken leg and fever. From the hospital, she returned to prison for another two months. She was released in September 1931, after a total of seven months in prison.

From 1931 through the overthrow of President Machado in 1933, Ofelia was a militant defender of the rights of student and labor dissidents. Wherever there was a crisis or a demonstration, Ofelia was present, either as a lawyer or a public speaker. When communist newspaper reporters were jailed, she took over the editorship of their newspapers. She was jailed again, although briefly, and after her release received a tip from Machado's brother that she was on the Porra's assassination list for speaking at the funeral of a fallen revolutionary, Mirto Miliam, which the government correctly viewed as inciting rebellion.

If Ofelia were to survive, she had to flee. In January 1933 she left for Mexico, the home of her parents, where she remained until Machado's overthrow in September. It was a crucial moment for the anti-Machado forces, and Ofelia wanted to help direct the Unión but to do so meant certain death. In Mexico she spoke to revolutionary student groups and to Cubans in exile, hoping to build support for the revolution and to oppose U.S. mediation and control of Machado's ouster.

From 1933 to 1940, no less than seven men occupied Cuba's presidential palace—men who were essentially appointed and replaced by the new commander in chief of the military, Fulgencio Batista. Batista's abandonment of social reform issues and his groveling for U.S. support repelled Ofelia. She sided with the dedicated revolutionaries who were demanding socialist reform. She was a member of the delegation that brought back Julio Antonio Mella's ashes and buried them in Cuba. She demanded amnesty for all political prisoners. She denounced labor practices and the subsistence wages paid to workers, in particular the female workers at the ten-cent stores. She protested Cuba's continued subservience to the United States. She encouraged tobacco union members to stiffen their armed resistance to police control, reminding them that they were more numerous and powerful than the rural police. She also encouraged other organizations, such as the needleworkers' union, to join international workers' shops to protect themselves against capital and labor exploitation. Her most continuous battle was with the Emergency Courts originally set up by Machado, and continued by subsequent governments, to try revolutionaries immediately after their arrest. They used no juries, and the judges were political appointees with questionable legal training. In effect, the courts were the government's tool for disposing of political dissidents.

Ofelia went to jail two more times before 1937 for her continued opposition and in 1937 fled again to Mexico. There she observed the reform government of Lázaro Cárdenas. In Mexico, she concluded that reform was possible without armed revolt, but only if socialists and communists could organize the workers' movement and only if the labor movement had significant access to political power. From 1937 to 1939, she worked in a legal and organizational capacity in Mexico to secure the nationalization of U.S. oil interests and to organize Mexican workers. Throughout her exile, Ofelia wrote for radical Cuban journals, denouncing Nazism and fascism.

Upon her return to Cuba, Ofelia maintained her communist affiliations, but she also took part in the 1939 Third National Women's Congress. Again she raised the issue of women's rights and of equality for children regardless of the legitimacy of their birth. She published her opinions about women's rights in newspapers and discussed them on a ten-minute radio program on Radio Salas. She also spoke out against Hitler's aggression and the coming world war. And in 1940, only a few days after the death of Leon Trotsky in Mexico, she offered to defend the murderer, Jacques Monnard. Although she could not act as a lawyer in Mexican courts, she helped the defense lawyer prepare the case.

Her pinnacle of international influence came in 1946, when Cuba organized its delegation to the United Nations planning meetings in San Francisco. Ofelia was the secretary-general of the Cuban delegation, a post she held for sixteen years. While a part of the Cuban delegation, Ofelia involved herself in programs for children affected by war devastation. She also created programs for improved international education.

Ofelia earned international recognition for her work at the United Nations. She also continued her opposition to the United States, a position that was not without consequences. In 1950, while traveling to New York as the Cuban delegate to the United Nations, she was detained, searched, and interrogated by FBI agents at the Miami airport. It was at the height of the McCarthy period, and the U.S. government was taking no chances with spies or communists visiting the country. The FBI kept Ofelia in Miami for ten days without her luggage or lodgings. She protested her detention to the president of the Cuban delegation, who finally gained her release.

In 1952, when Batista took over the government in a coup d'état, Ofelia protested. But she was no longer a young and vigorous woman, and her actions were not militant. Rather than participate in guerrilla movements, she concentrated on her work in the United Nations. When the 1959 Cuban revolution succeeded, however, she worked with the local block organizations, called the Committees for the Defense of the Revolution. In 1962 she resigned her post at the United Nations due to severe arthritis.

Ofelia was a woman of awesome courage, tremendous insight, and honesty. In 1971, when she published her autobiography, she described herself as old but basically at peace with herself. She neither cheered nor mourned the outcome of her struggles. She was grateful that she had maintained the strength to withstand imprisonment, and she knew that hardship had shaped her ideals. In the end, Ofelia rejoiced in a socialist Cuba because her and her nation's struggles had drawn her into international solidarity with other socialists and given her a commitment to humanity. She felt no remorse for losing the wealth that might have been hers nor bitterness for the planned austerity in Cuba's economy that she endured in her later years. She believed that she had lived well. She had been a socialist feminist and a revolutionary, but she was also a bit of a Quixote whose dreams reached beyond ideology.

SOURCES

This sketch is based on Ofelia Domínguez Navarro's autobiography, *50 años de una vida* (Havana: Instituto Cubana del Libro, 1971), her book about her imprisonments, *De seis a seis* (Mexico City, 1937), and newspapers and feminist publications from the period. To obtain these materials required my traveling to Cuba as well as the assistance of a number of Cubans. I would like to express my deepest appreciation to Tomás Fernández Robaina at the José Martí Library in Havana, for his support and interest. His excellent bibliography on Cuban women facilitated my research. Margy Delgado, Rita Perrera, and Marta Alberti from the Federation of Cuban Women invited me to Cuba and aided me with my work. Their trust and good faith have made this project possible; I remain in their debt.

10

George Westerman: A Barbadian Descendant in Panama

Michael L. Conniff

Populist leaders first caught the attention of Michael Conniff during his graduate studies in history at Stanford University and are the topic of his monograph, *Urban Politics in Brazil: The Rise of Populism, 1925–1945* (1981), and his anthology, *Latin American Populism in Contemporary Perspective* (1982). His interest in populism since has broadened from study of the leadership to study of the masses or, at least, of the generally inarticulate people of Latin America. In *Black Labor on a White Canal, 1904–1981* (1985), Conniff examines the rich social history of Panama, with its complex ethnic mosaic of blacks, whites, and West Indians.

In the biography that follows, Conniff describes the life of George Westerman, a Panamanian who found that the rough road caused by racism, U.S. political involvement, and ethnic opposition to West Indian immigrants could be negotiated through perseverance and self-determination. Undaunted by obstacles, Westerman used each one as an occasion to raise his aspirations. Not everyone of talent and ambition succeeds, but he has.

Conniff is a professor of history at the University of New Mexico. He is currently working with Alfredo Castillero Calvo on a study of U.S.-Panamanian relations since 1940.

INTRODUCTION

Between 1850 and 1914, some two hundred thousand West Indians migrated to Panama to work on various construction projects, culminating in the Panama Canal built by the United States. The immigrants created communities—enclaves really—along the route of the Panama Railroad and in the Canal Zone. They also took over many barrios in the adjoining cities of Panama and Colón. Over the course of several generations, the West Indians and their descendants created their own subculture, partly to preserve their families and communities and partly to defend themselves against discrimination and attacks from without. Eventually, they became fairly well integrated into the host society, but the road was long and often bitter.

Many persons emerged as guides and leaders in the immigrants' journey toward acceptance by the Latin Panamanians. Early on, Protestant ministers and teachers assumed positions of prestige and acted as mediators with outside groups, especially with the Panamanian government and the Canal Zone authorities. Labor leaders did so occasionally, but their roles proved difficult and even dangerous. Finally, a group of intellectuals arose to assume leadership of the West Indian community, which was made up of immigrants and their descendants. In some ways, the intellectuals labored as hard as their fathers who had wielded picks and shovels to dig the canal. No institutions, foundations, colleges, or academies hired them, so they had to work in other jobs, as teachers, journalists, politicians, or other professionals.

George Westerman typifies the intellectuals who emerged in the 1940s to lead the West Indians and their descendants in Panama. This account of his career uncovers the obstacles, hardships, discrimination, and disappointments his people experienced, but it also reveals the occasional triumph, of achievement or simply acceptance.

In reading his story, we should recall that the Americas are a land of immigrants—from the Mongolian migrations to the Caribbean boat people. The ruptures, upheavals, and cultural adaptations that always accompany such movements of people constitute a central theme of American history.

George W. Westerman was born in 1910 in Colón, which at the time was part of the Panama Canal Zone. His father had immigrated from Barbados to work on the canal; his mother was from St. Lucia. They baptized and raised their children in the Anglican church. When Westerman was still young, the family moved to La Boca, a major West Indian labor camp at the Pacific end of the Canal Zone. Westerman attended the canal-operated colored school in La Boca through the third grade and then studied for a time at a private West Indian institute in Panama, the Innis School. That was as far as his formal education progressed. Since English was the language of both the Zone and the West Indian community, Westerman learned little Spanish as a youth.

A major formative event in his life occurred in February 1920, during the Silver Roll labor strike.[1] Encouraged by black union representatives from the United States, the West Indian workers in the Canal Zone decided to call a strike. They had been led to believe that it would coincide with a railroad strike in the United States and that they were sure to win concessions from the government. Yet, when the canal workers walked out on February 23, they did not receive backing or even their own strike funds from their international in the United States. After nine days, the strike collapsed, an utter failure. For the next twenty-five years canal management prevented the non-U.S. laborers from unionizing.

When the strike broke out, Westerman's father was home in bed suffering from triple pneumonia. Canal police went door-to-door in the labor camps looking for strikers, with orders from the governor to evict them. The military police officers asked Westerman's father if he was on strike, and he responded, "No, I'm home because I'm sick, but if I *were* well I'd be on strike." The police proceeded to drag him, the family, and their belongings out into the street. The family took up temporary quarters in Panama until the end of the strike. When they returned, Westerman's father was given quarters again but rehired at a lower rate. The episode made an indelible mark on the ten year old, impressing him with the power and willfulness of the canal administrators. He would dedicate himself to promoting his people's welfare through compromise and reason, not through confrontation.

Like most families whose heads worked for the canal, Westerman's lived in old and cramped silver quarters in the Zone. They were assigned to housing that dated back to the French canal project of the 1880s. They were fortunate, however, to avoid the notorious "Titanic," as residents nicknamed a forty-eight unit barracks. To be sure, rents for silver quarters were kept low, and the canal provided basic services. The main reasons for living in the Zone, however, were proximity to jobs and access to the commissaries, hospitals, schools,

[1]"Silver Roll" was a euphemism for the nonwhite work force of the canal. Originally, it referred to locally hired persons who were paid in silver coin. Foreign, mostly U.S., employees formed the "Gold Roll," i.e., they were paid in gold. By 1910, however, the system evolved into one of racial segregation, in which virtually all facilities existed in duplicate, the "silver" set for nonwhites, the "gold" for whites.

and other facilities available to the workers and their families. Westerman, who never married, continued to live with his family in La Boca until the death of his father in the early 1950s.

Those who could not stand the regimentation of life in the Zone chose to live in tenements in Panama City and Colón (most of the latter reverted to Panama after World War I). The housing was just as bad and the rents low, yet outside the Zone they and their families had some freedom and could participate in the social and economic life of the two cities. There, vigorous West Indian communities arose, with a full complement of churches, private schools, businesses, social and charitable associations, and even newspapers. Although Westerman's family lived in the Zone until the 1950s, they often went into Panama City by streetcar or to Colón by train, an hour's journey.

As a teenager, Westerman took an entry-level job with the canal, that of messenger. Every day the complex operations of the canal required that thousands of communications be delivered throughout the five hundred square miles of the Zone. Westerman was both smart and inquisitive, and he quickly learned how the canal organization worked, and he developed his writing skills. His quest for personal improvement impressed his American bosses. In a short time, he was promoted to clerk.

Perhaps because of his own ambition and his father's disappointments working for the canal, Westerman soon took a job with the electric power company in Panama City. There he rose through the ranks, from typist to stenographer to secretary and, finally, to chief of the stenotypist section. In those days, much of the office work was done by males. Westerman won his employer's respect and appreciation in these roles.

Westerman's after-hours activities brought him even wider recognition. In 1928 he began what would become his principal career, newspaper writing. He submitted columns on sports, music, literary events, and general happenings to the *Panama Tribune*, a newspaper recently founded by Jamaican-born Sidney Young. The relationship proved long and fruitful; Young became a mentor for the aspiring writer.

Young had been in the newspaper business for many years and had risen to the position of editor of the English section of the *Panama American*, a bilingual daily owned by an American. In 1927 the owner called in the staff to announce the imminent folding of the paper. Young offered to conduct a fund-raising campaign in the West Indian community to save the paper. His readers responded generously, and the paper was saved from bankruptcy. Soon afterward, Young applied for a raise to bring his salary up to those of the other editors. The owner refused, saying, "Sidney, there is no doubt that you are a good worker and deserve a lot, but I don't think I could ever pay a Negro as much as a white man." Young quit and soon started his own paper, targeted at the West Indian community. His masthead slogan read, "Dedicated to the West Indians and the Panama Canal."

Young helped Westerman get his start, though he was able to pay very little. Over the next decades, Westerman rose to sports editor and eventually became associate editor. His specialty became the Canal Zone, where he had grown up and had many friends and neighbors. He often used contacts among the canal's messengers and clerical staff to get confidential papers and information, enabling him to scoop the other dailies. Although he often criticized decisions by Zone officials, he did so thoughtfully and responsibly, unlike the Spanish-language dailies, which saved their most vitriolic prose for denouncing the gringos. In this way, Westerman developed a working relationship with Zone administrators, who often consulted with or confided in him regarding changes in labor policy likely to affect the West Indian community.

In 1933, Westerman began publishing a column in the *Panama American* (undoubtedly to Young's displeasure) under his own byline. It was called the "Passing Review," and it broadened and developed Westerman's writing skills. First, he now had a much larger readership, including many Americans residing in the Canal Zone. This required him to moderate his prose and find a voice acceptable to a heterogeneous audience. He also wrote on a much broader range of topics, from current arts to politics, and from international affairs to life in the Zone labor camps. He developed an authority during these years that provided him with stature in the various communities of Panama, even among the Latin Panamanians. By the early 1940s his publisher even began to pay him a modest fee for the column.

During the 1930s, Westerman had begun assuming a leadership role in the black communities of the Zone and Panama City. For example, he was inducted into the Odd Fellows lodge and, later, served as president of his Masonic lodge for several years. He was one of Panama's tennis stars and also promoted sporting events. He was especially active in the 1938 Central American Olympic Games, hosted by Panama. In these and other ways, Westerman became known as a young man on the rise.

Westerman's career blossomed in the 1940s. He developed into a leader among the young of the Canal Zone and simultaneously gained a reputation as an intellectual. One of his major undertakings was to help found a library and high school in La Boca, his Zone neighborhood. The first step was the establishment of the "Black Hall of Fame." He wrote to a large number of black leaders in the United States—people like Ralph Bunche, W. E. B. Du Bois, and Paul Robeson—and requested ten-by-twelve-inch autographed photos. These were to be displayed in the school, as an inspiration to the Zone's black children. They also introduced the young intellectual to prominent blacks in the United States.

The second step was to convince school authorities that a library would be a good investment. Until that time, black children had little access to books and other reading materials. Westerman and the other library promoters argued that the facility would keep youngsters occupied in constructive ways and thereby reduce juvenile delinquency and idleness. They raised enough funds in the Canal Zone and among West Indian businesses to purchase a thousand books. The library, duly inaugurated in 1943, also housed the fifty Hall of Fame photographs Westerman had collected.

Then he and others campaigned to extend the Zone's colored school curriculum into the high-school grades, something that the racist superintendent had resisted for decades. As part of this campaign, Westerman published his first major writing, *A Plea for Higher Education of Negroes in the Canal Zone*, and he and his colleagues persuaded scores of people, including Eleanor Roosevelt, to support their proposal. The superintendent bowed to the pressure and added several grades during the war, and, in 1946, two full-fledged high-school buildings were inaugurated.

Finally, Westerman served as counselor for the Isthmian Negro Youth Congress, a YMCA-like organization formed in the early 1940s. Among other duties, he directed publication of the *Bulletin*, which was put out by the group and became a literary vehicle for bright youngsters of the next generation.

Not all of Westerman's activities focused on youth in these years. The entire West Indian community found itself threatened by an outbreak of chauvinism and racism. In 1941, President Arnulfo Arias (1940–41) promulgated a constitution and several laws that withdrew citizenship rights and employment freedom from the majority of the West Indians and their descendants. His successor, Ricardo Adolfo de la Guardia, continued to persecute members of the immigrant community. In response, West Indian leaders mobilized various petition campaigns, legal challenges, and political movements aimed at blunting the attack. Westerman took part in all of these actions, organizing several himself.

Out of these efforts emerged a local organization, the National Civic League (LCN), that played a role similar to that of the National Association for the Advancement of Colored People in the United States. It differed from the lodges and benevolent societies of the 1920s and 1930s in several ways: the LCN did not have formal ties to groups outside of Panama; it invited members from the more enlightened quarters of Latin Panamanian society; it sought to influence public opinion broadly, by publishing pamphlets in Spanish as well as English; and it moved toward active involvement in national politics. Westerman served as director of research for the LCN in the late 1940s and published several pamphlets in its series.

Westerman made an important employment change in the 1940s, becoming secretary to and office manager for the superintendent of Panama's national brewery. His boss, Ernestito de la Guardia (no relation to Adolfo), belonged to a prominent elite family and would eventually become president of Panama. Partly through his influence, Westerman would later be thrust into national politics.

The postwar years saw several important developments in the West Indian community, changes in which Westerman played key if controversial roles. First, canal management finally allowed the Congress of Industrial Organizations (CIO) to unionize its silver workers, under the auspices of the United Public Workers of America (UPWA), Local 713. The international sent a number of organizers to Panama, several of whom had leftist tendencies and promoted confrontation with Zone authorities. In 1949 and 1950, Westerman and others conducted a campaign against the leadership of Local 713 and managed to have them removed. Another CIO affiliate took over, and Westerman and his group gained considerable prestige.

Second, competitive politics had returned to Panama after the war, and the community of West Indian descendants came to play a pivotal part in elections. In recognition of this fact, candidates actively courted the "West Indian vote," more commonly called the criollo vote. Gradually, local leaders gained appointive and elective offices and worked precincts for Latin Panamanian politicians and parties. Criollo voters constituted a majority in Colón province and a substantial minority in Panama province, so they had a significant impact in national elections. In several contests, criollos voted in bloc for the winning side and acquired considerable leverage.

Westerman, who had been promoted to associate editor of the *Panama Tribune*, to which he had moved his "Passing Review" column, decided not to take sides publicly in politics. Young and he believed that the paper could play a more important part by remaining neutral and helping to define issues for the political debate. So scrupulously did they adhere to this policy that in 1948 they accepted paid ads for presidential candidate Arnulfo Arias, archenemy of the West Indian community.

Despite this official neutrality, Westerman played a major part in forming behind-the-scenes alliances and coalitions of criollo voters. He acted as broker and senior statesman, not as a politician. In recognition for such services, Westerman received Panama's highest honor, the Vasco Núñez de Balboa medal, in 1953.

Finally, in the late 1940s Westerman began to receive invitations to participate in international scholarly meetings. These were prompted by his publications in several journals and by his reputation among foreigners who visited Panama to teach or conduct research. For example, in 1950 and 1953 he attended the First and Second World Congresses of Sociologists and Political Scientists. He took advantage of these trips to make friendships and acquaintances throughout the Western world, especially with black and Third World politicians and intellectuals.

In the late 1950s, Westerman reached the pinnacle of his career in terms of breadth of activities and influence. His boss Ernestito de la Guardia won the 1956 election for president and took Westerman into his kitchen cabinet. The latter had been instrumental in lining up support for de la Guardia among criollo voters, and he soon was called upon to recommend appointments and other favors for leaders in the community. For the next four years, Westerman served as de la Guardia's assistant for West Indian affairs. One of his first initiatives was to draft a law, modeled on one in Brazil, prohibiting racial discrimination. The bill easily won legislative approval.

Westerman himself was appointed Panama's ambassador to the United Nations and attended General Assembly meetings between 1956 and 1960. This was not simply a reward for political favors: Westerman had gained a distinguished reputation in Panama and abroad, and he worked especially well with delegates from Third World countries. During and after his term as ambassador, Westerman represented Panama in a number of international capacities. He also tried to attract foreign investors to Panama.

Only the death of Sidney Young in 1959 marred the successes of these years. Westerman returned from New York to console the family, and he offered to buy the *Panama Tribune* from Young's widow. The agreement they reached allowed Westerman to keep the paper alive and provided savings from which the family could live.

The 1960s brought trouble to the West Indian community, and Westerman's authority began to fade as well. For one thing, the flag riots of 1964 led to treaty negotiations with the United States and a possible threat to the welfare of the black workers in the Canal Zone. The debates and insecurity drove wedges between leaders and followers and undermined the once-solid community. Moreover, Arnulfo Arias ran for president in the 1964 and 1968 elections and drew surprising support from criollo voters. They seemed no longer to remember his sins from the 1940s and believed that he would protect them. Westerman actively opposed Arnulfo in 1964 (he lost) but switched to his side in 1968 (he won). Westerman's about-face angered many blacks and caused them to desert him. A new generation of leaders asserted itself before its predecessor was ready to relinquish command.

A more subtle but equally erosive process, under way for some time but clearly visible by the 1960s, was the decline of the West Indian subculture. The community had been cemented together by church and club, school and team, as well as by a common language and heritage. Even those who had lived in the Canal Zone managed to keep alive the legacy of the Caribbean Islands. But by the time the third generation came of age, their collective memory of the West Indies had all but disappeared. Instead, social pressure from Latin Panamanians caused many to hispanicize their names, abandon English, and convert to Catholicism. Assimilationist influences were especially strong in the public schools. In this way, the West Indian community began to dwindle in importance, its leaders considered merely "old-timers."

Signs of the erosion of the West Indian subculture could be seen everywhere. The last of the benevolent societies closed. The Protestant churches reported shrinking congregations. A generation gap appeared, signaled when youths adopted black power symbols and provoked confrontations with their elders. Westerman deplored such developments and scolded readers in his editorials, but fewer and fewer persons listened. Bilingual newspapers cut back their English sections, and eventually the *Panama Tribune* went bankrupt in 1972 (due partly to government disfavor).

Since the early 1970s, Westerman has been semiretired and has dedicated himself to research and writing. In 1980, the government published a text of his in Spanish, *Los inmigrantes antillanos en Panamá.* He has been invited on several speaking tours, principally in the United States. Over the years, many Panamanians of West Indian descent have settled in the United States, and Westerman is an important contact for them. In the mid-1980s he worked on a full-scale book entitled *Fifty Years of West Indian Life in Panama, 1903–1953*.

Westerman is regarded as the senior statesman and intellectual of the West Indian community. He dedicated his life to helping his people make a home in Panama, using his considerable powers of explanation and persuasion. He fought discrimination with a fervor equal to that of his colleagues in the United States, with whom he remained in touch most of his career. He came to excel in the Latin Panamanian community and won recognition for his talents.

SOURCES

Virtually all material relating to George Westerman is based upon a series of interviews with him in 1981 and upon his correspondence, books, clippings, and back issues of the *Panama Tribune*. Information about the West Indians who worked for the Panama Canal is from Record Group 59, National Archives, Washington, DC. Perspectives on the relations between the West Indian community and the Latin Panamanians came primarily from newspapers and interviews.

BIBLIOGRAPHY

Biesanz, John, and Biesanz, Mavis. *The People of Panama*. New York, 1955.

Conniff, Michael L. *Black Labor on a White Canal: Panama, 1904–1981*. Pittsburgh, 1985.

LaFeber, Walter. *The Panama Canal: The Crisis in Historical Perspective*. 2d ed., rev. New York, 1979.

McCullough, David. *The Path between the Seas: The Creation of the Panama Canal, 1870–1914*. New York, 1977.

11

Ligia Parra Jahn: The Blonde with the Revolver

Judith Ewell

Judith Ewell first encountered the story of Ligia Parra Jahn as she thumbed through Venezuelan newspapers of the 1940s in search of news of the Venezuelan military dictator Marcos Pérez Jiménez. For Ewell, reading about Ligia's struggles with the traditional concepts of honor and *vergüenza* (shame) proved a welcome relief from Pérez's reorganization of the General Staff. Finally, Ligia's turn has come.

On one level Ligia's story belonged on a newspaper's last page, the one reserved for tawdry crimes and gory traffic accidents. Yet her respectability, her beauty, and her argument that a woman should be allowed to defend her own honor, vigilante-style, struck a chord among many of her compatriots. Women recognized some of their own dilemmas and humiliations in Ligia's plight. Venezuelan men often felt protective toward the young blonde and resentment toward the Basque adventurer who had disgraced her. Traditionalists believed that Ligia's freedom not only caused her tragedy but also threatened the web of custom and decency that binds society together.

Professor of history at the College of William and Mary, Ewell has published *The Indictment of a Dictator: The Extradition and Trial of Marcos Pérez Jiménez* (College Station, TX, 1981) and *Venezuela: A Century of Change* (Stanford, 1984).

Ligia Parra Jahn was born in 1927 at the moment when youthful challenges to the dictatorship of Juan Vicente Gómez (1908–35) indicated that the "autumn of the patriarch" had begun in Venezuela. Yet traditional cultural values lingered longer than did the caudillo system and filled the emerging modern political and economic system with contradictions. Women's roles and attitudes illustrate the tensions inherent in a system undergoing rapid political change. Women accepted jobs outside the home and responsibilities in the nascent political parties. The new political generations lauded women's political and economic participation without fully recognizing the challenge that it brought to the lingering cultural definitions of honor and *vergüenza*.

Hispanic custom dictated that a family's honor was intertwined with the chastity of its women. Legal codes granted the father of the family, or its oldest male, the exclusive right to guide and protect his family. If he attacked or killed another male who threatened his family, the law usually exonerated him. In particular, the patriarch of the family could not overlook the affront if another male had sexual relations with any of the women—his wife, sister, daughters—under his protection. The offense was compounded if others knew of the slip and ridiculed the man who had been unable to defend his family. Even though the suggestion of a woman's sexual activity shamed the entire family, women played an essentially passive role in the honor-*vergüenza* drama. Women, traditionally and legally considered weak, depended on male family members to protect them and their family's honor. What was to become of this network of traditions when women left the shelter of the family patio for the business office?

The beginning of commercial oil exploitation in Venezuela in the 1920s affected the nation and women's lives in unanticipated ways. The foreign companies, and the service economy they spawned, required a host of literate Venezuelan white-collar and clerical workers. Increased government revenues also supported the expansion of the Venezuelan government bureaucracy, especially after 1936 when the government put in place a minimal system of social services. Women became nurses for the oil camp hospitals, secretaries and receptionists and file clerks for the foreign companies and the new government offices, office workers for the burgeoning group of lawyers and other professionals who dealt with the companies, teachers for the schools in the camps and elsewhere, and clerks in the new commercial establishments which sprang up in the cities. Venezuelans did not immediately recognize the implications of these changes, but there came to be a small space in female society between the idle and respectable—and bored—upper-class women and their poorer sisters who enjoyed neither the luxury of male protection nor the social accolade of honor as they labored in fields, kitchens, bars, bedrooms. Subtly, the changes in the labor market would challenge the rather Manichaean way of viewing women as virgins or whores. Was a woman from a respectable family less respectable if she worked in public with men? Should she follow the behavior patterns and values of the sheltered upper-class or those of the less sheltered, more independent working-class women?

Like most children, Ligia Parra Jahn was oblivious to such weighty issues as she grew up in the 1930s. She lived near the colonial core of Caracas (population of 264,400 in 1936) and close to the Pantheon, the monument that sheltered the remains of Simón Bolívar and of other national heroes. The modest middle-class neighborhood evoked the sleepy past of the "city of the red roofs." It also lay near the new commercial and government offices that the petroleum wealth had spawned.

Ligia adored active games and romping about the neighboring plazas, but she also absorbed the Hispanic traditions of her neighborhood. She especially liked baseball and was one of the few girls who played the game with the neighborhood boys. She attended Amelia Cocking primary school for girls, where she organized a girls' basketball team and played enthusiastically. She also enjoyed bicycling. Even her youthful dreams turned around becoming a sports "star," and she fantasized about sports where a few women had achieved fame. The ritual drama of bullfighting drew her even more than the methodical game of baseball. Her imagination had been fired by seeing the famous bullfighter Conchita Cintrón, and Ligia pleaded to be allowed to take lessons. Her indulgent parents engaged the matador, Mario Núñez, who lived nearby, to tutor her, and she practiced faithfully on the flat roof of her house. Núñez later told a journalist that Ligia had shown promise as a bullfighter, but he must also have cautioned the young girl that the fraternity of *matadores* did not welcome women.

Ligia's love of activity and sports, and her fantasies, continued into her teens. If she had dreamed of a rather traditional Hispanic hero's career—that of bullfighter—she also turned her eyes to some of the newest heroes: airplane pilots. She knew of Amelia Earhart's exploits and determined to become the first woman pilot in Venezuela. The small Venezuelan air force had a training school in the nearby town of Maracay. One day, Ligia set out for Maracay to enlist in the school. On the way, she called home to tell her parents what she was about to do. Her father remonstrated that aviation was not a good career for a *hija de familia* (daughter of good family), for there would be no one to protect her. Señor Parra convinced Ligia that she should return home and prepare for an occupation more suitable to her gender and family position.

Denied the most active and iconoclastic of her fantasies, Ligia still insisted that she could not accept the boring and sheltered life of most middle- and upper-class young women. She dreamed of becoming a writer or a poet or an artist. Perhaps she thought of the romantic life of Venezuelan novelist Teresa de la Parra, who had lived in Paris and Madrid from 1923 until her death from tuberculosis in 1936. Ligia enrolled in painting and sculpture courses at the Escuela de Artes Plastícos, but more pragmatically, she also completed a secretarial course at one of the new business academies that had sprung up in Caracas. In 1947, at age nineteen, Ligia became one of the first secretaries of the dental division of the Social Security office. Her job had not existed a decade earlier, for there had been no social security system or state health care in Venezuela until after Gómez's death. Her parents were not enthusiastic about her job, but they may have decided that headstrong Ligia was better off as an office worker than as a bullfighter or an aviator. At least she still lived at home where her parents could protect her. While employed, Ligia enrolled in night school to work toward a high-school diploma, a mildly unusual ambition in a country in which only 16 percent of the high-school graduates were women. By 1948 she had successfully completed two years of high school.

Ligia's training and education set her apart from many of her contemporaries. She also could have confidently applied for any job that required that the employee be *de buena presencia* (attractive). Ligia was a striking blonde, fair skinned and slender, a younger edition of Evita Perón, who was then the first lady of Argentina. Ligia enjoyed buying new clothes with her earnings, and photographs of her in 1948 show a stylishly dressed and attractive young woman.

After a few months, Ligia left her job with the Social Security office and began to work at a wholesale drug firm owned by Pedro Penzini Hernández. She liked the job and her coworkers, and, by all accounts, she was a capable and responsible employee. Ligia still enjoyed being active, and she balanced the sedentary life of her clerical job by exercising at a Swedish gymnasium on Saturdays.

Although iconoclastic and restless in some ways, Ligia apparently paid little attention to the swirl of political activity about her. A joint military and civilian conspiracy had unseated General and President Isaías Medina Angarita on October 18, 1945. A civilian government headed by Rómulo Betancourt initiated the three years of unprecedented democratic government known as the *trienio*. Ligia's parents were not politically active, and perhaps they suggested to her, as some parents did, that attendance at political rallies and night meetings could compromise a young girl's reputation.

Women had played a larger role in politics since Gómez's death, both in women's organizations and newly legalized political parties, especially Acción Democrática (AD) and the Partido Comunista de

Venezuela (PCV). President Isaías Medina Angarita (1941–45) had allowed women to vote in municipal elections in 1945, and the *trienio* government decreed that women could vote for and hold office as delegates to the 1946 constituent assembly. Sixteen women won seats in the assembly. The new constitution, promulgated in 1947, granted the right of suffrage to all Venezuelans over the age of eighteen. Many women activists considered that their goals had been achieved with suffrage, and several women's groups dissolved. Other women, like journalist and activist Carmen Clemente Travieso, complained that more important issues of women's economic and civil rights still needed to be addressed.

The male leadership of the two major political parties, AD and the PCV, paid little heed to their women colleagues' tentative proposals to revise the civil and penal codes. Constituent delegates Mercedes Carvajal de Arocha (who wrote under the pen name Lucila Palacios), Panchita Soublette, and Mercedes Fermín, among others, had argued that the state, through a modern constitution and legal codes, should guarantee the civil and social rights of women and children. No longer should women have to rely on the goodwill and wisdom of the family patriarch for protection. When the female delegates offered specific resolutions to transfer to the state the protection of women's rights, their male colleagues sometimes refused even to second or to debate the proposals. More extreme proposals for economic equity also failed: equal pay for equal work, workplace protections for women workers, an eight-hour working day for women domestic servants, day-care centers in factories where women workers could nurse their babies, rural women's rights to the land they worked, and social security for women. In spite of the government's commitment to investment in Venezuela's human resources, none of these proposals received serious consideration.

Journalist Elba Isabel Arráiz concluded that women also contributed to the social climate that blinded the legislators to the dangers of patriarchical control.

> I believe that, in the depth of our souls, we all feel a kind of respectful veneration for the strong man, for the man who dictates the life of all the members of his family and demands that his decisions be respected. We have been brought up that way and most of us have not even thought of rebelling against that imposition.

Some of the female representatives to the constituent assembly also pondered ambiguities of social attitudes toward women. A lawyer with a doctorate in political science, Panchita Soublette Saluzzo, could debate a male colleague in the constituent assembly, but propriety dictated that she could not attend a dance alone with that same colleague. Communist Inés Labrador de Lara could go with fellow party member Gustavo Machado to Caracas jails to gather information about the treatment of prisoners, but she could not eat alone with him in a restaurant without being criticized and embarrassed. Obviously, more than legal codes affected women's behavior in this era of uneasy coexistence between modern and traditional values.

While well-educated and elite women struggled with the issues raised by a patriarchical legal and social system, some simpler women sought autonomy in more traditional ways. *El Nacional* reported the case of María Cristina Arguinzones, whose lover, José Angel Aponte, had left her when he got a good job in the nearby town of Los Teques. Angered and hurt at the abandonment, María Cristina prepared a spell in which she lit a candle, which had been stuck full of pins doused in sugar, in front of José's picture and next to one of his old shoes and some of her underwear. The spell was designed to compel José to return. José's mother, Julia, concerned about her son and his new job, denounced the young woman to the Jefe Civil. The authorities detained María Cristina for practicing witchcraft. Despite her detention, María Cristina must have had the satisfaction of knowing that she had not simply resigned herself to José's abandonment.

Meanwhile, Ligia Parra Jahn had discovered men. In spite of her attractiveness, she had had no *novios*, or boyfriends, before she went to work for Dr. Penzini in 1947. There she met the twenty-five-year-old José María—or Joseba, as he was called—Olasagasti, an accountant who worked in the same firm. Joseba was a Basque who had fought with Francisco Franco's Legión Blanca in Spain and had come to Venezuela in early 1947. Joseba became a well-known and popular member of the Basque community in Caracas, in part because of his skills at the game of jai alai. Charming, attractive, ambitious, foreign, athletic, Joseba attracted women easily, and Ligia was smitten.

The courtship of Ligia and Joseba followed the still traditional patterns of old Caracas. As members of the respectable middle class, Ligia and her family guarded her reputation and family honor as carefully as the more prominent political women of the constituent assembly did theirs. Ligia might have railed at some of the restrictions, but she too realized that eligible bachelors valued propriety—and virginity—highly for their wives, if not for their mistresses. For all of her heroic youthful fantasies, Ligia also dreamed of a happy marriage and children.

Ligia and Joseba saw each other at Dr. Penzini's shop, but they did not go out together alone. Caracas bustled with new nightclubs and excitement in the years following the war, but respectable people considered such "boîtes" as little more than covers for prostitution, as indeed many were. A couple might attend a movie, usually accompanied by family or friends. Most entertainment still revolved around the home and family.

It is worth stressing, however, how small a sector of the Venezuelan population actively shared, or lived by, many of the Parra Jahn family's notions of honor and shame with respect to sexual matters. Venezuela had not had the opulent colonial past that could have spawned a large number of elite families. Economic insecurity, civil wars, and disease conspired to keep the population small, poor, and scattered in the nineteenth century. Changes wrought by oil income, which had come in since the 1920s, and by the rush of foreigners, both those with the oil companies and the immigrants who followed World War II, further encouraged shifts and changes in the economic landscape. A father-patriarch who could not support an extended family often gave way to a household headed by a woman, at least for part of the year. Insecurity of life and income, and the comparatively weak hold of the Catholic Church, meant that relatively few unions were consecrated by matrimony, either ecclesiastical or civil. The case of María Cristina, the spell-caster, is illustrative; when her lover found a better job in a nearby town, he left her. The job may have been better than his Caracas one but perhaps not secure enough to support a family. In the 1940s, over half of all births were illegitimate.

Thus, the old values of honor and shame with respect to sexual purity had eroded considerably by 1948. Indeed, some would argue that they always had reflected the ideal more than the reality in Latin America. Only those families who had social status to preserve—or those who wished to climb up the social scale—could afford the luxury of protecting their women and family honor. Ligia Parra Jahn's virtue and attractiveness might improve her family's status through a successful match with a wealthier or more prominent family. In any case, public possession of honor would ensure that she would at least marry, unlike the less fortunate women who had no family to protect them or who had to work in more compromising situations.

Felipe Parra Barrios initially opposed Joseba's courtship of his daughter. Joseba was a worldly foreigner with no real roots in Caracas. Moreover, many Venezuelans retained a residual resentment of Basques dating from the eighteenth century when a Basque mercantile company had had a monopoly of Venezuelan trade; the Basque traders and governors had prompted hatred and rebellion because of their high-handedness and arrogance. The post–World War II flood of European immigrants in general also met with mixed reactions from Venezuelans.

Headstrong as always, Ligia pleaded for Joseba to be allowed to visit her. In August 1947, Sr. Parra allowed his reservations to be overcome and told Joseba that he was welcome as a guest in the Parra home. The paternal permission was tantamount to accepting him as a prospective son-in-law, a status of "engaged to be engaged." Ligia was radiant, forgetting all of her earlier heroic ambitions in favor of the more traditional one of marriage to the man she loved. Having won his case, Joseba probably paid little heed to Sr. Parra Barrios's admonition, "Be careful what you do in my home. . . . Be careful!"

After a few months, Joseba became restless, and he stopped visiting Ligia. She became despondent and depressed, causing her parents and friends to ask what was wrong. She finally confessed to her parents that Joseba had told her that he would not see her anymore, that his father opposed his getting married. More seriously, Ligia told her parents that she and Joseba had had sexual relations. Ligia's parents acted promptly, consulted a lawyer, and threatened Joseba that they would take legal action if he did not keep the pledge that had been implicit—but public—in his frequent visits to the Parra Jahn home. Cornered by Ligia's parents, Joseba returned and formalized his engagement to Ligia before parish officials. The lovers also exchanged rings. Ligia and her family accepted the young Basque back into the home, perhaps judging that he had just gotten nervous at the thought of marriage. In any case, Ligia's reputation and honor were safe if she married Joseba. Ligia even agreed to give up her job at the Penzini firm when Joseba said he did not want his future wife to continue working.

Joseba's promises and concern proved short-lived. In mid-July 1948, Joseba wrote Ligia:

> I have to confess to you that I have been acting out a role before your father. . . . I love you, that is true, but not enough to marry you. You deserve a better partner than I. It is best that you forget me. Forget me! I will not marry you now or ever.

Ligia did not tell her parents or her lawyer about Joseba's new treachery. She devised her own plan to try to save her honor and perhaps the man she loved. She wrote Joseba that she thought that she was pregnant. Desperately, she begged him in the name of their child to marry her just for a few days in a civil ceremony. She would release him later. If he would not, she told him that she was considering suicide, since life without honor would hold no future for her.

His veneer of patience and chivalry worn thin, Joseba wrote back that he had decided to break off with her definitively. Rubbing salt in her emotional wounds, he added that he did not care if she was the most disgraced, unhappy woman on earth.

Ligia heard rumors that Joseba was courting other women. He also gossiped with his friends about her. In the relatively small Caracas middle class, and with Joseba's prominence as a jai alai player, Ligia's reputation would be ruined. She was not only rejected but also humiliated by a man who had used her, thrown her aside, and then laughed about her to his friends. Joseba's father, who was also in Caracas, had referred to Ligia as a *mulata* and said that his son must marry someone of his own "race."

Ligia waited. Did she hope that Joseba would repent and return to her? Was she deciding whether again to ask her parents to have the lawyer threaten Joseba? Or was she simply hoping that her menstrual period would start and at least she would not have to suffer through a pregnancy? When she went to a clinic on August 4 for a pregnancy test, she was so nervous that a nurse prescribed a tranquilizer for her. Ligia had received a number of anonymous phone calls telling her about Joseba's activities. The one she received on Thursday, August 5, was different. The male voice taunted Ligia with the news that she would never win Joseba. He had booked passage back to Spain and would leave Venezuela in a few days. Then, humiliation again, the voice gave a loud laugh and hung up. The phone call ended Ligia's hope and her indecision. Recalling the moment later, she said that she had thought of a sports metaphor: "a player who risks nothing, neither wins nor loses."

The next day, Friday morning, Ligia dressed carefully in a gray cashmere suit with red trim, put on matching red shoes, picked up her red purse, and told her parents that she was going to visit a friend. She went to Penzini's office and entered to chat with some of her former colleagues at 9:15 A.M. Joseba was in an inner office with Dr. Penzini. He came to the outer office to fetch something, and Ligia greeted him. He didn't speak to her, only shrugging his shoulders disparagingly as he returned to Penzini's office. Ligia entered the inner office and nodded to Dr. Penzini. She stopped about six feet away from Joseba, drew a Smith and Wesson revolver from an inner pocket of her jacket, and shot Joseba twice before he had a chance to move. The bullets entered Joseba's neck and chest, and he died an hour and a half later at the Córdoba Clinic.

Ligia calmly walked out of the inner office, revolver in hand, and headed toward the street. When Adrian Urarte, a colleague of Joseba's, tried to take the revolver from her, she fired two more shots, which buzzed harmlessly about the office. Penzini's stupefied staff let her leave the building. The poised young blonde hailed a cab and told the driver to take her to the police station, for she had just killed a man.

The cab driver obediently drove her to the police station where she gave herself up. Her father and brother then met her at the judge's chambers where she rendered her first official statement. Her father asked her, "Ligia, why didn't you leave that job to me?" Ligia replied, "You are old and my mother needs you." She had not called on her brother to avenge her honor, because his career would have been ruined if he had had to go to jail. After all of her suffering and disgrace, Ligia said, going to jail meant nothing to her.

Word traveled quickly in Caracas, and Ligia faced a crowd of over one thousand curious *caraqueños* when she left Dr. Jesús Enrique González's courtroom at one o'clock. Dr. Panchita Soublette Saluzzo was in the crowd and one of the first to shake Ligia's hand and offer her sympathy.

The following day, Ligia again was closeted with judges and lawyers for seven hours to explain her actions. Ligia told the authorities that her love for Joseba had turned to hatred when she had been humiliated and taunted so publicly. She realized that her future was bleak, that Joseba had ruined her chances for a happy marriage and family. Only his death could compensate for the dishonor she had suffered. She concluded, "And let it be known that women too know how to defend their honor."

Ligia provided several challenges to the Venezuelan penal system. The most immediate dilemma was where to detain her during the long trial process. There was no jail for women, and only recently had the first female warden been appointed to supervise and discipline female prisoners. Ironically, the warden, twenty-one-year-old Delia Alemán, had been a school chum of Ligia's. Delia allowed Ligia to stay in her own apartment at the Cárcel Modelo (Model Jail).

Journalists avidly followed the sensational case and were fascinated by Ligia's apparent serenity and lack of tears. With her brother and sister and the warden and another friend, Ligia received reporters in the warden's office on August 7. She told the press that she had lived a happy and tranquil life until Joseba had publicly humiliated her, her family, and even the authorities before whom he had promised to marry her.

> What hope do I have now? To marry immediately, or never to marry. I had always dreamed of what all women dream of: a man to love me, an upright and virtuous home, children. If I had not dreamed so much of this, I believe that I would never have done what I did . . . but I was a dead woman morally. At least, that's how I felt.

Reporters, and Venezuelans, disagreed on what the real crime had been, who had committed it, who should be punished, and how. Part of the ambiguity lay with the seventy-six-year-old penal code, which retained much of the Mediterranean interpretation of honor and the patriarchical value system. A man who killed in order to defend, or repair, his own or his family's honor explicitly was exempted from punishment. The traditional code, however, did not recognize that a woman had honor that she could avenge on her own. Could Ligia, then, legitimately plead self-defense, or defense of her honor, as an extenuating circumstance?

Strict constructionists and traditionalists said that Ligia had shamed herself and her family by surrendering herself sexually to Joseba. She then compounded her offense by killing Joseba, in effect punishing him for her own weakness. The prosecuting attorney presented the strongest statement of the traditional argument. Poet and essayist Rafael Olivares Figueroa elaborated on the value of women's chastity when he wrote in *El País* that society had a responsibility to promulgate traditional moral and sexual education. Satisfaction of all desires did not bring happiness, he argued, especially for women. If women were allowed excessive sexual freedom, he believed that home and children would suffer. Those who had slipped, like single mothers, needed special guidance and rehabilitation.

In contrast, Ligia's defenders compared her to Joan of Arc and quoted from the seventeenth-century Mexican poet, Sor Juana Inés de la Cruz. "Hombres necios, que acusáis a la mujer sin razón, sin ver que sois la ocasión de lo mismo que culpáis." ("Ignorant men, who accuse women unjustly, without seeing that you are the cause of the crime that you reproach them for.") They argued that the penal code had not kept up with women's changing roles in society. Women journalists such as Juana de Avila, Teresa Troconis, Peregrino Pérez, Isabel Jiménez Arráiz de Díaz, and Ana Mercedes Pérez made the case that Ligia had been forced to act because the judicial system provided no protection for her. Women no longer remained at home where male relatives could defend them. The state should take on the patriarchical role and enact severe penalties for the breach of a prematrimonial contract. Juana de Avila argued that the tribunals did not recognize male sexual irresponsibility as a crime, even when a respectable woman had been publicly disgraced. Ligia Parra Jahn had taken justice into her own hands to punish a crime that men committed with impunity against women every day.

Isabel Jiménez Arráiz de Díaz added that Joseba had acted as if he had thought that a feudal, colonial right of conquest still existed. Ligia's action was especially justified against a foreigner who had abused Venezuelan hospitality. If men could defend their honor, then why couldn't women?

Teresa Troconis gave a popular reason for the state to intervene to protect women from Don Juans—at least until men became accustomed enough to the new social rules so that they could restrain themselves. She wrote:

> The feminine soul is made of passion; woman more than man lives for love; love is both an end and a means, since through it she achieves the realization of her destiny: motherhood. Thus, woman puts all in love, her heart, her honor and her courage. To deceive her when she has wholly given herself destroys all her strength, all her moral aspirations and all her emotional balance.

Male jurist Luis Cova García agreed that the legal system must give special consideration to women's nature. "In women to think and to feel are two inseparable actions, a thing which does not occur in men." Women's biological role so affects their psychology and their will that they should not be held fully accountable for crimes they commit. Women can vote, hold public offices, enter the liberal professions, compete with men, but their social salvation still is love and marriage.

Juana de Avila touched another chord when she asserted that many women saw Ligia as an avenging angel, a symbol of "just vengeance which has collected for all the pain and suffering that thousands of women have had to endure for their whole lives." Spokespersons for women's associations expressed a kinship with Ligia. Sra. Caridad de Novel, president of the Asociación Venezolana de Mujeres, said, "As a woman . . . it is my duty to be on the side of Ligia Parra Jahn, through a natural sense of fellowship not only feminine, but eminently human." Ana Senior de Delgado, of the Agrupación Cultural Femenina, said that she did not condone violence, but she thought that Ligia's action was a natural consequence of the omissions in the legal codes with regard to the rights of women. She hoped that the legislators would be encouraged to pass laws that are "more just and humane for those eternal social slaves that we women are."

Ligia's defense attorney, Dr. Juan Antonio Gonzalo Patrizi, in Ligia's October 13 court audience, confirmed some of the women's arguments when he said that he was acting not only for Ligia but also for all women. Ligia symbolized women who found that man-made laws did not aid them and those who had cried in silence or turned to prostitution when they had been dishonored by a man.

A few perceptive observers found the real root of the tragedy beyond the penal code, men's perfidy, or women's weakness. Cultural traditions and values, often nurtured by gossip, limited modern women as much as the laws did. Juana de Avila concluded that society must bear some of the responsibility. Society had instituted marriage for women's protection, and a woman who engaged in sex prior to marriage might be guilty of foolishly stepping beyond the boundaries of a shelter that was provided for her. But the same society that admired a man who had an active sex life punished a woman for her entire life for the same behavior. Why should it be a crime for a woman to give herself for love or to have a child without a father? Teresa Troconis agreed. Society, as well as the law, retained anachronistic whiffs of the past. Single mothers frequently could not even secure respectable jobs. Troconis pointed out that Ligia had killed Joseba not because he had left her but because he had left her in an unbearable social position. Avila and Troconis suggested that all those who ostracized single mothers bore some responsibility for actions like Ligia's.

While the debate continued about her, Ligia's body betrayed the surface calm with which she had handled the affair. She took tranquilizers to ward off nervous depression and to be able to sleep. Some of Joseba's Basque friends heightened her anguish. On August 8, an anonymous telephone call to the jail threatened, "You know that you have caused the death of a Basque and there are several of us who are ready to avenge his death. You will die to pay for your crime." Friends had told her brother Luis that they had heard of various people who had sworn to punish Ligia for her action. Her health continued to deteriorate during the long trial, especially when she had been moved from the relative comfort of the warden's apartment to a small, dark, and cold cell far in the back of the Cárcel Modelo. Her pregnancy had either been a false alarm, or her nervous state and poor health caused a miscarriage.

A hearing on October 13 established the defense arguments that Ligia had acted in self-defense to save her honor and thus should not be penalized. The prosecuting attorney rejected the plea of self-defense and asked for a five-to-six-year sentence. Lengthy court proceedings were normal, but the November 24 military revolt that terminated the democratic government may have been bad luck for Ligia. Her defenders had been more closely identified with the democratic opening than with the old caudillo system. The military junta headed by Carlos Delgado Chalbaud hardly represented a return to the caudillo past, but they did have more sympathy with the authoritarian and patriarchical codes. They quickly outlawed political parties and labor unions. In April 1949 they reestablished relations with Spain, not a good omen for a person charged with killing a Spaniard.

In January 1949, Ligia's defense attorney tested the waters. He asked the president of the junta to allow Ligia to transfer to a hospital or some similar institution, under full security. The penal code allowed such treatment for women prisoners who had already been sentenced. Since Ligia had not even been sentenced—and, of course, ultimately would be absolved because her action had been in defense of honor—she should be allowed to leave the Cárcel Modelo, not a good environment for a refined young woman.

Delgado Chalbaud turned a deaf ear to Ligia's plea, and she remained in jail while the process dragged on. Her lawyer died, and she secured a new one. On November 13, 1950, some thugs kidnapped and murdered Delgado Chalbaud. Marcos Pérez Jiménez became the obvious strong man, although he refrained from having himself named president. The political climate became more oppressive.

Two weeks after Delgado's assassination, the judge finally handed down Ligia's sentence. Reporters and an interested public packed the courtroom on November 30 to hear the judge read the sentence for two and one-half hours. Ana Mercedes Pérez heard gasps of disbelief when Ligia was sentenced to seven and one-half years in jail. The two years, three months, and twenty-four days that the trial had lasted would be subtracted from the sentence. The judge reasoned that Joseba had done nothing more serious than break a prematrimonial contract, a privilege that a person might take with any contract. Joseba's friends had testified that he was not sexually promiscuous. On the other hand, Ligia could not argue that Joseba had publicly shamed her; she had been the one to confess their relations when she had hired the first lawyer to force Joseba to honor his pledge. Ligia's plea of self-defense had no basis in law.

Ana Mercedes Pérez began lobbying in earnest to have the young woman released. In 1951, Pérez published an account of Ligia's tragedy entitled *Yo acuso a un muerto*. The book was a commercial success, but it also brought the journalist some hate mail and threats, especially from Basques and Spaniards. She followed up her first book with a second one, dedicated to Ligia's parents, which annotated and commented on Judge Monsalve's sentence. She hoped that her book might have some effect on any appeals. Pérez concluded that Judge Monsalve had "acted in favor of those of his own sex" and that he did Venezuela a great disservice to rule that, in effect, it did not matter if men did not keep their word.

The appeals fell on deaf ears until December 1952 when Ligia's sentence was reduced. She was allowed to leave jail after having served four years and four months of her sentence. She dropped from sight, after her time in the limelight. Newspapers devoted only a few lines to her quiet marriage to José Rafael Alfaro Ucero on March 21, 1953.

Venezuelans, however, did not forget Ligia Parra Jahn. In 1984 the Venezuelan essayist and playwright Elisa Lerner published "The Dangerous Criminality of Blondes." Lerner compared Ligia with the blonde Hollywood vamps of the 1940s or the gun molls in a Raymond Chandler novel, but with a Hispanic twist.

> The love story of the blonde Venezuelan girl was depressing. When she killed the boyfriend who had *dishonored her*—throughout masculine centuries the term has been used: female virginity was a sealed trunk that only the respectable key of matrimony could open—and had promised her eternal love (read: *legal love*), in part, she was killing herself.

Lerner continued, stating that "any society where blondes emerge sets in motion ill-omened threads of castastrophe. . . . Blonde hair—cooked up at the mischievous hairdresser's—in essence, is a strong warning that a country is going through an ambiguous or agonizing time."

SOURCES

For material directly pertaining to Ligia Parra Jahn, see two books by the journalist Ana Mercedes Pérez: *Yo acuso a un muerto* (Caracas, 1951) and *La sentencia "Ligia Parra Jahn"* (Caracas, 1951). Elisa Lerner's "La criminal peligrosidad de las rubias," in *Crónicas ginecológicas* (Caracas, 1984), is an evocative essay by a contemporary Venezuelan feminist. The newspaper *El Nacional* followed the Parra Jahn case closely in late 1948 and also devoted considerable attention to women's issues during the *trienio*. Other newspapers, such as *El Universal, El País, La Esfera, Ultimas Noticias*, and *Tribuna Popular*, also covered the Parra Jahn case. The more conservative papers, such as *El Universal*, gave minimal, rather matter-of-fact coverage to the case, whereas the papers with more leftist sympathies (the communist *Tribuna Popular*, *El Nacional*, the Acción Democrática's *El País*) covered the case extensively and openly sided with the young woman.

J. G. Peristiany and others discuss the concepts of honor and shame in J. G. Peristiany, ed., *Honour and Shame: The Values of Mediterranean Society* (London, 1966); and José Ramón López Gómez's *El culto a la virginidad* (Valencia, Venezuela, 1984) explores historical attitudes toward virginity.

Two novels by Venezuelan authors are useful for catching a glimpse of the lives of Venezuelan women: Teresa de la Parra, *Ifigenia: Diario de una señorita que escribió porque se fastidiaba* (originally published in 1924); and Antonia Palacios, *Ana Isabel, una niña decente* (originally published in 1949).

12

Carlos Gardel and the Tango

Harold Guy Bensusan

Guy Bensusan combines an interest in music and Latin American culture in his teaching at Northern Arizona University and as a visiting professor at Western Carolina University in Cullowhee, North Carolina, and in the Semester at Sea program. Bensusan used his expertise in the field of Latin American music to write, produce, and broadcast "Roots and Rhythms," fifty-two hour-long programs for National Public Radio on Latin America's varied musical heritage. This program, still being used by numerous colleges and schools, was broadcast in twenty-six states and nine foreign countries. With his wife, Lieselotte Hornung, Bensusan regularly gives lessons in Latin American dance at museums and cultural institutes. He also offers guitar lessons on public television. His love for the music of Argentina, where he lived and taught for some years, led Bensusan to the master of the people's music, Carlos Gardel, and to the tango.

The following biography of Gardel helps explain the popularity of the tango and of its greatest artist. Gardel regained an international audience in 1986 with the tremendously successful U.S. tour by the dance spectacular *Tango Argentino*. Today, from Toronto to Tierra del Fuego, Gardel's followers gather in the many Argentine restaurants that still display his photograph. Bensusan explains the rise of the tango, its popularity among migrants to the city, and the opposition to it from social elites.

What does the life of a Buenos Aires cabaret singer and cinema celebrity reveal about the human tradition in Latin America? Carlos Gardel became an international success. Audiences packed his colorful and dramatic presentations. Men as well as women of all ages adored and worshiped him. His personal journey from poverty as an immigrant child to slum street singer and then to fame, stardom, wealth, and friendship with the mighty symbolized the Argentine dream of individual opportunity. His life became a myth: people in the Americas and Europe sang his lyrics and imitated his gestures, his facial expressions, his haughty demeanor, his stance—and wept inconsolably at his fiery death in a still unexplained Colombian plane crash in June 1935.

Perishing as he did at a high point in a dazzling career, Gardel remains a success in retrospect. One cannot study the tango without focusing on Gardel's special contributions to that musical style. His tomb in Buenos Aires attracts tourists and residents even today. His movies are rerun, his recordings reprocessed and reissued, while a stream of books, verses, tangos and other songs, memorabilia, and articles continue to appear. He never faded away; we never had to see him old or failing. He is always in his prime.

Our fascination, however, is ironic. Gardel owed his success to the fact that he sang about hard times and tough lives, that he expressed the struggle of the "oppressed masses" in their own street slang, and that he postured and modeled for his public a stoic endurance of personal gain and emotional disappointment. He challenged fear. He flaunted anguish. He fought alone; in the symbolic bullring of life, he played the matador, a solitary figure facing the overwhelming beast, both real and figurative. Gardel defied the perils of progress.

Paradoxically, Gardel's very success was made possible through the technology and fabric of the modern life that his lyrics implicitly criticized. The transformation of Buenos Aires had occurred by the turn of the century because of the explosion of industry and commerce (especially, the modern meat-packing industry that arose with the invention of refrigeration); the flow of population to the city; the construction of houses, slums, wide streets, and avenues, with a modern urban transportation network to pull them together; and an unprecedented prosperity. This progress also gave birth to a diverse entertainment business, which both engaged the newly urban people and mirrored their conditions.

Through radio, personal appearances, movies, recordings, pamphlets, photographs, newspapers, and magazines, Gardel became an image, a role model. He personified sadness, squalor, suppression, struggle, sexuality, and solitude—a lower-class complex with which many Argentines, poor or rich, identified. The media broadcast the message, taking Gardel's drama from the pampas to Patagonia to the Andes and beyond. The public participated in and shared his image of defiance.

Technology also carried Gardel's image across the Atlantic to Europe, allowing him to appeal to a broader audience, caught up in the pessimism and disillusion that followed World War I. A sizable group of wealthy Argentines who lived in the revered and prestigious cultural setting of Paris, and whose lives in no genuine way reflected the "low-life" tango, now discovered it. They embraced it, and affected in their speech and comportment the soul of melancholy and blasé, impassive coolness popularized by their singing hero. The real Parisians applauded the antics of the rich visitors, participated in their dramatic, and sometimes outrageous, escapades, and privately remained convinced of the cultural inferiority of those "rustic, unrefined, neocolonials."

And so, the tango and Gardel traveled. By motion picture, recording, and personal appearance there was an influence that spread through the cities of Europe, across the Atlantic into Canada and the United States, and, on the other side of the Pacific, to Japan. The non-Latin nations, of course, did not comprehend well the meaning of the lyrics, although they might readily have identified with the sentiments expressed, especially during the Great Depression. They did, however, respond well to "The Master's Voice" and flocked to the ballroom to perform more refined and less lascivious steps than those danced in Buenos Aires and Paris. The effect was more graceful and romantic than macho and erotic. The tango slowly was purified.

By the end of World War II, zeal for the tango had declined. Hot jazz, then cool, and then progressive, and rock and roll prevailed. The tango seemed overly dramatic and antiquated. Dancers, real dancers, no longer touched each other. Gardel was dead; the Beatles were alive.

Then the sixties brought problems, unfulfilled expectations, instantaneous communications, confrontations—and a desire for, if not a retreat into, the past, a nostalgia for the simpler and perhaps safer days of yesteryear. People sought out identities, in some cases through ethnicity and in others through a revival of the sights and sounds of earlier days. Gardel returned. His sardonic image again smoldered at us from the screen, this time the television screen. Video cassette recorders made him constantly accessible. The old Gardel tangos, which had been released on 78 rpm discs, were enhanced by the electronic removal of surface noise and enriched by the addition of instrumental tracks providing modern, more complex harmonies more pleasing to late twentieth-century ears. Gardel and the tango seemed right up-to-date. A musical spectacle celebrating the tango—*Tango Argentino*—was commissioned for the Paris Festival d'Automne in 1983 and later became an international stage hit. An Argentine Nobel Prize winner accepted his scientific award "in the name of the Pampa and the Gaucho and the spirit of Carlos Gardel." Technology and nostalgia had given Gardel eternal life.

Yet, questions remain. Is he really "contemporary," or is he an artifact from another world? What does he mean to those whose parents had not been born when he died? Has immortality trivialized the man and his legend?

Whatever the meaning of Gardel and his tangos today, they certainly were central, vital, and internationally significant in the 1920s and 1930s. To understand them, we need to look at the interplay of the many forces and influences that led to their emergence, consumption, and meaningfulness. Audiences in the United States have become familiar with the context and backgrounds of Gardel's contemporaries—Rudy Vallee, Al Jolson—and their music. To appreciate Gardel, we must know Argentina and its musical tradition, Buenos Aires and its street life during the "roaring twenties" and depression thirties, and Gardel's own background.

Let us then explore five topics. First, let us describe the land and heritage that helped to create the conditions in which the tango and Gardel could emerge. Second, we shall examine the musical components themselves, and see how they reflect the interaction of the varied ethnic cultures that contributed to Buenos Aires's character and personality. Third, a glimpse of Gardel's own life and musical career will suggest how he personified the Buenos Aires cultural and economic reality. Fourth, we shall speculate on how and why the meanings and particular messages of Gardel's lyrics so poignantly touched his audiences. Finally, let us put it all together as a metaphor of historical process.

Argentina, the birthplace of the tango, is an elongated country, much of which borders the South Atlantic Ocean, and the southern tip of which, Tierra del Fuego, reaches almost to Antarctica. The mouth of the second largest river system in South America, La Plata, meets the famous pampas near the port and major city of Buenos Aires. The vast pampa land around Buenos Aires is flat, soggy, grassy, and infrequently dotted with huge Ombú trees. Skies are often cloudy and gray with frequent drizzles, which makes the pampa green. The endless stretches of the hinterland are quiet. Travelers have found them almost somber, melancholy. Their unbroken expanses dwarf and intimidate the solitary intruder.

Following the initial surge of Spanish exploration and settlement after 1519, the Plata region became a rather forgotten fringe of empire. There were no precious minerals and few Indians to force into servitude. The fierce, nomadic pampas tribes retreated to the southern regions of the nation until a series of military campaigns virtually wiped them out in the 1870s. Thus, the tango could not draw upon any of the indigenous qualities associated with the music of the Andes.

During the colonial period, Spain did not regard the shallow-water port city of Buenos Aires as intrinsically valuable. It served only the purpose of intercolonial defense: a counterpoise to the Portuguese in Brazil and a buffer or barrier against other foreigners (English, Dutch, and French) who might venture too close to the vital Spanish silver mines of Bolivia. Buenos Aires was an insignificant outpost, garrisoned by the army dregs, the passed-over officers, and the black militia. Even so, the Buenos Aires estuary was too large, too open, to eliminate foreign contacts. Spanish colonists and their officials welcomed the foreigners, smugglers, and pirates who contributed to their frontier, often illicit, economy. The inland cities such as Salta, Tucumán, and Mendoza enjoyed a mild prosperity by supplying the Bolivian mines with foods and wines, livestock, timber, and leather. The silver they earned in return often traveled eastward to Buenos Aires to purchase slaves and foreign manufactured goods. Thus, a small Afro-Argentine population could be found in Buenos Aires. They contributed an "African" quality of rhythmic syncopation to the music of Argentina, a quality that affected various styles, including the tango.

In the surrounding pampa, a new and marginal culture grew up, based on exiles, dropouts, and refugees. From the cities along the Andes came runaway slaves and mestizos who sought opportunity away from the rigidity of the inland Spanish colonial cities. Down the La Plata estuary came disgruntled military men, fugitives from Brazil and Paraguay, and even Europeans who tried to hide in the vast ocean of grass. They ate well from the huge herds of wild cattle and other livestock and washed down the meat with swigs of *yerba maté*. These pampas rebels—the gauchos, the cattle barons, the itinerant peddlers, the small farmers—gave birth to the uniquely Argentine spirit of freedom and defiance of authority that animated the national folk dances—*milonga, chacarera, candombe, malambo, payada*, and the like—from which the urban tango would derive.

Independence altered Argentina's social and economic context. During the nineteenth century, Buenos Aires drew away from the inland, traditional Spanish cities and intensified its trade and cultural ties with Europe. The technological revolution in Argentine cattle raising and the beginning of the prosperous wheat farming along the Litoral brought prosperity to the nation, but especially to Buenos Aires. The port became an immigrant haven for Italians, Germans,

Irish, English, and other Europeans who looked for jobs and opportunity. The population of Argentina expanded rapidly from some forty thousand in 1810 to over four million by 1895 and nearly eight million by World War I, when Gardel recorded his first songs. During the same time, the urban population grew from 25 percent of the national population to a dominant 53 percent. In 1909, Buenos Aires alone claimed 1,232,000 inhabitants, of whom slightly less than half (45.5 percent) were foreign born. Rural areas and rural people had been left behind. The city was the nation to the *porteño* cattle barons and to the new arrivals from Europe. The economy bloomed, but the wealthy elite who frequented the Buenos Aires Jockey Club kept the lion's share, oblivious to the poverty and slums around them in the city. This wave of European immigrants and the thriving economy contributed to a cultural shift, to extensive crowding and social pressures in the city, to an emerging political radicalism, and to a rapidly developing urban entertainment industry.

The sheer numbers of white immigrants changed the color of the population. Blacks and mulattoes had been a significant percentage of the colonial and early national scene and had contributed definable musical characteristics to the song and dance of port and pampa. Now the blackness became absorbed and whitened, even as the syncopated rhythm lived on. At the same time, the volume of European immigration created sprawling suburbs, extensive and packed colonies called *arrabales* (often slums) along the estuary shores, the dock region, around the packing plants, and on the outskirts of the ever expanding city. These people spoke various languages and regional dialects and helped to create not only a peculiarly *porteño* language (distinctive in vocabulary, diction, and inflection) but also the colorful street slang, or *lunfardo*, unique to Buenos Aires.

Many of the immigrants, having expatriated themselves from their European homes for political and economic reasons, found themselves equally frustrated with their new situation. Jobs were scarce, life was hard, pay was low, and Argentina lagged behind Europe in the "workers' revolutions." Expecting greater fulfillment of their egalitarian dreams in the new land of opportunity, unions and radical political parties pressed hard for a voice in the power structure. The conservatives, supported strongly by European and especially British investment capital, fought back with suppression, police intervention, and fraudulent control of elections, all of which would become grist for the underlying themes of tango lyrics. In this seductive world, both sides were alternately opposed and supported by groups of organized criminals. The tango made its first appearance in the netherworld of pimps and petty criminals who ran the brothels that sprang up around the fringes of Buenos Aires. Tango singer Carlos Gardel had many close personal contacts and friendships with people of the underworld. One might draw a parallel with gangsterism during the Prohibition years in the United States when contacts flourished between bootleggers, speakeasy or cabaret owners, and the musicians and entertainers who worked in these establishments.

The big city also evoked changes in entertainment. As in rural North America, pampa and ranch diversions and amusements had been homespun, nonprofessional, rustic, and based on an imitation of nature, livestock, and work habits. Argentines had created and enjoyed the rooster-hen dances like the *chacarera* and the horse prancing and cowboy slapping of the *malambo*. Urban Argentines, newly arrived from the pampa, met European immigrants in Buenos Aires and changed the character of music and dance. Song, dance, musical style, and instruments no longer focused upon nature; rather, they turned to urban culture for their form and content. The new home of the city provided the themes: crowded conditions, stresses, noise, struggle, taverns, hiring and firing, soot and garbage, streetcars, muggings, intimidations, vice, and a more complicated set of rules for casual encounters, romance, and courtship. In contrast to the relative informality of rural situations, men and women now had to deal with each other on city sidewalks, at the bank, in the streetcars, and in the bistros. Roles and expectations changed.

The impact of urbanization and immigration revolutionized the older forms of entertainment. Dance halls (where men would pay professional women by the dance), song-filled taverns or cabarets (with music and lyrics increasingly provided by paid performers rather than the customers themselves), and the new electric miracles of radio, records, and motion pictures all engendered a new class of worker—the entertainer: an individual who had learned the special skills of music, song, and dance performance. The audience watched rather than participated (although Latin audiences are often inspired to contribute to the performance). The birth of professional entertainment reinforced modern values because of the requirements for careful musical arrangements, the ability to read music, and choreography and rehearsal for precise and simultaneous movement.

If we turn now to the music and structure of the tango itself, we find ourselves following this cultural evolution. A Spanish rhythmic and instrumental triple-meter style called the *canción* entered Argentina (and the rest of Spanish America) and was modified by (1) the melancholy vastness of the pampa, (2) the ranching life and myth of the gaucho, and (3) the rhythmic play of the mulatto. What emerged first was the *milonga*, a song-dance style with a slightly elongated and syncopated gait, imitative of a limping horse. The lyrics of the *milonga* frequently praise the freedom of the open range, tell the local news to a nonliterate group of cowboys, and complain about getting cheated in the city. It is more for singing than for dancing.

Urbanization gives birth to dance halls and cabarets. The dance hall, rather than the cabaret, became the locale for the song. Dance requires a consistent, more constrained rhythm; in effect, form follows function. Instead of the one gaucho guitar, a new group of instruments appears: small ensembles of musicians playing violin, guitar, and flute, with piano or accordion often being added or replacing the guitar. The *milonga* style and form moved to the big city, but the instrumentation filtered down from an upper-class European chamber music environment patterned after Italian and French models. This latter and more "familiar" framework will facilitate the reverse immigration of the *milonga*, become tango, back to Europe.

At this juncture, Carlos Gardel (1887?–1935) enters the scene. Little is certain about his early life, and authorities differ on facts and dates. He may have been born in southern France (Toulouse is a strong possibility) in December 1887 and probably came to Argentina with his parents at the age of four. His parents later abandoned him. Apparently he had no formal education, grew up on the streets, was in and out of orphanages, and was frequently in trouble with the law. A woman by the name of Berthe Gardes or Berta Gardel took him in and became his foster mother. He learned to play the guitar, to sing and to dance, and earned his way on street corners by the time he was twelve.

Released from jail in 1907, he entered into partnership with other street performers and, with the help of local political bosses, began making recordings of popular songs in 1913. His underworld contacts helped to advance his career, and soon he was appearing in cabarets in the smaller cities of Argentina singing the laments of the people in popular ballads of the day.

The political campaigns of 1916, resulting in the election of Radical party leader Hipólito Yrigoyen as president, helped create the next transformation. Songs that were political in nature were recorded and became, in essence, Radical campaign endorsements. Populist necessity, which presided over the marriage of ideology, politics, and music, promoted the careers of both street musicians and "street" politicians.

In the election of 1916, Gardel campaigned through song for his candidate, Alberto Barceló. The following year he recorded "Mi Noche Triste" (My Night of Sadness) by Pascual Cantursi, a song that, in the view of some critics, marks the birth of the tango song, the particular genre through which Gardel would make his reputation.

While Gardel rose to stardom rapidly, his initial impact was *not* with the tango. Rather, in partnership with José Razzano, he performed in a wide variety of styles in cafes, elegant clubs, and the National Theater and toured Uruguay, Brazil, and Spain. In 1925, Razzano injured his throat, and the duo broke up. Only then did Gardel begin to develop the personal style that earned him the sobriquets, "the Magician," "the Thrush," and "the Sheik."

His personal popularity assured, Gardel carefully began to focus his talent and quickly became "Mr. Tango." Radio, records, and motion pictures gave him a wide audience as he sang the works of well-known composers such as Aieta, Le Pera, and Santos Discépolo. His trip to Paris in 1930 created a sensation. He made films and sang many of his popular compositions. Trips to New York and the Caribbean followed. Gardel's career came to a sudden end in 1935 with a tragic airplane accident in Medellín, Colombia. His was a meteoric and prolific career. He recorded more than seven hundred fifty songs, wrote (by himself and with others) more than one hundred twenty titles, and appeared in a dozen films.

Songwriters and composers befriended Gardel and wrote specifically for his voice and style. Gardel had no trouble arranging financial backing for his European films and tours. He was a good friend and a big spender. He loved horses, owned his own racing ponies, and socialized both with jockeys and the upper-class equestrian set. He worked hard, drank enthusiastically, played with zest, and made friends easily and kept them through his loyalty. Gardel never married, adding to the mystique and image that he often sang about: his total dedication and faithfulness to his foster mother.

Motherhood is a significant theme in the literature and song of many cultures. For the tango, however, it is very special. Tangos are not happy songs—in general they are as gloomy as the skies of the Argentine port and pampa. "Mother" offers the single bright spot in a man's development. As Deborah Jakubs observes: "A man's mother is the only truly good, generous, loving, and predictable female. She may be the only human being of value, the only one who deserves to be trusted. Mother embodies the true source of love and inspiration, the ideals that are lost in cruel adulthood . . . the inverse of all the evil the world inflicts upon us, the ultimate good, the only woman whose love is pure" (pp. 139–40).

Or, as José de la Vega expresses the sentiment in *Madre hay una sola* (There is only one mother):

> Kisses, lovers, good friends, good times,
> And fun-filled illusions, too bad
> The World is full of them.
> But you only have one mother;
> And though I forgot it for awhile,
> My life at last taught me
> That I had to return and love just her.

As for other women, they are "evil." Love and faith are all lies; there is only pain, and people must laugh or they will cry. Or, the woman I loved wanted things and I stole to get them for her, and, when the police came to take me away, she turned her back, went into the dance hall, and danced with all the others. The "innocent and gullible" Adam believes his Eve, but she either deceives and abandons him, or is a traitor to his body and love. Thus treated, what can a "real" man do? He must kill her, disfigure her, kill the male rival, or hate and hold himself back—or hopelessly wait alone, since the next woman will be the same. In the end, even his men friends will not stand by him.

Hopes and disappointment: in earning a living, in succeeding in a business or a career, in politics or friendship, all is doomed to fail. Who can understand the way of the world? Can we not go back to the "good old days at mother's knee," back "when the air was clear, skies were blue, and friends were faithful and women were true"? We can only be stoic: at least we have our own memories and our own manliness. And mother? Whatever the personal pain, we can sneer at the world and show everyone that we can take it. Whatever they throw at us, we will not cringe!

What dismal gloom and doom! And why? Was life really all that dreadful? Or was art exaggerating life?

Of course, one can make a case either way. Slum life was (and is) crowded and hard; employment was scarce, and when available, poorly paid. European immigrants suffered homesickness for their birthplace and frequent derision from their newly adopted compatriots. A boom in the teens was followed by a recession. The recovery in the twenties was followed by a world depression and then by World War II. Why should the lyrics of the tango not reflect the same pessimism that

Argentine writer Ezequiel Martínez Estrada did in *X-ray of the Pampa* (1933) or the same stoic fatalism that nineteenth-century poet José Hernández put into the Argentine national epic poem *El gaucho Martín Fierro y la vuelta de Martín Fierro* (1872, 1879)?

The tragic view of life was also a posture, a theatrical role, a safe and reliable stance that prevented one from having to reveal oneself. It was grand opera with the roles predetermined; the actions were expected and the responses were predictable. All the world was a stage, the actors all wore masks, and the show must go on.

Still, it was a long tradition—through the land, the early colony, the increasing dominance of Buenos Aires over the hinterland, the huge European immigration, the struggle for opportunity and for modernization. The tango dramatized past, present, and future, individual and nation. Educated Argentines are themselves divided about the merits of the theatrical excesses of the tango in image and words. Some, captivated by a nostalgia for the past and the search for authentic *lo argentinidad*, want to revive and promote the tango as part of the national folkways. Others reject the tango and its stylized, macho image as a negative stereotype that casts a tragic shadow over the face of the new, modern Argentina they long for.

José C. Ibáñez, author of the official eleventh-grade textbook *Historia de la cultura Argentina* (frequent editions since 1966), reaches an uneasy accommodation with the folklorists and the modernists. The book spends six pages on rural and historic folklore, songs, and dances but makes no mention at all of Carlos Gardel or the tango. Apparently, some Argentine historians, like many U.S. scholars, prefer the normative ideal of the simple, homespun agrarian myth and are uncomfortable with the vitality and complexity of urban heroes or folklore. The "authentic" is found in the pampas or the log cabin. The "aberrant" resides in the heterogeneous, pluralistic cities, where an abandoned street child like Carlos Gardel can find fame, fortune, and entry into the elite chambers of the Jockey Club.

SOURCES

For those interested in hearing the music of Carlos Gardel, the reissue recording of *La resurrección de Gardel, 1927/1933*, with the orchestra of Alfredo de Angeles, United Artists Records, UA Latino LT-LA 325-D, 1974, is available. Carlos Gardel and the tango are nearly inseparable as topics in both the English and Spanish literature. See especially Gerard Behague's "Tango," in *The New Grove's Dictionary of Music and Musicians*, vol. 18, edited by Stanley Sadie, 563–65, New York, 1980, which includes a representative reading list. See also Joseph Criscenti's "Carlos Gardel," in *Encyclopedia of Latin America*, edited by Helen Delpar, 249, New York, 1974.

BIBLIOGRAPHY

[Joseph Arbena, professor of history at Clemson University in South Carolina, prepared a presentation in 1985 on the occasion of the fiftieth anniversary of the death of Carlos Gardel. The following bibliography of available references is drawn from his unpublished manuscript.]

Arroyuelo, Javier, and López Sánchez, Raphael. "Tango-Mania." *Vanity Fair* 48, no. 10 (October 1985): 94–101.

Bernardi, Santiago. "The Tango." *Americas* 16, no. 12 (December 1964): 20–26.

Carrasco Pirard, Eduardo. "The *Nueva Canción* in Latin America." *International Social Science Journal* 34, no. 4 (1982): 599–623.

Castro, Donald S. "Popular Culture as a Source for the Historian: The Tango in Its Era of *La Guardia Vieja*." *Studies in Latin American Popular Culture* 3 (1984): 70–85.

Collier, Simon. "The Tango Made Flesh: Carlos Gardel." *History Today* 30 (October 1980): 36–41.

Growel, María. "Latest Tango in Buenos Aires." *Americas* 30, no. 1 (January 1978): 48–51.

Jakubs, Deborah L. "From Bawdyhouse to Cabaret: The Evolution of the Tango as an Expression of Argentine Popular Culture." *Journal of Popular Culture* 18, no. 1 (Summer 1984): 133–45.

Piazzolla, Astor. Interview by National Public Radio. Paris. Broadcast on "All Things Considered," November 27, 1984.

Pinnell, Richard. "The Guitarist-Singer of Pre-1900 Gaucho Literature." *Latin American Music Review* 5, no. 2 (Fall/Winter 1984): 243–62.

Rivero, Edmundo. "Lunfardo: Up from the Buenos Aires Underworld." *Americas* 35, no. 5 (September-October 1983): 2.

Roberts, John Storm. *The Latin Tinge: The Impact of Latin American Music on the United States*. New York, 1979.

Salmon, Russell O. "The Tango: Its Origin and Meaning." *Journal of Popular Culture* 10, no. 4 (Spring 1977): 859–66.

Skirius, John. "A Word with Borges." *Americas* 32, nos. 11–12 (November-December 1980): 13–16.

Sosa Pujato, Gustavo. "Popular Culture." In *Prologue to Peron: Argentina in Depression and War, 1930–1943*, edited by Mark Falcoff and Ronald H. Dolkart, 136–63. Berkeley, 1975.

"The Tango Cult." *The Economist* 193, no. 6070 (December 26, 1959): 1247.

Taylor, Julie M. "Tango: Theme of Class and Nation." *Ethnomusicology* 20, no. 2 (May 1976): 273–90.

Urbina, Leandro. "My Beautiful Buenos Aires." In *Chilean Writers in Exile: Eight Short Novels*, edited by Fernando Alegría, 132–38. Trumansburg, NY, 1982.

Von Schey, Lida. "Argentina: Radio-TV Boom, Answer to Inflation." *Billboard* 93, no. 42 (October 24, 1981): LA-6.

Ward, Catherine E. "Epic of the Gaucho." *Americas* 17, no. 11 (November 1965): 8–15.

Some significant references in Spanish are:

Astigueta, Fernando Diego. "La mentalidad argentina en el tango y sus modismos." *Journal of Inter-American Studies* 7, no. 1 (January 1965): 67–94.

Canton, Dario. "El mundo de los tangos de Gardel." *Revista Latinoaméricana de Sociología* (1968): 341–62.

Cerrutti, Raul Oscar. *El tango: Sus relaciones con el folklore musical y ubicación en la cultura argentina*. Resistencia, Chaco, 1967.

De Lara, Tomás, and Roncetti de Panti, Ines Leonilda. *El tema del tango en la literatura argentina*. 2d ed. Buenos Aires, 1968.

García Jiménez, Francisco. *Carlos Gardel y su época*. Buenos Aires, 1976.

Gobello, José. *Crónica general del tango*. Buenos Aires, 1980.

Mafud, Julio. *Sociología del tango*. Buenos Aires, 1966.

Matamoro, Blas. "Carlos Gardel." In *La historia popular*, vol. 24. Buenos Aires, 1971.

———. 'Historia del tango." In *La historia popular*, vol. 16. Buenos Aires, 1971.

Milkewitz, Harry. *Psicología del tango*. Montevideo, 1964.

Moreno, Miguel Angel. *Historia artistica de Carlos Gardel*. 2d ed. Buenos Aires, 1983.

Portogalo, José. "Buenos Aires: Tango y literatura." In *La historia popular*, vol. 93. Buenos Aires, 1972.

Sebato, Ernesto, et al. *Tango: Discusión y clave*. Buenos Aires, 1963.

Sobrino, Constantino. *Diccionario del tango*. Buenos Aires, 1971.

Ullá, Noemé. *Tango, rebelión y nostalgia*. Buenos Aires, 1962.

Vinas, David. *Carlos Gardel*. Madrid, 1979.

Two additional sources should be mentioned:

Castillo, Catullo. *Buenos Aires, tiempo Gardel*. Buenos Aires, 1966. Oversize volume of eighty-eight pages with extensive photographs of the city and of Gardel, his life, and his friends. Includes tango lyrics and eulogies.

Defino, Armando. *Carlos Gardel: la verdad de una vida*. Buenos Aires, 1968. Contains forty pages of photographs, an extensive biography, a list of Gardel's motion pictures, and a lengthy discography.

13

*Tomasa Muñoz de León**: *From* Precarista *to* Cooperativista

Lynne P. Phillips

Lynne Phillips, of the Centre for Research on Latin America and the Caribbean, York University, Toronto, has focused her research since her dissertation at the University of Toronto on gender and class in coastal Ecuador and, most recently, on the exclusion of women from agricultural production during the 1930s and 1940s. Her investigation has resulted in numerous conference presentations and journal articles.

This feminist-anthropologist says that she found it extremely difficult to write about another woman, one whose life was so different from her own. Repeatedly, Phillips could imagine "Tomasa saying, 'No, no, no . . . that's not what it's like. *This* is what it's like.'" Phillips overcame this obstacle by balancing what she wanted to say about life in coastal Ecuador with what Tomasa would rather she say. Thus, she explains, "understanding" becomes "an on-going, never-ending journey rather than a place at which one arrives." For this journey, Phillips has chosen Tomasa as her guide. She informs the reader: "The story I have written here is far from a compilation of 'facts.' Neither is it, however, an untrue story. It is, rather, a kind of negotiation. It is a story which has evolved, and continues to evolve, as Tomasa and I try to grapple with the strange and familiar aspects of each other's present lives, and as we both attempt to wrestle with our ever-changing pasts."

> Like those old trees in the countryside which, though damaged by axes, rebound and refuse to die, the coastal peasant, enduring tremendous injustices, holds on to life, just like the *matapalo* tree that takes hold of the earth, with deep and tenacious roots.
>
> —José de la Cuadra[1]

---

*Tomasa Muñoz de Léon is a pseudonym.

[1]"Como esos viejos arboles del agro que, heridos de hacha, rebotan y se resisten a morir, la gente montuvio, soportando males tremendos, se agarra a la vida, como

THE BANANA BOOM

Tomasa Muñoz was born in 1947, during the middle of the winter rains, in her parents' bamboo house. The countryside is hot and humid. Tomasa's father, Eduardo, is outside weeding the rice *pozas* of a local landowner when he hears the news that his firstborn is a girl. He smiles, thinking to himself: A *mujercita*;[2] Adela will be pleased. . . . I think she already has a *madrina* (godmother) in mind for the baby. Next week I must find a kind and generous *padrino* (godfather) for my new daughter. I have done a very good job on Don Felipe's rice this year. Perhaps he will do for me this one small favor and accept the honor.

At the house, Adela, Tomasa's mother, wraps the baby in layers of cloth to make the adjustment from the secure comfort of the womb to the open air of the outside world an easier one. Her tiny arms tucked mummylike beneath the cloth, Tomasa spends her first month being swung back and forth in the family's one worn-out hammock, her only view being the interwoven banana leaves that serve as the roof for the house.

Don Felipe agrees to the honor of being Tomasa's *padrino*. This means that he becomes the *compadre* (coparent) of her mother and father. He buys Tomasa a christening dress and a little something every year for her birthday. In return, Tomasa's father faithfully works on Don Felipe's land, sometimes with Adela's help when a sister or neighbor is at the house to mind the children. Even Tomasa helps in the fields occasionally once she becomes a little older.

Tomasa's father is a *precarista* (precarious tenant). This means that he owns no land of his own but rents land within a hacienda. Don Felipe, a hacendado who owns (it seems to Tomasa) an extraordinary amount of land, has dozens of *precaristas* cultivating his land. He expects each one of them to pay him two *quintales* of rice for every *cuadra* (three-quarters of a hectare) of land the *precarista* rents. Because Don Felipe is also a rice mill owner, almost all of the rice grown by the *precaristas* ends up in his hands. He pays the *precaristas* very little for their harvested rice, but Eduardo feels that he cannot complain too much since Don Felipe gives him permission to live on hacienda land, and, after all, they are now *compadres*.

---

los matapalos se agarran al subsuelo, con raices profundos y tenaces." José de la Cuadra, *El Montuvio Ecuatóriano* (Guayaquil, 1937), 42.

[2]Generally, "baby girl," although it literally translates as "little woman."

The closest town to the Muñoz residence is Vinces. Vinces is too far away for Tomasa to attend school, but it is close enough for her family to hear news of the outside world. And what they hear seems unbelievable. Suddenly large foreign companies such as United Fruit and Standard Fruit have begun paying large sums of money (fifty sucres a box) for Gros Michel bananas. After decades of economic stagnation in the region following the cacao collapse of the 1920s, rural life on the coast changes remarkably quickly. Banana trees seem to spring up everywhere, almost overnight, and within a short period of time there are plantations as far as the eye can see.

Because there are only very poor roads to Guayaquil in the early 1950s, the bananas grown in the Vinces area must be transported down the Vinces River to the port. The Coellos, a large landowning family in the area, decide to set up a transportation business, purchasing a number of flat *lanchas* made of bamboo poles, which navigate the windy river. During the busy season as many as four boats a day leave for Guayaquil.

Tomasa's father is fortunate in getting a job working part-time on one of the *lanchas*. The extra money helps out Tomasa's family tremendously; finally they do not have such a hard time making ends meet during that difficult season between the winter and the summer harvests. Don Felipe is not pleased at the prospect of Eduardo pursuing activities in addition to his rice growing, but by this time virtually everyone is involved in the banana trade.

Perhaps it is not surprising, then, that it is through the banana business that Tomasa eventually meets her future husband, Adolfo. By 1961, Adolfo León has spent his obligatory eleven months in the army and has returned to the countryside to find employment. He is eighteen and eager to "make some money and find a wife." He manages to obtain a *cupo* (contract) with Standard Fruit, buying an agreed-upon number of banana stalks from local farmers and ensuring that they arrive in the company's hands.

Tomasa, now fourteen, is quite taken by the worldly Adolfo when he starts to canvass the countryside near her home. By this time Eduardo and Adolfo have already met through the transportation business and get along well; in fact, Tomasa's father is sometimes able to give some preference to Adolfo's bananas on the *lanchas*. Only a year later Adolfo and Tomasa decide to get married.

It is unusual for rural women to marry their mates in this region. They prefer to form *compromisos*—socially sanctioned unions that involve neither the church nor the state. Tomasa says that the only reason she got married is because "Adolfo wanted to," although it is perhaps noteworthy that Tomasa is a more religious woman than most in this region. To this day, for example, she holds catechism classes in town twice a week and, unlike most other rural women, goes to church almost every Sunday. In fact, Tomasa occasionally complains about how the other people in the area do not like to take part in the activities involving the Catholic church because they think it is "communist." This image of the church exists in the minds of some because of the church's support of the cooperative movement and the struggles of the *precaristas* on the coast, although, as Tomasa says, the label itself is "ridiculous."

Adolfo and Tomasa move into the house in which Adolfo has lived all his life, in a hacienda owned by the Zapatier family located on the other side of the town of Vinces, about ten miles away. Tomasa brings with her two small pigs and some chickens, which she has raised while living with her parents. Adolfo has one cow (an uncommon animal to own at the time but soon to become an important commodity on the coast). Although the fact that Adolfo's parents also live in the house sometimes bothers Tomasa, a year later—when she has her first child—she is grateful for her mother-in-law's company as well as her knowledge about the needs of a baby.

Economic problems, however, loom ahead. Almost as suddenly as it had started, the banana "boom" collapses. This is in part because a new brand of banana (the Cavendish, which requires more investment on the part of the planters) is now in demand by the fruit companies, but river transportation from Vinces also takes too long and regions closer to Guayaquil, accessible by road, have begun to open up.

Suddenly only three *lanchas* take the trip down to Guayaquil, then two, and, finally, only one. *Cupos* with the large companies are quickly withdrawn. A number of local people who have invested heavily in the banana business lose a considerable amount of money; thousands of banana trees are pulled down to make way for rice growing, cattle grazing, or the (by then more reliable) cacao tree.

Adolfo is able to find a job through a friend working in the town jail, but Tomasa's father is forced to spend more time doing agricultural work. By this time, however, many aspects of the agricultural situation have drastically changed. By 1964 the government has passed an agrarian reform law to outlaw the *huasipungo* (peonage) system of the highland region of the country. The law formally affects the coast very little, but it does make landowners squeamish about renting out their land. Many begin to switch to cattle raising exclusively so as to avoid having obligations to *precaristas*, and it becomes more and more difficult to obtain agricultural work. By 1968 tension is high on the coast and land invasions are more frequent. Agricultural yields become dangerously low and for the first time ever, Ecuador, which had once produced so much rice it was actually able to export it, now has to import the product.

It is around this time that Eduardo begins having problems with his *compadre* Don Felipe. Felipe complains constantly about the quality of the care that Eduardo is giving his crops. He reminds Eduardo almost daily that he, Felipe, is doing Eduardo a favor by allowing him to farm his land. At the same time, Don Felipe becomes quite careless about his animals, allowing them to trample the fields and damage crops. Eduardo pleads with his *compadre* to keep the animals enclosed so that they will not do further damage, but Felipe pays little heed.

One day, after his *compadre*'s pigs have torn up some freshly planted seed in the fields, Eduardo herds the animals into a corral by the house. Felipe sees him doing this and, furious, accuses Eduardo of stealing his pigs. Eduardo strongly objects. He points out that he is only trying to protect the crops. Without hesitation, Felipe marches back to his house and hauls out a shotgun. Eduardo, a simple man who, many would say, had spent most of his life trying to please others, is dead within minutes.

The news spreads quickly across the countryside. Everyone is horrified, but it is not long before sides are taken. Was Eduardo really trying to steal Don Felipe's pigs? Was the stealing of private property a sufficient reason for Felipe to take such action? Is this to become a strategy for hacendados who want to be free of their *precaristas*?

Adela desperately tries to get some kind of compensation for the death of Eduardo. She accuses Don Felipe of murder. She wants someone in authority to recognize the injustice of the situation, to admit that what has taken place is unacceptable. Felipe, in fact, is given little more than a slap on the wrist for his behavior.

The realities of being responsible for three young children still living at home soon force Adela to concentrate on a more pressing matter: survival. Suddenly, and quite incredibly it seems to her, Adela finds herself working "like a man," planting, weeding, and harvesting rice in the hacienda where Tomasa and Adolfo live. This work is difficult for Adela to do, both physically and socially, since the sexual division of labor in the area strongly favors men working in the fields. But Adela has little choice: with so few employment opportunities available to women in the countryside, this is what she must do if she wants to "feed her babies."

Thereafter, Adela never tires of pointing out to her daughter Tomasa the extent to which the latter is dependent upon Adolfo. "Life is black," Adela assures her, "without a man."

AGRARIAN REFORM

Agrarian reform laws are introduced in the 1970s to ease tensions on the coast. The Ecuadorian government hopes that these laws will improve agricultural yields to help feed Guayaquil's burgeoning population and also bring some improvement to the lives of apparently disgruntled agricultural laborers and their families. In 1970 a decree is passed in the legislature to give *precaristas* secure access to land through the organization of cooperatives. Employing IERAC (Ecuadorian Institute for Agrarian Reform and Colonization) as a mediator, it is expected that landowners will be willing to sell, for a reasonable price, their least productive land to long-term renters. The BNF (National Bank of Development) will carry loans for the land purchases, and the *precaristas* will repay the BNF within ten years.

The plan in theory does not seem to be an unreasonable one, but the *precaristas* soon discover that forming a cooperative is not an easy task. Although some landowners may be willing to sell their land in order to invest in more lucrative pursuits, few are willing to sell to "their" *precaristas*. It is also quite clear that IERAC is not interested in intervening on the part of the *precaristas* unless land invasions or violence seem imminent.

Two people are killed when the first agricultural cooperative, San Vicente, attempts to form in the Vinces area. The original landowner of Hacienda San Vicente insists that he will only sell his land to "*gente culta*" (civilized people), and he brings in the police to throw the *precaristas* (now labeled by some "land stealers") off the land. He finally sells his hacienda to a family from outside the area. Although the new family promptly sells some land to the cooperative, this turns out to be a wise political move, since in total the cooperative receives barely a hectare of land for each cooperative *socio* (member), and today most of the *socios* of the cooperative find themselves working for the hacendado in order to make ends meet.

By 1974 the owner of the hacienda where Adolfo and Tomasa live is desperately trying to sell his land. He owes many of the workers back pay but says that he will only pay them when they move off his land. Adolfo decided to organize some of the hacienda workers into a cooperative. He quits his job at the town jail and devotes all of his time to organizing the workers, talking to IERAC officials, and visiting Ministry of Agriculture offices.

Zapatier, the hacendado, is, of course, furious. As head of the town council he has considerable influence over political matters, and the battle becomes a long and significant one. Adolfo and his friends construct a fence around what they believe should be the boundaries of the cooperative and begin planting rice seeds. Zapatier hires town thugs to tear it down and sends in his cattle to trample the workers' crops. In the end, with the intervention of IERAC, Zapatier admits defeat, although not before he is assured that Adolfo cannot legally be a *socio* of the cooperative. The argument is that because Adolfo was working as a town laborer, not a *precarista*, at the time of the cooperative's formation, he does not meet the legal requirements to be a *socio*.

When Zapatier, now a resident of Guayaquil, later questions the fact that the León family is still living in their original residence, he receives a letter from IERAC saying: "Adolfo León is not and never will be a *socio* of the cooperative in question. However, his wife, Tomasa, is."

Tomasa's mother, Adela, is also a *socia*. The cooperative is named "Together We Struggle."

That Tomasa and her mother have become *socias* is remarkable considering that both the state and local peasant men consistently discriminate against women on the question of cooperative participation. The laws themselves make it difficult for wives to become cooperative members, and from the beginning, the *precaristas* have made it clear that the cooperatives are "for the men, not the women." Since it is, at any rate, considered inappropriate for women to work in the fields, few people have disputed this decision; the overwhelming majority of *socios* in the area today are men.

However, Tomasa takes an active role in the formation of the cooperative from the beginning. Adolfo is arrested six times during the long struggle between the hacendado and the *precaristas*. During those times Tomasa sets up a makeshift stove outside the jail in town and daily prepares meals for Adolfo and many of the other jailed men. She takes over the necessary administrative work for the cooperative by visiting the appropriate authorities and still manages somehow to make ends meet at home.

Tomasa also becomes a prominent person in the organization of the Unión de Mujeres Trabajadores (UMT) in her area—the women's faction of the male-dominated UNOCAVB (Unión de Cooperativas). Within the UMT, which also has strong alliances with the Catholic

Church, women learn skills such as dressmaking in order to contribute income to the household. The twenty or so women members have varying reasons for belonging to the organization, although the most vocal of them will say that the UMT exists because "women should do more than have babies and sit around watching *novelas* [soap operas]."

The UMT holds meetings every week, and, while practicing their skills, the women often talk about the political issues being discussed by the UNOCAVB. Through informal and personal channels, they do not hesitate to suggest alternatives when they do not agree with the men's activities or decisions. The women could, but do not, run for political office in the UNOCAVB. As Tomasa puts it: "It just isn't necessary since the UMT tends to get what it wants anyway." Adolfo, it should be noted, holds an executive position in the UNOCAVB.

LIFE IN THE EIGHTIES

By the 1980s land invasions are less frequent and tensions between hacendados and the new *cooperativistas* have eased in the Vinces area. The kinds of troubles that the *cooperativistas* experience today are only indirectly related to the large landowners from whom they have purchased land; a more direct antagonism exists between the *cooperativistas* and the state.

Land reform was undertaken by the state not only to deflate a potentially militant peasant movement by offering *precaristas* land but also to gain control over the marketing and distribution of agricultural products. The two major features on the coast that the state identified as obstacles to the development of agriculture were the "feudal" character of production relations—that is, *precarismo*—and the power of *comerciantes* over the market. Promoting cooperatives, which were to operate alongside capitalist farms (now free of their less productive land), was to solve the first problem; creating a government marketing board for agricultural products—the Ecuadorian National Agriculture Exchange (ENAC)—was to solve the second.

ENAC was set up to enable small-scale rice farmers (including those within cooperatives) to bypass the *comerciante* and receive reasonable prices for their products. Today in Vinces, however, small farmers are largely ignored by ENAC. This is primarily because of ENAC's historical links to the BNF, the bank which was originally involved in the land purchase negotiations between hacendados and cooperatives and which today arranges agricultural loans. By the late 1970s the BNF began experiencing difficulties in collecting loan arrears, and in Vinces an informal arrangement was apparently made between ENAC and the BNF to ensure repayment: ENAC would only grant *cupos* to small farmers for the amount they might owe the BNF. ENAC buys an amount of rice the value of which will not exceed the value of the BNF loan and then transfers this money to the bank rather than paying the farmers themselves.

The farmers in the area are incredulous. Many are forced, once again, to sell their products to local *comerciantes* for reduced prices. (Such rice is eventually rerouted to ENAC through the *comerciantes*—who make a tidy profit—even though ENAC is only supposed to buy from "direct producers.") The situation worsens in 1982. In fact, Adolfo finds that the full value of his rice is not paid to him by ENAC because his *brother* owes money to the BNF. ENAC officials tell Adolfo that if he wants to be reimbursed he will have to talk to his brother about the matter. Adolfo is outraged.

Not long after this incident, UNOCAVB decides to tackle the marketing problems of the *cooperativistas*. However, not until after a long struggle between UNOCAVB and ENAC takes place does ENAC finally agree to buy rice in bulk from UNOCAVB (thus, the *cooperativistas* can sell their small harvests to UNOCAVB and still receive the official marketing board price). In the meantime, tension between "los ricos" and "los pobres" has arisen in Vinces once again, and some members of the community are by this time convinced that Adolfo is a troublemaker.

The whole situation makes Tomasa feel a little nervous. Adolfo's struggle with ENAC puts quite a substantial financial strain on the household, and she begins sewing frantically, day after day, in order to bring in some income. By this time she has sold one of her pigs to buy a secondhand sewing machine and has earned a reputation as an excellent seamstress.

At times like this, Tomasa's children are extremely important sources of labor for the household. She has now had six children: "five living and one in the grave," as she puts it. Two of her children are in *colegio* (high school), and the youngest still keeps her company at home. The child who died, Tomasa's last, was born with a number of physical handicaps; she still mourns this loss and badly wants to have another baby.

Every morning before the children go to school, they milk the fourteen cows now owned by Adolfo and his father, and, when they are not in school, the children help Adolfo with the agricultural work.

The children also cook, clean house, and wash clothes when Tomasa must focus on her income-earning activities.

"I can't imagine how women without their own *negocios* (businesses) can possibly manage," Tomasa comments. "How can one support one's family on only the one hundred sucres a day one's husband earns doing agricultural work?" In fact, Tomasa now has a small-scale pig business which is doing well, and she has just had two of her pigs inseminated in the hopes of expanding the business. It is through her pig *negocios* that she is also able to buy a kerosene-operated refrigerator (although Adolfo's cows are used as collateral). A neighbor, a close friend of Tomasa who owns a motorized canoe, picks up colas and beers for her in town and Tomasa stocks them in her fridge, selling them to passersby.

Tomasa keeps a notebook on the household's income and expenses. She keeps track of how much people owe her both for her sewing and the milk purchases. She, in fact, organizes the selling of milk from Adolfo's cows. The cows produce about twenty-five liters of milk a day, and Tomasa sells it for eight sucres a liter to neighbors and relatives. She keeps this money to pay for her sewing materials and the children's school needs.

Because of her UMT activities, Tomasa is in town fairly often, and she considers herself "lucky" to have a husband like Adolfo who gives her the freedom "to do what I want." Tomasa is aware of the fact that she has a considerable amount of power within the household, but she would deny any conscious use of it in her relationship with Adolfo. Yet not only do her *negocios* economically stabilize a household that is dependent on the whims of the market and *comerciantes*, but, more importantly, it is only through Tomasa that Adolfo has access to land. *She* is the *socia*.

In this region it is generally agreed that rural women should not walk about alone; many women have a difficult time negotiating with their *compromisos* to go shopping in town (almost all rural men in the area, Adolfo included, do the weekly shopping for the household), to take children to the town doctor, or to attend UMT meetings. In fact, locally the men circulate a joke about the *real* meaning of UMT: the Union of *Mujeres Tunanteras* (rascally women who loiter about), the clear implication being that they think this is a union of brazen women. Not surprisingly, the UMT has some difficulty attracting new members.

Such criticism seldom daunts Tomasa. In the meantime, she becomes one of the most vocal women from the area at the May 1st International Workers' Day march held in Babahoyo every year. A short, stout, and normally quiet, rather easygoing woman, Tomasa transforms herself before one's very eyes into an aggressive slogan chanter who marches boldly in front of the UMT banner. In a crowded pick-up truck, on the way back from the march, one can even find her sipping *puro* (raw alcohol) along with the men while reading her Bible.

Within the cooperative, Tomasa and Adolfo's household is a busy one. As is the case for most of the cooperatives on the coast, the *socios* of "Together We Struggle" (more commonly referred to as the León cooperative) seldom work collectively, spending most of their time on their own portion of land and other business pursuits. However, Adolfo, whose parents by this time have moved to another farm, is generally considered the most "knowledgeable" man in the cooperative, and people look to him for agricultural advice and to borrow tools and sometimes money. Tomasa also has close ties and lending arrangements with most of the women in the cooperative.

Through Tomasa, Adolfo has access to three *cuadras* of land within the cooperative on which to plant rice, corn, and beans. Adolfo often does not work this land himself. When he is not relying on unpaid family labor (Tomasa and the children harvested the beans the summer of 1986, for example), he hires labor, usually "family," from within the cooperative, to work his land for him when he has union business to do. In fact, Adolfo is primarily responsible for the arrival in the cooperative of a new family (kin of his) who were kicked off their land in a large hacienda nearby. The male adults in this family now work for Adolfo whenever there is extra work to be done.

Adolfo's work in the union begins increasingly to take him away from his agricultural work and from daily cooperative affairs, a situation that he does not seem to mind at all. For almost a year, in fact, Adolfo's general distaste for doing agricultural work prompts him to look for a nonagricultural job. He feels that he has a good chance of getting his old job back in the town jail, but this requires a considerable amount of time mobilizing his network in various parts of the country. As he spends more and more time away from the household, the activities of Tomasa and the children take on greater and greater importance. A year later, however, Adolfo is still unable to find permanent employment in town, and Tomasa, pregnant again and tired of running the household on her own, talks to him about taking a greater interest in the cooperative. She is not entirely successful; Adolfo, Tomasa has come to realize, is really much more interested in political concerns.

At the same time some unfortunate events occur within the cooperative, and tensions begin to rise between the families of Tomasa and Adolfo. Adolfo's younger brother, Guillermo, a *socio* of the cooperative, lives on cooperative land with his *compromiso*, María, and their three children. Before he met María, Guillermo had had a *compromiso* with a woman who lived in town. Problems start when Guillermo gets a job in town working for UNOCAVB, and rumors begin to float back to the countryside that Guillermo has taken up with another woman. Tomasa spends a lot of time talking to María about the problem. The two examine Guillermo's bankbook, María hoping that she can get access to some of the money in order to move away. Then one day Guillermo returns home early to find María in bed with a brother of Tomasa (also a *socio* of the cooperative). The scene is an ugly one. Guillermo beats María with a plantain stalk (Tomasa hears the screams from across the road and runs over to the house to stop the fight). Tomasa's brother quickly leaves town.

After this episode, Guillermo eats most of his meals and sleeps at Adolfo and Tomasa's house (María has moved back with her parents). Guillermo, apparently no longer interested in pursuing the relationship with his previous *compromiso*, begins seeing Tomasa's sixteen-year-old sister. Everyone, especially Adela, is extremely upset, primarily because Tomasa's sister is so young (she still attends high school) and Guillermo has shown himself to be exceptionally irresponsible in his relationships with women. Tomasa is appointed the unofficial mediator between Adela and the couple, but she is unsuccessful is convincing either her sister or Guillermo that they should wait awhile. When the two rent a place in town and move in together, it seems to Tomasa that the León cooperative is falling apart.

Meanwhile, Tomasa's wandering brother, Lorenzo, comes back to town. Tomasa is angry with him, but since he needs the money she convinces Adolfo to hire him to do some work on Adolfo's land. In addition, Lorenzo plants some of his own crops in the cooperative, while Adolfo attends to some problems his father is having on his farm on the other side of town (a nearby hacendado insists on letting his cattle wander aimlessly throughout the countryside, and over Adolfo's father's crops).

For a while Lorenzo eats his meals and sleeps at Tomasa's place. Soon, however, after urging from Tomasa, he agrees to set up a place for Adela in town. While continuing to work at the cooperative, Lorenzo establishes a *compromiso* with a young rural woman who, once she becomes pregnant, also moves in with Adela.

Adolfo fails to resolve the problem at his father's farm (the hacendado refuses to keep his cattle fenced in), and Adolfo calls Lorenzo over to help him deal with the matter. "Tell him to be careful," she tells Lorenzo. The familiarity of the situation concerns Tomasa; she can only think of the horrible fate that awaited her father. When Tomasa doesn't hear from Adolfo for two nights she becomes extremely worried.

Her worst fears are soon confirmed. The police in town tell her that Adolfo and Lorenzo have been "caught red-handed" stealing the cows of a hacendado. "Where are they?" she asks, afraid to know the answer. "Don't worry. We'll catch them," is the reply.

For several minutes there are only two things Tomasa can think of: they got away; they're safe.

But then it occurs to her that she has an enormous amount of work ahead of her. Suddenly she is responsible for two families, her brother's and her own. More immediately, she has to prove somehow her husband's and brother's innocence.

For a moment she considers the possibility that it is simply not possible for her to do all this. She walks slowly down the street toward the church, and then stops. She thinks of her mother and the years she spent battling with the authorities, long before the cooperatives existed. Was it worth the struggle?

Life here is black without a man.

She realizes: I have no choice. Tomasa turns down the footpath to her mother's place; Adela will know how much it will cost us to hire a lawyer.

SOURCES

On agrarian reform see C. Blankstein and C. Zuvekas, Jr., "Agrarian Reform in Ecuador: An Analysis of Past Efforts and the Development of a New Approach," *Economic Development and Cultural Change* 22 (1973): 73–94; Jorge Luna, *Los procesos de diferenciación campesina del contexto cooperativo* (Machala, 1979); Michael Redclift, *Agrarian Reform and Peasant Organization on the Ecuadorian Coast* (London, 1978); and Ximena Salcedo, "Estudios sobre el valle del Rio Daule" (Guayaquil, n.d.), typescript.

On social and economic history see José de la Cuadra, *El Montuvio Ecuatóriano* (Guayaquil, 1937); Carlos Larrea M., "El sector agroexportador y su articulación con la economía ecuatóriana durante la etapa bananera (1948–1972): Subdesarrollo y crecimiento desigual," in *Economía política del Ecuador: Campo, región, nación*, edited by Louis LeFebre (Quito, 1985); Olen Leonard, *Pichilingue: A Study of Rural Life in Coastal Ecuador*, Report no. 17 (Washington, DC, 1947); J. Maldonado Rennella, *La situación de la mujer casada en la legislación civil* (Guayaquil, 1974); N. Mayers, *Report on Economic and Commercial Conditions in Ecuador* (London, 1954); *Registro de propiedades* (Vinces, 1940, 1950, 1951, 1960, 1965, 1975–79, 1980–82); J. V. D. Saunders, "Man-Land Relations in Ecuador," *Rural Sociology* 26 (1961): 57–69; John Uggen, "Peasant Mobilization in Ecuador: A Case Study of Guayas Province " (Ph.D. diss., University of Miami, 1975); and A. Valverde, "El sistema de aparcería en el subsector arrocera ecuatóriana hasta antes de la aplicación de la ley de reforma agraria" (Quito, 1979), typescript.

14

*Soledad Fuente**

Oscar J. Martínez

As director of Latin American studies at the University of Texas at El Paso, Oscar Martínez works only three hundred yards from Mexico and from the border about which he writes. In *Border Boom Town: Ciudad Juárez* (Austin, TX, 1975) and *Fragments of the Mexican Revolution* (Albuquerque, 1983), Martínez examines the economic and political aspects of the border culture. Currently, he is comparing national frontiers of the Third World. The diversity of everyday life along the border has fascinated Martínez and prompted him to establish an oral history program at Texas–El Paso. The following interview is taken from the university's oral history collection and examines the tawdry life-style adopted by some residents in the infamous border town of Ciudad Juárez.

The biography of Soledad Fuente challenges the political rhetoric of Mexico's ruling Party of the Institutionalized Revolution that asserts that the idealism of the Great Rebellion continues. Soledad's prospects sadly reflect the desperate lot of many in Mexico today.

> "I have always had bad luck with men, always."

Prostitution has long been a well-known feature of life along Mexico's northern border. Tijuana and Ciudad Juárez, in particular, were famous as "centers of sin" not only during Prohibition in the United States but also during World War II when large numbers of American soldiers sought diversion south of the border. In recent years, the "sexual revolution" in the United States has diminished the prostitute's trade in the border cities. Nevertheless, prostitution remains important economically. Its social implications are equally significant.

When interviewed in Ciudad Juárez in 1976, Soledad Fuente worked in the tourist district. As revealed in this account, her difficult childhood caused her eventually to enter the world of prostitution. Although Soledad's experiences are tragic, in relating them she reveals her

*Soledad Fuente is a pseudonym.

strong will and sense of independence, traits that have helped her cope with trying circumstances.

I didn't know my father until I was ten years old. He and my mother split up because of my grandmother, who told many things to my father about my mother. He was always in the United States, in Los Angeles, because that is where he lived. When I finally met him, he was very nice to me. I would go see him every Sunday when he was staying in Juárez with my grandmother. My mother told me not to go looking for him, to just leave things as they were, but I couldn't. I would cry a lot, and I would tell my mother that it was her fault they were apart and that's why she didn't want me to see him.

When my father left for Los Angeles, my grandmother would want me to go visit her. I would go to her house, and at the same time I would go to other places. I would always be organizing parties in the neighborhood. When my mother and my aunts would go off to weddings or to dances I would cry because they wouldn't take me. Sometimes my grandmother would take me to where my mother was, at the dances, and I would be thrilled. When I was thirteen my father came to Juárez and they had a piñata for me. Everybody brought me gifts. I was spoiled.

My mother was always working in El Paso, cleaning homes, washing, ironing, and she left the baby with me. As best as she could my mother gave [me] everything I wanted. She would buy things for my brother and for me, so neither one would feel left out. At first I hated my brother, but after I took care of him I liked him. On one occasion my mother became ill, and I told a friend of mine, "I am going to work." But she told me not to, that I needed to stay in school. Frankly, my mother was sick because she had drunk too much; she had a hangover. I was desperate; I didn't know what to do. My grandmother would get angry with her because of her drinking. My uncle wanted to take my baby brother from her. I understood my mother very well, and I would tell my uncle, "Why do you want to take the baby from her if she is good to us? What's wrong if she drinks a beer once a week?" My uncle always meddled in our lives, and we were afraid of him. When I went dancing he would tell me I had to be home by midnight, and I would say, "All right."

But I was not satisfied to have to go home at that time. I would start partying at a *tardeada* (an afternoon party) and from there I would go someplace where there was music, where I could dance. I was fourteen at the time, and I went dancing everywhere, but I wouldn't drink. Once I was about to lose my virginity, but I didn't out of fear of my uncle. The first time he hit me was when someone spread gossip that I had had sex with the son of a teacher. My uncle pulled me by the hair across the patio, took me indoors, and beat me with his belt buckle. He hit me in the eye and shut it. When my mother got home she told him not to touch me again, and he never did. I would ditch school constantly. I liked basketball, and I would go to other schools to play. I would tell my mother that we had to go to such and such a stadium to practice. Of course, I was lying. I hardly cared about school. I would also go to the movies or to dances.

I never missed a party. I liked to hang around with older women, although I didn't pay much attention to their conversation. The first time I stayed out all night was when some women invited me to a party. I told my mother I would be home by twelve or twelve-thirty, and she let me go. But after the party was over we went to someone's house. Everybody started necking, and I did, too. But I was able to control myself because I was afraid of my uncle. That's when I started drinking, and the girls didn't want to let me go home because they didn't want my mother to see me drunk, so I stayed there. At four in the morning I got up to go to the bathroom and my period started. Later I told the girls I was leaving because I felt my mother was probably very worried, but they said to wait, that they would tell her that nothing had happened. A little while later, my mother found us and everybody was scared. The girls tried to explain but my mother didn't want to hear it. I had to leave. When we got home my aunts held my arms and my mother beat me with a piece of hose so hard that I urinated in my panties and stained the bed. When my mother saw that she said, "I wouldn't be surprised if you are no longer a virgin." I denied it and told her to take me to a doctor so she could be sure I was still a virgin.

The next time I left home I stayed out for two days with a girlfriend. My friend's mother then took me home and told my mother they had kept me there because I was sick, but my mother wouldn't believe her. Since my friend was a hairdresser, she had fixed my hair really nicely. I went in and sat at the edge of the bed, thinking, "They're going to beat me again." All of a sudden my mother came with the scissors and started cutting my hair. It was long. She cut it all off. I said, "Now that you have left me without hair, what do you want?" and she slapped me. I have never liked to be slapped, so I shouted at her that I hated her. I cried and cried. The next day I was still angry at her. She gave me a scarf and I put it on and went outside. I stood at the corner with some boys from the neighborhood and asked for a cigarette, although I didn't smoke. I knew my uncle would be passing by soon, and I was doing that deliberately to get revenge.

Sure enough, when he saw me, he said, "You are worse than a whore." He shouted those horrible words to me and then slapped me right in front of those boys. I laughed and laughed. "I don't care about any of you anymore. Why did you cut off my hair? Instead of straightening me out you are messing me up." I ran back into the house, and he came right behind, yelling at me. I said, "You take care of me, but you don't let me enjoy things. I am tired of everything." My uncles and aunts became silent. I shut them up and left them thinking.

My hair grew again and I went back to my old ways. My mother told me I just didn't understand, that she would need to put me in a school for girls. I didn't object. The first few days went fine, but then I got bored and escaped. I just walked away but they caught up with me and took me back. I escaped a second time and they caught me again. The third time they called my mother and told her they couldn't put up with me, that she would need to take me home. So I went home again. My mother asked me if I was going to behave and I said yes. But I felt like dancing. At the girls' school I had gotten everybody to dance. Soon my best friend from childhood came around and invited me out, and my mother let me go. My girlfriend was really naive. That night I danced all night and she went home by herself. In the morning, I went to her house and asked her to let me stay with her because I didn't want to go home. She said, "Soledad, go home now because the longer you stay out the longer will be the reprimand." But I insisted and she let me stay. Later I went home. They asked me where I had stayed, and I told them. But they wouldn't believe me, so they went and asked and were satisfied.

I became even more rebellious. My uncle tried both a hard and a sweet approach. On one occasion, he asked me if I wanted to give a party and I said yes. So I gave a party. But I was still dissatisfied because those kinds of parties ended early. Finally one day, I said to myself, "What I really want is to be free. I am tired of living in this house." That night I decided to carry out my plan. After I did the dishes, I wrote a letter, saying, "Don't look for me because you won't find me anywhere. Soledad." I stepped out of the house. It was raining very hard. They saw me and asked me where I was going. I said that a friend who was sick had sent for me. They asked me to wait until [it] stopped raining, but I said no, and took off running. I went to a friend's house, a girl who had several sisters. They let me in right away and gave me hot coffee and some dry clothes. Their mother really liked me. She asked me what was the matter and I started to cry. "They threw me out of the house." She said, "But how can that be? How could your mother do that?" That lady adored me because whenever I stayed at her house I would get up in the morning and do many things around the house, things her daughters never wanted to do. I sat there, crying and crying, and drinking coffee. I was just play[ing] the part. She said, "You can stay here with us. We are going to open up a new beauty salon and you can help out and we'll pay you a small salary. If they come to get you, tell them you don't want to go." I was really happy because the daughters went dancing every Saturday and Sunday.

One day the girls got an invitation to a wedding reception, and we decided to go. It turned out to be one of my aunts who had gotten married. As we were going up the elevator I saw people I knew. "My God, everybody from my *barrio* [neighborhood] is here." I got very nervous, but nobody saw me. As soon as we sat at a table I told the girls we should go, so [we] went to Curley's. I felt better there. My relatives were at their wedding and I was carousing around. After that they found me. I don't know who told them where I was. I really got chewed out, but they didn't hit me. I told my mother I had left because I was going to have a baby, and I knew they would kick me out as soon as they found out. Of course, that was a lie. My mother said, "So you're going to have a baby. Well, we're going to put you in a home for girls." I said, "That's all right, because I don't want to go with you." The following morning they took me to a home called the Girls' Refuge. My friends told me they kept the girls locked up at that place, but I said, "It doesn't matter."

The head nun introduced me to the girls, and I got to talking to one of them. She was chewing gum and asked me questions. I was quite apprehensive. Then [she] said, "We have a good time here. We can get *mota* [marijuana] and pills." Then she asked me to tell them why I was there. I told them my story, and she said she too had made up a story like mine, that she also was a virgin, and they asked me to tell them about that, so I invented a story. I told them I ran away with my boyfriend, but the *bato* [guy] didn't want to get married. Since I didn't want to tell my mother who the boy was, she decided to put me in the home. The girls asked me about the places where I danced, and when I told them one said, "Wow, how nice. I wish I were outside so I could go dancing." These girls were really crazy. I asked for a cigarette and they took me to a corral which had pigs in it. That's where we smoked like mad. They offered me *mota* and pills and I didn't want to at first, but then I accepted.

I really wasn't depressed there. I went to school, although I didn't study much. When I graduated from primary school my mother gave me a graduation dress. They had a Mass for us and took us to get our pictures taken. I got my diploma, even though I had skipped the fifth grade. I was happy that day. We borrowed a radio and I did quite a bit of dancing, whirling round and round, doing the "rock and roll." We all had a good time.

I got to be good friends with the girls. There was one in particular, Teresa, who liked to hang around with me. She was thirteen and I was fifteen. One day they took us to the doctor for a medical examination. Teresa claimed she was a virgin and of course I said I was not. After the examination, she said, "Well, you who claimed you were not a virgin turned out to be one, and I who claimed I was turned out not to be one." I explained to her that I knew the doctor would think I was a virgin, because my hymen had grown shut. That was simplistic on my part, but I was always saying things like that. My mother always told me I was simpleminded. Those of us who were virgins were separated from the others. We were in different dormitories and we were not allowed to leave the school.

I became very fond of Teresa, and when I saw her with other girls I became jealous. One night I was already in bed and Teresa came by to see me. She asked me why I was angry with her and I said I wasn't. It was one of those times that one doesn't want to express feelings, or doesn't know what to say. I didn't want to face it; I didn't want to believe it. I started crying, and then she cried also. We held each other, embraced, and kissed. She started fondling me and everything and I did the same to her. I asked her if she was repentant about what we were doing, but she said no, that she loved me. I told her I felt the same way. We got really excited, but didn't know how to do it. Then one of the other girls came in and asked, "What are you doing, dirty girls?" We got embarrassed, but she said not to worry, that she did the same thing with her girlfriend. We were eager to learn more and asked her how she did it. We talked and talked. Teresa and I became inseparable; I would play the role of the man and she of the woman. To make me angry, she would intentionally hang around with someone else. Later at the dormitory I would lock the door and I would slap her; the next day she wouldn't want to talk to me. One day she got real sick and was not supposed to leave the dormitory, but just to upset me she came down and started talking sweetly to someone else. I became so enraged that I grabbed her, scratched her, and threw her against the sofa. She became very angry; I had never seen her that way. She said, "Don't ever touch me again and don't ever speak to me." While she was sick they kept her locked up. I tried to see her, but she wouldn't let me.

There were other couples in the dormitory—Patricia with Margarita, Juana with Ramona. . . . I think Juana was angry with Ramona, and to make her jealous she would go up to see Teresa. Of course, that would make me jealous too, so I said to Ramona, "Let's escape. Let's go get the keys from the chapel. We'll tell the nun we want to clean it up." That was one of my jobs, to clean the chapel. We got the keys to the chapel and along with them the keys to the main door. Four of us then hid in the chapel for a while and then went out the front door and through the cotton fields to the highway. We caught a bus to Juárez and went to a friend's house. That night we went dancing. A week later my mother came by with some policemen and they caught us. She took me home and the police took the other girls back to the school. I was very angry. That night I found some pills in the refrigerator; they were red capsules. I swallowed about eight of them. I wasn't drunk or anything; I just wanted to die. I also ate a whole bunch of *chicharrones* [pig skins]. I got real sick; I didn't let anybody sleep. I don't know what they gave me so I would throw up. The following day they took me back to the Girls' Refuge.

Teresa was waiting for me at the front of the building. She said, "How cruel you are. Why did you leave me?"

I was in that place four years and I escaped four times. The last time Teresa went with me. When they caught us, Teresa was kept locked up and I became worried. I sneaked upstairs and knocked on the door. "Teresa, what happened?" She said, "Don't leave me, Soledad. My aunts want to take me away and I don't want to go." I said I wouldn't leave her, but what could I do? Her aunts came by and took her; they had money. I never heard anything else from Teresa.

After another year at the school I was taken out because I behaved myself. Then my mother heard gossip that I didn't care about school and that I had many boyfriends and all kinds of lies. So they sent me back. After a while they took me out again, and this time my uncle got stricter. He asked me what I wanted to study and I said English, so he enrolled me at the Lydia Patterson Institute in El Paso. I was there about a week, when I got myself a boyfriend, a married man. I was in love with him. I ditched school and went off to make out with him. As a married man he had a lot of experience; he was smarter than me. He was the one who dishonored me. They were strict at that school, so they sent a notice home that I was not attending classes. My mother suspected something and said, "This time I am going to take you to the doctor." I told her that wasn't necessary, that I was no longer a virgin. "What's more, I think I'm pregnant. I haven't menstruated in three months." She cried, "What are we going to tell your uncle?"

One day my mother and I were arguing and my uncle came in wanting to know what was going on. My mother told him I wanted to leave. He said, "Well, let her grab her rags and go to hell. But from there on our door will be closed to her." So I left and started suffering. I slept in the cab of one of those big trucks. The driver knew what had happened to me and he let me stay there. On Thursdays I went to a friend's house and she fed me. Later I just stayed there until I had my little girl. Then my boyfriend's mother wanted to take the baby from me because she didn't like the life I was leading. I wanted to keep my baby and so I started selling little baskets on the streets to earn money for a lawyer. By then I was a prostitute, but I stopped that way of life a while. My boyfriend's family had money. They hired a lawyer and took my daughter from me. I asked my family for help but didn't get it. I was really bitter about the whole thing and went to live with an aunt in El Paso, where I didn't go out for six months. I was sixteen then.

When I was back home in Juárez one of my girlfriends came by and we went dancing at Curley's. I got all dressed up and was feeling good. By then I didn't want to drink sodas; I only wanted hard liquor. I drank quite a bit and she wanted to take me home, but I said, "I'm staying here. I have no one, no home, nothing. Leave me alone." She left. After that I drank heavily every day. Then a friend said to me, "Look, Soledad, don't be dumb. If you're going to be doing that around there, take advantage of it. Don't just drink to drink; use it to make some money from the *gabachos* [Anglo-Americans]." I caught on to that and started making lots of money with the *gabachos*. Then I got a job as a "go-go" dancer at the Crystal Palace, even though I was a minor. There were six of us dancing there. One day the police raided the place and they took us to the juvenile hall, but they let us go and we continued to dance. I was arrested again and decided to go someplace else, but I had trouble getting work because I was a minor. Three months before I turned eighteen I was put in the juvenile hall. Since I was the oldest they put me in charge of making sure the girls took showers, but after having to hit someone who didn't want to shower I told them I didn't want to do that. They said I would have to and when I refused they shaved my head. I cried loudly.

That night one of the big shots came to the juvenile hall asking which girls had their heads shaved? I said to him, "Can't you see, you stupid man, you son of a bitch." That's what I told him. He said, "You know what, miss? Neither your mother nor I are at fault that you are here." I answered, "Then who is? The mother of your *chingada madre* [fucking mother]?" I was so mad because they had cut off my hair. He didn't say anything else, he just left. I didn't care if they put me in jail. Nobody else talked to him that way. The other girls got a big kick out of it.

When I turned eighteen they let me go. I remember I wore a red scarf over my bare head. My mother was told I was being released, but she didn't bother to pick me up. I said to myself, "So be it. Now where am I going to go without money or anything? And with a wig? Oh, my God!" I walked down the street, crying. I went to my grandmother's house, but it turned out she and her family were in Los Angeles, California. I decided to go to a friend's house, the girl with whom I had stayed the first time I ran away from home. When she saw me she said, "Jesus, what happened to you?" I explained everything to her and then I asked her mother if I could stay with them. She said yes, and I lived there for a while. They gave me a wig. But I would keep asking myself, "Why live off these people, always confusing this lady?" I thanked her for her help and told her I was old enough to find my own way in life. I returned to the bar Noa Noa. Three or four other *pelonas* [bald women] were there, but of course they had wigs on. Once one of them got drunk and became hysterical. She yelled and cried and took off her wig. She told me to take off mine, but I said no, that if she tried to take it off from me I would kill her. That would have been an embarrassment for me as a woman; hair is what adorns the face. The girls got scared. They told me not to pay any attention to her, that she was drunk and was only kidding. Nothing happened and she left.

At that time my ovaries began to hurt from all the relations I had with men. My stomach would become inflamed and I would shout like a crazy woman from the pain. When I danced it would hurt especially bad. One of the girls took me to a pharmacy and I got an injection; then I raised my feet and the pain eased. But I couldn't work very well; I would have to stay in my room at the hotel where I lived. I would run out of money and wouldn't have enough to pay the rent, so I would tell the manager to give me credit, that I would pay him later. I lived at that hotel for seven years.

Once the father of my daughter looked for me and found me in the hotel. I started to cry. I asked him why he had done that to me. "You were married and had your own kids. You had no need to take my daughter from me." He said, "No, it was my mother who did all that. I said nothing to her. Why would I want the child with me if I knew she was with you?" But I hated him and his mother. They would bring me my daughter so I could see her, but I would tell his mother not to come near me. He asked me for forgiveness but I said, "You think that will bring back what I loved so much, my first dream and all of that?" A child is a child; her blood is my blood. One loves them from the time one is carrying them. I cry a lot when I see my child.

In my life, the thing that bothers me the most is that I have always had bad luck with men, always. The first *bato* I lived with loved me very much; he gave me everything I wanted. He supported me and gave me a home. Then, wham! He went to California. When he returned he was crazy. So it was not meant to be with that man. And that's the way things continued to be. I have lived with *batos* who love me and everything, but then one thing or another happens and that's it.

I would cross into El Paso with Americanos, and one night I crossed with three of them. I hid on the floor of the car and they put their legs over me so the immigration inspector couldn't see me. I heard them say we were going to the airport, but when we stopped we were at the desert. They said, "Take off your clothes." I refused, so one of them threatened me with a knife. "So you won't take them off?" He scared me. I undressed and "laid" all three. Then they told me to give them a "blow job," but I said, "I won't do it. If I don't do that to a Mexican, why would I do it to you?" They put the knife to my stomach, but I said, "I will not do that." They tried to scare me. They then kicked me out of the car and threw my clothes at me. One of them hit me on the head and blood came out. They got scared and took off without turning their lights on. They must have thought I was going to look at the license plates. I walked and rocks kept getting into my sandals and stickers clung to my pants. I cried and cried and the blood just kept dripping out. Then a jeep full of soldiers came by and they tried to put me aboard, but, since I was still traumatized, I shouted and tried to scratch them. Only when they slapped me did I regain control. "What happened to you?" They forced me into the jeep and took me to an office where I was asked if I was a prostitute. I said, "No," but then one of them said, "Hi, Soledad." I thought, "I've had it."

A Puerto Rican soldier took me aside and cleaned my face. He thought he was translating for me, but I was answering all the questions in English. I was asked what punishment I wanted to see the soldiers get. I said three years in jail for the leader and six months for each of the other two. From there they took me to the base hospital where I was looked after. When the doctor was taking care of me, I thought to myself, "I feel like laying this guy right here." I still didn't realize what had happened to me. I was then taken to the border patrol and one of them kept asking me if I was a whore. I told him that it was none of his business, to leave me in peace. He wouldn't let up, so finally I complained that he was bothering me. He got chewed out and was told to leave. Then they took me home. Later they assigned a lawyer to my case and I would cross into El Paso and look at soldiers through a two-way mirror. They found the guilty ones because the police found my red brassiere in their car. That was the only thing they had not thrown to me. They must have hidden it in their car and thought that everything was over.

Even after that I continued to accept rides from strangers, from Mexicans or whoever. Sometimes when someone refused to pay me [after sex], I would leave the motel or wherever I was and start walking on the highway. Getting a ride was easy. Once I was taken away from the center of town and beaten by one guy while the other one just looked on. I asked him to help me, but the idiot didn't do anything. I yelled and the man bit me; I still have two scars from that. In a moment of anger I bit his ear as though I wanted [to] swallow it. We struggled and the other one finally said, "Leave her alone! Let's go!" But my attacker told him to stay out of it. I think he was drunk. They started driving and I hit the window with all the strength I had and I broke it. At that moment a police car came by and apprehended them. They really worked over that *bato.* The following day my arm was purple all over. After that I didn't ask for rides any more.

I worked independently, because if you worked for a bar they would charge you for everything, even the toilet paper. Those of us who worked clandestinely [unregistered] could keep all the money we made. The only one we paid was the man in charge of the bar, who protected us from being taken in by officers of the Sanitation Department. He would give them a *mordida* [bribe] and they would let us "hustle." It was a good deal for the bar owner because we would drink there. Before I worked out that deal I was arrested by Sanitation frequently, almost every other day. At times, I hardly had money to pay the fines. Once a new chief of Sanitation wanted to increase the fines, but the Chamber of Commerce would not go for it. That day all the girls who worked at Curley's were ready to hide in the back just in case they came. But they would come in and find you, even in the bathroom.

For a time I worked at Virginia's, where we were checked by Sanitation every Thursday. They would arrive and give each girl a number and ask us to form a line. One by one we would be examined by the doctor. Part of the exam consisted in opening your legs and having the *pato* ["duck," or examination instrument] inserted to see if you were well or not. It's called a *pato* because it is shaped like a duck's beak. They insert it in you and then open it once inside and they are able to see through small mirrors. You have to know how they do it so you can assume the proper position so it won't hurt. Some girls didn't clean themselves, and the doctor would get a whiff of their odor. But he would put up with it. I think they are used to it. Sometimes the doctor would tell some of the girls to clean themselves more often, even with just water, if soap was not available. After the exam we would get a card which proved we had passed. Sanitation would go around to the bars and call the girls by name and ask them for their cards. Those without cards would be fined two hundred pesos. If you were not there when they came by, they would look for you again. You were obligated to let the bar or Sanitation know that you would not be there. You had to stay in your own bar, otherwise Sanitation would give you problems. Even if you just wanted to have a drink someplace else, you couldn't do that. I had a friend who finally got a special permit from Sanitation allowing her to go drinking by herself because she was tired of the harassment.

I went looking for work in the *maquiladoras* [foreign-owned assembly plants], but I was asked for a high-school diploma and this and that. Why is that diploma so necessary? They put up those factories to provide work and to eliminate prostitution. But how are they going to eliminate it if the employers demand so much? Some of the girls who work in the *maquiladoras* make five hundred pesos per week, others more. Five hundred pesos is not enough, but what one wants is permanent work. At the end of the week you know they will pay you; your money is assured. Being a prostitute sometimes you make it and sometimes you don't. When things go well, great. But when they don't, there's not much you can do about it. Prostitution is not easy. You run the risk of being beaten, of being robbed, or getting killed, or of having things done to you that you don't like. You have to do it because you need the money. I spoke with a lawyer who helped some *camaradas* [friends] get jobs in a factory, and he said he would help me. Maybe he will. At the Sanitation office, they would tell us, "The president is going to put up some factories so you will stop being prostitutes." And we would say, "Well, build them. You've been saying that for a long time." Nothing happens.

15

Irma Muller

Marjorie Agosin
Edited and Translated by Nina M. Scott

The horror of the ordinary and the unexplained characterizes the chilling repression of society by Chile's military regime. The simple, terrible act of making someone disappear without elaborate, ghastly techniques or Nazi-inspired pogroms, just an abrupt, complete disappearance of someone from everyday life, numbs the sensibilities.

Marjorie Agosin has published her volumes of poetry, including *Witches and Other Things*, both in Latin America and in the United States, where she is often called upon to give public readings of her poems. She also publishes extensively in the fields of literary criticism and women's studies. After visiting her native Santiago, Agosin described her reaction to Chile under the rule of General Augusto Pinochet in *Wellesley Magazine* (Winter 1986). Currently, she teaches in the Spanish department at Wellesley College and continues to write poetry.

Nina Scott is a professor of Spanish at the University of Massachusetts. Her publications include criticism of both Latin American and peninsular literature and studies of women authors, including Sor Juana Inéz de la Cruz. A veteran of visiting professorships in Germany and Ecuador, Scott is a champion of the Fulbright exchange program. Recently, her research has been in the area of humor in literature.

INTRODUCTION

"To disappear is to vanish, to cease to be, to be lost forever." This is how Amnesty International defines this sinister invention, designed by repressive governments so that all opposition may cease to be, stop existing, or, better yet, so that those who are "missing" are swallowed up into the void of the inexplicable, the irrevocable, the uncertainty that someone has really been absolutely lost. To die is infinitely easier. Life comes to an end with the act of burial; there is a specific resting place for the remains of the loved one. However, for the relatives of those who have disappeared there is no one who knows where they are, in which prisons they have been tortured, and, above all, whether they are alive or dead.

When someone disappears, no one knows anything at all. There is only the indelible memory of the day on which that person disappeared, perhaps the street in which he or she was apprehended, the clothes worn. To disappear, then, becomes that inexplicable amalgam of the real—the act of vanishing—and the unreal: where has that person gone?

In 1966 the term *desaparecidos* was used to describe a specific practice of the Guatemalan government; this practice has been applied on a massive scale in Chile since September 1973 and in Argentina from 1976 to 1982. According to the governments involved, their practice of making people disappear has been implemented to safeguard order in their respective countries. However, it seems difficult to believe that order can be maintained in a country by means of repression, violence, and torture.

The story of Irma Muller, the mother of a missing person in Chile, is perhaps among the most concrete examples of what it means to have a member of one's family disappear. Statistics are utterly unable to transmit such a message or to express the pain felt by a mother, a sister, or other relatives when they discover that from one day to the next a loved one has passed to that feared and inexplicable category of "missing person."

Irma Muller is a middle-aged, middle-class woman. Ironically, she lived just half a block from my home in Santiago, but we never met until many years later, after our lives had taken different paths and acquired significantly different meanings.

As she recounts in her testimony, Irma Muller's life was transformed from one day to the next when her only son and his fiancée disappeared. Ever since their relatives disappeared, Irma and other women in similar situations have never ceased to search in jails, concentration camps, and ministries. They have appealed to international organizations for any answer at all, yet up to this time the whereabouts of her son and of the others is as uncertain and as indefinite as the very term "missing person" itself.

I met Irma Muller in the early 1980s, when I was working for the Vicariate of Solidarity and was writing a book on the *arpilleras*. *Arpilleras* are a type of small tapestry or wall hanging consisting of scraps of material appliquéd to a larger backing cloth made out of burlap;

they are also a direct product of the problem of the missing persons and form a part of Irma's story.

In 1974, when all means of aid for the needy and all of the channels of the protection of human rights were cut off, the Catholic Church assumed a leadership role in creating an organization, which, under its stewardship, would help the relatives, especially the wives, of missing persons. This is the Vicariate of Solidarity, an exemplary institution in the history of human rights in Chile. Through the Vicariate, the first *arpillera* workshops were organized in 1975. The participants, who are known as *arpilleristas*, were given a chance to fight the specific economic problem of hunger as well as other problems of a sociopolitical nature. Spurred on by their desire to denounce the country's political situation, they began to create the tapestries whose small scraps of material speak of torture, of missing persons, of the lack of schools for children. The tapestries became internationally famous and were more eloquent than any statistics about the number of tortured or missing persons in General Pinochet's Chile.

I got to know Irma in one of the twenty-five *arpillerista* workshops that exist in the poor neighborhoods of Santiago. Within the totality of these workshops, she belongs to the one that is both the oldest and involved in one of the most noteworthy activities in authoritarian Chile, the Association of Relatives of Detained-Missing Persons (Agrupación de Familiares de Detenidos-Desaparecidos). Irma is one of the principal founders and a leader of this group, which was started in 1974 and the majority of whose members are women. Among the association's numerous activities, including specific demands for information on the whereabouts of the approximately ten thousand persons reported missing between 1973 and 1986, this group manufactures *arpilleras* in order to protest political oppression as well as help alleviate the sorrow that comes from the loss of a loved one.

Irma is a quiet woman, but when she tells her story an enormous silence ensues. She says that her own destiny is linked to that of the women in her group as well as to the women in the country as a whole. It is impressive to hear the certainty with which she says, "I will find a way and I will find my son because of it." She describes an *arpillera* she is making that shows a mother and a little boy running freely on a beach. This child is Irma's, but the image is also a metaphor in order to strengthen the morale and the spirit of solidarity within her group.

Most of all, one is impressed by her accounts of the many times when, in search of her loved ones, she went to the different prisoner detention centers. Even though she knew that torture and murder were the norm in these places, she makes it a point of maintaining, "I never let the jailers see me cry."

When one hears Irma speak to her companions, one understands immediately that no one is immune from the threat of exile, of torture, of also becoming a missing person. Because of the awareness of this constant threat, group solidarity is essential both for survival itself and for the ability to deal with the deep wounds caused by their latent grief.

In order to bear witness to her suffering, Irma Muller has dedicated herself for almost fourteen years to the production of *arpilleras*. She feels that her pain moves beyond individual boundaries when it is shared not only by the others who are engaged in making *arpilleras* but also by those who see and buy the finished tapestries and who imagine the life stories behind what is truly an art form born of resistance.

The group's activities are endless, ranging from constant letters to numerous international organizations to nonviolent protests held in the corridors of the legislature, on the plazas, or at the detention centers. Aside from these activities Irma organizes handicraft classes for students who come from the disadvantaged sectors of the population; she is convinced that Chilean young people have been morally betrayed and emotionally crippled and need encouragement to reform their moral conscience. She maintains that, as grandmother to her daughter's children, it is her duty to tell them and show them what their country's history has been during the years of the dictatorship.

For about six years, during my trips to Chile, I have visited Irma Muller periodically and always find a smile and a kind voice. We sit and have tea, talk a great deal, and laugh together, but we always return to the same obsessive theme: the disappearance of her son and of so many others like him. I asked her to write an account in which she would relate what had happened, and, although it was exceedingly painful for her to recreate the horror of what she had been through, she agreed, saying, "Of course, I will do it because my story must be known and because silence is our worst enemy." This is her testimony.

After having lived for so many years under a dictatorship and having endured for almost all those years the disappearance of a loved one, one almost forgets how to write; so numerous are the thoughts of pain, anguish, rage, and impotence that the senses seem unable to do anything but to focus on all of that. I ask myself constantly, what can I do? How can I escape from the black well which is Chile? It seems that all I do is useless—as though one tries to keep a drop of water from slipping through one's fingers. I don't know where to begin to tell all that has happened to me since my son was arrested and made to disappear. I think there is not enough paper in the world to record what these years have been like.

My son Jorge was a movie cameraman. He studied at the School of Film at the Viña de Mar branch of the University of Chile and began to make films even before he finished his studies. He made documentaries about political events during the time of the Popular Unity government (Unidad Popular) of President Salvador Allende Gossens [1970–73]. In 1970 he toured various European countries to film the trip of the erstwhile minister, Clodomiro Almeyda. His work was steady even after the military coup. Early in 1974 he made his last picture, "In the Shadow of the Sun," in northern Chile. On November 28, 1974, this film premiered in the Las Condes Theater, in an exclusive neighborhood in Santiago. Even those in uniform attended. When I saw the film, I was so proud of what my son had done and said to my husband, "Jorge has a great future ahead of him," little realizing that [that] would be the last time we would see him. When the show was over, we met on the way out and he said, "I'm not coming home tonight because we're going to celebrate the film's success." We didn't ask him where he was going but later, when I began to look for him, we found out that the whole group had gone to the house of a woman friend of theirs and had stayed there all night. The next morning, when he and Carmen were going to Chile Film, that's when they were arrested. The same morning two men came to my home to ask where he was, and when I asked them who they were, they said friends from work; subsequently, I found out that they weren't colleagues at all, but that was a lot later, when I had gotten to know in general what types of men made the arrests—especially one of them who arrested many young people in those years and whose name is Romo . . . at this moment I can't remember his exact name, because it's as though part of me wants to blot him out of my mind, and on the other hand, I know how important it is not to forget him.

On November 29, 1974, when my son Jorge and Carmen should have gone to Chile Film and didn't get there, the office began to call and ask me where he was. I really didn't get too worried, because I spoke with a friend of his, and he told me that he thought that the whole group had gone to the beach, but in spite of that I had my doubts. Personally, I knew nothing about people who were detained;

it was Jorge who always told me everything that went on. Actually, at times I didn't want to believe everything he told me. I thought that I had always been partial to the military, all the more so because I have two half-brothers who are retired *carabineros* [Chilean national police] with the rank of captain; back then I thought that if someone had detained Jorge just because he thought differently from them, surely that person would be tried because, after all, that's what the courts are there for. Besides, we're pretty well off economically, and I have a brother-in-law who is a high United Nations functionary in Chile, so I thought nothing serious would come of the whole thing. So many relatives thought and believed just as I did, because nothing like this had ever happened in Chile before.

When there was no doubt as to his arrest, a friend advised me to go to the Committee for Peace [Comité Pro Paz] that had been in operation since the military coup of 1973, giving legal advice to those who had been arrested. From that instant on, this whole awful thing began. Every day I visited Los Alamos concentration camp, asking if he were being held there. Sometimes the guards said yes, he was there and could have visitors, and then when the time came to go into the camp they would tell me that he wasn't there, that he had never been arrested. Naturally, the camp was full of armed police, and whenever you got closer than you were allowed to they'd put a rifle to your forehead as though they were going to shoot. In the camp, I was once able to speak with a lieutenant whose last name was Azbaleta; he was a military lieutenant, and I didn't find out his first name. This man made me think he was nice and said, I'll go in to ask if your son has been arrested; naturally, he came back with the answer that he wasn't there. I kept going to Los Alamos more or less half a year until July or August 1975, in the hopes that they might tell me where they had taken him.

I went to the office where they were supposed to give out information about people who had been arrested. I went every day to ask about my son. The four branches of the military were in this office, and you had to sign in and leave your identity card; afterwards they went through all this farce of going to look at some lists their superiors had and naturally always came back with the same answer. In this office they also had a social assistant called Raquel Lois, who, according to them, was there to help the women who were imprisoned get freed. There was also a soldier named Jorge Espinosa Ulloa, who at one point saw me and told me that my son had not been arrested, that perhaps he, like so many others, had left the country, and then, right in the midst of everything he was telling me, said, "the act justifies the means." How can I ever forget it? And when he was leaving he held out his hand and I didn't know whether to take it or spit on it.

Another time I went to the Ministry of Defense. I already knew that the head of DINA [Directorate of National Investigations] was General Manuel Contreras Sepulveda, but the Contreras who appeared was very old and had absolutely nothing to do with DINA. Then he said, "I'm not the one you're looking for but go one floor down and ask to speak to General ———"; I can't remember his name right now, but I have it written down somewhere, because I remember very clearly what this general told me. After waiting for him a long time in a big lobby, I watched very attentively as military men went in and out; then they took me to a small room so I couldn't watch any more. Later on, this general comes, and I explain to him what I am looking for; then he says that he isn't from the DINA but from the military secret service, which is for the military only. He asks my son's age, and I tell him that he's twenty-six. Whereon he says, why are you so worried? Seems like your kid's a mama's boy. Then I got furious and asked him if he had any sons and if he planned to classify them as mama's boys when they got older. I asked him what kind of a father he was that led him to think that children reached a point where they didn't need their parents any more. I spoke to him of the pain of the Virgin Mary when she saw her son crucified, and I know that morally I shamed him at that moment, but I got nowhere.

I sent letters to all the members of the junta, to any general who was in charge of anything at all. I got answers, but they were always the same ones: he has not been arrested by this ministry. I even sent a letter to that Lucía person [the wife of General Augusto Pinochet], appealing to her love as a mother, and the reply she sent me said, "Submit all details to the appropriate agencies," and that's all I ever heard. Afterwards, I got so angry and the hurt was so dreadful that I didn't want to write anymore, except abroad, letting them know everything that had happened. I wrote to the United Nations, to Amnesty International, and so forth; each time I got a reply which said that they had reported the particulars of the case history to Pinochet but had so far received no answer.

My husband is German, in spite of having lived in Chile for forty years now. He never wanted to change his citizenship and I never asked him to because, after all, a piece of paper doesn't make you a citizen. Because of this my son had the possibility of going to Germany if he wanted to. We went to the German Embassy to ask for a residence permit in Germany in the event that he might turn up again and they gave it to me, saying that he could reside there when he was freed. I think the embassy knew perfectly well that my son was imprisoned but they didn't do anything either, just gave me the permit. Or did they already know the fate of the people who were detained or missing? I always wondered about that.

In 1976, Pinochet sent the case histories of the prisoners we were looking for to the United Nations. In these case histories it says that the one hundred fifty prisoners we were searching for had no legal status and were fictitious names. Jorge's name was on this list, and in light of this we went to the embassy and told them what monstrous things they were saying about these cases. Then the embassy sent a letter of inquiry to the Ministry of Foreign Affairs. They got a reply on letterhead stationery from the Ministry of Foreign Affairs and, among the other things they were answering for the embassy, [it] said that "because of an unfortunate error the name of Jorge Muller had been put on the list and they would check into it." The signature was a scrawl; nobody was responsible, and no one could be in any way identified. Those cowards, who from the beginning have hidden their evil faces!

The search for my son Jorge sent me on a road I never thought I would take. When I used to talk to my son, I always told him I was too old to begin to do new things. I wasn't even fifty years old then, and I thought that when you got to that stage in life you deserved a little peace and quiet and would wait for the grandchildren. Then he'd say to me, "Mama, at your age how can you possibly think you're too old to learn things? Look at Clotario Blest [founder of the Chilean labor movement in the 1930s]—he was already in his fifties." I had to go through my son's loss to realize that there's no age limit on being able to fight for something. Naturally, I wouldn't be able to go out and fire a gun, but, thank God, one has been given a brain and the ability to think in order to get things done. All the things I've accomplished these past years. . . . But I could never have just stayed home with my hands in my lap. The best memorial I can give my son is to take up his standard and fight, and in a way that's what I've done. I'm an active member of the Association of Relatives of Detained-Missing Persons and have been an officer in that same organization. I make *arpilleras* and use the embroideries as a method of denouncing the human-rights abuses, and this I've done practically from the moment my son disappeared. In the Committee for Peace, they taught us how to make *arpilleras*; they were always looking for ways to lessen the anguish we were living with. You could also do silk screening and knitting. As I said, for some women it was a means of easing their sorrow and for others, for those who were very hard up, it meant a way to earn a little money, because many of their menfolk were among the detained.

Another activity which helped me cope with my suffering has been teaching Chilean folk music, which I knew something about but never actually did anything with. In 1978, I was working in the eastern zone where the Vicariate of Solidarity had assigned us because we were from that area. I made contact with unemployed workers and their wives [who also made *arpilleras*] and with people from the slums who always come to the vicariate in search of solutions to many of their problems. Anyway, lots of people. Then I thought, why not make my knowledge of folk music available to them? People need so much to take their minds off their troubles in order to make them more bearable, and that goes as much for my own grief as for that of these good people. Many times I saw them faint with hunger and thought that perhaps it was sacrilege to put on something as festive as singing and dancing with all that was going on, but I gave myself the courage to do it. I spoke to a young man who is a very good musician so that he'd be in charge of the music and I of the rest, and that's how we got this group of regional music and dance from the area of Chiloé [a large island off the southern coast] going.

That was in August 1978, and in September we were already being asked to put on a show, and that's how it has continued until today, not only doing shows but also teaching youth groups in the villages. We've done all this alone, and it's been an uphill battle. This last year we got a contribution from a foreign organization that liked what we were doing, and the money allowed us to buy the instruments we needed. There's a great deal of solidarity in the group. We do shows in children's cafeterias, in villages, for striking syndicates, anywhere our presence is needed, only charging for transportation. The majority of the people who make up this group are unemployed, but their spirits are totally committed. Having gotten involved in this activity has been good for me in that it keeps me physically and morally strong to keep up the fight, because I know what happened to the people who were arrested and are missing.

The tasks of the association [Association of Relatives of Detained-Missing Persons] are numerous, for every day there is something to do. The morale of each and every relative is high, and everyone agrees that the fight must continue. We are constantly looking for ways to keep our cause alive, and for us the pressure that can be brought to bear from abroad by having them ask about our relatives is very important. We know that for Pinochet we are the crazy old women who stir things up, but he has no idea of the strength of spirit of each one of us. And this in spite of having been arrested, in spite of spending time in jail, as has happened to various of my companions; just recently one of the association's members was freed after having been under arrest for several months. Dictators may think that all this can frighten us, but they're totally wrong. They murder people who are supportive of our continual struggle and mean to frighten us as well, but what they don't realize is the groundswell of indignation that comes when people look at whose hands our poor country is in.

I am a believing Christian, and I pray that God will let me live a little longer, because I don't think I can die in peace if I don't know what has happened to my son. The years I have lived weigh on me as thought they were millennia. I wrote a poem about it:

My hair has gone white
My eyes are tired and sad
So many tears have flowed
In these past years.
I live in the question:
Will I see him some day?
I wait so anxiously—
It *must* happen.

It goes on from there. I have written a few other things. Somehow, I never thought that pain could be a source of inspiration. I only write popular poetry, because I don't have the training to write any other kind. It's folk poetry and says things very simply.

What I have done until now I will continue to do in the same way, because I think it's the only way I will be able to hold on. Sometimes I get so tired and would like not to do anything, but then I reproach myself for this attitude, take a deep breath, square my shoulders, and say to myself, "Jorge expects you to do what he was unable to do—and I shall, I shall."

Irma Silva de Muller
Santiago de Chile, April 1985

CONCLUSION

Chile has traditionally been one of the Latin American countries with a profoundly democratic heritage. In approximately one hundred fifty years the country had only one very brief period of dictatorship, under the government of Carlos Ibañez (1927–32). Aside from that, Chile has always been characterized by an influential middle class, something that is unusual in many other Latin American countries.

When Salvador Allende Gossens assumed the presidency in 1970, many Western nations, especially the United States, reacted with a mixture of admiration and astonishment to the fact that a Marxist could have been democratically elected. The process whereby Allende triumphed was not something that emerged all of a sudden or was created solely during the last years of his candidacy; rather, it was a gradual evolution with origins in the intense social changes that were already evident in the country during the period of Eduardo Frei's Christian Democratic government (1964–70).

Just as Allende represented a new democratic spirit for Chile, so has Augusto Pinochet been another radical change that has left a profound mark on the constitutional spirit of the Chilean people. Three years after he assumed power, in 1976, Pinochet began to wreak havoc in the country: leaders of the opposition disappeared, some died, and others had to go into exile. Torture was converted into a sophisticated system in order to subjugate all opposition to Pinochet's policies. Pinochet also proved himself a master at fostering the myth of internal conflict within the country, and for long periods of time he has been successful in keeping political leaders and their respective parties isolated.

Housewife Irma Muller is a part of all these violent changes affecting Chile. Owing to a particular historical event, she has assumed a leading role in the Association of Relatives of Detained-Missing Persons, a role she has stamped with her personal drive and with her inventiveness in creating ever new methods to manifest her opposition to the dictatorship.

Through her, we see how what is political is also personal and how a country's policies affect the lives of all of its inhabitants, those who choose to be silent in order to survive and those who speak out in order not to die and not to forget. Irma Muller is one of those who refuses to be silent and who is a leader of the relatives' association. In her we can observe and come to understand the way a housewife in Chile becomes involved in politics. Even if her son never reappears, her search will not have been in vain.

16

*Doña Sara and Doña Juana: Two Bolivian Weavers**

Mary Ann Medlin

Weaving represents one of the bonds of ethnic identity for the Calcha people of Bolivia's southern Andes. Handwoven cloth serves as an essential indicator of these people's culture. Although modern life (a money economy, male migration to Argentina for periods of work, the availability of cheap manufactured clothing, and other factors) has forced changes in the way these textiles are used, it has not altered the craft, or the pride, of the women who weave.

Mary Ann Medlin lived with the Calcha for nearly four years and returned later for additional stays as she investigated the place of handwoven cloth within the culture of those people. Medlin has examined in detail the interrelationships of weaving, social organization, gender roles, and division of labor in Calcha life. She also has served as a consultant and visiting curator for an exhibit on Bolivian textiles at the Muscarelle Museum, College of William and Mary; for the Folk Art Show of the Potosí Development Corporation, Potosí, Bolivia; and for folk textile exhibits in Sucre, Bolivia. She teaches anthropology at the University of North Carolina at Charlotte.

In the biographies of Doña Sara and Doña Juana, Medlin discusses the meaning of weaving, the impact of new demands made by contemporary life, and the resilience of the cultural importance of handwoven cloth for these women of two different generations.

When she was a small girl, Doña Sara, like all her kin and neighbors, had only the clothes that her mother had woven for her to wear. All the Calcha, a Quechua-speaking ethnic group in southern Bolivia, wore clothing woven by the women. They traded corn, the main crop of these subsistence farmers, for the wool of sheep raised in northern Argentina. Women and men worked together as members of families

*Doña Juana and Doña Sara are pseudonyms.

and settlements, doing all the tasks that needed to be done in order for their families to survive. Women and men worked at their distinctive tasks in the fields as they did in their household compounds. They still made their tools, houses, and clothing.

The Calcha have been an organized group living in southern Potosí, Bolivia, for hundreds of years. They felt the impact of the Inca conquest of their territory in the fourteenth century. In the sixteenth century, they were forced by the Spanish to supply labor for colonial silver mines and goods for the large, nearby mining city of Potosí. A Catholic church was established in the town, and there are records of baptisms and marriages from the 1700s. They were not isolated from the outside or from other ethnic groups with whom they had trade relationships. In the past, they met unavoidable demands from both Inca and colonial administrators. Today, they pay taxes and send their children to school and their young men to military service because they are required to by the state.

Doña Sara was born in 1914 into a household that worked to supply its own needs: family members grew their own food, traded with other groups, and processed raw materials into tools. As a young girl, she learned to weave by watching her mother, who wove clothing for her family and a very few gifts for individuals with close, long-term ties to her. By age ten Doña Sara had started her own first project, having already tried her hand at her mother's loom.

Doña Sara, as a teenager, wove all the textiles needed for a complete fiesta outfit. Respectable young women prepared their dress with care for the fiestas in the town. Young women and men from all of the dispersed hamlets attended the celebrations, which had four groups of musicians and dancers sponsored by the local political leaders. Crowds grew after dark and danced all night. Couples paired up late at night and evaluated one another as prospective marriage partners.

Youths attended with groups of cousins who could check on those thought to be attractive. They knew much about the families of those who were from nearby settlements, and many marriages were made with neighbors. Young men could also look at the fiesta dress of young women to get a good idea of the skill of the weaver, her industriousness, and the resources of her family, who had made weaving supplies available to her.

Doña Sara made a good marriage to a man who was one of five brothers. She inherited a small plot of land in a nearby settlement, which helped her new family, since her husband and his brothers had divided the little land their father had. One of her brothers decided to stay in Buenos Aires, where many young Calcha men went to work in construction. He arranged for Doña Sara and her husband to farm his land, so they had use of more land while the brother retained his right to the land in case he should return someday.

As a young man, Doña Sara's husband had crossed the Argentine border to work in the sugar harvest. Calcha men had to take off their ethnic clothing and put on manufactured clothes, because only "civilized" workers were allowed across the border. When the men returned, they put Calcha clothing back on. After her marriage, Doña Sara made all the clothing her husband wore. In the first year of marriage they had prepared a set of clothing for each other. The husband provided the wife with the materials, and she wove for them both. Dressed in these new outfits, they appeared before their families, who recognized the finalization of the marriage.

Doña Sara, who had moved to her husband's parents' house at her marriage, stayed there to take care of the house, family, and land when her husband worked in the city of Potosí for two years as a policeman. She says the city was too cold for him there alone, and even though he had gone with high hopes because he had so little land to farm, he returned to Calcha. His experience in Potosí led him to feel that he was better able to support his family by farming. He apparently made no permanent contacts in the urban area. When he died in 1981, the family said that his lungs had been permanently affected by the cold night winds of the city. There is no consistently available Western medicine in Calcha to treat the sick or identify diseases, but it is likely that he died of tuberculosis.

Doña Sara gave birth to seven children, but today she has only one surviving son and one daughter. She wove all the clothing for the young children and continued to clothe them until, as the times changed, the young men left the region to work for wages and were able to buy manufactured clothing. When she still had two sons alive, the older, working in construction in Buenos Aires where his uncle found him a job, decided to stay in Argentina permanently. He married a young Bolivian woman who had migrated from rural Chuquisaca with her brothers. Then his younger brother (Calcha families expect youngest sons to stay with their parents and take over their home) died in a truck accident. The son in Argentina returned to his parents with his wife and one son, who died soon after. Doña Sara's daughter-in-law says that the baby could not adjust to rural Bolivian life and food.

Doña Sara now lives with her surviving son, his wife, and their three children. The son says he wanted his children to be educated in Argentina rather than in rural Bolivian schools, but there was no one else to take care of his parents. Doña Sara occasionally goes to stay with her daughter in the town of Calcha when her son-in-law leaves to work in Buenos Aires. She helps with the care of her grandchildren and takes over household duties when they are born.

She has now turned over most of the responsibility for household chores to her daughter-in-law. Her son also makes short trips to Buenos Aires, because there is no local work from which he can earn the cash the family needs. They raise most of the food they eat and trade for much of the rest, but items like clothing and school supplies, fertilizers, and some building materials must be purchased with cash.

Doña Sara still directs the sorting of produce for storage and selects seed corn. Her daughter-in-law decides on the daily meals, and Doña Sara helps with food preparation. The daughter-in-law attends a local Mothers' Club and receives Catholic Relief Services food, which supplements the family's diet. She, and not Doña Sara, decides when manufactured products such as sugar, macaroni, and rice should be purchased. The daughter-in-law controls the money sent to the family by the son when he is in Argentina.

Doña Sara does most of the herding for the family. They have fewer than ten goats, but only the daughter-in-law is available as occasional relief. When her son is absent, Doña Sara is usually the one who brings fodder from the field for the family's mule and cow. She does much of the irrigation and shares other agricultural tasks with her daughter-in-law. Since his father's death, the son is always present for the planting and the harvesting.

In Calcha, families plant corn in cooperative work groups, *mink'as*, so all families have access to additional male labor at this crucial point in the agricultural cycle. This family's largest field is planted and harvested in a relatively small *mink'a*. Doña Sara helps her daughter-in-law make chicha, corn beer, and prepare the food. She and her husband were the primary hosts for the family's *mink'as*; they spoke the ritual greetings and thanked those who worked for them. Now Doña Sara speaks after her son and daughter-in-law, but she still makes sure all are properly served. During planting she is selected to direct the distribution of seed corn for her close kin; all families pick an older female relative to supervise the distribution of seed at planting. Doña Sara, like all women, performs essential tasks at planting, during the growing season, and at harvest.

The harvest of the house garden is supervised by the daughter-in-law, and either woman helps with the planting of the family's small plot of potatoes. The family has only three producing pear trees. Their peach trees, planted by the son, are now coming into full production.

The peaches are planted in the family's largest corn field; corn is planted between the young trees. Corn is served at the three daily meals and exchanged in trade. A family's fruit provides some additional cash income. The daughter-in-law now does most of the marketing of fruit and family trading. Doña Sara takes over the household chores in her absence.

Doña Sara, and her daughter-in-law, can turn to her husband's brother's son's household for help when necessary. Much of their daily interactions involve this household, which is next door. Doña Sara also has kin close enough so that they continue to work together. She expects her own son to continue to maintain her household while she is alive.

Doña Sara does necessary domestic and agricultural chores for the household. She also weaves. During 1979 and 1980 she made an overskirt, a belt, a small bag, a poncho, and a large storage sack. She spun for a neighbor, for me, and for her daughter-in-law. Doña Sara taught her daughter-in-law to weave and supervised her weaving of a *costal* and a poncho without design. The daughter-in-law hired a young woman to weave for her a mantle, which always has the more difficult-to-make woven designs. In her lifetime Doña Sara has woven eight ponchos, four blankets, five overskirts (an important item of female ethnic dress), and seven mantles. The ponchos were for her husband and sons, the blankets for her household, and the overskirts and mantles for herself. Mantles are also given as a wedding gift to a sister-in-law or a daughter-in-law.

When her son returned to stay with her, Doña Sara's relationship with her daughter-in-law did not start off well. The young woman could not weave at all. Not only did she not know the Calcha style of weaving but also her mother had died before she was old enough to begin to learn to weave. In Calcha a bride who cannot weave is still thought to be one who will not work hard for her husband and her family. This was the critical point upon which the conflict between the mother-in-law and daughter-in-law focused. With time, the conflict lessened, and after her husband's death, Doña Sara was satisfied with her daughter-in-law's efforts in weaving, with the hard work she did for the family, and with the grandchildren with which she surrounded her.

Weaving for the women of Doña Sara's generation has changed: by the 1960s they no longer produced all of their families' clothing. First, young men who had changed back to Calcha clothing at the border when returning from wage labor stopped wearing Calcha dress daily. Next, young women were given manufactured clothing for daily use by their brothers and husbands, who had returned from wage labor. Then the older men put on the clothing their sons had given them after having stored it in suitcases for years. Finally, by 1982, the older women, including Doña Sara, had carefully stored their daily Calcha dress and put on the manufactured skirts and sweaters that their sons' wages had purchased.

Doña Sara, now in her sixties, is a widow dependent upon her son, but an important laborer in his household and the fields. She is able to continue to weave and has taught her daughter and her daughter-in-law to weave. She wears the manufactured clothing she had stored for many years and stores her Calcha clothing, including the complete outfit in which she will be buried. As her weaving was used less and less by her family in daily life, she spent more and more time in agriculture, because her husband and son were away in cities working to earn cash.

Today, the weaving of Calcha women is not used as daily dress. Their families are not naked, because they can and do buy manufactured clothing, although it is often bought secondhand. It is cheaper for them to wear purchased clothing. Both the materials needed for weaving and the time women must invest at the loom have become increasingly scarce as men leave the region for wage labor.

Women today, because of changes in economic and political relationships both within and outside of their ethnic group, have other essential tasks that occupy the time they once devoted to weaving. Now Calcha men, rather than make the trading trips that took them weeks in the past, go to Argentina as wage laborers for months at a time. Women more often have primary responsibility for, or share significant aspects of, the agricultural labor that must still be done in order for their families to eat. When men go to work, their wages do not pay all the expenses of their families. Their mothers, wives, and children, who remain in Calcha, must still labor to provide the food the family will eat. Calcha women do weave the textiles that are necessary for their culture, but they must also see to it that other productive activities are carried out.

Dramatic changes have occurred in Doña Sara's lifetime. Unlike her mother, she does not weave to clothe her family, but the time that she spent in weaving in the past is not now free time. She works the long hours that her mother did, but the particular tasks that supply her family's needs have changed. She makes ethnic cloth for ceremonial and ritual purposes, rather than for daily dress. She has a major role in supplying her family's food.

Another Calcha weaver, Doña Juana, was born in 1948. She is a few years older than Doña Sara's surviving daughter and is now the mother of young children. Unlike the older woman, Doña Juana attended school in the hamlet for four years, but she remembers only a little of the Spanish she learned. All Calcha speak Quechua in their homes. Like other girls, she stopped school when she would have had to go to the central school, a two-hour walk from the settlement. She is one of the best weavers of her generation in the settlement. She learned to weave from her mother and an older sister who is also an expert weaver.

Doña Juana's courtship and marriage were similar to Doña Sara's, but there were fewer musicians and less elaborate fiestas. Still, the quality of her fiesta dress showed skill and willingness to work. By the time she married, when she was twenty-six, Doña Juana had woven as major pieces four overskirts and eight mantles. Six years later, she had woven three ponchos for her husband and two blankets. She complained that she had been a good weaver but that her small children no longer let her weave.

By 1980, when she had been married for five years, she had four young children: a son, a daughter, and twin boys born that year. One of the twins died when he was ten months old. Doña Juana had not been well enough nourished to nurse both babies and had supplemented feedings with unsanitary bottles, because she did not have the resources to buy formula or to prepare it properly. Her husband was seldom present when his children were born; he often did not see them until they were seven or eight months old. His return trips to Calcha were usually timed for the months of planting and harvest.

Doña Juana and her children were part of her husband's family's household where her father-in-law, mother-in-law, husband's father's sister, husband's sister, husband's two brothers (one of whom had cerebral palsy) and, occasionally, her husband, all lived. She went to live there when she married. The family's relatively large landholdings are located in several nearby hamlets.

Her husband and one of his brothers spent much of the late 1970s and early 1980s working in construction in Buenos Aires. Her father-in-law often worked in various parts of Bolivia until his death in 1980. Since his father's death, her husband and his brother spend more time in the hamlet. Doña Juana's husband began to build a house for his family in 1980. By 1982, Doña Juana had another daughter, and their house was almost ready for occupancy. Her husband's youngest brother married and was prepared to become the head of the household when Doña Juana, her husband, and her children left.

In addition to child care, domestic chores such as cooking kept Doña Juana occupied. She did most of the cooking for ten or more people until her brother-in-law brought his wife to the household. She did her share of herding, as well, and had brought her goats to the family's corral. She attended the Mothers' Club each week, received Catholic Relief Services food for her children, and had learned to knit, crochet, and do other handiwork.

The family lived without able-bodied males in the household for months at a time. The women carried out the routine activities in the house and fields. At this point in her life, Doña Juana, by concentrating on domestic chores and herding, freed the other women of the household for agricultural tasks.

During this time, Doña Juana, her husband, and children lived in separate rooms in her in-laws' house. There she stored her and her husband's belongings, including her considerable collection of textiles. She wore manufactured clothing for daily wear but was proud of her weavings, most of which she had made before her marriage. She had her complete and very well made fiesta outfit and an especially nice collection of mantles and matching small carrying cloth.

In 1979 she had managed to weave half a Calcha poncho for her husband, because other women in the household helped in child care. She was able to convince her sister to weave the other half, an action that shows that the two sisters are very close. After marriage, a woman often is so busy in her new household that she has little time to see her sister. These sisters were able to work and visit together since their houses and the fields that they and their families tended were near one another and, perhaps more importantly, their families also liked working together.

She enjoys talking about the weaving she has done. In discussing the materials she used, Doña Juana once said she was a real woman—she used sheep's wool in all of her weaving. The poncho she wove a year later, in 1979, was of synthetic yarn. The latter has practical appeal for Calcha weavers because the dyes don't run, the moths don't eat it, and it is already dyed and spun. Contradictions arise when women know what the superior weaving materials are but find that shortcuts are necessary if they hope to meet both the demands of household chores and a husband's need for a new poncho.

Doña Juana takes pride in the collection she has produced. When neighbors suggested that she sell some of her textiles, she was adamant in her rejection of the idea. She said she would never be able to weave so many textiles again, and this collection is her children's inheritance. She defended herself from a neighbor's disparaging remark about the Calcha poncho she was weaving as being part of "old, ugly customs" by saying that it would be a reminder to her husband of the weaving that she could do.

Even though synthetic yarn was used, she was a Calcha weaver. She made a fiesta poncho that proved how good a wife she was; it allowed her husband to appear before other members of the ethnic group dressed in the cloth that showed his allegiance to and willingness to work as a part of that group. That poncho not only showed what a good Calcha woman Doña Juana was; it also showed that her often absent husband had not forgotten his obligations to fellow Calcha.

Doña Juana's father lives with her brother's family and her unmarried sister in the house where Doña Juana was born. She has frequent contact with her family. When either her brother's household or the one in which she lives has meat, makes chicha, works in their fields, or goes on trading trips, the other family often participates. The two families' tie through this marriage is strong. Doña Juana receives a share of the crops from her own family's field but will not inherit land. Her husband's family has more land than most members of the settlement.

After five years of marriage, Doña Juana refers to the land of her husband's family as her land. She works in food preparation and chicha making for the family's *mink'as*. She participates in the other *mink'as* within the hamlet but does not travel outside the hamlet unless accompanied by her husband or a woman from her household. She never attends a fiesta without her husband. Her husband's father's sister does most of the long-distance truck trading. Doña Juana's kin and *compadrazco* ties (based on godparent-parent-baptized child relationships) take her out of the household compound, but her primary responsibilities at this time in her life are the tasks necessary for the well-being of her immediate family.

The household in which Doña Juana lived as a young bride was the largest in the hamlet. It broke up when her family moved to their new house. The large size of her husband's family meant that there were four adult women (five after the youngest son's marriage) who lived and worked together. By that point in her marriage, Doña Juana had worked out a relationship with the other adult women that minimized conflict, although she feels she was required to do an unfair share of the domestic chores.

Doña Juana assumed the position of the female head of household when she moved to her own compound. There she will have responsibility for all domestic chores until her daughter is old enough to help. Her family will receive some help from the household in which they lived before, but their land and household are separate. They will also be helped by members of Doña Juana's brother's family. It would now be difficult for her husband to leave for wage labor. Without another adult within the household, Doña Juana would not be able to supervise and work in agriculture as well as do all the domestic chores necessary in a house with four or more small children. When the children are older, he can leave again.

At this point in her life, Doña Juana is relatively confined to a household by responsibility for her children and domestic duties. She was helped when she was in a household with other women, but her daily activities changed after her family began living in their own home. For all women, those who move out of and those who inherit a household, the period of working under their mother-in-law is a temporary state during which they gradually assume more responsibility for the domestic maintenance of their own family. It is usually also a temporary stage, when a woman's small children make it difficult for her to weave. The time that children need frequent attention is shortened, because at an early age older daughters and sons learn to care for younger siblings. When their children are old enough to help in the house and the fields, the women have more time for weaving, but they still must supervise the children's work and have primary responsibility for agriculture as well when their husbands are absent.

Doña Juana's husband, a man two years younger than she, faced a radical change in lifestyle. For the last twelve years, he spent more time outside Calcha than living in his hamlet. He left for military service at eighteen and, until his father died, was seldom in his family's household for more than a couple of months at a time. After his younger brother began working in Buenos Aires, Doña Juana's husband, with his father, bought land in Tarija, another department in southern Bolivia, which they worked for a time. He also worked in construction in Cochabamba, a Bolivian city, but found that unprofitable because of the high cost of living there.

Extended households are able to continue working together after a son marries, while the young couple lives with the husband's family. When there is more than one adult woman in the household, the women can manage both domestic and agricultural tasks while the male members are absent. Men can bring back cash and explore alternative avenues for securing more land for their families. Women have only a little time for weaving.

Young and older women have essential tasks. Both usually manage to weave the basic textiles a household needs. Even when they are involved in local politics, men still need ponchos. All households need certain textiles for planting, for holding *mink'as*, and for weddings. Because there are other tasks which no one else is available to do, women weave less. The purchase of clothing does free them from having to weave, but it also more tightly binds their families to a market economy and to other purchased goods, which may only be obtained when men leave the region to work for wages.

With the continued deterioration of the Bolivian economy, most families in Calcha will need increased cash incomes not available within the region. Kinships and previous experience make work in Argentina attractive to young men in Calcha. Doña Juana and Doña Sara know that their families need money, that they can no longer survive just by farming. They also realize from their own experience of social and economic change in Bolivia that it is their farming that feeds their families while many in Bolivia's cities are increasingly hungry. Farming feeds them, but the men's wages buy the goods they cannot make themselves. These weavers understand that, even though their families will not be able to make or trade for everything they need, their weaving still is a very important resource.

The weaving of Calcha women represents them as individuals and as members of an ethnic group. It is a major part of these women's efforts to keep their families working together. Their gifts of cloth make these ties stronger. They obligate kin to help one another as a family and as an ethnic group. While women are doing more in agriculture, they also weave the cloth that binds their families together. They weave only for their kin.

SOURCES

This essay is based on anthropological fieldwork carried out in Calcha, Bolivia, from October 1978 to July 1, 1981, and during a return trip in September and October 1982.

17
Leoncio Veguilla

Harold E. Greer

With a Ph.D. in history from the University of Alabama and a Th.M. from New Orleans Baptist Theological Seminary, Harold Greer is uniquely prepared to investigate the experience of Cuban Protestants under Fidel Castro's revolution. Greer has previously written on the general topic of Southern Baptists in Cuba from the first missionary effort in 1886. This research led him to the career of Leoncio Veguilla. Currently, Greer teaches history at Virginia Commonwealth University.

Veguilla's experience deserves comparison with that of his fellow Cuban Ofelia Domínguez Navarro and of others, such as María Ferreira dos Santos and Irma Muller, who have used religious institutions as part of their strategy for responding to their society. Veguilla's imprisonment receives careful consideration from Greer, as do his efforts to adjust to Cuba's new society in the making.

He is an unlikely hero, this smiling, soft-spoken Cuban Baptist preacher. Leoncio Veguilla's love of God and country, while causing him anguish and suffering in revolutionary Cuba, have brought forth a man with quiet confidence in himself, a man whose leadership is sought out by his fellow Cubans and Baptists. His faith in his God and in his calling to serve the Cuban people sustained him through almost four years of imprisonment at the hands of Castro's government and prohibited his fleeing his native Cuba and its people for a more secure life in the United States.

As a ten year old, Leoncio Veguilla was a troublemaker. In his native village of Regla, the Baptist worship services led by missionaries Herbert and Marjorie Caudill were a prime target for his antics. The Baptists met in a large old colonial home near the center of Regla. Often passersby would stop and listen to the services through an open window or the screen door—but not Leoncio. While Dr. Caudill preached, Leoncio shouted and knocked on the door. Once he threw a bag of roaches into the service, another time a dead crab. Finally, Dr. Caudill threatened to take him to the police.

"Please, Dr. Caudill, no, don't take me to the police station," Leoncio pleaded in a pitiful voice. "I won't ever do it anymore." Unconvinced that he was repentant, the Caudills nevertheless gave the child another chance.

One Wednesday evening during choir practice, Mrs. Caudill looked up from the piano and saw Leoncio standing there, watching her hands. Ignoring her suspicions of his motives, she asked him if he liked music. He replied that he did, and Mrs. Caudill invited him to attend Sunday school, where he could learn the songs he had been hearing.

Leoncio began attending activities at the Baptist Church, which also was the Caudills' home. The front room where services were held contained benches, a small platform, and the piano, but the modest setting was alive with programs to engage the young people of the community. Leoncio especially enjoyed Royal Ambassadors, an organization for boys, and the junior choir. Gradually the mischievous boy changed into a committed young man, and at the age of fifteen he was baptized as a member of the Regla Baptist Church. He had become a part of the religious group that would be the focal point of his life and for which he would be a crucial leader in the troubled years ahead.

Baptist ideas had been introduced into Cuba by Alberto J. Díaz, a Cuban who had organized the first Baptist church in Cuba in Havana in 1886. Díaz, a native Cuban, had become a Baptist while a refugee in the United States during the unsuccessful attempt at Cuban independence known as the Ten Years' War (1868–78). The Home Mission Board of the Southern Baptist Convention, learning of Díaz's work, established contact with him and provided support.

Political conditions in Cuba at the time encouraged the growth of Baptist and other Protestant mission work. The people of Cuba had given nominal allegiance to Roman Catholicism ever since the island was colonized by Spain. However, the Catholic church, allied politically with the colonial government and served by Spanish priests, alienated those who advocated Cuban independence. The Liberal party, which favored independence from Spain and separation of church and state, supported Baptist principles. Baptist beliefs and policy, such as the congregational form of church government, emphasis on the individual, and the provision of funerals and other religious services without charge, drew support from the liberal Havana press.

The pressure for independence erupted in fighting again in 1895. To the consternation of the officials at the Baptist Home Mission Board, Díaz threw himself into the fray by enlisting as commander-in-chief of the insurgent forces in Havana Province. He was imprisoned by the colonial government but later released as the result of pressure from the United States. The United States became increasingly involved in the conflict, which culminated in the Spanish-American War. Cuba won its independence by the treaty ending that war in 1898.

Immediately after the war, Protestantism was enthusiastically received in Cuba, as the island nation set about restructuring its economic and social institutions. To take advantage of this favorable climate, Southern Baptists sought to restore and enlarge their work begun before the war. The Cuban pastors, many of whom had fled the island during the war to work among Cubans in the United States, returned to Cuba. In addition, missionaries from the United States joined the Baptist mission in Cuba. Protestants were aided by the constitution of 1901, which provided for separation of church and state, religious freedom, and universal suffrage.

Southern Baptists, agreeing with the American Baptists on a division of the Cuban field, focused their work in the island's four western provinces—Matanzas, Havana, Pinar del Río, and Santa Clara. The basis for a denominational structure was created with the organization of the West Cuba Baptist Convention in 1905. The cadre of U.S. missionaries grew slowly during the years following the war. M. N. McCall of Georgia joined the Cuban mission as its superintendent in 1905, a position he was to hold for forty-two years until his death in 1947. Herbert Caudill became McCall's associate in 1929 and would succeed him as superintendent in 1947, also serving for more than forty years. It was in his role as pastor of the small Baptist congregation at Regla that Caudill first encountered Leoncio Veguilla.

Leoncio was born July 31, 1930, in Regla, a smelly, rough-hewn fishing village across the bay from Havana. The aroma of fish often filled the air, for most residents earned a livelihood from fishing in the bay, then selling their catch in Havana. Others took the launch to cross the bay and work in Havana or perhaps earned a livelihood at the nearby tannery. Leoncio's mother struggled to provide for her large family, as the father had left them. Their modest home fronted right on the street, as did the other houses, leaving no yard. Leoncio played in the streets or nearby parks with his friends, most of whom were as poor as he was. Good public schools, both a primary and a middle school, were provided in Regla, and Leoncio was an eager student who always did extremely well. When he graduated with a bachelor of letters degree from the Institute of Havana in 1952, he had amassed a brilliant record, the equivalent of all A's.

Feeling that God was calling him to be a preacher, Leoncio approached the Caudills for assistance in arranging for him to attend the Baptist Seminary in Havana. By then the Caudills were living in an apartment in the seminary complex. As one of about twenty students, Leoncio studied at the seminary for three years. In addition to his regular curriculum, Leoncio studied music with Mrs. Caudill. By the time he graduated from the seminary in 1955, he could play the piano and direct music for congregational worship. Mrs. Caudill commented: "He could take a big congregation at a meeting like the annual Baptist Convention and make a choir out of it."

The summer of 1955 was an eventful one for Leoncio. Following his graduation from the seminary, he began the work to which he was to devote his life. He became pastor of the little Tapaste Church, sixty miles from Havana. He had been licensed to preach earlier that summer at the Baptist camp at Yumurí and was ordained by the church in Regla on July 20, 1955. Dora Sánchez Ruíz joined him as his wife and partner in his work. They had met at the seminary when Dora's church in Matanzas sent her there for a special short session. Chance encounters in the hallways were followed by lunches together in the cafeteria; soon they knew that they would spend their lives together, partners in the church work to which they both were committed. They were married July 1, 1955, in Colón, Matanzas.

Leoncio described his feelings toward the pastorate as a strong desire to serve, and such was a pastor's role in Cuba. He might be called a combination social worker, economic adviser, comforter, and friend. A typical day in Leoncio's ministry might include helping a church member find a job, obtaining food for a family experiencing hard times, getting a church member admitted to the hospital, or helping the son of a friend of a church member who had gotten into trouble. The Cubans saw the pastor as someone they could go to in time of need. Leoncio was committed to his people. They knew they could count on him with any kind of problem they might have.

The church at Tapaste grew under Leoncio's leadership. He developed all the church organizations and a particularly good choir. He had similar successes at all the churches he served. The church at Cienfuegos, where he was pastor from 1960 to 1969, had a particularly fine group of young people. He has served as pastor of the Cerro Church in Havana since 1969.

Early in his pastorate, the denomination also began calling on Leoncio for leadership. He became national counselor for the Royal Ambassadors in 1957, and in 1961 he was named to the Junta Directiva (Cuban Mission Board). This administrative board was elected by the annual West Cuba Baptist Convention and met several times during the year to carry on convention business.

The denomination continued to develop strength during the years prior to the Castro Revolution. The number of baptisms broke prior records year after year, and Sunday-school enrollment reached its peak. By the time Castro took over in 1959, there were 84 churches and 176 missions in the four provinces served by the convention, with a total membership of 8,561; Sunday school enrollment was 14,604. In addition to a full range of organizations for adults and children in the churches, the convention supported the seminary in Havana, a Baptist clinic in Havana staffed by six doctors, a home for the elderly, a bookstore in Havana, four primary schools, and the ninety-acre Baptist Assembly at Yumurí. Summer conferences for various age groups at the assembly grounds were highlights of spiritual growth for many. The Baptist Student Union's work at the University of Havana had been interrupted when the university was closed by the government. There were 158 Cuban Baptist pastors and workers and eight U.S. missionaries working in Cuba. Another retired missionary had elected to remain in Cuba.

The revolution, which Fidel Castro had been leading from the mountains in the eastern part of the island since 1956, made aggressive moves against the Batista government in three parts of the country in 1958. As the war moved closer to the people, their preoccupation with it increased, as did government restrictions on meetings and movement. Attendance, baptisms, and offerings were down in most Baptist churches that year. Several evangelistic campaigns were canceled, and attendance at Camp Yumurí was small. The government restricted the importation of literature for use in the churches.

When Fulgencio Batista fled Cuba in the early morning hours of January 1, 1959, allowing Castro to take control of the government, there was almost ecstatic rejoicing that the fighting was over. Baptists looked forward to a brighter day for Cuba and for their work. Some Baptists had participated in the revolution; several had given their lives.

Baptists, like most Cubans, reacted positively to the plans and projects announced by the provisional government of Fidel Castro and President Urrutia. Mrs. Urrutia, wife of the provisional president, called in three Catholic priests and three evangelical ministers—a

Baptist, a Presbyterian, and a Methodist—to ask for their cooperation with plans to clean up politics and lift the moral life of the nation. Never before in Cuba had those in such high positions asked for the opinions or the cooperation of the evangelicals. Protestants occupied several prominent positions in the new government. A Presbyterian physician served in the cabinet. One of the three commissioners appointed to govern Havana was a Baptist. Many felt that a new era of acceptance and opportunity was opening for the evangelicals in Cuba.

This optimistic outlook was confirmed in denominational reports for 1959: membership, baptisms, Sunday-school enrollment, and total gifts were all up. In 1960, Baptist work in Cuba experienced the most rapid growth and development in its history. Hundreds were attending Baptist churches for the first time. In 1961, Fidel Castro's sister, Augustina, was married in one of the Baptist churches. Mrs. Caudill was an invited guest.

However, for some the optimism about the revolution was to be short-lived. Disillusioned with the revolution, the first Cuban Baptist pastor left the country with his family at the end of 1959. And early in 1960 the pastor of the largest Baptist church in Cuba emigrated to the United States.

Although the Caudills' daughter and her husband, David Fite, were admitted as missionaries in April 1960, Mr. and Mrs. Tom Law left in October. Most of the members of the English-speaking church Law had pastored in Havana had left. The U.S. State Department warned American citizens to leave for their own safety, but the Home Mission Board gave the missionaries the option of staying or being reassigned. At that time all eight decided to stay. When the United States and Cuba broke diplomatic relations in January 1961, Mr. and Mrs. Hubert Hurt decided to leave Cuba "because of the uncertainty of travel between the island and the United States." All of the missionaries working in eastern Cuba under the American Baptist Convention also left.

The Cuban government, as it moved to solidify its control in 1961, took over all public schools, including the four that belonged to the West Cuba Baptists and their four school buses. Since the schools were held in church buildings, they were later returned for church use but could not be used for schools. Dr. Caudill reported that atheistic teaching was being pushed and regretted that the young people were having to bear the brunt of this.

Thousands of Cubans had fled, especially members of the middle and upper classes who had been hurt by the economic policies of the revolution. In January 1963, Dr. Caudill reported that practically all of the churches had lost members. More than one thousand members had emigrated, many of whom had been leaders in their churches. A number of Cuban pastors had also gone to the United States. In spite of that, the churches continued to win others; besides the work of individual congregations, student work at Havana University and the seminary program were continuing, and large numbers were attending the summer encampment at Yumurí.

However, still greater restrictions were soon to follow. Evangelicals were shocked when a shipment of Bibles was seized and ground to pulp. A shipment of two thousand hymnbooks to the Baptist Book Store in Havana met the same fate. Literature that was published outside Cuba could no longer be used. The Baptist radio broadcast, after being temporarily suspended earlier, was now altogether prohibited. Nearly all religious activities were confined to church buildings. Several pastors, including Leoncio, were fined for "proselytizing." Government observers became frequent visitors to services.

The Home Mission Board missionary staff in Cuba dwindled to four in the summer of 1963 when the Cuban government expelled Lucille Kerrigan and Ruby Miller, who had been working for eighteen years at Cabanas in Pinar del Rio Province. No explanation was given for their expulsion.

The ideological conflict throughout these years was felt intensely in the Cuban church. Leoncio observed that both the proponents of the revolution and those opposed to it were outspoken in their attacks. All the denominational papers were full of their arguments. Brochures and books were published and meetings were held to discuss issues or persuade toward a point of view. No one seemed to be indifferent. Nevertheless, there was a group that determined early in the discussion to focus on the centrality of the Gospel. They would avoid purely political stands, and no matter what happened they would stay with the work. Leoncio numbered himself with this group.

Because Dr. Caudill needed an operation to repair a detached retina, he and Mrs. Caudill flew to Atlanta in the summer of 1964. While in Atlanta, Dr. Caudill reported that "in many ways the 'Word of God' meets with greater acceptance today than at any time during the 35 years I have been in Cuba." He added, "There's the same opportunity to preach the Gospel we've always had, though there are more restrictions on the number of services outside the buildings. More young people than ever are flocking to the churches, and we had our largest beginning class in our theological institute this September." However, hard times lay just ahead for Dr. Caudill, Leoncio, and the Baptists of Cuba.

After recuperating from surgery, Dr. Caudill returned to Cuba in December 1964. A few days before he arrived in Havana, the Cuban security police had arrested a Baptist pastor. The government had evidence of his involvement in currency exchange for his own profit and of his membership in a counterrevolutionary organization. He had enrolled four or five other pastors in that organization. The government presented its evidence—pictures and other papers—and threatened his life. To try to save himself, the pastor invented a story implicating missionary Herbert Caudill as an agent of the Central Intelligence Agency and head of a spy network made up of Cuban Baptist pastors. He claimed that this organization, headed by Dr. Caudill, in addition to teaching counterrevolutionary ideas, was assisting counterrevolutionaries and supplying information about geography and weapons to the CIA.

Four months later, just after midnight on April 8, 1965, Dr. Caudill and fifty-two other Baptist leaders, pastors, and laymen, including four women, were arrested. Among those arrested were Dr. Caudill's son-in-law, David Fite, and the young pastor at Cienfuegos, Leoncio Veguilla. All were affiliated with the West Cuba Baptist Convention. The Baptists were taken to various jails or prisons across the country, with the largest number being committed to facilities in Havana.

On the morning of the arrests, two policemen came to Leoncio's home in Cienfuegos and searched the house thoroughly, scrutinizing every paper and every book. Leoncio was taken to a house in the city where Ineida Reyes, a Cuban missionary working in Cienfuegos, was also being held. She had been arrested in a similar manner. They were both transported later that day to the provincial capital, Santa Clara. Seven other Baptist pastors were being detained there. Despite being interrogated relentlessly, Leoncio was otherwise well treated at the Santa Clara prison. His family was allowed to visit him once each week.

After thirty-five days Leoncio was transferred to a larger state prison where he was to face trial. There he discovered that he and the other pastors had become famous due to newspaper and television publicity about their arrests.

After lengthy, repeated interrogations during the thirty-six days they were held, the Cuban government brought forty-one of the original fifty-three Baptist leaders to trial as political prisoners who had conspired to overthrow the government. Some were not informed of the charges against them until just before the trial; others were never informed. The Americans were furnished a lawyer by the Swiss Embassy but were only able to meet with him briefly at the start of the trial. Cuban defendants were represented by a court-appointed attorney whom they had not previously met.

The trials for Dr. Caudill and the others imprisoned in Havana were held on Friday, May 14, followed on Saturday with the trials for Leoncio and the other pastors imprisoned at Santa Clara. The outcome of Leoncio's trial on Saturday was thus already determined by what had happened in the Havana court. The official charges against all the pastors were:

1) conspiracy against the security and integrity of the nation;
2) collaboration with the Central Intelligence Agency;
3) helping people get out of the country illegally;
4) ideological diversion;
5) covering up the activities of others; and
6) illegal currency exchange.

Dr. Caudill denied the validity of all the complaints except the ideological diversion charge and the currency exchange charge. He stated that he had continued to preach and teach the Gospel as he always had since he had been in Cuba. He and David Fite admitted in the public hearing on May 14 that they had exchanged dollars for Cuban pesos. It was easy to justify this action in their own minds. Restrictions on the flow of currency between the United States and Cuba had placed hardships on Cubans leaving the country and on the Home Mission Board in supporting its work on the island. An informal exchange process had assisted both groups in accomplishing their objectives. In exchange for Cuban money that could be used to support the Baptist work in Cuba, Dr. Caudill would have the Home Mission Board give dollars to a relative in the United States. The board was thus able to support its work indirectly, and Cubans leaving the country could have a resource of funds available when they reached the United States. Although seeming to obey the letter of the law, in that no Cuban money ever left the island, this humane and convenient currency exchange scheme was, in fact, illegal. Some Cuban pastors who helped people with currency exchange had also profited personally from the exchange; some also confessed to being involved in counterrevolutionary activities.

The terms handed down to the thirty-three who were tried in Havana ranged from thirty years of imprisonment to two years of house arrest.

Caudill received a ten-year sentence rather than the recommended thirty-year term because of his age. Fite was sentenced to six years in prison. At Santa Clara, Leoncio and three other pastors were sentenced to nine years in prison. Two pastors received twelve-year sentences and two others, twenty years. Ineida had been released earlier.

Leoncio had fully expected the government to free him and the others once they learned the absurdity of the charges rumored to have been made against them. He was never formally informed of those charges. When he faced the trial on that Saturday, he was unprepared to defend himself and had no attorney. Believing in his own innocence and that of his fellow pastors, Leoncio was stunned by the sentences. It seemed that the major charge, which could be given substance in some cases, was the illegal exchange of currency. However, since this offense carried a sentence of six months to two years, the length of the sentences far exceeded his worst expectations.

Seventeen more days passed. The miserable depression of the situation weighed heavily on Leoncio. He had expected release; he now faced instead what seemed a lifetime of imprisonment. Approximately one thousand persons occupied this crowded prison; water was scarce, and Leoncio was allowed only one bath in the seventeen days at this location. Food was both inadequate and unappealing. Not a large man, Leoncio lost fifty pounds during these first weeks in prison. Being separated from his family was especially hard on him. He spent his time reading, praying, and talking with other prisoners. Besides his miserable personal condition, his family would suffer real hardship without his support. These were the bleakest days of his imprisonment.

Reaching into the depths of his faith and his personal resources, Leoncio determined to make the best of the situation. Being transferred to a country place where conditions were much improved helped. Although he worked hard in the sugarcane fields, there was plenty of food and water. He was able to bathe daily, and the opportunity to be outside in the sunshine was welcome. Most important, he was only three miles from home; his wife and children were able to visit him each Sunday.

Eventually, Leoncio and the other pastors were invited by the prison officials to teach other inmates to read. They worked in the fields in the morning and prepared their lessons in the afternoon. At night they taught reading and writing as well as history and geography to the other prisoners. The men were interested, enthusiastic students. By the time Leoncio moved to another prison two and one-half years later, his students were reading at about the eighth-grade level.

At first, the pastors were allowed to hold daily religious services. However, because the guards feared the large crowds attracted to the services, the pastors decided to divide the group, with each pastor leading a small group. These times of singing, preaching, and sharing continued to be popular with the Cuban prisoners.

After two and one-half years in the prison near Cienfuegos, Leoncio was told that he was to receive an early release. Prior to being freed, he was to be transferred to Camagüey Province, far from his home, to work for another ten months. Leoncio was cook for the prisoners at Camagüey. The work was difficult. He was the only pastor at Camagüey, and he missed the camaraderie of his fellow Baptists. However, he was allowed to preach to the other prisoners. His family was allowed to visit two or three times a month, but the trip was difficult for them. Still, the anticipation of being released from prison buoyed his spirits. He dreamed of liberty every night. After nine months at Camagüey, Leoncio was transferred back to his home province, given more liberty, and paid for his work. One month later he was freed.

His church at Cienfuegos was eager to have him return as its pastor, and he longed to resume his chosen work, but first he had to convince the government officials, who insisted that he must take a civilian job. Various alternatives were open to him, including teaching. His relatives in the United States urged him to join them. Finally, Leoncio was able to persuade the officials that his work as pastor helped "to bring about the new man," which was also a goal of the revolution.

Leoncio had spent three and one-half difficult years in prison. The separation from his family was hardest. Being subject always to the will of those in authority depressed the human spirit. The physical restraints, deprivations, and humiliation were not easy to adapt to, yet Leoncio guarded himself against responding with bitterness. After reflecting on his experience, Leoncio felt he had profited from his years in prison in a number of ways. The time he had had to reflect and to think deeply on many subjects provided him mental and spiritual resources for his later work. He had learned useful skills and had become acquainted with aspects of daily life that he had never before encountered. He also had had opportunities to share his faith with other prisoners and felt he had been an effective witness. He would have a deeper understanding, a more empathetic spirit in pastoring his people than ever before.

Dr. Caudill had been released from prison two years before Leoncio, on November 25, 1966, because he was steadily losing his vision. The surgery for his detached retina had not been successful, and now the same problem threatened the other eye. Because Dr. Caudill was unwilling to leave Cuba while his son-in-law, David Fite, remained in prison, the Cuban government assisted with arrangements for an Atlanta physician to come to Cuba and perform the needed surgery to save his vision.

Dr. Caudill's activities were severely restricted during the two years he was to remain in Cuba. He was not allowed to participate in Baptist work or attend any of the church's activities. Fite was released on December 16, 1968, and the Caudills and Fites left Cuba on February 7, 1969. On the day the Caudills left Cuba, Leoncio, only a few months out of prison himself, traveled the 230 miles from Cienfuegos to tell them goodbye. Their parting was full of emotion. Leoncio had come to regard the Caudills as his mother and father, and there was no expectation that they would see each other again or perhaps even be able to communicate.

The 1965 arrest and imprisonment of half the pastors and most of the leaders of the West Cuba Baptist Convention had caused some to question whether the Baptists' work would endure in Cuba. Some did give up the faith and leave the churches; others left Cuba, as the migration of those disenchanted with the revolution continued. However, the majority of the church members had stayed and demonstrated an even deeper consecration. The wives of the imprisoned pastors were heroic in the way they carried on the work in the churches, taking leadership roles and often doing the preaching themselves. Laypersons developed into strong, effective leaders, and many loyal members increased their giving to 20 percent of their modest incomes.

Eventually, all the pastors would be released. The longest prison term served by any of them was twelve years. The imprisoned pastors had had a positive influence in the prisons and prison farms. For many of these pastors, the maturing process meant that they returned to their churches even more effective as leaders. Leoncio believed the experience caused many in the Cuban government to understand the humane quality of the Christians. Although motivated by different ideologies, the two could both work for the good of society.

With the departure of the Caudills and Fites in February 1969, leadership of the West Cuba Baptist Convention fell totally into the hands of the Cuban Baptists. Leoncio Veguilla was to play a role in that leadership. He became pastor of the Cerro Baptist Church in Havana in 1969 and continued as a member of the Junta Directiva for the West Cuba Baptist Convention. In 1971 the West Cuba Baptist Convention elected him vice president. After serving in that position for a year, he was elected president in 1972 and served until 1974. Mounting ideological pressures within the convention made this a difficult period. Efforts to maintain the apolitical status of the Baptist Student Union's work at the University of Havana ultimately failed, and the program was discontinued in 1973. Even personal and moral problems assumed political overtones in these tense times. Anyone charged with such an offense seemed to grasp quickly at the defense that he was being charged merely because of his political views. The convention was also faced with serious financial difficulties due to previous unauthorized spending for an automobile. Because of the mounting dissension within the convention, Leoncio resigned as president in 1974.

Despite the stressful times, Baptists were continually building, and during Leoncio's presidency six churches were organized and nine pastors were ordained. Four hundred and nine were baptized in 1972, the largest number since 1961. Convention giving reached $94,766.14, the largest amount in its history. The convention was able to secure authorization for the entrance of hymnals, books for the seminary, and Lord's Supper sets. The Baptists began to send delegates to international events: the Baptist World Alliance, the Evangelistic Congress in Lausanne, the Young People's Conference in Puerto Rico.

Leoncio became director of Christian education for the West Cuba Baptists in 1976. In that capacity, one of his major tasks was to provide literature for religious education programs in the churches. The convention was not allowed to have printing presses, and such literature could not be imported. Therefore, Leoncio wrote much of the lessons, compiled other materials, typed the lessons, ran copies on the mimeograph machine, and sent the materials to the churches.

In 1969, Leoncio began serving as a professor at the Baptist Seminary in Havana. He eventually became vice rector and then rector. In addition to theological education for pastors, the seminary offered programs in religious education and music and short programs for laymen and for pastors' wives. Students lived at the seminary, and the churches provided food for them. The teachers were mostly pastors and taught without pay.

In 1984, twenty-five years after the Castro Revolution, Leoncio could report that the Baptists in western Cuba had maintained their denomination as a vital part of Cuban life, although they had come through some difficult years. One reason was the leadership of Cubans like Leoncio. With the West Cuba Baptist Convention being devastated of leadership by the emigration of pastors and the departure of missionaries, the development of an educated, indigenous leadership was crucial. Through his positions as director of Christian education and as rector and professor at the Baptist Seminary, Leoncio led in providing the Christian education vital to the survival of the denomination.

In a situation that is sometimes volatile, Leoncio Veguilla is not a leader who seeks confrontation; his style is rather that of the negotiator who weighs and balances the possibilities, then quietly plots a path. He has focused his life on sharing his faith in God with the Cuban people he loves. With this goal as his beacon and his confidence in God's leadership, he is able to adapt and work within the restrictions that exist. Tested by his prison years and tried by the hard times under the revolution, Leoncio is not afraid. He moves with quiet confidence. He has determined his priorities. He knows what is important.

BIBLIOGRAPHY

Caudill, Herbert. *On Freedom's Edge.* Atlanta, 1979.

———. Interviews with author. July 1984.

Caudill, Marjorie. Interviews with author. July 1984.

Home Mission Board Archives (Atlanta). Minutes of the Home Mission Board of the Southern Baptist Convention, 1884–1984, and various other items, including reports, correspondence, and news releases.

Southern Baptist Convention. *Annuals of the Southern Baptist Convention.* 1884–1984.

Veguilla, Leoncio. "Desenvolvimiento histórico de la educación Cristana entre los Bautistas de Cuba Occidental." Master's thesis, Seminario Teológico Bautista Mexicano, 1983.

———. Interviews with author. Havana, December 1984.

18

*María Ferreira dos Santos**

Warren E. Hewitt

Before taking a professorship in sociology at the University of Lethbridge in Alberta, Canada, Warren Hewitt studied at McMaster University in Hamilton, Ontario, and the Universidade de São Paulo in Brazil. His academic preparation has emphasized sociological theory, industrialization and modernization, and religion, resulting in his publications on the basic Christian communities in Brazil.

Hewitt's examination of the new religious movements in Latin America, especially the Comunidades Eclesiais de Base in São Paulo's archdiocese, has concentrated on the local improvement strategies used by these groups as the primary method to initiate social change. He finds that in the midst of the widely discussed revolutionary potential of these movements there are certain limitations too often neglected by proponents of liberation theology.

Resourceful and enthusiastic, María dos Santos demonstrates the potential for helpful social change through one Comunidade Eclesiais de Base. Her activities challenge age, gender, and class stereotypes that would seem to eliminate her as a leader in her community. Yet she has been successful, even when faced with opposition from the local government, from her neighbors, and from conservative elements in the Roman Catholic church. Like many other women in this volume, María has overcome the limitations placed on her by a male-dominated society, and, like Irma Muller of Chile, she has refused to let age prevent her from doing something in which she believes.

Once or more per week in at least half the countries of Latin America, men and women Catholics meet together in small, informal lay circles known as basic Christian communities or CEBs (*comunidades eclesiales* or *eclesiais de base*). Currently, there are well in excess of one hundred thousand of these groups in the region, some two-thirds of which are located in just one nation—Brazil.

---

*María Ferreira dos Santos is a pseudonym.

In essence, the CEBs are religious associations, which engage in a range of devotional practices, but they also have profound socio-political implications for the societies in which they operate. This is because group members, most of whom belong to the least privileged social classes, often use their faith to guide them in an attempt to resolve the concrete social problems that affect them. In rural areas, for example, the CEBs actively promote the cause of land reform, while urban groups are frequently involved in neighborhood improvement projects designed to secure basic amenities such as running water, street lights, and garbage collection.

A number of studies have recently appeared that attempt to describe the organizational structure and orientation of the CEBs as they exist in Latin America today. This essay focuses instead upon the human content of the CEBs, to investigate the forces that create and sustain their vitality. To this end, we shall examine the role of one individual who, through her attempts to stimulate political awareness and action within her own group, demonstrates the power of the human spirit. This person is María Ferreira dos Santos, the leader of a basic Christian community located in a working-class district in the Brazilian city of São Paulo.

The origins of the CEB phenomenon of which María dos Santos and her neighbors are a part can be traced to the early 1960s. According to most CEB analysts, the groups emerged in response to a host of both religious and political factors unique to this period. On the one hand, the rise of the phenomenon can be partially attributed to the influence of new and socially progressive church teaching emerging from important sources such as the Second Vatican Council. The council, consisting of over two thousand Catholic bishops summoned to Rome by the pope in 1962, called for an enhancement of lay participation within the church and greater attention to the problems of the least privileged social classes. This theme, broadened to include support for the CEBs directly, was reemphasized at subsequent meetings of the Latin American episcopate at Medellín, Colombia (1968), and Puebla, Mexico (1979). On the other hand, to a considerable extent the CEBs can be seen as the product of a desire for political expression on the part of the poor and oppressed themselves in Latin America. As the military took power in a series of countries after 1960, cutting off traditional avenues of protest, the lower classes increasingly turned to the church for guidance and protection. In response, the church offered the CEBs as secure spaces from which the poor could voice their dissatisfaction with repressive government policies.

Support for the CEBs has varied from country to country, but it has always been especially strong in Brazil, where the church has wholeheartedly embraced the dictates of the "new" Catholicism that arose in the wake of Vatican II. Here, the bishops have taken full responsibility for the groups and have been on the front lines of CEB formation and development. Measures adopted by the episcopate to promote the CEBs over the past twenty years include the publication of official statements justifying the existence of the groups within religious and secular spheres and the creation of CEB Pastoral Commissions offering moral and material support to the phenomenon. Quite often, within individual dioceses, money has also been spent to acquire land for local CEB meeting places and to provide the CEBs with basic liturgical, discussion, and organizational materials.

Another extremely effective way the bishops have encouraged CEB information in Brazil is through the designation of priests and nuns to serve as pastoral agents. These individuals, who tend for the most part to be rather young and politically progressive, are dispatched to parishes in rural and semiurban areas where the poor and oppressed are concentrated. Their goal is not so much to stimulate the CEBs directly but to seek out potential lay leaders and encourage them to interest their neighbors in group activation.

In the Nossa Senhora das Dores parish of the São Miguel Episcopal Region on the eastern flank of the Archdiocese of São Paulo, one lay Catholic who has firmly taken up this call to action is María Ferreira dos Santos. Within a period of less than a year, María almost single-handedly revitalized a fledgling group known as the Comunidade Santana, which was struggling to survive in a dusty, sprawling, working-class neighborhood with the exotic name of Jardim Copacabana.

Born in 1933 in the interior of São Paulo State, María is a *doña de casa* (housewife) who lives with her husband and two children in a small but comfortable home on one of the few paved streets in the area. In many ways, she is an ideal candidate for CEB leadership. Unlike most of her neighbors, who are semiliterate at best, María has acquired a primary-school education, and although currently at home, she has gained valuable organizational experience in the working world as both a salesperson and a dressmaker. María's husband, she herself claims, has never worked steadily, yet between her own savings, and her son's income from a job at a local bank, the family maintains a higher-than-average income. This allows María the freedom to engage full-time in CEB promotion.

Like others in the vanguard of the CEB movement, María dos Santos is also an active supporter of the cause of social justice. Brazil, she claims, has been for too long in the grip of self-interested political leaders who have served only to perpetuate inequality. "In our country," she states, "the rich get richer and the poor get poorer. . . . Those in power don't want to leave; the people protest, but who eventually decides [things] are two or three men at the top, and everything remains the same."

To alter this seemingly intractable situation, Maria places her total faith in popular organizations such as labor unions, neighborhood groups, and other associations, which, she claims, serve to channel and intensify the inherent strength of the organized masses. Before becoming involved with the CEBs, María had long been an active supporter of the working-class Partido dos Trabalhadores (Workers' party) and was involved with the Unified Workers' Center, an organization that represents several local trade unions.

This commitment to the cause of justice through social action has been fortified through María's association with the Catholic church. In some ways, it is true, she is very much a part of the "traditional" church, attending Mass regularly and taking the sacraments. Nevertheless, she finds her principal inspiration in the teachings and actions of the "new" church of the post-Vatican II era. As is the case for many of her fellow laypersons, and indeed many clergy, for example, she prefers to interpret the figure of Christ as "liberator of the poor and oppressed" and thus as the guiding light and principal impetus for the popular takeover of unjust social structures. Moreover, María strongly supports the efforts of the institutional church in Brazil to bring about social transformation, through its attempts to resolve not only spiritual problems but also this-worldly, concrete social issues such as unemployment, low wages, hunger, racial and gender discrimination, abandoned youth, and so forth. An especially significant development, in María's view, is the church's role in promoting the CEBs. In a very fundamental way, she believes, the CEBs help awaken the poor to the reality of socioeconomic oppression and encourage them to participate actively in the secular world, thus making Brazil a more just and egalitarian society.

Although she may feel greatly inspired and encouraged by the church's active role in the social transformation process, María is not entirely noncritical of the institution as it operates today. Just as she would like to see greater emphasis on justice and equality in society, so too would she like to see the church open its own doors to the poor and oppressed. She is especially critical of the power of the hierarchy, which has been conducive to a continuing blind acceptance of clerical authority on the part of the laity. "The priest," María states, "is a man equal to all others. He is like us. He is nothing special. But there are a lot of people who think the opposite. And the heads of the Church, there in Rome, they want us to think that way."

Even those priests most active in the people's struggles have not escaped María's criticism. Unfortunately, she claims, their middle-class origins prevent them from a true appreciation of the plight of the poor. "The priest doesn't know poverty like we do," she asserts. "He is never hungry, never lacks comforts, such as a car and a telephone." "Even women," she adds whimsically, are rarely lacking for the clergy. "I don't know why, but a priest is always one of the most sought-after men around here!"

As we shall see, María is also critical of the way that religious personnel involved directly with the CEBs in her own area attempt to control the groups without consulting the membership. Before discussing these and other CEB-related problems, however, let us first examine María's relationship with those members of the institutional hierarchy with whom she interacts on a daily basis.

One cleric for whom María does have a great deal of respect is Dom Angélico Sândalo Bernardino. Dom Angélico is bishop of the Episcopal Region of São Miguel, where María's neighborhood and CEB are located. Over the years, María has worked closely with the bishop not only as a representative of her own Comunidade Santana but also as CEB coordinator for her sector and as a member of the Regional Pastorate of Vocations (formed to bolster the local church's institutional ranks).

The area over which Dom Angélico presides is one of nine ecclesiastical subunits in São Paulo. It has a population of approximately 1.9 million and is territorially divided into seven subregional sectors, and twenty-three parishes, some containing well over a quarter of a million people. The majority of the region's inhabitants are quite poor, earning at or slightly above the monthly minimum wage, and reside in self-constructed housing in sprawling dusty neighborhoods like María's, lacking even the most basic services, such as running water, street lights, and sewers.

São Miguel Region is well known in São Paulo as an area of intense CEB activity. In 1983 about one hundred twenty CEBs, similar to María's Comunidade Santana, were officially reported to be operating here, more than in any other single region. The success of the CEBs is partly attributable to the youthful zeal of pastors working in the area (the mean age of the pastors is forty-three as compared to fifty-two for the archdiocese), and to the fact that most (63 percent) were ordained in the progressive wake of the Second Vatican Council.

According to María, though, the greatest impetus for CEB formation in the region has been the bishop himself, Dom Angélico. Born in the same year as María (1933), Dom Angélico has been in charge of São Miguel Region since its creation in 1975. Unlike many of his counterparts in other areas of São Paulo, he has embraced the church's "preferential option for the poor" with extreme passion, and much to María's satisfaction, has moved to initiate CEB activity on a number of fronts. To begin with, he has encouraged decentralization of the region and of its parish system. This has been undertaken to allow the CEBs, and CEB leaders such as María, to have more say in the everyday internal workings of the church. Second, he has called frequent CEB conferences to stimulate dialogue between the church and the CEBs, and among the CEBs themselves. In María's view, this latter forum for communication and cooperation is extremely important to the development of effective political strategies within the groups. Finally, Dom Angélico has furthered CEB activities through the publication of highly politicized documents and statements. Material promoting the work of the CEBs is published by the region itself and is distributed both internally, to groups like the Comunidade Santana, and to other parts of the archdiocese.

The admiration that María shows for Dom Angélico and his accomplishments does not, however, extend to her local pastor, Pe. Franco, who ministers to the three hundred thousand residents of María's Nossa Senhora das Dores parish with the help of some ten religious and diocesan priests. On the surface, Pe. Franco appears to have a good deal in common with his immediate superior, where the poor and oppressed are concerned. In Pe. Franco's view, for instance, the will of the people is inviolable, and he claims to approve of any and all means whatsoever that the poor might choose to overthrow their oppressors. In his interpretation of the CEBs, Pe. Franco is even somewhat more radical than his bishop and follows a strictly Marxist line. "The CEBs," he claims, "attempt to realize and confront their class position, their common situation. The aim is to perceive their common enemy [which is] American imperialism and capitalism, although not the American people per se."

In spite of Pe. Franco's rhetoric and apparent conviction, however, María is extremely wary of his motives. His concern, she believes, is political and self-serving, and he cares very little for the everyday problems of the people. Furthermore, in his dealings with parishioners, including herself, he is arrogant. One day, at lunch in her home with Pe. Patrick, an Irish priest who accompanies María's CEB, she explained her feelings this way: "He [Pe. Franco] wouldn't eat with us here, like Pe. Patrick is doing; not even go into a café to have a coffee with us. He talks a lot about the people, but is not of the people."

María is also bitter that, unlike Dom Angélico, Pe. Franco has done little to actually promote the CEBs in the area and rarely even stops to visit her Comunidade Santana. Nevertheless, María's own contribution to the group would seem to more than compensate for the local pastor's lack of interest.

María dos Santos did not initiate the Comunidade Santana. In fact, she is a latecomer to the CEB, becoming involved some three years after it was formed in 1980. Originally, the CEB was designed to provide religious services to the local population (the nearest church is located several miles away), and over the years it has grown from five or six to about forty full-time members. Presently, about two-thirds of these are women, and about one-half are under thirty years of age. Like María, virtually all are poor.

In its relatively brief history prior to María's arrival, the Comunidade Santana was basically a CEB in name only. While the group did pursue a number of both devotional and political functions, these had traditionally been rather limited in scope. Its principal religious activities included the preparation of the local Mass (which is still said each Sunday by the local priest, Pe. Patrick), charity work, religious instruction, Bible study and reflection, and the planning of occasional religious festival days. Baptisms or weddings were not usually performed, nor were there training courses, as exist in some other groups, to prepare individuals to take these two sacraments.

The CEB's political involvement was essentially limited to consciousness-raising, where members would discuss matters pertaining to the reality of poverty and oppression at the local level and beyond. This was characteristically carried out during the Mass, or sometimes at special membership meetings. Though popular in many other CEBs, neighborhood improvement projects, designed to improve the quality of the local infrastructure by petitioning civic authorities, were rarely initiated.

In support of its functions, the Comunidade Santana had created a rather elementary organizational structure. Separate subgroups, for example, were established to help Pe. Patrick prepare the weekly Mass, for religious instruction, for charity work, and so forth. In addition, small nuclei known as *grupos de rua* (street groups) were formed to encourage reflection and political consciousness-raising in a more intimate setting. Some of these teams, especially the *grupos de rua*, met in the homes of individual members, while others met in the CEB's own community center. This building, initiated by the membership in 1982, is still under construction on land owned by the central curia.

The leadership of the Comunidade Santana was invested in a *conselho* (council) consisting of a small number of lay volunteers and the priest who accompanies the CEB, Pe. Patrick. This steering body was officially charged with coordinating the various subgroups, as well as undertaking certain other special functions, such as fund-raising, and representing the CEB at the level of the institutional church.

What had been a rather sleepy, almost inactive little CEB was, however, completely transformed with the arrival of María Ferreira dos Santos in 1983. She was originally invited to join the group by a friend and, in recognition of her experience with other popular movements, was elected almost immediately by group members to serve as president of the *conselho*. Since that time, she has come to be the principal driving force behind virtually all of the CEB's activities.

Initially, María attempted to convince the other *conselho* members to join her in her efforts to breathe desperately needed new life into the group. Her call for revitalization, however, very quickly fell upon deaf ears, leaving much of the responsibility for leadership on María's shoulders alone. To this day she feels a certain bitterness toward the CEB's *conselho*. "This conselho," she rails,

> is weak, without a brain. They do whatever I suggest. "Let's launch a youth group," I say, for example, and they all think that's a great idea; but nobody actually participates, they leave all that up to me. "We need a person for catechism classes—María; a person for liturgy—María; a representative for the next sectoral conference—María."

Undaunted, María has moved unilaterally to push the Comunidade Santana to action. Her first step was to become personally involved with already established group activities, such as liturgy preparation, religious instruction, charity work, and Bible study, giving their respective teams new importance and impetus and encouraging them to meet regularly. Moreover, María has initiated two additional subgroups, for the discussion of issues of importance to women and to young people. Admittedly, both of these do not yet meet regularly, and there is still a high degree of internal turnover. Nevertheless, they have proven extremely popular and do serve a definite need within the community.

María also has involved the CEB for the first time in neighborhood improvement projects, or *revindicações*. Such projects are especially important to María and, in her view, should be the principal concern of all CEB participants. "Our neighborhood," she explains, "lives in total abandonment by the public authorities." Remedial efforts to improve the basic infrastructure, she asserts, are not only desirable but also absolutely necessary to the betterment of the quality of life in the area. Yet, despite the obvious benefits to all, what successful attempts have been made to obtain better services in the area (for improved bus service, a health care post, road paving, and sewers) are largely a result of initiatives undertaken alone by María, who has taken the lead in circulating petitions and arranging seemingly endless meetings with civic officials. Not even the *conselho* of the Comunidade Santana has offered significant support to María in her efforts to improve local living standards. Recently, for instance, it met and agreed to lend material and moral support to a group of local *favelados* (slum dwellers) who wished to appropriate a publicly owned piece of land for the construction of new homes. When the time came for the invasion, however, not one *conselho* member showed up; not one, that is, except for María. In addition, in accordance with the wishes of the local bishop, Dom Angélico, María was forced to move unilaterally to take over the local ratepayers' association, successfully having herself elected to its presidency and then integrating its functions with those of the Comunidade Santana. This ratepayers' group is one of dozens in São Paulo known collectively as SABs (Friends of the Neighborhood Societies). In essence, they are a type of citizens' complaint group but possess little autonomy, as they are funded and monitored by the São Paulo city hall. More often than not, the SABs are simply used by politicians and bureaucrats to neutralize, rather than stimulate, public involvement. Normally, this is accomplished by careful dispensation of favors to members considered influential in the community. In taking control of the SAB, María has sought primarily to use its established ties to local authorities to promote the Comunidade Santana's neighborhood improvement projects.

Another area of intense involvement for María has been the cause of the Comunidade Santana's community hall, which she hopes will someday become the true spiritual and organizational center of not only the CEB but also of the entire neighborhood. As previously mentioned, this structure was initiated in 1982 but remains largely unfinished. Upon entering the CEB, María had attempted to interest group members in pooling their labor to ensure a swift completion of the building. Offers of assistance, however, were never forthcoming, and, consequently, a local stonemason was hired to complete the structure all by himself.

Finding money to keep the project alive, though, has not been easy. Having taxed the generosity of the membership (admittedly quite limited to begin with), María has been forced to solicit contributions from a variety of alternative sources. She has managed to convince Pe. Patrick, for example, to appeal to his friends in Ireland to send money. So far, the priest's old soccer team has made at least one generous donation. In addition, María has organized bazaars and bake sales and has made frequent trips to the pastors of more affluent parishes in central São Paulo in search of support. To date, however, little has been forthcoming from the local clergy, many of whom María describes as "tightwads." More recently, she has even appealed to charitable sources outside Brazil, including Catholic Development and Peace in Canada.

These fund-raising activities, it might be mentioned, have landed María in considerable hot water with local authorities, including Dom Angélico. The bishop, rather paternalistically, has repeatedly stressed that efforts by the groups to secure funds from charitable sources should be discouraged and that the CEBs must operate within their own means. Ostensibly, this is to ensure that the groups do not simply become welfare recipients as opposed to self-sufficient popular organizations. For María, such suggestions are unfortunate and merely represent an effort by the church to maintain its influence over the CEB movement. Adequate funding of the groups, from whatever source, María asserts, is absolutely crucial to their successful operation. "If we had the money," she states, "we could do good work, with youth and their families, with the women of our neighborhood, with the unemployed, and so many other things. . . . it's a real shame, when you have a desire to work for the conscientization of the people, but don't have the funds, only goodwill."

One more way María has contributed to the revitalization of the Comunidade Santana is through her efforts to reduce the often overbearing ecclesiastical control exercised by the group's *pastoral agent*, Pe. Patrick. In some respects, María is a great admirer of the priest and strongly praises his efforts at raising the political consciousness of group members at the weekly Mass. "As you noticed in the Mass," she related approvingly, "the priest really has to speak strongly to motivate the people here." María also defends him from frequent criticisms, often emanating from more elevated sources, about his national origin. "You know," she explains, "they want to remove him from the sector because he is a foreigner. There are even people around here who ask why we have a foreign priest among us. He must know this. He is so good, but everybody talks about him."

It is Pe. Patrick's rather authoritarian and paternalistic attitude with respect to the group and its activities, though, that profoundly disturbs María. By his own admission, Pe. Patrick attempts to shield the CEB from "undesirable" or "harmful" influences. "I don't allow the *comunidade* to be used," he warns, "for specific ends, be they political or personal." In the period leading up to the general elections of 1982, he claims to have demonstrated this intent by denying politicians from all political parties the right to speak to the congregation following Sunday Mass. The researcher himself was similarly denied access to the group until such time as he had thoroughly discussed with the priest the nature and purpose of this study. Even after Pe. Patrick's approval was granted, many CEB members remained reluctant to speak with the researcher and refused to cooperate until they had received Pe. Patrick's verbal permission. For María, such tendencies are both distasteful and inappropriate and have no place in a democratically formed association of the people. Liberty, she asserts, should not be limited to the secular sphere.

The priest's attitude also had had an effect on one of María's most cherished undertakings—the formation of a viable, active youth group. Young people, she claims, are difficult enough to organize, but as a representative of the church, Pe. Patrick compounds this difficulty. Often, María explains, young people feel constrained and limited by church teaching, especially that related to sexual behavior. Though they are attracted by the church's call to political action, they are constantly reminded by Pe. Patrick that matters such as birth control, premarital sex, and abortion are not open for discussion or interpretation. As a consequence, she observes that "at first, they [young people] become involved with full force, but drop out just as quickly. Because they are young, they wish a certain degree of liberty, and feel constrained by the Church; the Church is holding them and they want freedom." This state of affairs, she adds, is truly a shame, since it is young people, with their zeal for justice and liberty, who represent the real hope for the future of Brazil.

One might assume, then, that María's rather solitary efforts on behalf of what is a rather apathetic membership would lead to a certain degree of bitterness and disillusionment. In fact, however, her work with the poor has been personally rewarding in a number of respects. In joining the CEB, she claims, her faith in God and in the church (despite its faults) has been strengthened. She has become more aware of the poor's problems and has developed a strong interest in those problems. Such awareness, moreover, has given her a firm objective in life that had been formerly lacking: raising the consciousness of the people.

The only regret she has is with respect to her family life. Her active involvement with the Comunidade Santana has left her little time to devote to her own husband and children and to their problems. Sadly, as well, she was left with little time to grieve for her eldest child, a married daughter, who was violently murdered with her husband by men who María believes were drug dealers, who had become involved with her son-in-law. The fact, incidentally, that she learned of her own daughter's death not from the police but through word of mouth several days after the event greatly intensified both her disdain for local government officials and her commitment to the cause of social justice.

In the current cold war atmosphere of the developed world, with its narrow focus on East-West relations, there are many who would suggest that María Ferreira dos Santos is a communist, rebel leader, or potential urban guerrilla. Indeed, there are those within the Brazilian Catholic church who share this view. Contrarily, there are still others on the political left who would praise her as a saint, a visionary, or a great revolutionary figure. In actual fact, however, as María herself will readily tell you, she is none of these things. Rather, she is an ordinary person who is engaged in an extraordinary struggle to help the poor of Brazil to become full citizens in their own country. In effect, she seeks no more for herself and her neighbors than most North Americans take for granted—a chance to participate equally in all aspects of social, economic, and political life. María Ferreira dos Santos is the kind of person who, like countless others working in thousands of CEBs throughout Brazil and the rest of Latin America, will likely never be cited in history books but who, in their own way, will help in some measure to transform their societies.

SOURCES

The data for this biography of María Ferreira dos Santos were gathered as part of a larger research project conducted in Brazil in the spring of 1984. The purpose of the research was to investigate the organizational structure and orientation of a select sample of twenty-two CEBs located in the Archdiocese of São Paulo. Information was obtained over a five-month period from representatives of the institutional church, CEB leaders like María dos Santos, and ordinary CEB participants using interviews, self-administered questionnaires, and participation observation.

With the exception of Dom Angélico Sândalo Bernardino, bishop of São Miguel Episcopal Region, the names of all persons and places in this report have been changed to protect those involved, especially María dos Santos, from possible recriminations by local authorities.

FOR FURTHER READING

Adriance, Madeleine. *Opting for the Poor: Brazilian Catholicism in Transition.* Kansas City, 1986.

Barreiro, Alvaro. *Basic Ecclesial Communities.* Translated by Barbara Campbell. Maryknoll, NY, 1982.

Bruneau, Thomas C. "Basic Christian Communities in Latin America: Their Nature and Significance." *Churches and Politics in Latin America,* edited by Daniel H. Levine, 225–37. Beverly Hills, 1980.

———. *The Church in Brazil.* Austin, TX, 1982.

Cox, Harvey. *Religion in the Secular City.* New York, 1984.

Deelen, Gottfried. "The Church on Its Way to the People: Basic Christian Communities in Brazil." *Cross Currents* 30 (1980): 385–408.

Hewitt, W. E. "Basic Christian Communities in Brazil." *The Ecumenist* 24 (September-October 1986): 81–84.

———. "Strategies for Social Change Employed by Comunidades Eclesiais de Base (CEBs) in the Archdiocese of São Paulo." *Journal for the Scientific Study of Religion* 25 (March 1986): 16–30.

Mainwaring, Scott. *The Catholic Church and Politics in Brazil, 1916–1985.* Stanford, 1986.

Torres, Sergio, and Eagleson, John. *The Challenge of Basic Christian Communities.* Translated by John Drury. Maryknoll, NY, 1981.

Welsh, John R. "Comunidades Eclesiais de Base." *America* (February 8, 1986): 85–88.

19

*Leticia**: A Nicaraguan Woman's Struggle*

Dianne Walta Hart

In the middle of the Sandinista revolution to overthrow the Somoza dictatorship and the continuing struggle against the contras, life for everyday Nicaraguans has gone on, complete with all the frustrations and the pleasures common to most people in contemporary society. Leticia has her ambitions and her problems: difficulties with her husband drive her to make an illegal entry into the United States, but the lure of her family brings her back to Managua. The Sandinista success has meant new opportunities for Leticia and others like her and, also, new hardships for them as they attempt to earn their livelihood.

Leticia's story is told with warmth and humor by Dianne Walta Hart of the Spanish department of Oregon State University. Spanish, linguistics, and adult education are Hart's teaching specialties, while her research since 1984 has concentrated on the oral history of a Nicaraguan family. She has published articles on Nicaraguan women and Sandinista society. Besides serving as executive secretary of the Pacific Northwest Council on Foreign Languages, Hart has found the time to act as adviser to Oregon State's Japanese Traditional Karate Club.

This vignette reveals the balance between personal needs and national goals that Leticia and others maintain in Nicaragua. Her experience adds a human dimension and female perspective to the Sandinista struggle for social justice in Nicaragua.

> Nicaragua's crisis is so long, so long . . . we walk each day so near to hope and to despair.
> —Uriel Molina, *Barricada*, Managua, Nicaragua, August 1986

> I would like to discuss with you
> how now I live in the catacombs
> and how determined I am to kill the hunger
> that is killing us
> when you discuss this
> discuss it long and hard

*Leticia is a pseudonym.

when no one who sows hunger is around
nor a spy for those who sow hunger
nor a guard for those who sow hunger.
—Leonel Rugama, Estelí poet killed at the age of twenty in 1970 by Somoza's Guards[1]

In July 1979 the Nicaraguan people overthrew the forty-six-year-long dictatorship of the Somoza family and, in its place, established the Sandinista government. In 1981 the U.S. government created a counterrevolutionary group, the contras, on Nicaragua's borders in an attempt to overthrow the Sandinistas. I met Leticia and her family in 1983 and began an oral history of them in 1984. They have requested that pseudonyms be used and that minor details be changed because they fear retaliation from the contras.

Leticia's story begins in Estelí, Nicaragua, capital of the province of the same name. It is a city of fifty thousand people that has been her home most of her life. In Estelí, she can chat with old friends on the street, describe the histories of families and buildings, go down to the river where her mother used to make her living washing clothes, and stop by the cemetery where a tall tree has grown from a seed the family planted to shade her brother's grave.

Estelí is two hours north of Managua in Nicaragua's hilly tobacco country. The Pan-American highway cuts through the town, bringing with it motorcycles and four-wheel drive vehicles that seem both to bounce and roar on the rough streets. Bordering the lively central park are government buildings, a run-down theater, and vendors selling vegetables. Sloths hang from the park trees and children chase each other around the swings. Sophisticated helicopters drone over the city by day and at night one can hear distant gunfire.

Leticia describes the people in Estelí as nicer, more hospitable, and less prejudiced than other Nicaraguans. They don't gossip and criticize each other, but, at the same time, they know where everyone lives, and they are concerned about their neighbors. They have few luxuries, but they like to dress well, even if only inexpensive fabric is available. The climate is cooler than Managua's, and the people are

[1]Leonel Rugama, *The Earth Is a Satellite of the Moon*, trans. Sara Miles, Richard Schaaf, and Nancy Weisberg (Willimantic, CT, 1984), 101.

lighter skinned, not as burned by the sun. Many people have green or blue eyes, and it is said that the women of Estelí are beautiful.

There is another dimension to Estelí, though. Popular tee shirts proclaim Estelí as a *pueblo heroico* for several well-fought reasons. It is one of the towns that most openly defied the Somoza government, causing Estelí to be bombed more than any other city in Nicaragua. Many of the downtown buildings still show the scars of the battles that destroyed most of Estelí's businesses. Out of those battles has come a feeling that the city and its people will never give in, never be defeated. They view themselves as warriors. The young poet and early martyr, Leonel Rugama, came from Estelí, and his attitude represents the spirit of the city. His finest verse, some say, was his profane last words in defiance of Somoza's Guards just before they killed him: "Tell your mother to surrender!"

Leticia's story, and that of her mother, brother, and sister, started in Estelí in desperate hunger and poverty. Their mother, Dora, lived with five different men in her life. All but one beat her, and all of them abandoned her. Landlords often chased them out of shanty homes, their few possessions on their backs. At the age of six, the children began working fourteen hours a day. They shined shoes, picked tobacco, and sold food door-to-door in an attempt to add to the money Dora made. As hard as they all worked, it often was not enough. "Some days," according to Leticia, "we would wake up in the morning and there was nothing to eat. Sometimes we didn't even have wood to start a fire. Sometimes we'd eat a piece of bread in the morning, with a cup of coffee; that was all until night, when—if my mother had washed and if the clothes had dried and if she had been able to deliver the clothes—we would eat again."

All of them fought, in different ways, to overthrow the Somoza dictatorship that had controlled Nicaragua since the early 1930s. As a teenager, Leticia's brother, Omar, fought for two years in the mountains. Her sister, Marta, was forced to stand for a month in a foot of water in a government prison because she refused to tell Somoza's guardsmen her brother's whereabouts. Leticia, born in 1948 and at least ten years older than her sister and brother, provided a safe house in Managua for Omar, burying his dirty clothes in the backyard, providing him with clean ones, and hiding him, although such actions endangered her three young daughters and husband. A second brother died in the struggle.

Today, Leticia, Marta, and Omar are still committed to the revolution. Leticia volunteers for AMNLAE (the national women's organization) and takes her turn watching over her barrio at night.

Marta and Omar are Sandinistas; she works for AMNLAE, and he is still in the military.

Leticia and her family have been actively involved in the social changes that have taken place in Estelí and in all of Nicaragua since the revolution. As children in prerevolutionary Nicaragua, Leticia and her siblings went to school at night whenever they could find time, because they had to work during the day. Leticia remembers those years with sadness: "A child cannot study without food. When I would pick up a book to study a lesson, I wouldn't remember anything. My head would start to ache. It would feel heavy, and I would have to stop studying." Now children like those of Leticia, Marta, and Omar go to school with full stomachs and go to school during the day. At night the schools are attended by adults.

With a voice in their community, better access to medical care, and better education for their children, Leticia and her family, for the first time, share in the responsibility for their own lives and that of their community. They are proud of Estelí and proud of Nicaragua. They are also happy that the leadership and courage shown by many Nicaraguan women during the struggle has not been forgotten, as evidenced by the laws protecting women and their enforcement by the Sandinistas. Even though the legal status of women has been improved, many old attitudes persist.

The Sandinista government built subsidized housing in the years after Somoza's overthrow, and today Dora and Marta live together in a government-built duplex. It is the first time that either woman has lived in a house where the front door locks. It is also the first time that they do not have to worry that someone will come along and chase them out.

Leticia lives a block away. She is small, quick to cry, and an important member of the family. Within the family, her ninth-grade education is surpassed only by that of her university-educated husband. As a teenager, she took a correspondence course in cosmetology, worked in a SONY store, and met her first boyfriend, an intense young man named Antonio, nine years older than she. When they first met, she did not know that he was already working with the Frente Sandinista. Often he disappeared for days, and she believed that he had another girlfriend. He denied this and told her that he visited a family in Santa Clara. On her fifteenth birthday in 1963, he gave a party for her and presented her with fabric for a dress, white cloth with golden stripes. Although Antonio knew the law required permits for private parties, he did not get one, and Somoza's Guards broke up Leticia's only birthday party. "Soon after that, he asked me if we could have a civil marriage. I don't know why, but I became afraid and told him that at fifteen, I was too young. I was nervous; my teeth even chattered. It wasn't that I didn't love him because I did. He was my first boyfriend, and I loved him a lot. But he didn't think I loved him." Not long after, Antonio "went to the mountains," that is, he joined the guerrillas. She never saw him again. He became a *comandante*, a national hero, and, upon his death in 1979, an official martyr. In Estelí, there is a barrio named after him.

Leticia went on to a cosmetology school in Managua. She lived with the owner, a woman who fed her *gallo pinto* (beans and rice) three times a day in return for Leticia's working seven days a week. When she finished school, she moved to Matagalpa, not far from Estelí, took out a loan to buy a mirror and a dryer, hired someone to make a table, and placed a sign, *Centro de Belleza Leticia*, outside her apartment. She was twenty years old and in business.

"I felt good about it. I felt liberated. Whenever I had a slow day, I would come and see my mother. I would come to leave her a little money. Then I would leave. I liked Estelí, and I wanted to stay there because it was where I was born, but I don't know—[at that time in my life], Estelí brought back a lot of bad memories for me. I felt sad whenever I went to Estelí, probably due to my childhood, due to all the difficulties we went through with my mother. We suffered hunger because my mother was on her own. She has always been on her own. I have always admired her, maybe because I was the eldest and could understand the situation a bit better. She always had to wash and iron to support us; this would make me feel sorry for her. It would make me sad to think of all the things that we went through.

"And then I met Sergio. One day his sister came to my beauty parlor and invited me on an outing to a farm. She and her friends didn't know me and weren't even my friends, but I thought that maybe they liked me, and that's why they invited me. That was not so—there was more to it. Sergio's sister was jealous of her boyfriend. She thought her boyfriend was in love with me. But that was not true. He was a friend of mine because he worked with my roommate. They both worked at PROLASA, a dairy product factory. We were friends, and he would come to visit, but he wasn't in love. She thought he was in love with me, so she came to the beauty parlor. It was part of her plan. Sergio's sister and her friends invited me on the trip so that I could see that she was his girlfriend. I went, but took it very naturally because there wasn't any truth in the rest.

"When I was going to the farm, when I got into the truck that we used for the trip, Sergio was in it. He moved so that I could sit down.

So I sat down beside him, and then we drove off. We started to talk about everything, but nothing related to falling in love and all those things. We went to the farm on the fourteenth of February 1970.

"We spent the day there; we walked and had a party and a *piñata*. The farm was very nice because it had a big river where we went swimming. Then I realized that he had fallen in love with me and I with him. We returned home that same day, at night. He went home to bathe and returned later that night to see me. The girls who had invited me to the party were very happy and became good friends of mine. They were happy because they no longer worried about the boyfriend.

"Sergio started to visit and soon, during the first week of March, they planned another trip to the farm for Holy Week. So we went back again and spent a whole week on the farm. It was during that week that we became engaged. He was just starting his first year at the university; he was twenty-one and I was twenty-two.

"When he told his mother that he wanted to marry me, she said, no, that if he married me, she wouldn't help him with his studies and that he would have to leave her house. He left, and we were married on the fourth of April. We married quietly, without his family knowing. I wrote to my mother and told her all about it—that I had found a man and was going to marry, that I was having only a civil wedding to see if it would work. I hadn't known him for too long, but I was sure that I was in love because I had had another boyfriend before for two years and had never felt so in love with someone as to get married."

During the next few years, Sergio attended the Universidad Autónoma de Nicaragua in Managua while Leticia continued her work as a hairdresser in Matagalpa. They saw each other on weekends. Her first daughter was born on May 22, 1971; three of her four daughters would be born before 1979. Leticia eventually moved to Managua to be with her husband.

After Sergio finished the university, he worked for Sears, Roebuck and Company and later for the Bank of America. Politics did not interest him. Leticia did not tell him that her brothers were working with the Sandinistas in the struggle to overthrow Somoza. Later, she learned that he knew all along but said nothing to her.

One night, when Leticia's brothers had sneaked into Managua and were sleeping at her house, she woke up after hearing a jeep go around the block several times. She worried about her innocent husband and children. She had not meant to endanger them. "The guards stopped in front of my door and got out of the jeep. They kept the jeep running.

I could hear them get their guns ready to shoot. I got up quickly and, without turning on a light, I ran to my brothers. They slept with their clothes on, ready for what might happen. After I warned them, I went to the living room in the dark and knelt on the floor. I asked God to help us, to please not let the guards come to our house. I heard one guard say, as he came closer to us, that he thought people were there, but the other one said that there was no one. They got in their car and left."

In July 1979, after a month of fierce fighting, there was a moment of calm as troops withdrew. Leticia, along with her husband, children, and friends, took advantage of this time to scout for refuge from the battle—someplace outside of Managua. They stopped at a small farm owned by a friend of Sergio's. As they rested, they heard a helicopter above and then watched with horror as it landed next door, at a farm owned by a *comandante* in Somoza's Guard. When they realized that the helicopter was full of guardsmen, they hid under beds and in closets, certain that they would be killed. But instead of coming to look for them, the guardsmen waited for the *comandante* who left his house with the few bags he had packed. The guardsmen loaded the suitcases into the helicopter, the *comandante* got in, and they flew away. At that moment, Leticia knew, without hearing it officially, that the revolution had been successful. Much earlier she had made a red-and-black flag for this victorious moment and had hidden it in her purse. Now she pulled out the flag, ran to their car, and tied it to the antenna. They laughed and cried and began the victory drive into Managua on roads full of people singing, shooting guns, and playing mariachi music to celebrate the triumph of the revolution.

In time, Sergio accepted a government position, so once again Leticia moved her table, dryer, and mirror to a new Centro de Belleza Leticia. This time their move was to Estelí, her hometown. Later, the Sandinista government sent Sergio to study in Cuba for a year. They both considered a divorce during his absence. Leticia thought they had gone their separate ways; her community involvement had become time-consuming. Sergio did not understand and occasionally beat her. She felt that he wanted her to be his slave, not his companion for life. In Cuba, Sergio watched men and women interact and was impressed with how different it was from Nicaragua, how men and women treated each other more as equals. He wrote that it changed his attitude and that he wanted a second chance. She agreed.

In 1981 the U.S.-backed contras began their war against Nicaragua; the battle often touched the lives of Leticia and her family. Omar was usually in the battlefield and often suffered from nightmares and fears.

The stress and war-related anxiety eventually debilitated him for a year, causing the Sandinistas to take away his rifle and relieve him from actual battle responsibilities until his emotional health improved. Marta's work, similar to a paramilitary position, placed her near the war zone where the Sandinista soldiers fought the contras. She was in the border town of Santa Clara in 1984 when U.S. mercenaries from the Alabama-based Civilian-Military Assistance attacked by air and were shot down by the Sandinistas. It seemed never to end. The father of the family in the other side of their duplex was killed fighting the contras. The rumors of children with slit necks, of dead bodies in the river, and of random and senseless contra attacks on civilians added to the tension, as did the low car with a loudspeaker on the top, making its way through the barrio, announcing the latest death of someone from Estelí. They wondered if they would ever have peace.

The symbolic importance of Estelí was not lost on the contras. They attacked it in August 1985, knowing how significant the defeat of Estelí would be. During the attack on the city, Marta was in charge of coordinating the civilian defense of the city's perimeters. Omar sat helplessly immobile in his tiny ramshackle hillside home with a cast on a broken leg, painfully reliving, in an emotional sense, his wartime horrors as he heard the Sandinista helicopters strafe the nearby hills in their attempt to repel the contras. Leticia stood watch over her barrio at night, as she had done once a week since 1979, to protect the area. She made coffee and food for others, when she was not on watch, and worried as Estelí buried ten people in one day. Eight days later, the contras retreated. The people of Estelí felt that once more they had been victorious.

By this time, Leticia had become the emotional center of the family. She had, by everyone's account, assumed the dominant role. She was the one in whom the family members traditionally confided; she, in turn, worried about them and advised them. That she struggled with this responsibility and their confidence in her was evident in her overall sadness.

Leticia and her four-year-old daughter left Nicaragua three months later, in November 1985, leaving behind not only her mother, brother, and sister but also three teenaged daughters and her husband. She had never before been outside Nicaragua had only vague knowledge of the location of the cities and countries that lay ahead of her. She had never seen a map. She said that her reason for leaving was not Nicaragua: "I am convinced that the revolution is for us, for the poor, for those of us who were always marginalized." She added that, as a Nicaraguan, her duty was in her country.

If her duty was in Nicaragua and the reason she left was not Nicaragua, why then did she leave? She left to get away from Sergio. She could no longer tolerate having him come near her. A cousin in Nevada had invited her to the United States and offered to pay her way. A friend had advised her that maybe she would feel better about Sergio if she left for a couple of months. The invitation came at the perfect time.

However, in a way, the problem *was* Nicaragua. Danger from the contras to family and friends is omnipresent in the towns far from Managua; it strains relationships like no other stress can. Every day Leticia heard of a sorrow unimagined the day before. And Leticia visibly suffers more than others; she has said, "I am one of those people who is always worrying about what is happening to others." She remembers as a child watching one of Somoza's Guards hit an old man with his rifle butt. She stood on the street corner screaming at the guard, telling him that the old man was a drunk. But the beating continued, and Leticia ran to her house, crying over her inability to help. When she was in Nicaragua, no orphaned child or abandoned mother went unhelped by Leticia. She volunteered for AMNLAE, went to two weekly meetings of her Christian base community where they discussed a practical approach to being Christians, and stood watch over her neighborhood. However, her marital problems, exacerbated by her family responsibilities and the anxieties caused by the last contra attack on Estelí, had become too great.

Sergio and their daughters took her to the Nicaraguan-Honduran border where she joined eight other Nicaraguans, all with Mexican visas but with no intention of staying in Mexico. They rode in a van, mostly in silence, through Honduras, El Salvador, Guatemala, and Mexico. They missed, by a few minutes, a military confrontation in El Salvador. At night they stayed in small hotels or slept in the van.

When they reached the U.S.-Mexican border, they waited until 5:00 A.M. to begin their illegal entry into the United States. Carrying a small suitcase brought from Nicaragua, Leticia and her daughter climbed over a wall and walked through heavy rain, mud, and standing water for one and a half hours until they reached an abandoned house. Later, they made the three-hour trip to Los Angeles in two cars, the men in the trunks and the women and children lying down in the back.

Then the confusion began. When her cousin invited her, he thought she was emigrating. He had no intention of paying for a mere visit. As for her child, Leticia had told someone to ask another person about the advisability of taking her daughter along but had interpreted the response—"No hay ningún problema"—to mean there would be no charge. As a result of these misunderstandings, Leticia was presented with a bill for $1,500. She had no money and no way of earning enough to repay this unexpected debt.

Leticia and her daughter moved to Nevada with her cousin where they shared an apartment with other Nicaraguans who had entered illegally. She worked for a few weeks in a factory. Later, they were invited to Oregon by friends and spoke with groups of university students about the Nicaraguan revolution. She said, "I think it was a bad decision [to leave Nicaragua] but it is done. I have analyzed all this and I think that God always has His plans; a leaf on a tree does not move except by His will." She added that maybe what God had wanted her to do was talk with students and tell them about Nicaragua.

Her responsibilities had followed her: "I know that my sister and brother feel that I am their second mother. My mother will be able to die peacefully because she knows she has me. I cannot make decisions about my life . . . because my life doesn't belong to me but to my family."

Leticia and her daughter made their way to Miami where they could easily drop unnoticed into a world of illegal aliens and where, she hoped, she could find employment, earn plane fare back to Nicaragua, and maybe even make a few extra dollars. Although she had friends from Estelí there, Miami was difficult. Everyone spoke Spanish, but, she said, most of them were Cubans who spoke too fast and all the time. Even the Nicaraguans in Miami were always agitated, in a hurry, and running to catch a bus. She got a job cleaning and cooking in the house of a *señora*. Next, she worked with a *señor* whom she accompanied to the docks, greeting incoming tourist ships from Latin American countries and selling perfume, clothes, and souvenirs in her struggle to make enough money for the return ticket. As time went on, she found work in the evenings as an Avon lady, using her stylish good looks to advertise her products and her cosmetology background to sell them. She could keep 50 percent of what she brought in; the first night out, she sold $300 in Avon products and made $150 for herself. Finally, the perfect job.

Leticia did not hear very often from Nicaragua, but she did know that Sergio had accepted a promotion and had moved, along with their three teenaged daughters, from Estelí to Managua. She also heard that a niece had been killed by the contras and that a stepsister had died of a stroke. She sensed that even more was wrong. When she telephoned Sergio, he almost always was the first one to suggest that the call end. He seemed not to be very interested in talking with her, and she wondered if there was another woman. In May, on her thirty-ninth birthday, a friend in Miami called to congratulate her and added that she had heard from a relative that Leticia's husband was going out with another woman, publicly, in front of everyone. No one had told her because they did not want her to worry.

A few weeks later, in June, Leticia called Sergio's Managua office and found out that he had quit his job. When she asked for him, the secretary said, "He no longer works here, but if you wish to leave a message for him, I can ask the driver to take it to him." Leticia asked if the secretary had the address. The answer was, "Not of his house, but I know the address of the woman he lives with." Leticia was stunned. She asked that he call her in Miami: "I wanted the secretary to think everything was normal, that it didn't matter, but that was a lie. I thought that I was dying."

Sergio did not return the call. Instead, his sister came to Miami and called Leticia, telling her that Sergio was leaving that week for Mexico. "It was another blow, because I still had the hope that it was a passing thing for him, and that when I returned, everything was going to be normal, as before. I was ready to forgive him because I thought he had done it because I wasn't with him. The majority of Latin men are *machistas*, and they say they cannot be without a woman. But when I heard he was leaving for Mexico, this meant it was serious. He hadn't even called me to tell me that he was going, or that I should come because the children would be alone. I knew I had to hurry and return before I had planned, even though I had hoped to stay a couple of months longer to make money. I called a relative to find out if he had actually left; she said he hadn't, so I asked her to tell him that he should wait for me."

Later that month, the U.S. House of Representatives voted to give $100 million to the contras. That meant the war against Nicaragua would continue. Leticia, eight months after entering the United States, was finally on her way back to Nicaragua, spurred more by her husband's impending departure to Mexico than by political reasons. She had often worried about various aspects of her return. One was how she would be received after spending so much time in the country that was, in effect, at war with her country. The other problem was her lack of papers. Leticia had entered the United States illegally. If, on paper, she had not entered, how could she leave? No one seemed to know the answer to that question.

Entering Nicaragua and reestablishing her life there, from a political point of view, presented no problems. Oddly enough, neither did the lack of papers. No one asked for them when she left the United States and, in Nicaragua, the officials asked for no more than the form she filled out on the plane. She must have looked like most Nicaraguans who return from extensive shopping trips abroad because the fourteen boxes she brought back with her caused her no trouble at customs.

The return itself turned out to be the easy part. It was her relationship with Sergio that presented the most difficulty. In his new position in Managua, he had been earning the maximum monthly wages (80,000 córdobas, equal to U.S. $57) that one could earn from a government job in Nicaragua, but it wasn't enough. In Leticia's absence, the córdoba had lost much of its value; in addition, living in Managua was more expensive than in Estelí.[2] Even if one could afford it, everything from meat to beans to beauty care products was difficult to find, more so than in the countryside, where the people were more affected by the war and where the government, as a consequence, maintained better food distribution and lower prices.

Nicaragua had changed in the eight months that Leticia had been in the United States. Nicaraguans had begun calling their country the land of "no hay" (there isn't any), so severe were the shortages of beans, corn, and spare parts. Basic goods were to have been available at low prices, but the impact on Nicaragua of the war with the U.S.-backed contras and the effect of the U.S. government embargo, compounded by inefficiency and corruption in the Nicaraguan distribution system, had resulted in frequent shortages. Even one of Nicaragua's newspapers, *El Nuevo Diario*, called Managua's prices exorbitant. At the same time, an "increased flight of the technical-professional sector" was predicted, along with continued labor indiscipline and inflation, already at the astonishingly high level of more than 1,000 percent.[3] Nicaraguans lived in what was now being called a "survival economy."

---

[2]In August 1983 the exchange rate was 25 córdobas to one U.S. dollar. In August 1984 it was 74 córdobas to a dollar; in August 1985 it was 600; and in August 1986 it was 1,400. The black market paid a thousand more than that.

In Leticia's absence (November 1985 to July 1986), a tortilla went from 10 córdobas to 50 córdobas in Managua. The price of five pounds of beans rose from 16 córdobas to 300. When beans were otherwise unavailable, they could be obtained on the black market at 1,100 córdobas for a 1 lb.-4 oz. bag.

[3]"Slow Motion toward a Survival Economy," *Envío*, Instituto Histórico Centroamericano, Managua, Nicaragua, 5, no. 63 (September 1986): 14.

The family met Leticia and her daughter at the airport. "We went to the house, talked a lot, and they asked me a lot of questions about what had happened in the United States. I began to tell them how hard life there really is because the majority of the people who go to the United States talk big—how there is everything and how everything is pretty and how much money they make. That is the mistake, to not tell the truth. Because I believe that if all the world knew how it really is, very few people would want to go there. It is not for everyone."

Leticia and Sergio made love that first night but after that he became cool and distant. He accompanied her to Estelí where she went to see her mother and other family members, but he returned early to Managua. She struggled to find the answers. When she asked her daughters about the woman with whom her husband had had the affair, she learned that she was about the same age as Leticia but "shorter and not especially pretty." "Then why," she asked her children, "do you think that your dad went out with her?" "We don't know," they answered, "but you know how men are." The children told her that there were several nights that he did not come home while she was in the United States. Even some weekends. But they added that he checked on them often.

"Then one day," according to Leticia, "I went to Estelí again, to see my mother and that very day, he went with the woman, when I wasn't here. I had reached a limit; I couldn't stand it anymore—I couldn't bear the humiliation. I packed his bags and asked him to leave. I told him that even though I was a woman, I still had dignity."

She and Sergio argued. She accused him of leaving her for the other woman. He denied it, saying that he did not love the woman; he loved Leticia. Besides, the woman had two children and under no circumstances would he remake his life with a woman who had two children when he had four of his own he could no longer support on his salary. He was leaving to find work and to have time to think. And maybe, or so thought Leticia, to get even. She had left, and now he would.

Sergio planned to leave with his brother, starting out from Managua on an August evening. He was going to take his university diploma and other papers with him, hoping to get a position in Mexico for which his degree in business administration had prepared him. Other members of the family wondered if he intended to enter illegally the United States, much as Leticia did. She said no, that since she had told him how hard life is in the United States, his goal was to stay in Mexico. Since 1979 he had supported the revolution and worked for it; but he, unlike the others in Leticia's family, had not actually fought for it. Politics had never interested him and still did not.

Leticia had no definite plans. The children had to stay in Managua to finish the school year. Maybe she could leave them with Sergio's sister and return to Estelí. Certainly when the school year finished in early December, they would return. But how to support her family? The beauty shop that she left in Estelí had been poorly managed in her absence and no longer existed. Maybe she could set up a beauty shop in her house, but it would not be easy. In the years following 1979, the government purchased beauty products and distributed them to beauty salons. As the economic situation worsened, the government was unable to continue this, and salon owners had to find a way to purchase beauty products out of the country, a feat that was easier for owners of large salons than it was for Leticia. The products she had brought back with her would not last long. She knew life would improve if she could just get back to Estelí, if only for the ease with which she could get beans and rice.

Dora, Marta, and Omar still live in Estelí, and Leticia still considers it home. She is more comfortable there than she is in Managua or Miami. During her eight months in the United States, people in Estelí often asked about her and then commented that she would never return. Such remarks for a family committed to the revolution provided many awkward moments.

Estelí was also the home of the man who had driven Leticia and her daughter in his van to the United States and who supported himself by making such trips. She still owed him $1,500. He had called her in Miami, and she told him that she was working and would repay him when she could. A concern of hers had always been that he would damage her reputation by telling people in her hometown that she had not paid. Later, when she ran into him on a Nicaraguan street, she assured him that she had come back only to attend to family problems and that when she returned to the United States, even though she had no intention of doing so, she would earn the money to pay him. Repaying U.S. $1,500 when one makes córdobas would take a lifetime, and he understood that. A few weeks later, as he attempted to leave Nicaragua for Mexico by plane, this time taking several young draft evaders with him instead of people from Estelí, he was arrested and put in prison. As a result, the debt was not a problem, at least not for the moment, and Leticia's reputation and credit in Estelí remained intact.

In the month that she had been back, Leticia's visits to her mother's house had been brief. She appeared to be distracted when she did come to Estelí and often spent her time with other friends and relatives. She hadn't even had lunch with Dora, Marta, or Omar. To them, she seemed changed by her experience in the United States, and her absence had affected their attitude toward her. They knew that she was having trouble with her husband because he had not tried to keep his infidelity a secret. Such problems, though, did not make her family more sympathetic. Marta, commenting on Leticia's behavior of the past year, said that a woman can always get another man, but she has just one mother. Dora, who is slowly succumbing to heart failure, feels abandoned by the very daughter who earlier had shouldered the worries of the entire family.

Leticia's problems are not separate or isolated from those of her country. The inability of her husband to support his family on his managerial wage, the strains that long separations bring, and the fear of death and loss that come with war—while striving to retain the improvements they have made in Nicaragua and to ensure a better future for Nicaragua's children—have affected Leticia and all those around her. Each day Leticia walks close to hope and to despair along with her country. The struggle continues. As the epitaph of Estelí's martyred poet, Leonel Rugama, reads:

> Leonel Rugama
> rejoiced in the promised land
> in the hardest month of the planting
> with no choice but the struggle
> very near death
> but nowhere near
> the end.

20

Majito and Carlos Alberto: The Gamín *Legacy*

Michael Shifter

When Michael Shifter first interviewed Majito and Carlos Alberto in Bogotá, Colombia, he was a representative of the Inter-American Foundation. He has since become the human rights-social justice program officer for the Ford Foundation in Lima, Peru, with responsibility for Chile, Peru, and Argentina. This appointment utilizes his doctoral training in sociology at Harvard University and his experience at the Woodrow Wilson International Center for Scholars, the Foundation for American Communications, and the Harvard Institute for International Development.

Shifter has investigated squatter settlements in Colombia, peasant organizations in Venezuela, and nonformal education in Chile. In his Inter-American Foundation work he evaluated studies of grass-roots programs grappling with the problems of modern life in Latin America. Not surprisingly, his interest turned to the culture of the streets and the efforts that were being made to save children from street life. This interest resulted in his interviews with the former *gamines* in Bogotá that follow.

Although Majito and Carlos Alberto are distinctly Colombian, the early experiences that led them to the streets and their lives as *gamines* are similar to those of many youngsters in all the cities of the region. But no other program exceeds Bosconia-La Florida in assisting *gamines* to improve their lives through self-motivation and self-discipline.

Scarcely a *gamín* in Bogotá, it seems, does not know Majito. As Bosconia-La Florida's blue van makes its nightly rounds from barrio to barrio, the street children become animated—Majito is inside. We pass a grassy area and spot a large sheet of plastic. To me, it appears lifeless; Majito's instincts tell him otherwise. After a quick glance, he steps out of the van and strides confidently forward. Eight young boys—ranging in age from seven to twelve—spring to their feet and throw off the cover, shouting exuberantly, "Majito! Majito!"

In a world marked by terror, where survival is an overriding impulse, Majito, for twenty-five years, has offered a measure of security, however fleeting, to Bogotá's *gamines* (street children). A bearded man, around fifty, he knows the *gamín* subculture as well as anyone. "I was one myself in the early 1950s," he explains, "but then we were known as *muchachos de la calle* (boys of the street). The term *gamín* did not become fashionable until the late 1950s, the early 1960s."

Majito is now the director of El Patio, first stage of the Bosconia-La Florida program, a place where the *gamines* can bathe, receive medical attention, and get something to eat. He joined the program at its inception in 1973, when Cinerama (another organization that fed the *gamines* and gave them temporary lodging) folded. "Cinerama," he says, "had no sequence, no philosophy behind it. There were no stages: all we had to offer was some food and perhaps a brief stay. Bosconia-La Florida has a progression, there's something to aim for. Nothing else is like it, either in the old days or now. It is special."

Known as "Father Javier's program" to some, in recognition of the Salesian priest who is its founding director and guiding force, Bosconia-La Florida is engaged in an innovative campaign to enable Bogotá's *gamines* to become productive members of Colombian society. Over the past dozen years, Javier de Nicoló's efforts have evolved into four successive and complementary stages, each designed to serve a specific purpose—from providing meals and medical attention for thousands of younger boys to housing and education for some five hundred high-school students. A final stage will emphasize technical training and will be completely self-supporting. Moving from principles of self-motivation to self-discipline to community responsibility to financial independence, the guiding belief throughout has been Father de Nicoló's view that "to be effective in taking care of the child, you must respect his freedom."

In his work with Cinerama some fifteen years ago, Majito met Carlos and Eduardo when both were *gamines*. Carlos is now a charismatic twenty-two-year-old who is the *alcalde* (mayor) of the program's last stage, La Florida; Eduardo is a twenty-six-year-old graduate of La Florida who has studied in the Soviet Union and now works as an *educador* in El Patio. Tonight, both have joined Majito in the van for Operación Amistad (Operation Friendship). The three will approach scores of *galladas* (bands of *gamines*) during the next few hours, talking to the boys, asking them how they've been, suggesting they drop by El Patio during the day. Majitos, Carlos, and Eduardo are all strangers to the hard sell—their approach is easygoing, almost nonchalant, devoid of moralizing.

The *gamines* are excited as they board the van. They know they will be treated to a cup of coffee, a bowl of soup, some bread at one of the outdoor food stands that dot the city. When we stop, the boys, far from foolish, ask the man at the window for chicken and hamburgers; but Majito sternly waves his hand, no: he has a limited budget and many hungry mouths to feed. Still, the *gamines* wait patiently in line, thanking Majito as they receive their food.

Carlos and Eduardo look up to Majito and strive to follow his example. They play with the *gamines*, roughhousing with them, chasing them around. When Carlos asks a ten-year-old for his knife, the boy hands it over. Carlos inspects it briefly, then returns it. Almost half of the boys carry containers of glue, often partially concealed in the sleeves of their oversized coats. Carlos and Eduardo show an interest in the boys' containers, but they do not confiscate them.

As soon as all the *gamines* have been taken care of, Majito brings them back to the doorways, street corners, and grassy areas where he found them. Inside the van on the return trip, the smell of glue hangs in the air. After the group of fifteen boys gets out, Carlos turns to me and asks, "How do you like the sweet fragrance of *gamín* life?"

Many of the *gamines* we picked up, according to Majito, have already been to the first stage of Bosconia-La Florida. How many will make it to the community where Carlos is now *alcalde*? With most of the boys, Majito claims, "you can look into their eyes and tell who will go through the program and who will end up back on the streets or in jail. You're a sociologist, you say? You must be able to tell, can't you?" I made a few wild guesses, but my graduate training and fieldwork are no match for his twenty-five years of experience with Bogotá's *gamines*. Majito can predict even their physical movements and facial expressions.

In southern Bogotá at 1:00 A.M., we spot a young boy walking alone. Majito tells me the boy is a *pregamín* who has just left his home, probably for the first or second or third time. The boy is terrified, and Majito predicts, with astonishing precision, how many steps he will take, which way he will turn and look. It is almost as if Majito has him programmed. Overcome with fear, the boy eventually approaches the van; Majito and Carlos have told him that we are "friends of the boys of the street" and have coaxed him to get in. Trembling, he climbs aboard and somehow manages to tell us his father has beaten him. The boy has strayed far from home, so Majito promises him lodging for the night. The next day the boy will be returned to his parents.

Carlos is visibly moved. Seeing this frightened child evokes memories of his own initiation into Bogotá's street life—that first week without sleep, the constant fears for his life. Victim of many robberies,

Carlos was forced to join a *gallada* for his own protection. This pattern—this process of becoming a *gamín*—has long been the same.

Obviously street smart, Majito is also highly analytic about the world he knows so well. Describing changes in Bogotá's street culture over the past twenty-five years, he focuses on the progressive strength and intensity of the dominant *vicios* (vices). When he was a *gamín*, he remarks, drugs were unknown; now *bazuka* (a mixture of cocaine paste, gasoline, and a variety of acids) is a staple. For former *gamines* like Carlos and Eduardo—now in their twenties—marijuana was the most widely used drug; *bazuka* today is more prevalent still.

Majito and Carlos tell me that the widespread use of *bazuka* has dramatically transformed Bogotá's street scene. Highly toxic, it has inflicted significant physiological damage on many *gamines*. "For them," Majito laments, "we have no solution." Further, the high cost of *bazuka* relative to marijuana—and the natural impulse to consume it in ever-increasing quantities—has led the *gamines* into more serious, organized crime. Carlos notes that petty larcenies such as watch and hubcap snatching are on the decline in Bogotá; instead, victims are well targeted, and the crimes are more vicious and better planned. The period of being a *gamín* (as commonly conceived) is thus becoming shorter and shorter as many of the boys quickly become full-fledged, sophisticated criminals.

Majito ponders a host of subjects bearing on Bogotá's street life, and he has a penchant for typologies. He talks with authority about the three discrete stages of *gaminismo*—the *pregamín*, the *gamín* of the barrio, and the full *gamín* who gravitates to the *centro* (center of Bogotá). He knows where the children go and how they are distributed throughout the city. He can discuss the *gamines* of the north, the south, and the *centro* according to the intensity and prevalence of their drug use and the aggressiveness of their behavior. He notes that fewer and fewer girls are seen on Bogotá's streets, a trend he attributes to their abrupt initiation into prostitution.

Perhaps one of the most salient divisions in Bogotá's street life exists between the *largos* (the older boys) and the *chinches* (the younger boys). Each group tends to go its separate way, although it is not uncommon for the *largos* to prey on the *chinches*. The *chinches* thus must seek protection and are apt to locate in an area patrolled by the police, since police treatment—by no means benign—generally seems preferable to the more predictable brutality of the *largos*. In contrast, the *largos* deliberately assemble in places far removed from where the police are stationed. Their long criminal records and dangerous behavior make them prime police targets.

The police are known to harass street children and throw them in jail, yet they can provide an evening's shelter and, for the *chinches* particularly, protection against the city's perils. This evening of Operación Amistad is marked by several police attempts to round up the *gamines*. The police back off, however, when Majito, Carlos, and Eduardo explain they are working for "the program of Father Javier."

By the time we decide to call it a night, we have visited numerous *galladas* in various parts of Bogotá. The van has carried roughly seventy or eighty *gamines*, and Majito has helped nourish them all with food and with his friendship. At 3:00 A.M., Carlos, Eduardo, and I return Majito to his home, to his wife and three daughters.

As we continue on our way, I recall the previous morning. Carlos, who has "custody" of me for the day, is telling me about his own childhood, an all-too-familiar one among the *gamines*: a family life of extreme poverty, alcoholism, relentless beatings, and abandonment that was followed by a street life of drugs, crime, and violence. Despite Majito's comforting street visits—and even after joining Javier's program at the age of eleven—Carlos kept returning to drugs and thievery. As we retrace the steps of his extraordinary life—from the Twelfth Street doorways in which he slept to the progressive phases of Bosconia-La Florida—Carlos is reflective, never bitter or sorry.

As we walk along, I ask him, "Do you think you'll ever see your father again?"

"I think I will," Carlos replies, "though I'm not sure when."

"What will you say to him?"

Carlos responds without hesitation: "I'm going to help him out. I'll offer everything I have. It wasn't his fault that he beat me. He couldn't read or write and he had a miserable job. I'll tell him I now understand why he did what he did."

When we arrive at El Patio, Eduardo is telling some fifty or sixty young boys what Bosconia-La Florida is all about. He is articulate, his delivery impassioned yet controlled. Though the boys are attentive, few will be sufficiently motivated to go on the next phase—Liberia and Camarín, places where they stay for thirty days and agree to give up drugs and to participate in a range of activities throughout the city. Most of the *gamines* will go back to the streets after washing and eating. Life is too painful for them to give up drugs entirely.

Carlos guides me through these facilities, as well as the next phases of Bosconia—Chibchalá, a manual arts workshop, and Arcadia, the program's school. We then briefly visit and have lunch at La 78, a program for girls, most of whom also have brothers at Bosconia-La

Florida. Indeed, the creation of La 78 was a response to the boys' concern about the strong pull of prostitution on their sisters.

At each place, I look at the classrooms, the workshops, the dining rooms. In the dormitories the beds are lined up, sometimes forty or fifty in a room, each one tidy and proper, everything in its place. The girls are a bit timid, but the boys are generally more gregarious, eager to welcome a stranger. They are deeply proud of their work, their paintings, and their various small projects.

Carlos shows me around La Industria, where he will soon complete his studies for a high-school degree. There are no dormitories here, only classrooms and workshops for carpentry, mechanical repair, and the like. The equipment is advanced, and the boys are thoroughly immersed in their work. They greet us warmly, but they are highly disciplined and quickly return to their tasks. In an office here, Carlos shows me his diploma that has just been printed, which he will soon receive; pride is written all over his face as he holds it tightly in his hands.

Throughout Bosconia–La Florida, Carlos is well known, both to children and staff. He moves about briskly and gracefully, exhibiting concern for others and an easy wit. He makes his presence felt from Operación Amistad to La Industria, but it is at La Florida that he is most plainly in charge.

For the past year, Carlos has been the mayor of this self-governing community of five hundred former *gamines*. Many of the boys of La Florida address him as "*alcalde*" and treat him with deference. As Carlos and I pass through the modern complex—its plant, at least, comparable to that of a small liberal arts college in the United States—many of the boys rush up to ask him a favor, to ask advice about a medical or family problem, or to complain about some decision or policy. The concerns of La Florida's residents are nearly inexhaustible, and Carlos addresses them all with efficiency and self-assurance.

Carlos governs with a firm hand. He regularly applies sanctions for such transgressions as stealing and drug use. One boy known for his talent as an artist was caught smoking marijuana; Carlos suspended him from the community. Several boys mention that Carlos is perhaps too tough and has gotten carried away, yet he is widely liked and respected, despite the harshness of his penalties. The boys may take issue with a particular decision he has made, but their *alcalde*'s authority is unquestioned.

The most common problem for the boys at La Florida is a return to drugs. This is most likely to occur during holiday breaks, Carlos observes, when the boys leave the community and return to their families and the streets. Many have brothers and sisters in jail, mothers working as prostitutes, fathers who are alcoholics and hardened criminals. The temptation to call it quits and revert to old, familiar ways is great. Carlos believes that having no family will help him get ahead in life. He claims he is "more privileged than the rest," that he can focus on his own development without being dragged down by hopeless family circumstances or lured astray by Bogotá's street culture.

La Florida bears all the features of a showcase, which seems entirely fitting for such accomplished showmen as its residents. Carlos is more keenly aware of this than most—before becoming *alcalde* he headed La Florida's public relations office. The boys have spoken with reporters from the *New York Times, Wall Street Journal, Washington Post,* and *Chicago Tribune*, not to mention scores of distinguished visitors from Europe and Latin America. Moreover, La Florida is a regular feature of Colombian newspapers and television.

Could these boys have ever looked like the *gamines* I saw on the streets during Operación Amistad? They are, by and large, polished, quick, and disciplined. They thrive on entertaining visitors and can fire questions on every imaginable subject—from the latest fashions in New York to the famine in Ethiopia.

It may seem perplexing that these boys were steeped in Bogotá's seamy street culture not so long ago, but maybe their present behavior should not seem so surprising. They should be accustomed to adhering to a strict code of behavior, exercising and relying on their wits, pursuing a goal with dogged determination, working with others, and demonstrating a profound understanding of liberation and freedom. Is there, perhaps, a central thread linking the agreeable community of La Florida to the harsh world I saw during Operación Amistad? Maybe the key to the program is precisely its ability to cultivate and redirect the qualities endemic to *gamín* subculture.

All of the boys I meet at La Florida are impressive in some way; Carlos is exceptional. Perhaps this is only because I spend enough time with him, get to know him better than the others. When we visit the music room at La Florida, Carlos plays Beethoven and Mozart on the piano, modern jazz on the saxophone, Andean folk music on the guitar. His versatility seems inexhaustible. He has a keen eye for art and a talent for dance and athletics. He has given talks at two highly respected Colombian universities—Javariana and Los Andes—on the philosophical underpinnings of Bosconia–La Florida. To such subjects as North American culture, Latin American literature, and the mores of Colombia's upper-class youth, he brings irony and shrewd insight.

Carlos is an avid reader with a special interest in literature and political philosophy. He comes close to being the most widely read twenty-two-year old I have ever met, including the many students I encountered during my four years of teaching at Harvard. It is not that he invokes the names of Shakespeare, Dostoevsky, Cervantes, Machiavelli, Nietzsche, García Márquez, Fuentes, or Vargas Llosa; it is that he discusses their works with such sophistication and zeal. His notebook is packed with reflections, original poetry, and quotations, especially from Nietzsche and Machiavelli. These plainly inspire his life and guide his personal philosophy. The *alcalde* of La Florida is engaged in what the American sociologist C. Wright Mills called intellectual craftsmanship.

I again notice these qualities while Carlos and I have a beer together at Unicentro, a North American-style mall in northern Bogotá. I ask him how long Unicentro has been open. (I knew it was not here when I lived in Bogotá eight years ago.) "I think about four or five years," he replies. Carlos pauses for a moment, then begins to grin. "I wish this place had been here when I was a *gamín*," he says. "Just think of all the possibilities for a good thief . . . look at all those rich people!"

21

*Ivonne Rivero: Urban Squatter**

Enrique del Acebo Ibáñez

Professor Enrique del Acebo received his training in sociology and political science in Argentina, Italy, and Spain, where, at the Universidad Complutense de Madrid, he wrote his dissertation, "Urban Living as Space and Temporal Roots." He is now on the faculty of the Universidad de Buenos Aires, and his publications include *The City: Its Essence, History and Pathology* (1984) and *Space and Society in Georg Simmel* (1984). Acebo has combined his academic career with positions in the public sector as coordinator of research on the quality of life in geriatric institutions, sponsored by the National Institute of Social Services for Retirees and Pensioners, and as an independent researcher for the National Council for Scientific Research.

In the following vignette, Acebo describes the life of an Uruguayan migrant to Buenos Aires. Ivonne Rivero, despite hardships as an unwed mother without permanent residence or adequate income, testifies to the tenacity of the human spirit, to the desire for independence and the strength of will to find dignity even in adversity. This woman demonstrates the resourcefulness that is required of those living on the margins of modern life. Many urban migrants have established shanty towns on the edges of great cities, called *villas miserias* in Argentina, *favelas* in Brazil, *callampas* in Chile, *barriadas* in Peru, and *canteguiles* in Uruguay. Others, like Ivonne, have found housing by seizing and taking possession of abandoned buildings.

In 1974, Ivonne Rivero, at the age of twenty-two, left the city of Montevideo, Uruguay, where she had lived with her parents and four siblings. Their house was located in La Barra de Santa Lucía, a peripheral suburb of Montevideo. Ivonne is the fourth of five children (three sons and two daughters). While she was living with her parents, she worked in the center of Montevideo in a fish cannery that required

*Translated and edited by William H. Beezley.

sixteen hours of work per day. She began working there when she was fifteen.

Her father was a trucker and her mother a housewife. Her brothers and sisters also worked. Ivonne worked for herself, as she said, "to cover her personal expenses." The house that her parents occupied was their own, built by the municipality of substantial material, in a modest neighborhood. Ivonne was born and reared in this house in La Barra de Santa Lucía. Nevertheless, as she grew older, and especially when she obtained some independence by working, she wanted to "get out of the neighborhood." She did not like it any more, she was tired of it, and she did not see any possibility to better herself.

Ivonne was bored because her life seemed "predetermined," partly because of the life in her neighborhood. Both her parents were literate and would have practically nothing to do with their neighbors. The father, by virtue of his job, was away from home for weeks at a time. No relatives lived in La Barra de Santa Lucía, although a few did in downtown Montevideo. Ivonne's family did not visit relatives, friends, or neighbors, nor did Ivonne visit, "given that she had few friends." With an incomplete elementary education of five years, she had little opportunity to finish school or to make friends, because she worked sixteen hours each day and traveled a two-hour round trip from her home to Montevideo. Her job left Ivonne little free time. Her social life was practically nil. On weekends she often put in "overtime" at the factory. She began looking for an escape. "The day I can go," she said, "I'm leaving."

After a brief period of seven months, during which she lived in downtown Montevideo, Ivonne returned to her parents' house and to her daily factory job. This was her only experience on her own before she migrated to Argentina. When she was twenty, she got to know a married man with children who was living in Montevideo, and she established a relationship with him. They decided to leave Uruguay together. She left her parents' house, and he left his wife and children as well as the office job he had taken after completing his secondary studies. They went to Buenos Aires because it was the closest big city and because Ivonne had never been to Argentina.

In February 1974 they crossed the Rio de la Plata and found a room in a cheap hotel in the Once district of Buenos Aires. The relationship with her companion[1] was marked by instability. He returned to Montevideo fifteen days after leaving, rejoining his wife and children. Ivonne found a job and moved from the Once district

---

[1]*Compañero*, in contemporary usage, indicates a live-in sexual relationship.

to the Ramos Mejía locality some twenty kilometers from Buenos Aires, where "the hotels were cheaper." Ivonne took what jobs she could get. At first, she was a vendor in the town's central district, and then she worked cleaning a restaurant. Meanwhile, her companion returned with his three children. He was thirty-six years old (fifteen years older than Ivonne). They eventually had three children together, the first of whom died almost immediately after birth.

Ivonne's children grew up in the hotel, where they lived for five years. From there they moved to a house she rented in the neighborhood of Cáseros, close to Buenos Aires. In 1979 her companion, who had been unemployed (Ivonne had been the sole support of the family for about five months), found a job at a banking cooperative, allowing Ivonne an opportunity to be with her children. Before she had only stopped working long enough to nurse the children when they were born.

Ivonne constantly searched for independence. She and her family lived in Cáseros for one year, at the end of which they were evicted from their house because her companion "didn't want to pay the rent; he wanted to go back to Uruguay." Ivonne vowed to stay in Buenos Aires no matter what he decided. "I am discredited," she told him, "and can't go back to Uruguay." The "bright lights" of the big city, often only an illusion, offered her a chance for independence, success, and fulfillment. Whatever sadness she felt when she decided to emigrate was more than compensated for by the hope of a better life.

Ivonne's commitment had force, and she stayed in Buenos Aires, but the relationship between the children and their father in Montevideo was poor. "He didn't worry much about the children; he didn't leave enough money and I had to work." So in 1980 she decided to return to Montevideo. Back in Uruguay, Ivonne permanently broke off the relationship with her companion and momentarily moved with her two children into her parents' house. She got a job as a domestic, working eight hours per day. Later, she went to work at a fish cannery, taking advantage of her previous experience. Nevertheless, she decided to leave this job because she did not like the work. "It was a very dirty job, and I didn't feel comfortable doing it." She left the cannery but continued to work as a domestic.

Living in her parents' house and leaving the children with them allowed Ivonne to begin a second job cleaning in a biscuit factory. As a result, she spent almost all of her waking hours working. "I continued working as a domestic during the mornings, and in the afternoons I was employed in the factory, arriving at my parents' house at midnight." Finally, she decided to work only in the biscuit factory, where she was employed every day from six in the morning until ten at night. She could see her children on weekends, but, she explained, "I would sleep practically all those days, so that I didn't see my children."

The children received little attention or affection except from their grandparents. They never saw their father, and their mother was either away at work or asleep. This entire situation made Ivonne think about returning to Buenos Aires. She had begun to receive more wages from the biscuit factory through a government program of "family pay." She was able to save some money, thereby hastening her decision to leave Montevideo for a second time.

In January 1981, Ivonne and her children left for Buenos Aires without knowing where they would live or where she would work. The security of a job and a home in Montevideo to Ivonne meant being dependent on her parents. "I was uncomfortable in my parents' house," she maintains. "We used to sleep all stacked up there. Besides, I felt the need for independence. And I also wanted to get the furniture that I had left in Buenos Aires the first time that I was there."

Newly returned to the Once neighborhood, Ivonne settled with her children in a small hotel. After a short time she moved to a cheaper hotel in the Congreso neighborhood, still in Buenos Aires. Both neighborhoods were "old" zones of the city, inhabited, in general, by the middle class but with working-class people. She earned her living expenses as a domestic. She discovered that her children could eat in the parochial dining room of the Regina Roman Catholic Church, and this greatly helped her financial condition. She also enrolled the children, now six and seven, in primary school. However, "they were left by themselves all afternoon" while she worked. Since the dining room where Ivonne took her children was a long way from where she lived and from the school, she located another free dining room closer to her home, this one run by the Cáritas, a charitable society of the Catholic church.

Ivonne's life settled into a routine in Buenos Aires. "I would get up at five in the morning; at six I would leave the hotel to take the children to school and at eight I would start working in a private home as a maid. At twelve-thirty, I would go get them to take them to the dining room; later I would leave my children in the hotel, where they used to stay alone, and I would go back to work, returning home at six in the evening."

Ivonne's income did not stretch far enough to pay for both food and hotel. For a time, the Cáritas helped her pay for lodging. At the same time, she tried to obtain aid from the National Children's Agency to pay for housing, but she was unsuccessful. Her poverty became more severe in 1983 when she was evicted from the hotel. That day she and her children slept in the plaza. Finally, through a friend, she arranged for a place for her family in an occupied building, but she did not stay there very long. "I didn't like the situation; when I don't like it, I leave. They had bad habits." Ivonne resolved to take the initiative to get "her" housing free and thus alleviate her economic situation.

Ivonne saw a house burning in the Congreso neighborhood and learned from the neighbors that the building was unoccupied. "Officially" unoccupied, that is, because in reality it was full of street people and vagrants. After the fire was extinguished, Ivonne contacted the fire department and the commissioner of the ward, asking them for information about the house and its residents. "The firemen as well as the commissioner recommended that I not go in the house because there were vagrants, and, at times, thieves." But Ivonne had now found her house. After a long discussion, she convinced the police watchman that she had been staying in the front hall of the three-story building and succeeded in getting in. The fire had been on the second floor. The street people stayed on the first floor, and there had been some on the second. But these old residents of the building were no more than "usurpers" to Ivonne since to her this was, or should be, her house. With the help of a chain and padlock, she made herself the landlady of the building, threatening to call the police if the vagrants did not get out. Ivonne succeeded in her plan and took effective possession of the second floor of the building in December 1983. Putting the chain and padlock on the first floor's street door was her first victory in the pursuit of her own home. The night Ivonne padlocked the doors, the street people returned, but when they saw the door barred, they decided to move on. Ivonne had become the "owner"; she had chosen the life of an "urban squatter."

She then persuaded a friend from one of the hotels where she had previously lived to move into the first floor of the building. Her friend, together with her husband and two children, occupied that floor and were made into "desirable" residents by Ivonne. Positive about what she was doing, she took another step and went to the office of the ward commissioner and informed him that she had "taken over" the building, assigning one of the floors to her friend. The commissioner "told me that I had charge of the house, as long as the owner didn't turn up."

In the meantime, Ivonne continued to work as a domestic. Her children changed schools and now attended one with double classes—

that is, they spent more than one-half of their day in school. Simultaneously, Ivonne's neighbors in the district became her unexpected allies, supporting her in everything. "When the police asked for reports about me, the neighbors backed me up. They decided that they were lucky to have found a good neighbor, like me, who took care of the house and kept it clean, getting rid of the street people living in it."

Ivonne decided to turn over the third floor of the building to a young married couple since "she had to bring in people, and they seemed like good people." Of course, she dug in her heels about the need for them to "look after the house for me." The floor occupied by Ivonne offered conveniences and room that she had not had in her previous dwelling. In addition to a small kitchen and pantry, there was a dining room with a balcony on the street, three bedrooms, and two bathrooms. There she arranged her furniture and the radio on which she relied for news and pleasure.

Ivonne's uneasiness about what the future might bring her became worse in February 1984, when a gentleman appeared in the building and claimed to be its owner. But, when Ivonne asked him for the title to the property, he said he did not possess it. "I did it to threaten him; I told him not to dare enter the house again, and, besides, not to knock at the door because I would take care of him." The man gave up. Another time a police patrol took Ivonne to the ward commissioner's office on a charge of trespassing. However, later she was released. "Since I saw myself out in the street, I took dangerous risks. And I explained this very thing to them in the precinct office. The police congratulated me for my courage." Feeling like she had the backing of the police authorities, although not formally, Ivonne took great pains caring for "her" house: "I waxed the floors; I put the house in good shape."

During this time Ivonne's family increased. In the last hotel where they had lived, she met the man who would be the father of her third child, a little girl who was born with serious heart and respiratory problems. This man, together with his brother, moved in with Ivonne on the second floor of the seized house. Her new companion was from Salta and worked as a folksinger and as a private security guard. "There I was pregnant with the baby girl. In my seventh month, my companion left me."

About the middle of 1984 the real owner showed up at the building. "We were heaped up to the top, on the third floor," Ivonne relates. "The married couple to whom I had given lodging had put a married couple with children in each room. It was extremely filthy." The police summoned all the residents of the squatters' house before the owner.

Ivonne asked him to rent the house to her, but he refused. From that moment, every day the police went to "Ivonne's house" and reminded her that the residents had to get out within one month. Ivonne never stopped fighting. "How much money did they give you to do this?" she asked the police inspector. "If not, why would you have such interest in evicting us? Otherwise, the owner would be acting through the courts. I am not leaving if they don't begin judicial proceedings." Her attitude and the suggestion of bribery annoyed the inspector. "The police threatened to take my children away from me if we didn't leave. They told me that my children would be placed in the care of the National Children's Agency."

Not yet resigned to leaving the building, Ivonne went to court, where she found out that the owner had actually begun eviction proceedings. At this juncture there were no other residents in the building. "Those on the third floor had left; the policeman threatened the man because he was a thief. My friends on the first floor left, too. I left the last day, the day of the eviction date." Ivonne then called Montevideo and told the father of two of her children that he had to take them because she had been evicted. Her former companion took them, and Ivonne remained alone and pregnant.

The same police officer who had evicted Ivonne's family told her that "there was another house that we could occupy a few blocks from the other house. It was a kind of abandoned laboratory. I lived there alone for three months. In February 1985 the children's father returned with them; he left them with me and then went away." In December, Ivonne's daughter was born. She continued to live with her baby and her other two children in this newly occupied house. However, the dwelling did not satisfy Ivonne. "It was an ugly place. There were many people. I like peaceful places, with few people."

This uncomfortable feeling pushed Ivonne to find another house. The Cáritas society told her that there was an occupied building that had previously been part of the University of Buenos Aires and was located near her earlier residence. Together with one of the Cáritas, Ivonne spoke with the residents of this so-called abandoned dwelling and was successful in getting a room. In April 1985 a new stage began in the life of Ivonne and her children.

Twenty-seven families presently live in the occupied former school building. There is little interaction among them. However, "in cases of necessity," says Ivonne, "there is solidarity among the majority of the people when there is some misfortune or the danger of eviction. Otherwise, no! There is a minority that are bad people. There are prostitutes who are working here inside the building; there are also thieves and dope addicts. Therefore, the children don't go out of my room. They are always with me. Regularly, the police come."

There is a meeting of the squatters only when some problem develops. They once tried to form a tenants' committee, but it did not work successfully. "Here nothing works because the people don't do their share, in any sense. They all have two faces; they are insincere." The physical closeness of those living in the building does not become togetherness; theirs is a closeness that divides rather than brings together. The anxious situation in which each family lives turns the residents to suspicion, to individualism, and to unsociable behavior. "I stay put in my rooms. I don't meddle with anyone; everyone has her life. Although everyone knows what I am doing, I don't know what the rest of them are doing."

Ivonne still works as a domestic, but she receives economic help from the Cáritas. Her children attend catechism classes in the Catholic parish and go to Mass on Sundays. Ivonne says, "I don't go to Mass, but I believe in God." She defines herself as independent, "a little possessive of myself," and as having great drive. "Now I have it in my head that I have to leave this occupied building. Partly it is because I don't want to have problems with a neighbor woman who bothers me and is looking for a fight. Nevertheless, I will endure. I know my character."

The building in which Ivonne presently lives consists of three floors. There are two bathrooms on each floor. The water and sewage pipes are found outside the improvised apartments. The kitchen stove works on a tank of gas. There is electricity in these apartments, and each of the tenants pays to use it. "In the other places, in the other two occupied houses where I lived, instead we stole the electricity."

Ivonne's life does not include many social relationships. In her birthplace of La Barra de Santa Lucía, she had little social interaction. "I didn't have friends; only one" that was not a relative. Her jobs demanded long hours and prevented her from spending much time in the neighborhood. She does, however, maintain a strong bond to her parents. "My relationship with my parents has been and is good. I wouldn't say very good, but good. I try not to let my mother find out my present problems and, if they are reported to her, I tell her that I have already overcome them. For example, my parents were not acquainted with the serious health problem that my daughter had. My mother visited me once in Buenos Aires, in July 1986."

Ivonne continues to see her girlfriend from the hotel who had lived with her in the first occupied house. "Now my friend lives in Moreno, some fifty kilometers from Buenos Aires; it is better economically;

they are owners of their residence. She is the godmother of my baby." Ivonne does not worry about the nationality of the people she knows. "I have few friendships; I talk with everyone and I don't court anyone. In case of an emergency, I turn to Charlie of the Cáritas."

The level of information about Uruguay available in Buenos Aires, through the newspapers and the mass media, has improved. Ivonne did not read the daily newspapers or watch television in her parents' home in Montevideo, partly because of the amount of time that her job demanded. Now, however, she listens to the radio every morning and watches television in the afternoon and evening, "especially the news and some movies that I like."

Ivonne does not miss Uruguay. On the contrary, she says, "when I am in Uruguay, I miss Buenos Aires. Buenos Aires is different; it has another rhythm of life." She likes this great city; in it she feels better, more comfortable. Even so, Ivonne knows little or nothing about Buenos Aires. She almost never goes outside her neighborhood, except to work or to take her children to school. "I'm not interested in going out. Here I am in my place, in my house, with my things, with my bed." On rare occasions she takes the children for a walk or to the plaza. In the mornings she works as a domestic, and the rest of the day she spends in her apartment with her children. An important reason for this isolation is economic: "I can't go out with the children without money. My income only stretches for food, beyond that nothing else, and the costs for light and gas."

Ivonne does not think of the neighborhood where she presently lives as her own; she does not like it. "I don't think of myself in the slightest as a neighbor of the people in the neighborhood, nor do they think of themselves as our neighbors." Her lack of interaction with the urban space has other causes besides the economic, some of them psychological. "The street is always dangerous," maintains Ivonne; "you don't know if you will return or not when you go out." Her attitude affects the children, who have practically no friends among the residents of the building in which they currently live, or in the neighborhood. Ivonne does not leave them with anyone. At their primary school the children do have some friends whom they visit in their homes, but these friends do not visit Ivonne's children in the occupied building. On Saturdays she lets them go with the Boy Scouts: "They treat them well, and teach them about life in the countryside. And at the end of the year they go with them for ten days of vacation. I also get that through the Cáritas." Ivonne sends her sons to church, to the parish, and to the Boy Scouts "because I want them to mix with good people."

Ivonne, currently thirty-two years of age, with children eleven, ten, and two, displays an independent, strong personality. She does not want to return to her parents' house precisely in order to safeguard her independence, even though with them her life would be less burdensome. "I don't like to depend on my family; I like to make my own life." She confronts her problems, and it is evident that much of her confidence comes from the help and support that the Cáritas gives her. "I feel that there is something supporting me when I have the rope around my neck. The health problems of my little daughter required a couple of hospitalizations which demanded large payments, in part assumed by this Catholic charitable society."

Her present circumstances, in spite of her problems, do not stop her from seeing a positive future. "A future," says Ivonne, "that will be better than what I have now and than I have had. It is going to have to be better." She is optimistic. In 1988 she has plans to change her life completely. "I am going to send my children to a school with all-day classes, and I am looking for a monthly job, the kind so that I would only work as a domestic when I have free time." This attitude, with its vision of the future, is important in helping Ivonne cope with her present situation. Usually, marginality orients a person primarily toward the present, which makes shreds of the possibility of rational planning for the future.

Urban squatters have captured the attention of social agencies in many cities. Charitable institutions, the police, and other social offices regard the occupied dwellings as evidence of marginal conditions, and in some cases they help squatters locate buildings. This implies a weakness in the existing social institutions.

Ivonne lives with constant anxiety over circumstances such as the need to throw out street people, the sudden appearance of the owner, and the possibility of eviction by public authorities for simply moving into someone else's house. She persuades herself that the building in which she lives is compensation for living in an unresponsive society. She also contends that she has more rights than the street people and vagrants who sometimes occupy an inhabitable building. Her attitude is that the squatter, like herself, with children and a job is *inside* the system, while the street people are *outside* of it. Rather than any feelings of class awareness, Ivonne believes in a rank ordering of society in which she looks down on those whom she sees as her "subordinates," in this case the street people.

Ivonne's unstable residence as an urban squatter limits her possibilities for developing relationships with the local community. This difficulty of becoming integrated into the neighborhood makes her an urban nomad. She is not one of the "intellectual nomads" described by the historian Oswald Spengler as that person in the great city who declares independence from others and from the location where she lives. Clearly not Spengler's nomad, Ivonne Rivero represents a new form of urban nomad, one who must endure both marginality and misery, yet she perseveres and trusts in the future.

Suggestions for Additional Reading

The following readings are recommended for those who want additional information on the historical circumstances of the persons in this book. We have not repeated the titles mentioned in the introduction or in the prefatory remarks before each vignette. Insofar as possible, we have suggested only books and articles in English.

General

Bergquist, Charles. *Labor in Latin America: Comparative Essays on Chile, Argentina, Venezuela, and Colombia.* Stanford: Stanford University Press, 1986.

Crahan, Margaret E., ed. *Human Rights and Basic Needs in the Americas.* Washington, DC: Georgetown University Press, 1982.

Hardoy, Jorge, ed. *Urbanization in Latin America: Approaches and Issues.* Garden City, NY: Doubleday, 1975.

Johnson, John J. *Political Change in Latin America: The Emergence of the Middle Sectors.* Stanford: Stanford University Press, 1958.

Landsberger, H. E., ed. *The Church and Social Change in Latin America.* South Bend, IN: University of Notre Dame Press, 1970.

Lavrin, Asunción. *Latin American Women: Historical Perspectives.* Westport, CT: Greenwood Press, 1978.

Levine, Daniel H., ed. *Churches and Politics in Latin America.* Beverly Hills: Sage Publications, 1980.

Lewis, Oscar. *Five Families: Mexican Case Studies in the Culture of Poverty.* New York: Basic Books, 1959.

Loveman, Brian, and Davies, Thomas M., Jr. *The Politics of Antipolitics: The Military in Latin America.* Lincoln: University of Nebraska Press, 1978.

Nash, June, and Safa, Helen Icken, eds. *Sex and Class in Latin America.* New York: Bergin, 1980.

Skidmore, Thomas E., and Smith, Peter H. *Modern Latin America.* New York: Oxford University Press, 1984.

Veliz, Claudio. *Obstacles to Change in Latin America.* New York: Oxford University Press, 1969.

Wolf, Eric R., and Hansen, Edward C., eds. *The Human Condition in Latin America.* New York: Oxford University Press, 1972.

Argentina

Alexander, Robert J. *The Perón Era*. New York: Russell, 1965.

Constantini, Humberto. *The Long Night of Francisco Sanctis*. New York: Plume Books, 1986.

Mangin, William. "Latin American Squatter Settlements: A Problem and a Solution." In *Contemporary Cultures and Societies of Latin America*, edited by Dwight Heath. Boulder, CO: Westview Press, 1982.

Navarro, Marysa, and Fraser, Nicolas. *Eva Perón*. New York: W. W. Norton, 1980.

Potash, Robert A. *The Army and Politics in Argentina, 1945–1962: Perón to Frondizi*. Stanford: Stanford University Press, 1982.

Rock, David, ed. *Argentina in the Twentieth Century*. Pittsburgh: University of Pittsburgh Press, 1975.

Scobie, James R. *Argentina: A City and a Nation*. 2d ed. New York: Oxford University Press, 1971.

Smith, Peter H. *Argentina and the Failure of Democracy*. Madison: University of Wisconsin Press, 1974.

Bolivia

Carter, W. E. *Aymara Communities and the Bolivian Agrarian Reform*. Gainesville: University of Florida Press, 1964.

Klein, Hubert S. *Bolivia: The Evolution of a Multi-Ethnic Society*. New York: Oxford University Press, 1982.

Malloy, James. *Bolivia, the Uncompleted Revolution*. Pittsburgh: University of Pittsburgh Press, 1970.

———, and Thorn, R. S., eds. *Beyond the Revolution: Bolivia Since 1952*. Pittsburgh: University of Pittsburgh Press, 1971.

Rout, Leslie B., Jr. *Politics of the Chaco Peace Conference, 1935–1939*. Austin: University of Texas Press, 1970.

Brazil

Bourne, Richard. *Getúlio Vargas of Brazil, 1883–1954*. London: C. Knight, 1974.

Bruneau, Thomas C. *The Political Transformation of the Brazilian Church*. London: Cambridge University Press, 1974.

Burns, E. Bradford. *A History of Brazil*. New York: Columbia University Press, 1970.

Dean, Warren. *The Industrialization of São Paulo, 1880–1945*. Austin: University of Texas Press, 1969.

DeJesus, Carolina Maria. *Child of the Dark*. New York: Mentor Books, 1964.

della Cava, Ralph. *Miracle at Joaseiro*. New York: Columbia University Press, 1970.

Kadt, Emanuel de. *Catholic Radicals in Brazil*. New York: Oxford University Press, 1970.

Lever, Janet. *Soccer Madness*. Chicago: University of Chicago Press, 1983.

Levine, Robert M. *The Vargas Regime: The Critical Years, 1934–1938*. New York: Columbia University Press, 1970.

Love, Joseph L. *Rio Grande do Sul and Brazilian Regionalism*. Stanford: Stanford University Press, 1971.

Wirth, John L. *The Politics of Brazilian Development, 1930–1954*. Stanford: Stanford University Press, 1970.

Central America

Cabezas, Omar. *Fire from the Mountain: The Making of a Sandinista*. New York: Plume Books, 1986.

Coleman, Kenneth M., and Herring, George C., eds. *The Central American Crisis: Sources of Conflict and the Failure of U.S. Policy*. Wilmington, DE: Scholarly Resources, 1986.

Gettleman, Marvin E., et al. *El Salvador: Central America in the New Cold War*. New York: Grove Press, 1981.

Jonas, Susanne, and Tobis, David, eds. *Guatemala*. New York: NACLA, 1974.

LaFeber, Walter. *Inevitable Revolutions*. New York: W. W. Norton, 1983.

Macaulay, Neil. *The Sandino Affair*. Chicago: Quadrangle Books, 1967.

Millett, Richard. *Guardians of the Dynasty: A History of the U.S.-Created Guardia Nacional de Nicaragua and the Somoza Family*. Maryknoll, NY: Orbis Books, 1977.

Montgomery, T. S. *Revolution in El Salvador: Origins and Evolution*. Boulder, CO: Westview Press, 1982.

Pearce, Jenny. *Under the Eagle: U.S. Intervention in Central America and the Caribbean*. London: Latin America Bureau, 1982.

Walker, Thomas W., ed. *Nicaragua in Revolution*. New York: Praeger, 1982.

Woodward, Ralph Lee, Jr. *Central America: A Nation Divided*. New York: Oxford University Press, 1976.

Chile

Bauer, Arnold J. *Chilean Rural Society: From the Spanish Conquest to 1930*. Cambridge, England: Cambridge University Press, 1975.

Loveman, Brian. *Chile: The Legacy of Hispanic Capitalism*. New York: Oxford University Press, 1979.

Mamalakis, Markos J. *The Growth and Structure of the Chilean Economy: From Independence to Allende*. New Haven: Yale University Press, 1976.

Sigmund, Paul. *The Overthrow of Allende and the Politics of Chile, 1964–1976*. Pittsburgh: University of Pittsburgh Press, 1977.

Smith, Brian H. *The Church and Politics in Chile: Challenges to Modern Catholicism*. Princeton: Princeton University Press, 1982.

Cuba

Caudill, Herbert. *On Freedom's Edge*. Atlanta: Home Mission Board, 1979.

Domínguez, Jorge I. *Cuba: Order and Revolution*. Cambridge, MA: The Belknap Press of Harvard University Press, 1978.

Goodsell, James Nelson, ed. *Fidel Castro's Personal Revolution*. New York: Alfred Knopf, 1975.

Greer, Harold E. "Southern Baptists in Cuba, 1886–1916." In *Militarists, Merchants, and Missionaries: United States Expansion in Middle America*, edited by Eugene R. Huck and Edward H. Moseley. University, AL: University of Alabama Press, 1970.

Hageman, Alice L., and Wheaton, Philip E., eds. *Religion in Cuba Today*. New York: Association Press, 1971.

Knight, Franklin W. *Slave Society in Cuba during the Nineteenth Century*. Madison: University of Wisconsin Press, 1970.

Lockwood, Lee. *Castro's Cuba, Cuba's Fidel*. New York: Random House, 1969.

Mesa-Lago, Carmelo. *The Economy of Socialist Cuba: A Two Decade Appraisal*. Albuquerque: University of New Mexico Press, 1981.

Pérez, Louis A., Jr. *Army Politics in Cuba, 1898–1906*. Pittsburgh: University of Pittsburgh Press, 1976.

Randall, Margaret. *Women in Cuba: Twenty Years Later*. New York: Smyrna Press, 1981.

Ruiz, Ramón. *Cuba: The Making of a Revolution*. New York: W. W. Norton, 1970.

Suchlicki, Jaime. *Cuba from Columbus to Castro*. New York: Charles Scribner's Sons, 1974.

Thomas, Hugh. *Cuba: The Pursuit of Freedom*. New York: Harper and Row, 1971.

Ecuador

Crespi, Muriel. "Changing Power Relations: The Rise of Peasant Unions on Traditional Ecuadorian Haciendas." *Anthropological Quarterly* 44 (1971): 223–40.

Ehrenreich, Jeffrey, ed. *Political Anthropology of Ecuador: Perspectives from Indigenous Cultures*. Albany: State University of New York Press, 1985.

Franklin, Albert. *Ecuador: Portrait of a People*. Garden City, NY: Doubleday Doran, 1943.

Griffin, Keith. *Land Concentration and Rural Poverty*. London: Macmillan and Company, 1976.

Hurtado, Osvaldo. *Political Power in Ecuador*. Albuquerque: University of New Mexico Press, 1980.

Larrea, M. Carlos. "Transnational Companies and Banana Exports from Ecuador, 1948–1972: An Interpretation." *North/South* 7 (1982): 3–42.

Luzuriaga, Carlos, and Zuvekas, Clarence, Jr. *Income Distribution and Rural Poverty in Ecuador*. Tempe: Arizona State University Press, 1983.

Martz, J. "The Regionalist Expression of Populism: Guayaquil and the CFP, 1948–1960." *Journal of Inter-American Studies and World Affairs* 22 (1980): 189–314.

Phillips, Lynne. "Women, Development, and the State in Rural Ecuador." In *State Policy and Women in Latin America and the Caribbean*, edited by Carmen Diana Deere and Magdalena Leon. Sage Press (forthcoming).

Plaza, Galo. *Problems of Democracy in Latin America*. Chapel Hill: University of North Carolina Press, 1955.

Redclift, Michael. "Agrarian Reform and Peasant Organizations in the Guayas River Basin." *Inter-American Economic Affairs* 30 (1976): 3–27.

———. "The Influence of the Agency for International Development (AID) on Ecuador's Agrarian Development Policy." *Journal of Latin American Studies* 2 (1979): 185–201.

Weiss, Wendy. "The Social Organization of Property and Work: A Study of Migrants from the Rural Ecuadorian Sierra." *American Ethnologist* 12 (1985): 468–88.

Whitten, Norman, ed. *Cultural Transformations and Ethnicity in Modern Ecuador*. Urbana: University of Illinois Press, 1981.

World Bank. *Ecuador: Development Problems and Prospects*. Washington, DC: World Bank, 1979.

Mexico

Ankerson, Dudley. *Agrarian Warlord: Saturnino Cedillo and the Mexican Revolution in San Luis Potosí*. DeKalb, IL: Northern Illinois University Press, 1984.

Falcón, Romana. *Revolución y caciquismo: San Luis Potosí, 1910–1938.* Mexico: El Colegio de Mexico, 1984.

Friedrich, Paul. *Agrarian Revolt in a Mexican Village.* Englewood Cliffs, NJ: Prentice-Hall, 1970.

Jacobs, Ian. *Ranchero Revolt: The Mexican Revolution in Guerrero.* Austin: University of Texas Press, 1982.

Meyer, Michael C., and Sherman, William L. *The Course of Mexican History.* 3d ed. New York: Oxford University Press, 1987.

Raat, W. Dirk, and Beezley, William H. *Twentieth Century Mexico.* Lincoln: University of Nebraska Press, 1986.

Ruiz, Ramón. *The Great Rebellion.* New York: W. W. Norton, 1983.

Womack, John. *Zapata and the Mexican Revolution.* London: Penguin Books, 1972.

Peru

Albert, Bill. *An Essay on the Peruvian Sugar Industry, 1880–1920.* Norwich, England: University of East Anglia, 1976.

Bauer, Arnold J. "Rural Workers in Spanish America: Problems of Peonage and Oppression." *Hispanic American Historical Review* 59, no. 1 (1979): 34–63.

Davies, Thomas M., Jr. *Indian Integration in Peru: A Half-Century of Experience, 1900–1948.* Lincoln: University of Nebraska Press, 1974.

Duncan, Kenneth, and Rutledge, Ian, with Harding, Colin, eds. *Land and Labour in Latin America.* Cambridge, England: Cambridge University Press, 1977.

Gonzales, Michael J. *Plantation Agriculture and Social Control in Northern Peru, 1875–1933.* Austin: University of Texas Press, 1985.

Hammel, Eugene A. *Power in Ica.* Boston: Little, Brown, and Company, 1969.

Mallon, Florencia. *The Defense of Community in Peru's Central Highlands: Peasant Struggle and Capitalist Transition, 1860–1940.* Princeton: Princeton University Press, 1983.

Miller, Rory. "The Coastal Elite and Peruvian Politics: 1895–1919." *Journal of Latin American Studies* 14, no. 1 (May 1982): 97–120.

Morner, Magnus. *The Andean Past: Land, Conflicts, and Societies.* New York: Columbia University Press, 1985.

Pike, Frederick B. *The Modern History of Peru.* New York: Praeger, 1967.

Stein, Steve. "Soccer and Social Change in Twentieth Century Peru." *Studies in Latin American Popular Culture* 3 (1984) and 5 (1986).

Thorp, Rosemary, and Bertram, Geoffrey. *Peru, 1890–1977: Growth and Policy in an Open Economy.* New York: Columbia University Press, 1978.

Venezuela, Colombia, and Panama

Bernstein, Harry. *Venezuela and Colombia.* Englewood Cliffs, NJ: Prentice-Hall, 1964.

Dix, Robert H. *Colombia: The Political Dimensions of Change.* New Haven: Yale University Press, 1969.

Fluharty, Vernon L. *Dance of the Millions.* Pittsburgh: University of Pittsburgh Press, 1957.

Friedmann, John. *Venezuela: From Doctrine to Dialogue.* Syracuse: Syracuse University Press, 1965.

Kamen-Kaye, Dorothy. *Venezuelan Folkways.* Detroit: Blaine Ethridge, 1976.

Kolb, Glen L. *Democracy and Dictatorship in Venezuela, 1945–1958.* Hamden, CT: Connecticut College, 1974.

Liss, Sheldon B. *The Canal: Aspects of United States–Panamanian Relations.* Notre Dame, IN: University of Notre Dame Press, 1967.

Martz, John D. *Acción Democrática: Evolution of a Modern Political Party in Venezuela.* Princeton: Princeton University Press, 1966.

Index